KB145715

KOREAN GRAMMAR

한 번에 끝내는 문법 기본서

한국어 문법

KOREAN GRAMMAR : A ONE-STOP REFERENCE BOOK
Volume Ⅱ
Clausal Conjunctions and Sentence Connectors

Copyright © 2020 by Cho, Won Seok

Published March 6, 2020
by Pagijong Press, Inc.
4, Cheonho-daero 16ga-gil, Dongdaemun-gu,
Seoul, Republic of Korea 02589

Tel : 82-2-922-1192
Fax : 82-2-928-4683
www.pjbook.com

Publisher : Park Chan-ik

979-11-5848-433-0 94710
979-11-5848-431-6 (SET)

Printed in Korea

A ONE-STOP REFERENCE BOOK

KOREAN GRAMMAR

Volume II

Clausal Conjunctions and Sentence Connectors

Cho, Won Seok

Pagijong Press, Inc.

Preface (머리말/서문)

I will never forget what happened in my first class teaching Korean grammar to non-native speakers in a formal classroom setting. It was on November 11, 1998. At that time, I was teaching Korean to US service men and women who were in the second week of learning the language. The topic of the grammar lesson was how to identify and indicate the subject of a Korean sentence. At the beginning of the class, I introduced the Korean subject case markers "~이/가" to the students and explained how they are used in a given sentence. Soon after that, the students were supposed to do a ten-minute speaking practice using the script of the basic conversational exchanges from the textbook. Of course, all the sentences on the script were written for pedagogical purposes and each of the individual sentences was grammatically flawless as shown below.

Speaker A: 고향이 어디십니까? (=Where are you from?)
Speaker B: 제 고향이 _____ 입니다. (=I am from _____.)
Speaker A: 가족이 어떻게 되십니까? (=How many are there in your family?)
Speaker B: 제 가족이 모두 ____명입니다. (=Altogether there are ____ in my family.)
Speaker A: 나이가 어떻게 되십니까? (=How old are you?)
Speaker B: 제 나이가 ____살입니다. (=I am ____ old.)
Speaker A: 직업이 어떻게 되십니까? (=What do you do for a living?)
Speaker B: 제 직업이 _____ 입니다. (=I am _____.)

Once the students became familiarized with these expressions enough to utter them in their own words, I asked the students to stand up and continue to practice these expressions with their partners. I was walking around the classroom during the speaking practice to provide them some extra help whenever they needed me. Everything went smoothly for a while as planned. Meanwhile, one student approached me and tried to engage in a conversation with me using the scripted questions. So, I kindly interacted with him by taking the role of Speaker B. All of a sudden the student seemed to look puzzled and showed signs of frustration. Right at that moment, I sensed that something went wrong. I immediately realized that I was the culprit of the unpleasant situation which ruined his first and bold attempt to have a conversation with a native speaker. It was all because I inadvertently provided him the following natural answers to his questions instead of using the purported sentence frames above.

Speaker A: 고향이 어디십니까? (=Where are you from?)

Speaker B: 제 고향은 서울입니다. (=I am from Seoul.)

Speaker A: 가족이 어떻게 되십니까? (=How many are there in your family?)

Speaker B: 제 가족은 모두 세 명입니다. (=Altogether there are three in my family.)

Speaker A: 나이가 어떻게 되십니까? (=How old are you?)

Speaker B: 제 나이는 서른 다섯 살입니다. (=I am thirty-five years old.)

Speaker A: 직업이 어떻게 되십니까? (=What do you do for a living?)

Speaker B: 제 직업은 선생님입니다. (=I am a teacher.)

When the student returned to his seat, he asked me a question regarding whether it is possible to create a statement without a subject, which is not possible in English. Since I already knew why he asked me such a question, I admitted that it was my fault not to use the appropriate subject case markers in my answers. Then, just to clarify, I continued to say that a subject in Korean can often serve as the topic of a sentence and in that case, it can be alternatively marked by the topic markers "~은/는," which can be rendered as "As for" in English. After having made that comment, I wanted to get back to the main theme of the lesson to cover the rest of the material assigned for the class. Unfortunately, another inquisitive student raised his hand and asked me a very challenging question. He said his Korean wife often uses "~은/는" for the noun that cannot be interpreted as "As for." I cannot recall the exact sentence, but it was something like "나는 커피는 좋아해." To quench his academic thirst and curiosity, I briefly explained that the first occurrence of "~는" is the topic marker and the second one is the contrastive focus marker. Therefore, the sentence could be rendered as "As for me, I like coffee, but not others such as tea, juice, milk, and so on." Again, the student was not completely satisfied with my explanation and made a series of legitimate questions. As far as I can recall, the questions were like "Why does the same case marker behave differently in the given sentence?," "Why was it used more than once in the same sentence?," and "In what way can I distinguish between the two different functions?" Since I realized that I had already sidestepped way too much and could not come up with any satisfactory answers to the questions, I abruptly ended the discussion and promised to the class that I would get back to it later.

After that class, I conducted very extensive research on the Korean topic/contrastive focus markers "~은/는." I made an all-out effort to search for the answers using all available resources ranging from a large number of published Korean grammar books and professional journals to personal communications with many Korean grammar experts. Unfortunately, I was not able to find any systematic or at least persuasive explanation on their proper usage. The mystery of this extremely important grammar feature has survived a series of my unending academic pursuits and the numerous attempts even made by other renowned Korean grammarians. Thereafter, whenever I was supposed to talk about this seemingly unconquerable grammar feature, I had no choice but to beat around the bush and intentionally not go into any detailed discussion.

This book now attempts to keep the nearly two-decade-old promise that I had made to the students in my first Korean grammar class. With my sincere apology to them for this belated response to their insightful questions, I hope this humble work can at least partially alleviate their pending emotion that might have been left behind in their course of learning the Korean language. The same apology also applies to the countless number of my former and current students who have been under my supervision for the last twenty-one years.

Another driving force that has propelled me to write this book is to fulfill my responsibilities as a Korean language educator who has received so many benefits from this academic field since I embarked on my predestined journey. As a small token of appreciation to all the passionate Korean language learners around the world who have relentlessly dedicated their time and efforts to the mastery of Korean grammar, I decided to give top priority to this somewhat arduous work among the items on my bucket list. Now after three years of strenuous journey, I am about to cross the finish line with the hope that this book can be used as a one-stop reference guide for all serious learners of Korean at all proficiency levels.

The following is a list of the unwavering tenets deeply engraved in this book.

(1) The readers of this book can have access to clear and systematic explanations on a wide range of Korean grammatical phenomena that they may encounter in the course of learning the language. They can be empowered with all necessary grammatical knowledge while reading this book without seeking any extra help from outside resources.

(2) This book must provide explanations for all essential Korean grammar features that are being used for both written and spoken language. Especially, the grammar patterns commonly used in spoken expressions deserve to receive more special attention. They are indeed the real things that most Korean language learners are going to be exposed to while interacting with native speakers in real-life situations.

(3) The readers should be given at least an opportunity to gain native-level intuition to discern the alternative grammar patterns that are being used in similar, but somewhat different situations. To facilitate this process, closely related grammar features are grouped together with the explanations of their similarities and different restrictions on their usage.

(4) Instead of simply making a sales pitch of a jargon-free book, if some grammatical terms are indispensable to explain and understand core grammar features, they should be welcomed to be used to appreciate the deeper understanding of grammatical phenomena. At the same time, unless otherwise deemed necessary, most grammatical terms are going to be simplified or rephrased in layman's terms.

(5) The syntactic, semantic, and pragmatic treatment of grammatical phenomena should be integrated in describing and explaining important grammatical features whenever applicable.

(6) To accommodate a more diverse group of Korean language learners, English is chosen as a medium of communication with the readers of this book. In addition, if Korean grammar features have their English equivalents, they are being compared side by side to expedite the explanation process.

I am greatly indebted to my colleagues who have participated in my weekly Korean grammar forum during the last two years. I would like to thank Taek Jun Chung, Soyoung Jeong, Kyong Hee Lee, Yusun Jung, Raeshik Myung, Pyong Gag Ahn, Mi-Ra

Karrer, Gloria Lee, Josephine Petkovski, Eun Young Suh, SeongOak Paek, Seunghyun Yoo, So Young Kim, Anne Lim, Imsuk Berger, Seung B Baek, Seung Jae Oh, Estel Kahuila, Eunjin Joo, Young Ae Shin, Jungok Becker, David Yoon, Bo Y Park, and Inhae Kim. Their impeccable grammatical intuition and expertise, fruitful suggestions, and constructive criticisms are all reflected on this final product in one way or another. I would also like to thank Samuel Lee, Jewel Lee, Youngju Koo, Gilyun An, Sung Joong Kim, Iksoo Jeong, Kyoung-Kook Kim, Jang-Il Kim, Chong S Kim, Meesun Cho, Byung-Joon Lim, and Dukhyun Cho. Their constant support and warm encouragement helped me reorient myself whenever I was going through a tumultuous period.

This book would not have been possible to see the light of the world without the unending support of the publishing company Pagijong Press. I would like to express my special thanks to the executive editor, Yi Jun Kwon, who gave me the golden opportunity to communicate with the readers of this book. I am also profoundly grateful to my long-time colleague, S. C. Silverman, for her diligent proofreading of all the English sentences in this book.

Special thanks are due to my great mentors at the Department of Linguistics at the University of Chicago who shaped and honed my linguistic intuition and grammatical knowledge during my graduate studies: James D. McCawley, Amy Dahlstrom, John Goldsmith, Jerry Sadock, and Salikoko S. Mufwene.

Lastly, I have always felt bad for not having carried out my familial duty during the time of writing this book. The very first copy of this book with my deepest love will be delivered to my wife, Woo Kyung Park.

Won Seok Cho
Monterey, California

Table of Contents

chapter 02 Clausal Conjunctions II (구절 접속사 II)_ 148

chapter 03 Sentence Connectors I (문장 접속사 I)_ 264

CHAPTER 1 Clausal Conjunctions I (구절 접속사 I)

A sentence (문장) can be classified as a simple sentence (단문), a compound sentence (중문), and a complex sentence (복문) in terms of the number of clauses it contains and how clauses are linked together when two or more clauses are connected. A simple sentence contains one independent clause which consists of a subject (주어) and a predicate (서술어).

John	[is a student.]
Subject	Predicate
Mary	[studies Korean.]
Subject	Predicate

In the case of a compound sentence and a complex sentence, two or more clauses are combined together by clausal conjunctions (구절 접속사)[1] to express a complex idea and at the same time to enrich the grammatical structure of the given sentence. A compound sentence is made up of two or more independent clauses. They are connected with a comma and a coordinating conjunction (등위접속사) or with a semicolon. English examples of coordinating conjunctions are "and, but, or, so, for, yet, nor."

John is a student, and he is studying Korean.
Mary is living in Seoul, but she cannot speak Korean.
John wants to buy a house, or he will rent an apartment.
I was very tired, so I went to bed early.
I need to buy a jacket, for the weather is getting cold.
John studied hard, yet he didn't pass the test.
Mary cannot sing, nor can she dance.
I saw a monkey; it was eating a banana.

A complex sentence is a sentence that contains one independent clause and one or more dependent clauses. The former is also called "a main clause (주절)" and the latter "a subordinate clause (종속절)." They are connected with subordinating conjunctions (종속접속사). Some of the English examples of subordinating conjunctions are "because, since, although, while, until, after, before, etc."

I went to a restaurant because I was hungry.
I have been working here since I came to Korea.
Although John left early, he was late for the meeting.
Mary came to my house while I was eating dinner.
I cannot go back home until I finish this work.
John took a rest after he worked for an hour.
Mary finished her homework before she went to bed.

There are also other types of complex sentences including sentences with relative clauses, quoted clauses, and that-clauses.

John met the woman who wrote this book. (Relative clause)
Mary told me that John already ate dinner. (Quoted clause)
That John is a genius is so obvious. (That-clause)
Mary thinks that John is a genius. (That-clause)

In the next two chapters, we will investigate the various types of Korean clausal conjunctions and explore how they are used effectively to connect two or more clauses focusing on the precise relationship between the two connected clauses.

Note:

1. Clausal conjunctions can be subcategorized into coordinating conjunctions (등위접속사), subordinating conjunctions (종속접속사), and correlative conjunctions (상관접속사). English examples of coordinating conjunctions and subordinating conjunctions were already discussed above. Correlative conjunctions are the combination of two elements that work together such as "either _ or _", "neither _ nor _", "not only _ but also _", etc.

1. Expressing "And": ~고

Function	Expressing "And"		
Form	~고		
Meaning	And		
Distribution	Present	Past	Future
Action Verb Stem — After a consonant	~고	~았/었고[*]	
Action Verb Stem — After a vowel	~고	~았/었고[*]	
Action Verb Stem — After "ㄹ"	~고	~았/었고[*]	
Stative Verb Stem — After a consonant	~고	~았/었고[*]	
Stative Verb Stem — After a vowel	~고	~았/었고[*]	
Stative Verb Stem — After "ㄹ"	~고	~았/었고[*]	

[*] The preceding verb can take its own tense suffix, or its tense can be determined by the tense of the last verb.

The Korean coordinating conjunction "~고" can be used to link two or more clauses, which can be rendered as "and." It can be freely used with both action verbs and stative verbs. In addition, it can also be used to connect clauses with the same subject or with different subjects.

존이 체육관에서 운동하고 메리가 도서관에서 책을 읽습니다.
(=John is doing exercise at the gym, and Mary is reading books in the library.)

존이 그 프로젝트를 시작하고 메리가 완성을 했습니다.
(=John started that project, and Mary finished it.)

존이 회사를 설립하고 메리가 지금까지 회사 일을 운영했습니다.
(=John founded the company, and Mary has run the business up until now.)

존이 회사를 설립하고 지금까지 회사 일을 운영했습니다.
(=John founded the company and has run the business up until now.)

존이 뚱뚱하고 메리가 날씬합니다.
(=John is fat, and Mary is slender.)

존이 똑똑하고 운동을 잘 합니다.
(=John is smart, and he is good at sports.)

The main function of "~고" is to link two or more clauses without imposing any specific sequence or order on the connected clauses. Therefore, all six sentences below basically carry the same meaning.

시간이 있으면 보통 영화도 보<u>고</u> 음악회에도 가<u>고</u> 친구하고 커피를 마십니다.
(=When I have time, I usually watch a movie, go to a concert, and drink coffee with my friend.)

시간이 있으면 보통 영화도 보<u>고</u> 친구하고 커피도 마시<u>고</u> 음악회에도 갑니다.
(=When I have time, I usually watch a movie, drink coffee with my friend, and go to a concert.)

시간이 있으면 보통 음악회에도 가<u>고</u> 영화도 보<u>고</u> 친구하고 커피를 마십니다.
(=When I have time, I usually go to a concert, watch a movie, and drink coffee with my friend.)

시간이 있으면 보통 음악회에도 가<u>고</u> 친구하고 커피도 마시<u>고</u> 영화도 봅니다.
(=When I have time, I usually go to a concert, drink coffee with my friend, and watch a movie.)

시간이 있으면 보통 친구하고 커피도 마시<u>고</u> 영화도 보<u>고</u> 음악회에도 갑니다.
(=When I have time, I usually drink coffee with my friend, watch a movie, and go to a concert.)

시간이 있으면 보통 친구하고 커피도 마시<u>고</u> 음악회에도 가<u>고</u> 영화도 봅니다.
(=When I have time, I usually drink coffee with my friend, go to a concert, and watch a movie.)

With regard to the tense of each connected verb, it can either be separately marked on each verb or can be marked only on the last verb which determines the tenses of all the preceding verbs.

존이 어렸을 때 농구를 잘<u>했고</u> 메리가 배구를 잘<u>했</u>습니다.
존이 어렸을 때 농구를 잘하<u>고</u> 메리가 배구를 잘<u>했</u>습니다.
(=John was good at basketball, and Mary was good at volleyball when they were little kids.)

존이 피자를 먹<u>었고</u> 메리가 샐러드를 먹<u>었</u>습니다.

존이 피자를 먹<u>고</u> 메리가 샐러드를 먹<u>었</u>습니다.

(=John ate pizza, and Mary ate salad.)

어렸을 때 존이 뚱뚱<u>했고</u> 메리가 날씬<u>했</u>습니다.

어렸을 때 존이 뚱뚱하<u>고</u> 메리가 날씬<u>했</u>습니다.

(=John was fat, and Mary was slender when they were little kids.)

존이 1년 전에 회사를 설립<u>했고</u> 지난 달에 파산<u>했</u>습니다.

존이 1년 전에 회사를 설립하<u>고</u> 지난 달에 파산<u>했</u>습니다.

(=John founded the company a year ago and went into bankruptcy last month.)

On the other hand, "~고" can also be used to express the sequence of immediate actions, which can be rendered as "and then/after." But this is not the inherent function of "~고," but rather it is the grammatical function of "~고 (나)서 (and then/after)" whose contraction form happens to be the same as "~고." It will be discussed in more detail below.

존이 저녁을 먹<u>고</u> **나서**/먹<u>고서</u>/먹<u>고</u> TV를 봅니다.

(=John eats dinner and then watches TV.)

(=John watches TV after eating dinner.)

메리가 옷을 갈아입<u>고</u> **나서**/갈아입<u>고서</u>/갈아입<u>고</u> 운동을 합니다.

(=Mary changes her clothes, and then she does exercise.)

(=Mary does exercise after changing her clothes.)

존이 도서관에서 공부를 하<u>고</u> **나서**/하<u>고서</u>/하<u>고</u> 집에 갑니다.

(=John studies at the library and then goes home.)

(=John goes home after studying at the library.)

2. Expressing concurrent actions or states: ~(으)며

Function		Expressing concurrent actions or states					
Form		~(으)며					
Meaning		And also/And at the same time			While		
Distribution		Present	Past	Future	Present	Past	Future
Action Verb Stem	After a consonant	~으며	~았/었으며		~으며*		
	After a vowel	~며	~았/었으며		~며*		
	After "ㄹ"	~며	~았/었으며		~며*		
Stative Verb Stem	After a consonant	~으며	~았/었으며				
	After a vowel	~며	~았/었으며				
	After "ㄹ"	~며	~았/었으며				

*The preceding verb cannot take its own tense suffix, and its tense is determined by the tense of the last verb.

The Korean coordinating conjunction "~(으)며" can be used to express that the listed actions or states take place more or less at the same time in a certain time period, which can be rendered as "and also/and at the same time." It can be used with both action verbs and stative verbs to link two or more clauses with the same subject or with different subjects. Due to its formality, however, it is generally limited to use in written text or in formal speech.

존이 도서관에서 공부하**며** 메리도 집에서 공부합니다.
(=John is studying at the library, and at the same time Mary is studying at home.)

존이 똑똑하**며** 메리도 똑똑한 편입니다.
(=John is smart, and Mary is also kind of smart.)

존이 공부도 잘하**며** 운동도 잘한다.
(=John is good at studying, and he is also good at sports.)

이 집은 거실이 아주 넓**으며** 전망도 좋습니다.
(=As for this house, it has a large living room, and it also has a good view.)

메리가 얼굴도 예쁘**며** 마음씨도 착합니다.
(=Mary is pretty, and she is also kind-hearted.)

When "~(으)며" is used with the copula "~이다," it expresses that the subject is holding two different titles at the same time.

존이 대학원생이**며** 조교로 일을 한다.

(=John is a graduate student, and at the same time he works as a teaching assistant.)

메리가 변호사(이)**며** 대학교수이다.

(=Mary is a lawyer, and at the same time she is a college professor.)

On the other hand, the default tense rule of "~(으)며" is that each verb must take its own tense suffix. But when "~(으)며" is linking clauses with the same subject, it is also possible that the tense suffix can be attached only to the last verb, which determines the tense of the preceding verb.

어제 **존이** 도서관에서 공부했으며 **메리도** 집에서 공부했다.

어제 **존이** 도서관에서 공부하며 **메리도** 집에서 공부했다. (NOT OK)

(=Yesterday John studied at the library, and Mary was also studying at home.)

어렸을 때 **존이** 똑똑했으며 **메리도** 똑똑한 편이었습니다.

어렸을 때 **존이** 똑똑하며 **메리도** 똑똑한 편이었습니다. (NOT OK)

(=John was smart, and Mary was also kind of smart when they were little kids.)

어렸을 때 **존이** 공부도 잘했으며 운동도 잘했다.

어렸을 때 **존이** 공부도 잘하며 운동도 잘했다. (OK)

(=John was good at studying, and he was also good at sports when he was a little kid.)

어렸을 때 **메리가** 얼굴도 예뻤으며 마음씨도 착했다.

어렸을 때 **메리가** 얼굴도 예쁘며 마음씨도 착했다. (OK)

(=Mary was pretty, and she was also kind-hearted when she was a little kid.)

Another primary function of "~(으)며" is to express that the subject is carrying out two different actions simultaneously, which can be rendered as "while." This function of "~(으)며" can be freely used in both written text and in conversation.

존이 항상 밥을 먹**으며** TV를 본다.

(=John always watches TV while eating food.)

존이 노래를 부르**며** 춤을 춥니다.

(=John is dancing while singing a song.)

In this usage of "~(으)며," the preceding verb cannot take its own tense suffix, and its tense is determined by the tense of the last verb.

존이 웃**으며** 메리에게 **다가갔다**.

(=John approached Mary while smiling.)

존이 웃**었으며** 메리에게 **다가갔다**. (NOT OK)

존이 비틀거리**며** 집에 **돌아왔다**.

(=John came back home while staggering.)

존이 비틀거**렸으며** 집에 **돌아왔다**. (NOT OK)

메리가 울**며** 살려달라고 **애원했다**.

(=Mary begged for her life while crying.)

메리가 울**었으며** 살려달라고 **애원했다**. (NOT OK)

3. Expressing concurrent actions or states: ~(으)면서

Function		Expressing concurrent actions or states					
Form		~(으)면서					
Meaning		And also/And at the same time			While		
Distribution		Present	Past	Future	Present	Past	Future
Action Verb Stem	After a consonant	~으면서[*]			~으면서[*]		
	After a vowel	~면서[*]			~면서[*]		
	After "ㄹ"	~면서[*]			~면서[*]		
Stative Verb Stem	After a consonant	~으면서[*]					
	After a vowel	~면서[*]					
	After "ㄹ"	~면서[*]					

[*] The preceding verb cannot take its own tense suffix, and its tense is determined by the tense of the last verb.

"~(으)면서" can be used to express that both the situation in the preceding clause and the situation in the following clause hold true at the same time, which can be rendered as "and also/and at the same time." To compensate for the limited usage of its equivalent grammar feature "~(으)며," "~(으)면서" can be freely used in both written text and conversation.

> 존이 공부를 잘하**면서** 운동도 잘한다.
> (=John is good at studying, and he is also good at sports.)
>
> 이 집은 거실이 아주 넓**으면서** 전망도 좋습니다.
> (=This house has a large living room, and at the same time it also has a good view.)
>
> 메리가 똑똑하**면서** 마음씨도 착합니다.
> (=Mary is smart, and at the same time she is also kind-hearted.)

It can also be used with the copula "~이다" to express that the subject is holding two different titles at the same time.

> 존이 시인이**면서** 소설가다.
> (=John is a poet, and at the same time he is a novelist.)
>
> 메리가 치과의사**면서** 대학교수다.
> (=Mary is a dentist, and at the same time she is a college professor.)

Another main function of "~(으)면서" is to express that the ongoing action in the following clause occurs simultaneously with another ongoing action in the preceding clause, which can be rendered as "while." It is fully interchangeable with "~(으)며." The only difference is that "~(으)면서" focuses more on the ongoing action itself, whereas "~(으)며" puts more emphasis on the description of the ongoing state of the action.

> 존이 노래를 부르**면서** 춤을 춥니다.
> 존이 노래를 부르**며** 춤을 춥니다.
> (=John is dancing while singing a song.)
>
> 메리가 지금 음악을 들**으면서** 공부합니다.
> 메리가 지금 음악을 들**으며** 공부합니다.
> (=Mary is studying now while listening to music.)

Unlike "~(으)며," however, "~(으)면서" in all of its usage cannot be used with different subjects.

존이 공부를 잘하**면서** 운동도 잘합니다.

(=John is good at studying, and he is also good at sports.)

존이 공부를 잘하**면서** 메리가 운동도 잘합니다. (NOT OK)

존이 밥을 먹**으면서** TV를 본다.

(=John is watching TV while eating food.)

존이 밥을 먹**으면서** 메리가 TV를 본다. (NOT OK)

메리가 여기 저기를 구경하**면서** 쇼핑을 한다.

(=Mary is shopping while looking around here and there.)

메리가 여기 저기를 구경하**면서** 존이 쇼핑을 한다. (NOT OK)

In addition, the tense of the preceding verb is always determined by the tense of the main verb.

존이 웃으**면서** 메리에게 **다가갔다**.

(=John approached Mary while smiling.)

존이 웃었**으면서** 메리에게 **다가갔다**. (NOT OK)

존이 비틀거리**면서** 집에 **돌아왔다**.

(=John came back home while staggering.)

존이 비틀거렸**으면서** 집에 **돌아왔다**. (NOT OK)

메리가 울**면서** 살려달라고 **애원했다**.

(=Mary begged for her life while crying.)

메리가 울었**으면서** 살려달라고 **애원했다**. (NOT OK)

4. Expressing "But": ~(으)나

The Korean coordinating conjuction "~(으)나" can be used to contrast two different clauses, which can be rendered as "but." It can be used with both action verbs and stative verbs to link clauses with the same subject or with different subjects. Due to its formality, however, it is more likely to be used in written text or in formal speech.

Function	Expressing "But"		
Form	~(으)나		
Meaning	But		
Distribution	Present	Past	Future
Action Verb Stem — After a consonant	~으나	~았/었으나	~겠으나
Action Verb Stem — After a vowel	~나	~았/었으나	~겠으나
Action Verb Stem — After "ㄹ"	~나[*]	~았/었으나	~겠으나
Stative Verb Stem — After a consonant	~으나	~았/었으나	~겠으나
Stative Verb Stem — After a vowel	~나	~았/었으나	~겠으나
Stative Verb Stem — After "ㄹ"	~나[*]	~았/었으나	~겠으나

[*] If the verb stem ends with "ㄹ," "ㄹ" will be dropped before we attach "~나" according to the rule of "ㄹ" deletion that says "the consonant "ㄹ" at the end of a verb stem is dropped before "ㄴ, ㅂ, ㅅ." (See Chapter 12 Verbs)

팔다 (to sell): 팔→파나, 멀다 (far): 멀→머나

존이 수영을 잘하**나** 여동생이 수영을 못한다.

(=John is good at swimming, but his younger sister isn't.)

존이 공부를 열심히 **했으나** 시험에 떨어졌다.

(=John studied hard, but he failed the test.)

존이 잘생**겼으나** 남동생이 못생겼다.

(=John is handsome, but his younger brother is ugly.)

존이 메리를 만**났으나** 아무 말도 하지 않았다.

(=John met Mary, but he didn't say a word to her.)

존이 돈은 많**으나** 남에게 전혀 베풀 줄을 몰라요.

(=John has a lot of money, but he doesn't spend money on others at all.)

메리가 얼굴은 예쁘**나** 너무 말랐다.

(=Mary has a pretty face, but she is too skinny.)

내일은 전국이 대체로 맑**겠으나** 오후 한 때 비가 조금 내리겠습니다.

(=Tomorrow it must be mostly clear nationwide, but it must be raining occasionally in the afternoon.)

With regard to the tense rule, the preceding verb can take its own tense suffix which is independent of the tense of the main verb.

존이 공부를 열심히 **했으나** 이번 시험에 합격할지 모르겠다.
(=John has studied hard, but I am not sure whether he is going to pass this exam.)

메리가 전에는 피아노를 잘 **쳤으나** 지금은 잘 못 친다.
(=Mary was good at playing the piano before, but she doesn't play well now.)

존이 어렸을 때 키가 **컸으나** 지금은 작은 편이다.
(=John was tall when he was a kid, but now he is short.)

메리는 돈을 좀 벌**겠으나** 다 써버릴 겁니다.
(=Mary must be making some money, but she may waste all of it.)

On the other hand, "~(으)나" can be used in most sentence types, but it cannot be used in questions.

시장하시겠**으나** 조금만 더 기다리세요. (Imperative)
(=You must be hungry, but please wait a little more.)

시간은 없**으나** 좀 더 기다려 보자. (Proposition)
(=We don't have much time, but let's wait for him/her a little more.)

존이 키가 작**으나** 농구를 잘 합니까? (Question: NOT OK)
(=John is short, but is he good at basketball?)

존이 부자이**나** 다른 사람들을 위해 돈을 씁니까? (Question: NOT OK)
(=John is rich, but does he spend money on others?)

To compensate for its limited usage in question, "~지만 (even though)" or "~는/(으)ㄴ데 (given that)," which are more or less equivalent to "~(으)나," can be used in questions instead.

존이 키가 작**지만** 농구를 잘 합니까?
(=Even though John is short, is he good at basketball?)

바쁘시겠**지만** 조금만 더 기다려 주시겠습니까?
(=Even though you must be busy, could you please wait a little bit longer?)

존이 키가 작**은데** 농구를 잘 합니까?

(=Given the condition that John is short, is he good at basketball?)

존이 부자**인데** 다른 사람들을 위해 돈을 씁니까?

(=Given the condition that John is rich, does he spend money on others?)

5. Expressing "Even though": ~지만

Function	Expressing "Even though"		
Form	~지만		
Meaning	Even though		
Distribution		Present	Past	Future
Action Verb Stem	After a consonant	~지만	~았/었지만	~겠지만
	After a vowel	~지만	~았/었지만	~겠지만
	After "ㄹ"	~지만	~았/었지만	~겠지만
Stative Verb Stem	After a consonant	~지만	~았/었지만	~겠지만
	After a vowel	~지만	~았/었지만	~겠지만
	After "ㄹ"	~지만	~았/었지만	~겠지만

"~지만" can be used to contrast two different clauses in which the situation in the following clause occurs although the situation in the preceding clause is true, which can be rendered as "even though." It can be used with both action verbs and stative verbs to link clauses with the same subject or with different subjects. Unlike its more or less equivalent grammar feature "~(으)나," however, "~지만" can be freely used in both written text and conversation.

새 컴퓨터를 사고 싶**지만** 돈이 없어서 못 사요.

(=Even though I want to buy a new computer, I can't buy one because I don't have money.)

밖에 비가 오**지만** 우산은 필요 없다.

(=Even though it's raining outside, I don't need an umbrella.)

존은 날씨가 춥**지만** 항상 반바지만 입는다.

(=Even though the weather is cold, John always wears short pants.)

존은 똑똑하**지만** 여동생은 머리가 나쁘다.

(=Even though John is smart, his younger sister is not smart.)

존은 부자가 아니**지만** 가난한 사람들을 도와준다.

(=Even though John is not a rich man, he helps poor people.)

메리는 똑똑하**지만** 남들한테 자랑을 하지 않는다.

(=Even though Mary is smart, she is not snobbish.)

With regard to the tense rule, the preceding verb can take its own tense suffix which is independent of the tense of the main verb.

밥을 먹었**지만** 아직 배가 고프다.

(=Even though I ate some food, I am still hungry.)

(아까) 약을 발랐**지만** 온 몸이 가렵다.

(=Even though I applied the medicine a while ago, I am itching all over my body.)

Although "~지만" can be used in most sentence types, it cannot be used in an imperative sentence.

존이 키가 작**지만** 농구를 잘 합니다. (Statement)

(=Even though John is short, he is good at basketball.)

존이 키가 작**지만** 농구를 잘 합니까? (Question)

(=Is John good at basketball even though he is short?)

배가 고프**지만** 조금만 기다리자. (Proposition)

(=Even though we are hungry, let's wait a little more.)

배가 고프**지만** 조금만 기다려라. (Imperative: NOT OK)

(=Even though you must be hungry, just wait a little more.)

피곤하**지만** 샤워하고 자라. (Imperative: NOT OK)

(=Even though you must be tired, take a shower and go to bed.)

But if we attach the probability suffix "~겠" to the preceding verb, "~지만" will become fully compatible with imperative sentences.

배가 고프**겠지만** 조금만 기다려라. (Imperative: OK)

(=Even though you must be hungry, just wait a little more.)

피곤하**겠지만** 샤워하고 자라. (Imperative: OK)

(=Even though you must be tired, take a shower and go to bed.)

6. Taking the given situation into consideration: ~는/(으)ㄴ데

Function	Taking the given situation into consideration		
Form	~는/(으)ㄴ데		
Meaning	Given that _		
Distribution		Present	Past	Future
Action Verb Stem	After a consonant	~는데	~았/었는데	~겠는데
	After a vowel	~는데	~았/었는데	~겠는데
	After "ㄹ"	~는데*	~았/었는데	~겠는데
Stative Verb Stem	After a consonant	~은데	~았/었는데	~겠는데
	After a vowel	~ㄴ데	~았/었는데	~겠는데
	After "ㄹ"	~ㄴ데*	~았/었는데	~겠는데

*If the action verb stem ends with "ㄹ," "ㄹ" will be dropped before we attach "~는데, ~ㄴ데" according to the rule of "ㄹ" deletion that says "the consonant "ㄹ" at the end of a verb stem is dropped before "ㄴ, ㅂ, ㅅ." (See Chapter 12 Verbs)

알다 (to know): 알→아는데, 멀다 (far): 멀→먼데

"~는/(으)ㄴ데" can be used to contrast the situation in the following clause with the given situation in the preceding clause, which can be rendered as "Given that _." It can be used with both action verbs and stative verbs to link clauses with the same subject or with different subjects. It can be freely used in both written text and conversation.

메리는 공부하**는데** 존은 밖에서 놉니다.

(=Given that Mary is studying, John is playing outside.)

존은 키가 작**은데** 농구를 잘한다.

(=Given that John is short, he is good at playing basketball.)

존은 사람은 착**한데** 말이 너무 많다.

(=Given that John is kind-hearted, he is too talkative.)

With regard to the tense rule, the preceding verb can take its own tense suffix which is independent of the tense of the main verb.

존은 열심히 공부**했는데** 시험에 불합격했다.

(=Given that John studied hard, he failed the test.)

In addition, it can be used to express that the situation in the preceding clause is taken into consideration for the situation in the following clause, which can also be rendered as "Given that _."

In addition, it is also compatible with all sentence types.

돈이 조금 모자라**는데** 좀 깎아 주시겠습니까? (Question)
(=Given that I am a little short of money, could you give me a discount?)

가격은 괜찮**은데** 품질은 어떻습니까? (Question)
(=Given that the price is ok, how about the quality?)

목이 마**른데** 물 좀 주시겠습니까? (Question)
(=Given that I am thirsty, could you give me some water?)

운동하**는데** 방해하지 마세요. (Imperative)
(=Given that I am exercising, please don't disturb me.)

다 좋**은데** 빨리 일을 마무리하세요. (Imperative)
(=Given that everything looks good, please get it done quickly.)

밤이 늦**었는데** 빨리 가서 자라. (Imperative)
(=Given that it's late at night, go quickly and get some sleep.)

지금은 시간이 없**는데** 나중에 이야기합시다. (Proposition)
(=Given that I don't have time now, let's talk about it later.)

배가 고**픈데** 어디 가서 밥이나 좀 먹읍시다. (Proposition)
(=Given that I am hungry, let's go some place to eat.)

날씨도 더**운데** 바닷가에 놀러 갑시다. (Proposition)
(=Given that the weather is hot, let's go to the beach to have some fun.)

7. Expressing "Before/After": ~기 전에, ~(으)ㄴ 후에/다음에

Function		Expressing "Before/After"					
Form		~기 전에			~(으)ㄴ 후에/다음에		
Meaning		Before			After		
Distribution		Present	Past	Future	Present	Past	Future
Action Verb Stem	After a consonant	~기 전에[*1]			~은 후에/~은 다음에[*1]		
	After a vowel	~기 전에[*1]			~ㄴ 후에/~ㄴ 다음에[*1]		
	After "ㄹ"	~기 전에[*1]			~ㄴ 후에/~ㄴ 다음에[*1,2]		
Stative Verb Stem	After a consonant						
	After a vowel						
	After "ㄹ"						

[*1] The preceding verb cannot take its own tense suffix, and its tense is determined by the tense of the main verb.

[*2] If the verb stem ends with "ㄹ," "ㄹ" will be dropped before we attach "~ㄴ 후에, ~ㄴ 다음에" according to the rule of "ㄹ" deletion that says "the consonant "ㄹ" at the end of a verb stem is dropped before "ㄴ, ㅂ, ㅅ." (See Chapter 12 Verbs)

놀다 (to play): 놀→논 후에, 논 다음에

"~기 전에" can be used to express the sequence of two different events such that the event in the following clause occurs before the event in the preceding clause, which can be rendered as "before." "전에" can only be used with a noun or a noun equivalent such as gerund. Therefore, the preceding verb must be changed into a gerund form by attaching the gerundival suffix "~기" to its verb stem.

존은 밥을 먹**기 전에** 손을 씻습니다.

(=John washes his hands before he eats food.)

메리는 자**기 전에** 이를 닦습니다.

(=Mary brushes her teeth before she goes to bed.)

존은 한국에 오**기 전에** 한국말을 배웠습니다.

(=John learned Korean before he came to Korea.)

메리는 결혼하**기 전에** 남자친구가 있었습니다.

(=Mary had a boyfriend before she got married.)

With regard to the tense rule, the preceding verb cannot take its own tense suffix, and its tense is determined by the tense of the main verb.

존은 시험을 보**기 전에** 준비를 철저히 했습니다.

(=John thoroughly prepared for the test before he took it.)

존은 시험을 봤**기 전에** 준비를 철저히 했습니다. (NOT OK)

메리는 자**기 전에** 불을 껐습니다.

(=Mary turned the light off before she went to bed.)

메리는 잤**기 전에** 불을 껐습니다. (NOT OK)

On the other hand, "~(으)ㄴ 후에/다음에" can be used to express that the event in the following clause occurs after the event in the preceding clause, which can be rendered as "after." "후에/다음에" require the preceding verb to be in a modifying form. In addition, since the event in the preceding clause occurs before the event in the following clause, the past-tense modifying suffixes "~(으)ㄴ" are attached to the preceding verb stem.

존은 저녁을 먹**은 후에**/먹**은 다음에** TV를 봅니다.

(=John watches TV after eating dinner.)

존은 도둑을 잡**은 후에**/잡**은 다음에** 경찰에 신고했습니다.

(=John reported to the police after he captured the burglar.)

메리는 설거지를 **한 후에**/**한 다음에** 책을 봅니다.

(=Mary reads books after washing dishes.)

메리는 집을 **판 후에**/**판 다음에** 아파트로 이사 갔습니다.

(=Mary moved into an apartment after she sold her house.)

8. Expressing the sequence of actions or the cause and effect relationship: ~아서/어서

"~아서/어서" can be used to express the sequence of actions in which the action in the preceding clause occurs before the action in the following clause, which can be rendered as "and then." It is frequently used with verbs of locomotion and verbs of posture. The second syllable "서" can sometimes be deleted in casual speech.

Function	Expressing the sequence of actions			Expressing the cause and effect relationship		
Form	~아서/어서					
Meaning	And then			And so		
Distribution	Present	Past	Future	Present	Past	Future
Action Verb Stem — After "오" or "아"	~아서[*]			~아서[*]		
Action Verb Stem — Otherwise	~어서[*]			~어서[*]		
Stative Verb Stem — After "오" or "아"				~아서[*]		
Stative Verb Stem — Otherwise				~어서[*]		

[*] The preceding verb cannot take its own tense suffix, and its tense is determined by the tense of the main verb.

Verbs of locomotion: 가다(to go), 오다(to come), 나가다(to go out), 나오다(to come out), 돌아오다(to come back), 돌아가다(to go back), 들어가다(to go in), 들어오다(to come in), 뛰어가다(to go running), 뛰어오다(to come running), 출발하다(to depart), 도착하다(to arrive), 이민 가다(to emigrate), 이민 오다(to immigrate), 들르다(to stop by), 다가가다(to approach), 다가오다(to come close), etc.

Verbs of posture: 일어나다(to get up), 앉다(to sit), 서다(to stand), 일어서다(to stand up), 눕다(to lie on your back), 엎드리다(to be on the ground), 구부리다(to hunker), 웅크리다(to crouch), 펴다(to spread), etc.

존은 도서관에 **가서** 공부를 했습니다.

(=John went to the library, and then he studied there.)

메리는 집에 **와서** 저녁을 먹었습니다.

(=Mary came home, and then she ate dinner.)

존은 집에 들어**가서** 돈을 가지고 나왔습니다.

(=John went inside the house, and then he came out with some money.)

메리는 고향을 떠**나서** 한국에 왔습니다.

(=Mary left her hometown, and then she came to Korea.)

존은 아침 일찍 일어**나서** 아침을 먹습니다.

(=John gets up early in the morning, and then he eats breakfast.)

메리는 의자에 앉**아서** 노래를 불렀습니다.

(=Mary sat on the chair, and then she sang a song.)

존은 줄을 **서서** 차례를 기다리고 있었습니다.

(=John stood in line, and then he was waiting for his turn.)

메리는 소파에 누**워서** TV를 봅니다.

(=Mary is lying on the sofa, and then she is watching TV.)

내일 만나**서** 그것에 대해서 자세히 얘기합시다.

(=Let's meet tomorrow and then talk about it in more detail.)

선물을 사**서** 선생님께 드렸어요.

(=I bought a present and then gave it to my teacher.)

"~아서/어서" can also be used with other action verbs to express that the action in the following clause can be fulfilled by carrying out the action in the preceding clause.

고구마 두 개를 삶**아서** 먹었습니다.

(=I steamed two sweet potatoes and then ate them.)

닭 한 마리를 기름에 튀**겨서** 먹었습니다.

(=I deep-fried a whole chicken and then ate it.)

존은 집을 팔**아서** 빚을 갚았습니다.

(=John sold his house and then paid off his debt.)

메리는 돈을 모**아서** 집을 샀습니다.

(=Mary saved her money and then bought a house.)

존은 메리를 만**나서** 저녁을 먹었다.

(=John met Mary and then ate dinner.)

신청서를 작성하**셔서** 이달 말까지 제출하세요.

(=Please fill out the application form and then submit it by the end of this month.)

저희 프로그램에 등록하**셔서** 한국어 능력을 향상시키세요.

(=Please register for our program and then improve your Korean proficiency.)

On the other hand, "~아서/어서" can also be used to express the cause and effect relationship in which the situation in the preceding clause is the main cause for the situation in the following clause, which can be rendered as "and so." The preceding verb can be either an action verb or a stative verb.

저는 점심을 늦게 먹**어서** 배가 고프지 않습니다.
(=I had a late lunch, and so I am not hungry.)

존은 열심히 공부**해서** 시험에 합격했습니다.
(=John studied hard, and so he passed the test.)

존이 도와**줘서** 일을 끝낼 수 있었습니다.
(=John helped me, and so I could finish the work.)

공항에 늦게 도착**해서** 비행기를 놓쳤습니다.
(=I arrived late at the airport, and so I missed the flight.)

비가 많이 **와서** 길이 미끄럽습니다.
(=It rained a lot, and so the roads are slippery.)

날씨가 좋**아서** 기분이 좋습니다.
(=The weather is good, and so I am in a good mood.)

너무 피곤**해서** 일찍 잠을 잤습니다.
(=I was so tired, and so I went to bed early.)

너무 아파**서** 병원에 갔습니다.
(=I was so sick, and so I went to a hospital.)

In addition, "~아서/어서" can be used in conversational idioms to express the reason for the speaker's current feeling about a given situation.

만**나서** 반갑습니다.
(=It's nice to meet you.)

늦**어서** 죄송합니다/미안합니다.
(=I am sorry for the late.)

도와주**셔서** 감사합니다/고맙습니다.
(=Thank you for your help.)

9. Expressing "Upon the completion of": ~고 나서, ~고(서)

Function		Expressing "Upon the completion of"		
Form		~고 나서, ~고(서)		
Meaning		And then		
Distribution		Present	Past	Future
Action Verb Stem	After a consonant	~고 나서/고(서)*		
	After a vowel	~고 나서/고(서)*		
	After "ㄹ"	~고 나서/고(서)*		
Stative Verb Stem	After a consonant			
	After a vowel			
	After "ㄹ"			

* The preceding verb cannot take its own tense suffix, and its tense is determined by the tense of the main verb.

"~고 나서" and its contraction form "~고(서)" can be used to express that the action in the following clause takes place upon the completion of the action in the preceding clause, which can be rendered as "and then."

존이 떠나고 **나서**/떠나**고서**/떠나**고** 메리가 공항에 도착했다.
(=John left, and then Mary arrived at the airport.)

존은 저녁을 먹고 **나서**/먹**고서**/먹**고** 스타벅스에서 커피를 마셨다.
(=John ate dinner and then drank coffee at Starbucks.)

메리는 숙제를 하고 **나서**/하**고서**/하**고** TV를 봤습니다.
(=Mary finished her homework and then watched TV.)

존은 일을 다 끝내고 **나서**/끝내**고서**/끝내**고** 집에 갔다.
(=John finished his work and then went home.)

메리는 올림픽에서 금메달을 따고 **나서**/따**고서**/따**고** 관중들 앞에서 흐느껴 울고 있었다.
(=Mary won the gold medal at the Olympics, and then she was sobbing in front of the audience.)

With regard to the tense rule, the preceding verb cannot take its own tense suffix, and its tense is determined by the tense of the main verb.

존이 저녁을 먹고 **나서**/먹<u>고서</u>/먹<u>고</u> TV를 봤습니다.

(=John ate dinner, and then he watched TV.)

존이 저녁을 먹<u>었고</u> **나서**/먹<u>었고서</u>/먹<u>었고</u> TV를 봤습니다. (NOT OK)

메리가 존과 데이트를 하고 **나서**/하<u>고서</u>/하<u>고</u> 집에 돌아왔습니다.

(=Mary went on a date with John, and then she came back home.)

메리가 존과 데이트를 <u>했고</u> **나서**/<u>했고서</u>/<u>했고</u> 집에 돌아왔습니다. (NOT OK)

10. Expressing "After the completion of an action/the precondition for taking action": ~고(서)는

"~고(서)는" can be used to express that the situation in the following clause happens some time after the completion of the action in the preceding clause, which can be rendered as "(some time) after."

Function		Expressing "After the completion of an action"			Expressing the precondition for taking action		
Form		~고(서)는					
Meaning		(Some time) After			Unless		
Distribution		Present	Past	Future	Present	Past	Future
Action Verb Stem	After a consonant	~고서는/고는[*]			~고서는/고는[*]		
	After a vowel	~고서는/고는[*]			~고서는/고는[*]		
	After "ㄹ"	~고서는/고는[*]			~고서는/고는[*]		
Stative Verb Stem	After a consonant						
	After a vowel						
	After "ㄹ"						

[*] The preceding verb cannot take its own tense suffix, and its tense is determined by the tense of the main verb.

존은 나한테 화풀이를 하<u>고서는</u>/하<u>고는</u> 밖으로 나갔다.

(=John went outside after he took his anger out on me.)

메리는 술을 마시<u>고서는</u>/마시<u>고는</u> 갑자기 소리를 지르기 시작했다.

(=Mary suddenly started shouting after drinking.)

존은 메리가 다른 남자친구가 있다는 사실을 알<u>고서는</u>/알<u>고는</u> 무척 화를 냈다.

(=John went off the deep end after he found out that Mary has another boyfriend.)

메리는 존의 사정을 듣<u>고서는</u>/듣<u>고는</u> 용서해 주기로 했다.

(=Mary decided to forgive John after she heard about his situation.)

The preceding verb cannot take its own tense suffix, and its tense is determined by the tense of the main verb.

존은 나한테 화풀이를 했<u>고서는</u>/했<u>고는</u> 밖으로 나갔다. (NOT OK)

(=John went outside after he took his anger out on me.)

On the other hand, "~고(서)는" can also be used in a double negative sentence with "~(으)ㄹ 수 없다" to express a strong positive statement that the situation in the preceding clause is the precondition to carry out the action in the following clause, which can be rendered as "unless."

부모님의 허락을 받지 않<u>고서는</u>/않<u>고는</u> 존과 결혼**할 수 없다**.

(=I cannot marry John unless I get permission from my parents.)

수면제를 먹지 않<u>고서는</u>/않<u>고는</u> 잠을 **잘 수 없다**.

(=I cannot sleep unless I take a sleeping pill.)

존은 수술을 받지 않<u>고서는</u>/않<u>고는</u> 오래 **살 수가 없다**.

(=John cannot live long unless he gets a surgery.)

신분증을 보여 주지 않<u>고서는</u>/않<u>고는</u> 여기에 출입**할 수가 없어요**.

(=You cannot have in-and-out privileges unless you present your ID.)

11. Expressing "In the middle of carrying out an action": ~는 (도)중(에)

"~는 도중(에)" and its contraction form "~는 중(에)" can be used to express that the situation in the following clause occurs at some point in the middle of carrying out the action in the preceding clause, which can be rendered as "while one is doing something."

Function		Expressing "In the middle of carrying out an action"		
Form		~는 (도)중(에)		
Meaning		While one is doing something		
Distribution		Present	Past	Future
Action Verb Stem	After a consonant	~는 도중(에)/중(에)[*1]		
	After a vowel	~는 도중(에) /중(에)[*1]		
	After "ㄹ"	~는 도중(에) /중(에)[*1,2]		
Stative Verb Stem	After a consonant			
	After a vowel			
	After "ㄹ"			

[*1] The preceding verb cannot take its own tense suffix, and its tense is determined by the tense of the main verb.

[*2] If the verb stem ends with "ㄹ," "ㄹ" will be dropped before we attach "~는 도중(에)/중(에)" according to the rule of "ㄹ" deletion that says "the consonant "ㄹ" at the end of a verb stem is dropped before "ㄴ, ㅂ, ㅅ." (See Chapter 12 Verbs)
놀다 (to play): 놀→노는 도중(에)/노는 중(에), 살다 (to sell): 살→사는 도중(에)/사는 중(에)

존은 학교에 가**는 도중(에)/**가**는 중에** 메리를 자주 만난다.

(=John often sees Mary while he is going to school.)

메리는 내가 공부하**는 도중(에)/**공부하**는 중에** 자꾸 방해를 한다.

(=Mary repeatedly disturbs me while I am studying.)

존은 운동하**는 도중(에)/**운동하**는 중(에)** 발목을 삐었습니다.

(=John sprained his ankle while he was doing exercise.)

메리는 쇼핑하**는 도중(에)/**쇼핑하**는 중(에)** 친구를 만났습니다.

(=Mary met her friend while she was shopping.)

공부하**는 도중(에)/**공부하**는 중(에)** 전기가 나갔습니다.

(=The power went out while I was studying.)

The preceding verb cannot take its own tense suffix, and its tense is determined by the tense of the main verb.

존이 메리와 이야기하**는 도중(에)/**이야기하**는 중(에)** 내가 끼어들었다.

(=I cut in on the conversation while John and Mary were talking to each other.)

존이 메리와 이야기**했는 도중(에)/**이야기**했는 중(에)** 내가 끼어들었다. (NOT OK)

한국에서 유학하<u>는 도중(에)</u>/유학하<u>는 중(에)</u> 여러가지 예절을 배웠습니다.

(=I learned various kinds of etiquette while I was studying in Korea.)

한국에서 유학<u>했</u><u>는 도중(에)</u>/유학<u>했</u><u>는 중(에)</u> 여러가지를 배웠습니다. (NOT OK)

12. Expressing "During the given period of time": ~는/(으)ㄹ 동안(에)

Function	Expressing "During the given period of time"		
Form	~는/(으)ㄹ 동안(에)		
Meaning	During the time that _		
Distribution	Present	Past	Future
Action Verb Stem — After a consonant	~는 동안(에)[1]		~을 동안(에)[1]
Action Verb Stem — After a vowel	~는 동안(에)[1]		~ㄹ 동안(에)[1]
Action Verb Stem — After "ㄹ"	~는 동안(에)[1,2]		동안(에)[1]
Stative Verb Stem — After a consonant			
Stative Verb Stem — After a vowel			
Stative Verb Stem — After "ㄹ"			

[1] The preceding verb cannot take its own tense suffix, and its tense is determined by the tense of the main verb.

[2] If the verb stem ends with "ㄹ," "ㄹ" will be dropped before we attach "~는 동안(에)" according to the rule of "ㄹ" deletion that says "the consonant "ㄹ" at the end of a verb stem is dropped before "ㄴ, ㅂ, ㅅ." (See Chapter 12 Verbs)
놀다 (to play): 놀→노는 동안(에), 살다 (to sell): 살→사는 동안(에)

"~는 동안(에)" can be used to express that the situation in the following clause continues to happen during the given period of time that one is carrying out the action in the preceding clause, which can be rendered as "during the time that _."

존은 메리와 사<u>는 동안(에)</u> 아주 행복했다.

(=John was very happy during the time that he was living with Mary.)

존은 제가 숙제하<u>는 동안(에)</u> 자꾸 방해를 해요.

(=John repeatedly disturbs me during the time that I am doing my homework.)

이따가 존이 자<u>는 동안에</u> 빨래를 할 겁니다.

(=I will do my laundry during the time that John will be sleeping sometime later.)

With regard to the tense rule, the preceding verb cannot take its own tense suffix, and its tense is determined by the tense of the main verb.

> 존은 메리가 한국에 있는 동안(에) 한 번도 연락을 안 했다.
>
> (=John did not contact Mary at all during the time that she was in Korea.)
>
> 존은 메리가 한국에 있었는 동안(에) 한 번도 연락을 안 했다. (NOT OK)

On the other hand, "~으(ㄹ) 동안(에)" can be optionally used instead of "~는 동안(에)" to emphasize that one's carrying out the action in the preceding clause will actually happen at a future time.

> 한국에 있을 동안(에) 여기 저기를 구경해 보고 싶다.
>
> 한국에 있는 동안(에) 여기 저기를 구경해 보고 싶다.
>
> (=I want to try to visit here and there during the time that I will be staying in Korea.)
>
> 내일 인터뷰할 동안(에) 전화 걸지 마세요.
>
> 내일 인터뷰하는 동안(에) 전화 걸지 마세요.
>
> (=Don't call me during the time that I will be having the interview tomorrow.)

13. Expressing "At the time that": ~(으)ㄹ 때(에)

Function		Expressing "At the time that"		
Form		~(으)ㄹ 때(에)		
Meaning		When		
Distribution		Present	Past	Future
Action Verb Stem	After a consonant	~을 때(에)	~았/었을 때(에)*	
	After a vowel	~ㄹ 때(에)	~았/었을 때(에)*	
	After "ㄹ"	때(에)	~았/었을 때(에)*	
Stative Verb Stem	After a consonant	~을 때(에)	~았/었을 때(에)*	
	After a vowel	~ㄹ 때(에)	~았/었을 때(에)*	
	After "ㄹ"	때(에)	~았/었을 때(에)*	

* The preceding verb can take its own tense suffix or its tense can be determined by the tense of the main verb.

"~(으)ㄹ 때(에)" can be used to express that the situation in the following clause happens when the action or state in the preceding clause takes place, which can be rendered as "when."

메리는 웃**을 때(에)** 정말 귀엽다.
(=Mary looks so cute when she smiles.)

존은 메리와 데이트**할 때(에)** 항상 그 레스토랑에 간다.
(=John always goes to that restaurant when he goes on a date with Mary.)

날씨가 좋**을 때(에)** 야외수영장에서 수영을 합니다.
(=I swim at the outdoor swimming pool when the weather is good.)

존은 우울**할 때(에)** 친구와 술을 마십니다.
(=John drinks with his friend when he gets depressed.)

With regard to the tense rule, the tense of the preceding verb is determined by the tense of the main verb. But sometimes the past-tense suffix can be optionally used to emphasize the completion of the situation in the preceding clause.

존이 상을 받**을 때** 메리가 옆에 있었다.
(=Mary was next to John when he was receiving the award.)

존이 상을 받았**을 때** 메리가 옆에 있었다.
(=Mary was next to John when he received the award.)

메리는 어제 냉장고를 **살 때** 가격을 흥정했다.
(=Mary haggled over the price when she was buying the refrigerator yesterday.)

메리는 어제 냉장고를 샀**을 때** 가격을 흥정했다.
(=Mary haggled over the price when she bought the refrigerator yesterday.)

어제 날씨가 좋**을 때(에)** 야외수영장에서 수영을 했습니다.
(=Yesterday I swam at the outdoor swimming pool when the weather was good.)

어제 날씨가 좋았**을 때(에)** 야외수영장에서 수영을 했습니다.
(=Yesterday I swam at the outdoor swimming pool when the weather was good.)

날이 어두워**질 때** 집에 도착했다.
(=I arrived at home when it was getting dark.)

날이 어두워<u>졌을 때</u> 집에 도착<u>했</u>다.

(=I arrived at home when it was dark.)

14. Expressing "By the time": ~(으)ㄹ 적에

Function		Expressing "By the time"		
Form		~(으)ㄹ 적에		
Meaning		By the time		
Distribution		Present	Past	Future
Action Verb Stem	After a consonant		~았/었을 적(에)*	~을 적(에)
	After a vowel		~았/었을 적(에)*	~ㄹ 적(에)
	After "ㄹ"		~았/었을 적(에)*	적(에)
Stative Verb Stem	After a consonant		~았/었을 적(에)*	~을 적(에)
	After a vowel		~았/었을 적(에)*	~ㄹ 적(에)
	After "ㄹ"		~았/었을 적(에)*	적(에)

* The preceding verb can take its own tense suffix or its tense can be determined by the tense of the main verb.

"~(으)ㄹ 적에" can be used to express that the situation in the following clause applies by the time the situation in the preceding clause happens, which can be rendered as "by the time." It is more likely to be used in conversation, whereas the equivalent expression "~(으)ㄹ 때(에)" can be freely used in both written text and conversation.

어른이 이야기 **할 적에** 말대꾸하지 말아라.

(=Don't talk back by the time an elderly person is talking to you.)

개가 밥을 먹**을 적에** 절대 건드리지 마세요.

(=Don't ever touch a dog by the time it is eating.)

여기가 제가 어릴 **적에** 살던 곳입니다.

(=This is the place where I used to live by the time I was a kid.)

With regard to the tense rule, the tense of the preceding verb is determined by the tense of the main verb. But sometimes the past-tense suffix can be optionally used to emphasize the completion of the situation in the preceding clause.

여기가 제가 어**렸을 적에** 살았던 곳입니다.

(=This is the place where I used to live by the time I was a kid.)

15. Expressing "Until, Whenever": ~(으)ㄹ 때까지, ~(으)ㄹ 때마다

Function		Expressing "Until"			Expressing "Whenever"		
Form		~(으)ㄹ 때까지			~(으)ㄹ 때마다		
Meaning		Until			Whenever		
Distribution		Present	Past	Future	Present	Past	Future
Action Verb Stem	After a consonant			~을 때까지[*]			~을 때마다[*]
	After a vowel			~ㄹ 때까지[*]			~ㄹ 때마다[*]
	After "ㄹ"			때까지[*]			때마다[*]
Stative Verb Stem	After a consonant			~을 때까지[*]			~을 때마다[*]
	After a vowel			~ㄹ 때까지[*]			~ㄹ 때마다[*]
	After "ㄹ"			때까지[*]			때마다[*]

[*] The preceding verb cannot take its own tense suffix, and its tense is determined by the tense of the main verb.

"~(으)ㄹ 때까지" can be used to express that the situation in the following clause continues until the completion of the situation in the preceding clause, which can be rendered as "until."

이 은혜 죽을 **때까지** 잊지 않겠습니다.

(=I will not forget what you have done for me until I die.)

회의가 끝날 **때까지** 밖에서 기다리세요.

(=Please wait outside until the meeting is over.)

저는 한 번 일을 시작하면 지**칠 때까지** 계속합니다.

(=Once I start working, I continue to work until I get exhausted.)

존은 메리를 만날 **때까지** 여자친구가 없었다.

(=John had had no girlfriend until he met Mary.)

경찰은 범인이 잡**힐 때까지** 집 근처에서 잠복근무를 했다.

(=The police had been on stakeout near the suspect's house until he/she was captured.)

With regard to the tense rule, the preceding verb cannot take its own tense suffix, and its tense is determined by the tense of the main verb.

> 존은 대학에 **갈 때까지** 열심히 공부했다.
> (=John had studied hard until he entered the college.)
> 존은 대학에 <u>갔</u>을 **때까지** 열심히 공부했다. (NOT OK)
>
> 메리는 이혼 신청**할 때까지** 남편한테 모든 것을 바쳤다.
> (=Mary had devoted herself to her husband until she filed for divorce.)
> 메리는 이혼 신청<u>했</u>을 **때까지** 남편한테 모든 것을 바쳤다. (NOT OK)

"~(으)ㄹ 때마다" can be used to express that the situation in the following clause occurs whenever the situation in the preceding clause happens, which can be rendered as "whenever."

> 존은 점심을 먹**을 때마다** 학교 식당에 간다.
> (=John goes to the school cafeteria whenever he eats lunch.)
>
> 메리는 존이 그리**울 때마다** 존을 처음 만났던 장소를 찾아갑니다.
> (=Mary goes to the place where she met John for the first time whenever she misses John.)
>
> 존은 부모님에게서 용돈을 받**을 때마다** 다 써버린다.
> (=John uses up the money whenever he gets his allowance from his parents.)
>
> 메리는 시험을 **볼 때마다** 항상 실수를 합니다.
> (=Mary makes mistakes whenever she takes a test.)
>
> 존은 힘**들 때마다** 항상 제 곁에 있어 주었습니다.
> (=John has been always with me whenever I had a hard time.)

With regard to the tense rule, the preceding verb cannot take its own tense suffix, and its tense is determined by the tense of the main verb.

> 존은 점심을 먹**을 때마다** 학교 식당에 갔습니다.
> (=John went to the school cafeteria whenever he ate lunch.)
> 존은 점심을 먹<u>었</u>을 **때마다** 학교 식당에 갔습니다. (NOT OK)

메리는 시험을 **볼 때마다** 항상 실수를 했습니다.

(=Mary made mistakes whenever she took a test.)

메리는 시험을 **봤을 때마다** 항상 실수를 했습니다. (NOT OK)

16. Expressing "Since": ~(으)ㄹ 때부터

Function	Expressing "Since"		
Form	~(으)ㄹ 때부터		
Meaning	Since		
Distribution	Present	Past	Future
Action Verb Stem — After a consonant	~을 때부터	~았/었을 때부터*	
Action Verb Stem — After a vowel	~ㄹ 때부터	~았/었을 때부터*	
Action Verb Stem — After "ㄹ"	때부터	~았/었을 때부터*	
Stative Verb Stem — After a consonant	~을 때부터	~았/었을 때부터*	
Stative Verb Stem — After a vowel	~ㄹ 때부터	~았/었을 때부터*	
Stative Verb Stem — After "ㄹ"	때부터	~았/었을 때부터*	

* The preceding verb can take its own tense suffix or its tense can be determined by the tense of the main verb.

"~(으)ㄹ 때부터" can be used to express that the situation in the following clause has continued up to the present time since the situation in the preceding clause occurred, which can be rendered as "since."

이 신발은 처음 신**을 때부터** 아주 불편했다.

(=These shoes have been very uncomfortable since I wore them for the first time.)

존은 태어날 **때부터** 몸이 약했다.

(=John has been physically weak since he was born.)

존은 어릴 **때부터** 공부를 잘 했습니다.

(=John has studied very well since he was a kid.)

이 세탁기는 **살 때부터** 좀 문제가 있었다.

(=This washer has had some problems since I bought it.)

With regard to the tense rule, the tense of the preceding verb is determined by the tense of the main verb. But sometimes the past-tense suffix can be optionally used to emphasize the completion of the situation in the preceding clause.

이 신발은 처음 신었을 **때부터** 아주 불편했다.

(=These shoes have been very uncomfortable since I wore them for the first time.)

존은 태어났을 **때부터** 몸이 약했다.

(=John has been physically weak since he was born.)

존은 어렸을 **때부터** 공부를 잘 했습니다.

(=John has studied very well since he was a kid.)

이 세탁기는 샀을 **때부터** 문제가 있었다.

(=This washer has had some problems since I bought it.)

17. Expressing "Right at the moment that": ~는/(으)ㄴ 순간(에), ~는 찰나에

Function		Expressing "Right at the moment that"					
Form		~는/(으)ㄴ 순간(에)			~는 찰나에		
Meaning		Right at the moment that _					
Distribution		Present	Past	Future	Present	Past	Future
Action Verb Stem	After a consonant	~는 순간(에)	~은 순간(에)		~는 찰나(에)		
	After a vowel	~는 순간(에)	~ㄴ 순간(에)		~는 찰나(에)		
	After "ㄹ"	~는 순간(에)*	순간(에)		~는 찰나(에)*		
Stative Verb Stem	After a consonant						
	After a vowel						
	After "ㄹ"						

* If the action verb stem ends with "ㄹ," "ㄹ" will be dropped before we attach "~는 순간(에), ~는 찰나(에)" according to the rule of "ㄹ" deletion that says "the consonant "ㄹ" at the end of a verb stem is dropped before "ㄴ, ㅂ, ㅅ." (See Chapter 12 Verbs)
알다 (to know): 알→아는 순간(에), 팔다 (to sell): 팔→파는 찰나(에)

"~는 순간(에), ~는 찰나에" can be used to express that the situation in the following clause occurs right at the moment that the situation in the preceding clause happens, which can be rendered as "right at the moment that _." "~는 순간(에)" can be freely used in both written text and conversation, whereas "~는 찰나에" is more likely to be used in casual speech.

> 존은 앞 차와 부딪치려**는 순간**(에)/부딪치려**는 찰나에** 얼른 브레이크를 밟았다.
> (=John quickly hit the brake right at the moment that he was about to hit the car in front of him.)

> 기차가 역에 도착하**는 순간**(에)/ 도착하**는 찰나에** 그 사람이 갑자기 철로에 뛰어들었다.
> (=All of a sudden the person jumped onto the railway track right at the moment that the train was arriving at the station.)

> 잠깐 한 눈을 파**는 순간**(에)/파**는 찰나에** 사고가 났다.
> (=I got into an accident right at the moment that I took my eyes off the road for a split second.)

> 적이 방심하고 있**는 순간**(에)/있**는 찰나에** 기습공격을 해야 한다.
> (=We must make a surprise attack right at the moment that the enemy forces are off guard.)

> 범인이 막 도망치**는 순간**(에)/도망치**는 찰나에** 경찰이 그 집에 들이닥쳤다.
> (=The police stormed into the house right at the moment that the suspect was about to flee.)

With regard to the tense rule, the tense of the preceding verb is determined by the tense of the main verb. But sometimes "~(으)ㄴ 순간(에)" which contains the past-tense modifying suffix can be optionally used to emphasize the completion of the situation in the preceding clause.

> 잠깐 눈을 감**은 순간**(에) 누가 내 가방을 훔쳐 갔다.
> 잠깐 눈을 감**는 순간**(에) 누가 내 가방을 훔쳐 갔다.
> (=Somebody stole my bag right at the moment that I closed my eyes for a brief moment.)

> 그녀를 처음 **본 순간**(에) 나는 사랑에 빠졌다.
> 그녀를 처음 보**는 순간**(에) 나는 사랑에 빠졌다.
> (=I fell in love with her right at the moment that I first saw her.)

18. Expressing "At the same time": ~는/(으)ㄴ 동시에

Function	Expressing "At the same time"		
Form	~는/(으)ㄴ 동시에		
Meaning	At the same time that _		And at the same time
Distribution	Present	Past	Future
Action Verb Stem — After a consonant	~는 동시에[1]		
Action Verb Stem — After a vowel	~는 동시에[1]		
Action Verb Stem — After "ㄹ"	~는 동시에[1,2]		
Stative Verb Stem — After a consonant	~은 동시에[1]		
Stative Verb Stem — After a vowel	~ㄴ 동시에[1]		
Stative Verb Stem — After "ㄹ"	~ㄴ 동시에[1,2]		

[1] The preceding verb cannot take its own tense suffix, and its tense is determined by the tense of the main verb.

[2] If the verb stem ends with "ㄹ," "ㄹ" will be dropped before we attach "~는 동시에, ~ㄴ 동시에" according to the rule of "ㄹ" deletion that says "the consonant "ㄹ" at the end of a verb stem is dropped before "ㄴ, ㅂ, ㅅ." (See Chapter 12 Verbs)
팔다 (to sell): 팔→파는 동시(에), 멀다 (far): 멀→먼 동시(에)

"~는 동시에" can be used with an action verb to express that the situation in the following clause occurs simultaneously when the situation in the preceding clause happens, which can be rendered as "at the same time that _."

존이 그 여자와 결혼하**는 동시에** 메리도 다른 남자와 결혼했다.

(=Mary got married to another man at the same time that John married that woman.)

존은 대학을 졸업하**는 동시에** 삼성에 취직이 됐다.

(=John got a job at Samsung at the same time that he graduated from a college.)

그 사람이 그 곳을 떠나**는 동시에** 폭탄이 폭발했다.

(=A bomb exploded at the same time that that person left the place.)

북한은 ICBM을 개발하**는 동시에** 핵실험도 계속하고 있다.

(=North Korea has continued to conduct nuclear tests, and at the same time it is developing an ICBM.)

On the other hand, "~는/(으)ㄴ 동시에" can also be used to express that the situation in the following clause applies in addition to the situation in the preceding clause, which can be rendered as "and at the same time."

이 약은 고혈압을 치료하<u>**는 동시에**</u> 우울증 치료에도 효과가 있다.

(=This medicine cures high blood pressure, and at the same time it can also cure depression.)

메리는 리더십이 있<u>**는 동시에**</u> 공부에 대한 열정도 대단하다

(=Mary has good leadership, and at the same time she has a great passion for her studies.)

이 제품은 품질이 좋<u>**은 동시에**</u> 가격도 아주 합리적이다.

(=This product has good quality, and at the same time the price is also very reasonable.)

메리는 마음이 따뜻<u>**한 동시에**</u> 얼굴도 아주 예쁘다.

(=Mary is kind-hearted, and at the same time she also has a very pretty face.)

19. Expressing "As soon as, Soon after": ~자마자, ~자

Function		Expressing "As soon as"			Expressing "Soon after"		
Form		~자마자			~자		
Meaning		As soon as			Soon after		
Distribution		Present	Past	Future	Present	Past	Future
Action Verb Stem	After a consonant	~자마자[*]			~자[*]		
	After a vowel	~자마자[*]			~자[*]		
	After "ㄹ"	~자마자[*]			~자[*]		
Stative Verb Stem	After a consonant						
	After a vowel						
	After "ㄹ"						

[*] The preceding verb cannot take its own tense suffix, and its tense is determined by the tense of the main verb.

"~자마자" can be used to express that the action in the following clause takes place immediately upon the completion of the action in the preceding clause, which can be rendered as "as soon as."

존은 일어나**자마자** 아침을 먹습니다.

(=As soon as John gets up, he eats breakfast.)

사고가 나**자마자** 경찰이 사고 현장에 도착했습니다.

(=As soon as the accident occurred, the police arrived at the scene.)

메리는 결혼식이 끝나**자마자** 신혼여행을 떠났습니다.

(=As soon as the wedding ceremony was over, Mary left for her honeymoon trip.)

The preceding verb cannot take its own tense suffix, and its tense is determined by the tense of the main verb.

존은 일어났**자마자** 아침을 먹었습니다. (NOT OK)

사고가 났**자마자** 경찰이 사고 현장에 도착했습니다. (NOT OK)

메리는 결혼식이 끝났**자마자** 신혼여행을 떠났습니다. (NOT OK)

On the other hand, "~자" can be used to express that the action in the following clause occurs after a certain period of time, but not immediately, upon the completion of the action in the preceding clause, which can be rendered as "soon after."

존은 복권에 당첨되**자** 새 차를 뽑았습니다.

(=John bought a new car soon after he won the lottery.)

메리는 결혼식이 끝나**자** 신혼여행을 떠났습니다.

(=Mary left for her honeymoon trip soon after the wedding ceremony was over.)

남편은 돈이 생기**자** 다시 도박을 시작했습니다.

(=My husband started gambling again soon after he got some money.)

Again, the preceding verb cannot take its own tense suffix, and its tense is determined by the tense of the main verb.

존은 복권에 당첨되었**자** 새 차를 뽑았습니다. (NOT OK)

메리는 결혼식이 끝났**자** 신혼여행을 떠났습니다. (NOT OK)

남편은 돈이 생겼**자** 다시 도박을 시작했습니다. (NOT OK)

20. Expressing "About the time":

~(으)ㄹ 쯤(에), ~(으)ㄹ 즈음(에), ~(으)ㄹ 무렵(에)

Function		Expressing "About the time"		
Form		~(으)ㄹ 쯤(에)	~(으)ㄹ 즈음(에)	~(으)ㄹ 무렵(에)
Meaning		About the time _		
Distribution		Future	Future	Future
Action Verb Stem	After a consonant	~을 쯤(에)[*]	~을 즈음(에)[*]	~을 무렵(에)[*]
	After a vowel	~ㄹ 쯤(에)[*]	~ㄹ 즈음(에)[*]	~ㄹ 무렵(에)[*]
	After "ㄹ"	쯤(에)[*]	즈음(에)[*]	무렵(에)[*]
Stative Verb Stem	After a consonant			
	After a vowel			
	After "ㄹ"			

[*] The preceding verb cannot take its own tense suffix, and its tense is determined by the tense of the main verb.

"~(으)ㄹ 쯤(에), ~(으)ㄹ 즈음(에), ~(으)ㄹ 무렵(에)" can be used to express that the action in the following clause occurs about the time when the situation in the preceding clause happens, which can be rendered as "about the time _." The preceding verb cannot take its own tense suffix, and its tense is determined by the tense of the main verb. "~(으)ㄹ 쯤(에)" can be freely used in both written text and conversation, whereas "~(으)ㄹ 즈음(에), ~(으)ㄹ 무렵(에)" are more likely to be used in written text.

아이를 낳**을 쯤(에)**/낳**을 즈음(에)**/낳**을 무렵(에)** 어머님이 산후조리를 하러 집에 오셨습니다.

(=My mother came to my house for my postpartum care about the time when I gave birth to my baby.)

날이 어두워**질 쯤(에)**/어두워**질 즈음(에)**/어두워**질 무렵(에)** 집에 도착했다.

(=I arrived at home about the time when it was getting dark.)

존은 보통 해가 **질 쯤(에)**/**질 즈음(에)**/**질 무렵(에)** 알바를 하러 나갑니다.

(=John usually goes to work for his part-time job about the time of sunset.)

21. Expressing "To the point that" or "To make sure that": ~도록

Function		Expressing "To the point that"			Expressing "To make sure that"		
Form		~도록					
Meaning		Until			So that _ can _		
Distribution		Present	Past	Future	Present	Past	Future
Action Verb Stem	After a consonant	~도록[*]			~도록[*]		
	After a vowel	~도록[*]			~도록[*]		
	After "ㄹ"	~도록[*]			~도록[*]		
Stative Verb Stem	After a consonant						
	After a vowel						
	After "ㄹ"						

[*] The preceding verb cannot take its own tense suffix, and its tense is determined by the tense of the main verb.

"~도록" can be used to express that the action in the following clause continues to be carried out until its outcome gets close to the situation in the preceding clause, which can be rendered as "until." It is commonly used as a metaphorical expression to exaggerate one's feeling over the given situation. The preceding verb cannot take its own tense suffix, and its tense is determined by the tense of the main verb.

존은 죽**도록** 일을 했다.

(=John worked to death.)

손발이 부르트**도록** 열심히 일을 했습니다.

(=I worked hard until my hands and feet got swollen.)

존은 메리를 죽**도록** 사랑합니다.

(=John loves Mary to death.)

메리는 존을 미치**도록** 사랑합니다.

(=Mary loves John like crazy.)

메리는 귀청이 떨어지**도록** 소리를 질렀다.

(=Mary shouted until my eardrums popped.)

집이 떠나가**도록** 비가 내렸다.

(=The rain poured down until my house may float away.)

비 오는 날 먼지 나**도록** 맞았다.

(=I got beaten until the air got dusty on a rainy day.)

배가 터지**도록** 밥을 먹었습니다.

(=I ate until my stomach was about to explode. =I ate way too much.)

동해 물과 백두산이 마르고 닳**도록** 하느님이 보우하사 우리나라 만세 (**From Korean National Anthem**)

(=Until the water in the East Sea drys up, and Mt. Baekdu wears away, long live our nation because God protects us.)

On the other hand, "~도록" can also be used to express that the action in the following clause must be carried out to make sure that the condition in the preceding clause is to be met, which can be rendered as "so that _ can _." Again, the preceding verb cannot take its own tense suffix, and its tense is determined by the tense of the main verb.

존은 메리가 따라올 수 있**도록** 천천히 걸었습니다.

(=John walked slowly so that Mary could catch up with him.)

뒤에서도 볼 수 있**도록** 스크린을 좀 크게 해 주세요.

(=Please make the screen bigger so that people in the back can also see it.)

좀 알아들을 수 있**도록** 천천히 얘기해 보세요.

(=Please speak slowly so that I can understand it.)

제가 따라 할 수 있**도록** 천천히 읽어 주세요.

(=Please read it slowly so that I can repeat after you.)

22. Expressing "To Make sure that": ~게(끔)

"~게(끔)" like "~도록" can be used to express that the action in the following clause must be carried out to make sure that the condition in the preceding clause is to be met, which can be rendered as "to make sure that _." The preceding verb cannot take its own tense suffix, and its tense is determined by the tense of the main verb. "~게(끔)" is more likely to be used in conversation, whereas "~도록" can be freely used in both written text and conversation.

Function	Expressing "To make sure that"					
Form	~게(끔)					
Meaning	To make sure that _					
Distribution		Present	Past	Future	Present	Past	Future
Action Verb Stem	After a consonant	~게끔[*]			~게끔[*]		
	After a vowel	~게끔[*]			~게끔[*]		
	After "ㄹ"	~게끔[*]			~게끔[*]		
Stative Verb Stem	After a consonant						
	After a vowel						
	After "ㄹ"						

[*] The preceding verb cannot take its own tense suffix, and its tense is determined by the tense of the main verb.

좀 알아들을 수 있**게(끔)** 자세히 말씀해 주세요.

(=Please tell me in more detail to make sure that I can understand it.)

돈이 모자라지 않**게(끔)** 넉넉히 가져 오세요.

(=Please bring enough money to make sure that you will not be short of money.)

뒤에서도 들을 수 있**게(끔)** 스피커를 크게 틀어 주세요.

(=Please turn up the speaker volume to make sure that people in the back can also hear it.)

23. Expressing the cause and effect relationship: ~기 때문에, ~(으)니(까)

In Korean, there are various types of grammatical conjunctions that can be used to express the cause and effect relationship between two adjoining clauses. "~아서/어서, ~기 때문에, ~(으)니(까)" are the most commonly used ones. They are generally interchangeable, but they differ in terms of the grammatical restrictions imposed on their actual usage.

(1) ~아서/어서

As we discussed before, "~아서/어서" can be used to express the cause and effect relationship between the preceding clause and the following clause, which can be rendered as "and so."

Function		Expressing the cause and effect relationship					
Form		~기 때문에			~(으)니(까)		
Meaning		Because					
Distribution		Present	Past	Future	Present	Past	Future
Action Verb Stem	After a consonant	~기 때문에	~았/었기 때문에		~으니(까)	~았/었으니(까)	
	After a vowel	~기 때문에	~았/었기 때문에		~니(까)	~았/었으니(까)	
	After "ㄹ"	~기 때문에	~았/었기 때문에		~니(까)*	~았/었으니(까)	
Stative Verb Stem	After a consonant	~기 때문에	~았/었기 때문에		~으니(까)	~았/었으니(까)	
	After a vowel	~기 때문에	~았/었기 때문에		~니(까)	~았/었으니(까)	
	After "ㄹ"	~기 때문에	~았/었기 때문에		~니(까)*	~았/었으니(까)	

*If the verb stem ends with "ㄹ," "ㄹ" will be dropped before we attach "~니(까)" according to the rule of "ㄹ" deletion that says "the consonant "ㄹ" at the end of a verb stem is dropped before "ㄴ, ㅂ, ㅅ." (See Chapter 12 Verbs)
팔다 (to sell): 팔→파니(까), 멀다 (far): 멀→머니(까)

존은 돈을 많이 벌**어서** 강남에 집을 샀습니다.

(=John made a lot of money, and so he bought a house in the Gangnam district.)

쇼핑을 오랫동안 **해서** 다리가 아팠습니다.

(=I did the shopping for a long time, and so my legs hurt.)

날씨가 아주 좋**아서** 산책을 했습니다.

(=The weather was so good, and so I took a walk.)

배가 고**파서** 식당에 갔습니다.

(=I was hungry, and so I went to a restaurant.)

피곤해**서** 일찍 잤습니다.

(=I was tired, and so I went to bed early.)

But there are some grammatical restrictions on this usage of "~아서/어서." The preceding verb cannot take its own tense suffix, and its tense is determined by the tense of the main verb.

존은 돈을 많이 벌었**어서** 강남에 집을 샀습니다. (NOT OK)
쇼핑을 오랫동안 했**어서** 다리가 아팠습니다. (NOT OK)
날씨가 아주 좋았**어서** 산책을 했습니다. (NOT OK)

배가 고팠**어서** 식당에 <u>갔</u>습니다. (NOT OK)

피곤했**어서** 일찍 <u>잤</u>습니다. (NOT OK)

Another restriction is that"~아서/어서" cannot be used in imperative or propositional sentences.

날씨가 좋<u>아서</u> 산책을 해라. (Imperative: NOT OK)

(=The weather is good and so take a walk.)

배가 고<u>파서</u> 식당에 가라. (Imperative: NOT OK)

(=You must be hungry and so go to a restaurant.)

피곤해<u>서</u> 일찍 자라. (Imperative: NOT OK)

(=You must be tired and so go to bed early.)

쇼핑을 오랫동안 해<u>서</u> 집에 가자. (Proposition: NOT OK)

(=We have been shopping for a long time and so let's go home.)

배가 고<u>파서</u> 식당에 가자. (Proposition: NOT OK)

(=I am hungry and so let's go to a restaurant.)

피곤해<u>서</u> 일찍 자자. (Proposition: NOT OK)

(=I am tired and so let's go to bed early.)

(2) ~기 때문에

"~기 때문에" can be used to express the cause and effect relationship between the preceding clause and the following clause, which can be rendered as "because."

존이 학교에 항상 늦게 오**기 때문에** 선생님한테 혼납니다.

(=Because John always comes to school late, he is scolded by his teacher.)

메리가 늦게 일어나**기 때문에** 항상 지각을 합니다.

(=Because Mary gets up late, she is always late for her class.)

Unlike "~아서/어서," however, the preceding verb can freely take its own tense suffix which is independent of the tense of the main verb.

존은 돈을 많이 벌**기 때문에** 강남에 집을 <u>샀</u>습니다.

(=Because John <u>is</u> making a lot of money, he <u>bought</u> a house in the Gangnam district.)

존은 돈을 많이 벌었**기 때문에** 강남에 집을 <u>샀</u>습니다.

(=Because John <u>made</u> a lot of money, he <u>bought</u> a house in the Gangnam district.)

배가 고팠**기 때문에** 식당에 갑니다.

(=Because I <u>was</u> hungry, I <u>am</u> going to a restaurant.)

배가 고팠**기 때문에** 식당에 <u>갔</u>습니다.

(=Because I <u>was</u> hungry, I <u>went</u> to a restaurant.)

But "~기 때문에" still cannot be used in imperative or propositional sentences.

돈을 많이 벌**기 때문에** 저녁을 사라. (Imperative: NOT OK)

(=Because you are making a lot of money, buy me dinner.)

날씨가 좋**기 때문에** 산책을 해라. (Imperative: NOT OK)

(=Because the weather is good, take a walk.)

피곤하**기 때문에** 일찍 자라. (Imperative: NOT OK)

(=Because you must be tired, go to bed early.)

쇼핑을 오랫동안 **했기 때문에** 집에 가자. (Proposition: NOT OK)

(=Because we did the shopping for a long time, let's go home.)

배가 고프**기 때문에** 식당에 가자. (Proposition: NOT OK)

(=Because I am hungry, let's go to a restaurant.)

피곤하**기 때문에** 일찍 자자. (Proposition: NOT OK)

(=Because I am tired, let's go to bed early.)

(3) ~(으)니(까)

"~(으)니(까)" can be used to express the cause and effect relationship between the preceding clause and the following clause, which can be rendered as "because." The last syllable "까" can sometimes be deleted in conversation.

존이 학교에 항상 늦게 오**니까** 선생님한테 혼납니다.

(=Because John always comes to school late, he is scolded by his teacher.)

메리가 늦게 일어나**니까** 항상 지각을 합니다.

(=Because Mary gets up late, she is always late for her class.)

In addition, the preceding verb can freely take its own tense suffix which is independent of the tense of the main verb.

존은 돈을 많이 버**니까** 강남에 집을 <u>샀</u>습니다.

(=Because John <u>is</u> making a lot of money, he <u>bought</u> a house in the Gangnam district.)

존은 돈을 많이 벌었**으니까** 강남에 집을 <u>샀</u>습니다.

(=Because John <u>made</u> a lot of money, he <u>bought</u> a house in the Gangnam district.)

Unlike "~아서/어서, ~기 때문에," "~(으)니(까)" can be used in all types of sentences including imperative and propositional sentences.

날씨가 좋<u>**으니까**</u> 산책을 해라. (Imperative)

(=Because the weather is good, take a walk.)

돈을 많이 버**니까** 저녁을 사라. (Imperative)

(=Because you are making a lot of money, buy me dinner.)

피곤하**니까** 일찍 자라. (Imperative)

(=Because you must be tired, go to bed early.)

쇼핑을 오랫동안 **했으니까** 집에 가자. (Proposition)

(=Because we did the shopping for a long time, let's go home.)

배가 **고프니까** 식당에 가자. (Proposition)

(=Because I am hungry, let's go to a restaurant.)

피곤하**니까** 일찍 자자. (Proposition)

(=Because I am tired, let's go to bed early.)

(4) Summary

We have so far discussed the three different types of clausal conjunctions that can be used to express the cause and effect relationship between two adjoining clauses. There are many cases where the grammatical conditions for all these three clausal conjunctions are fully met so that each of them can be freely used, as in the following sentences.

Cause and Effect Conjunctions	Grammatical Restrictions
~아서/어서	1. The preceding verb cannot take a tense suffix. The tense will be determined by the main verb. 2. It cannot be used in imperative or propositional sentences.
~기 때문에	1. The preceding verb can take its own tense suffix. 2. It cannot be used in imperative or propositional sentences.
~(으)니(까)	1. The preceding verb can take its own tense suffix. 2. It can be used in imperative or propositional sentences.

날씨가 좋아서 산책을 합니다.

날씨가 좋기 때문에 산책을 합니다.

날씨가 좋으니까 산책을 합니다.

(=Because the weather is good, I am taking a walk.)

배가 고파서 식당에 갔습니다.

배가 고팠기 때문에 식당에 갔습니다.

배가 고팠으니까 식당에 갔습니다.

(=Because I was hungry, I went to a restaurant.)

Aside from some slight differences in nuance, the sentences above are fully interchangeable. But one mysterious fact arises as to the native speaker's choice among the three available options. Without any clear reason, native speakers tend to use the more restricted one over the less restricted ones in the case that all three options are equally available. This is exacly the opposite of the non-native speakers' natural choice among the options. They tend to use the least restricted one a lot more than the other options partly because they want to avoid making any unnecessary grammatical errors.

~아서/어서   〉   ~기 때문에   〉   ~(으)니(까)

most restricted   least restricted

more likely used by native speakers   more likely used by non-native speakers

Therefore, if you want to achieve native level Korean proficiency regarding these grammatical features, it is highly recommended that you practice using the more restricted one rather than the less restricted ones whenever they are equally available.

24. Expressing the cause for a negative outcome: ~느라(고)

Function		Expressing the cause for a negative outcome		
Form		~느라(고)		
Meaning		Because one is/was doing something		
Distribution		Present	Past	Future
Action Verb Stem	After a consonant	~느라(고)[*1]		
	After a vowel	~느라(고)[*1]		
	After "ㄹ"	~느라(고)[*1,2]		
Stative Verb Stem	After a consonant			
	After a vowel			
	After "ㄹ"			

[*1] The preceding verb cannot take its own tense suffix, and its tense is determined by the tense of the main verb.

[*2] If the action verb stem ends with "ㄹ," "ㄹ" will be dropped before we attach "~느라고" according to the rule of "ㄹ" deletion that says "the consonant "ㄹ" at the end of a verb stem is dropped before "ㄴ, ㅂ, ㅅ." (See Chapter 12 Verbs)

팔다 (to sell): 팔→파느라고, 살다 (to live): 살→사느라고

"~느라(고)" can be used to express the cause and effect relationship between the preceding clause and the following clause regarding the way in which one is carrying out the action in the preceding clause, which results in the negative outcome in the following clause. It can be rendered as "because one is/was doing something."

숙제를 하느라(고) 한 숨도 못 잤습니다.

(=Because I was doing my homework, I could not sleep at all.)

공부하느라(고) 밥 먹을 틈도 없다.

(=Because I have been studying, I don't even have time to eat.)

Unlike other cause and effect conjunctions such as "~아서/어서, ~기 때문에, ~(으)니(까)," "~느라(고)" cannot be used with a stative verb.

존은 키가 작느라(고) 농구를 잘 못한다. (NOT OK)

존은 키가 작아서 농구를 잘 못한다.

존은 키가 작기 때문에 농구를 잘 못한다.

존은 키가 작으니까 농구를 잘 못한다.

(=Because John is short in height, he is not good at basketball.)

Some may raise the question regarding this restriction because of the following sentence in which "~느라(고)" is used with the stative verb "크다 (tall)."

존은 키가 <u>크느라(고)</u> 밥을 많이 먹는다. (OK)

However, this is not the counterexample against the exculsive usage of "~느라(고)" with action verbs, but rather it is another strong supporting example for its restricted usage. In Korean, the stative verb "크다 (tall)" is a homonym (a word with the same pronunciation, but with a different meaning) of the action verb "크다 (to grow)." The interpretation of the sentence above is only possible on a par with its action verb usage.

존은 키가 <u>크느라(고)</u> 밥을 많이 먹는다.
(=Because John is growing, he is eating a lot.) (OK with the action verb "크다 (to grow)")
(=Because John is tall, he is eating a lot.) (NOT OK with the stative verb "크다 (tall)")

On the other hand, the preceding verb cannot take its own tense suffix, and its tense is determined by the tense of the main verb.

숙제를 하<u>느라(고)</u> 한 숨도 못 <u>잤</u>습니다.
(=Because I had to do my homework, I could not sleep at all.)
숙제를 <u>했느라(고)</u> 한 숨도 못 <u>잤</u>습니다. (NOT OK)

In addition, "~느라(고)" can be used to link clauses with the same subject, but not with different subjects.

<u>메리가</u> 공부를 하<u>느라(고)</u> 한 숨도 못 잤습니다.
(=Because Mary was studying, she could not sleep at all.)

<u>메리가</u> 공부하<u>느라(고)</u> <u>존이</u> 한 숨도 못 잤습니다. (NOT OK)
(=Because Mary was studying, John could not sleep at all.)

Moreover, "~느라(고)" cannot be used in imperative or propositional sentences.

밖에 비가 <u>오느라(고)</u> 우산을 가지고 가라. (Imperative: NOT OK)
(=Because it's raining outside, take the umbrella with you.)

밖에 비가 <u>오느라(고)</u> 우산을 가지고 가자. (Proposition: NOT OK)

(=Because it's raining outside, let's take an umbrella.)

Lastly, there is also a semantic restriction on the usage of "~느라(고)." The outcome of the action specified in the following clause must be a negative one, not a positive one.

하루 종일 일하<u>느라(고)</u> 아주 피곤하다. (OK with Negative Outcome)

(=Because I have been working all day, I am so tired.)

하루 종일 일하<u>느라(고)</u> 돈을 많이 벌었다. (NOT OK with Positive Outcome)

(=Because I have been working all day, I made a lot of money.)

25. Expressing an unexpected outcome due to an uncontrollable situation: ~는 바람에

Function	Expressing an unexpected outcome due to an uncontrollable situation		
Form	~는 바람에		
Meaning	Because		
Distribution		Present	Past	Future
Action Verb Stem	After a consonant	~는 바람에[1]		
	After a vowel	~는 바람에[1]		
	After "ㄹ"	~는 바람에[1,2]		
Stative Verb Stem	After a consonant			
	After a vowel			
	After "ㄹ"			

[1] The preceding verb cannot take its own tense suffix, and its tense is determined by the tense of the main verb.

[2] If the action verb stem ends with "ㄹ," "ㄹ" will be dropped before we attach "~는 바람에" according to the rule of "ㄹ" deletion that says "the consonant "ㄹ" at the end of a verb stem is dropped before "ㄴ, ㅂ, ㅅ." (See Chapter 12 Verbs)

팔다 (to sell): 팔→파는 바람에, 살다 (to live): 살→사는 바람에

"~는 바람에" can be used to express that the unexpected situation in the following clause occurs due to an uncontrollable situation in the preceding clause, which can be rendered as "because."

돌에 걸려 넘어지**는 바람에** 피가 났습니다.

(=Because I tripped over a stone, I was bleeding.)

아버님이 부도가 나**는 바람에** 대학에 진학할 수 없었습니다.

(=Because my father declared bankruptcy, I could not go to a college.)

존은 복권에 당첨되**는 바람에** 갑자기 부자가 되었다.

(=Because John won the lottery, he suddenly became rich.)

"~는 바람에" can only be used with an action verb, but it cannot be used with a stative verb.

존은 키가 작**는 바람에** 농구를 잘 못한다. (NOT OK)

존은 키가 작**느라(고)** 농구를 잘 못한다. (NOT OK)

존은 키가 작**아서** 농구를 잘 못한다.

존은 키가 작**기 때문에** 농구를 잘 못한다.

존은 키가 작**으니까** 농구를 잘 못한다.

(=Because John is short in height, he is not good at basketball.)

On the other hand, the preceding verb cannot take its own tense suffix, and its tense is determined by the tense of the main verb.

돌에 걸려 넘어지**는 바람에** 다리가 부러졌다.

(=Because I tripped over a stone, I was bleeding.)

돌에 걸려 넘어졌**는 바람에** 다리가 부러졌다. (NOT OK)

Moreover, "~는 바람에" cannot be used in imperative or propositional sentences.

밖에 비가 오**는 바람에** 우산을 가지고 가라. (Imperative: NOT OK)

(=Because it's raining outside, take the umbrella with you.)

밖에 비가 오**는 바람에** 우산을 가지고 가자. (Proposition: NOT OK)

(=Because it's raining outside, let's take an umbrella.)

26. Expressing the main reason for a given situation: ~(으)므로

Function		Expressing the main reason for a given situation		
Form		~(으)므로		
Meaning		And therefore		
Distribution		Present	Past	Future
Action Verb Stem	After a consonant	~으므로	~았/었으므로	~겠으므로
	After a vowel	~므로	~았/었으므로	~겠으므로
	After "ㄹ"	~므로	~았/었으므로	~겠으므로
Stative Verb Stem	After a consonant	~으므로	~았/었으므로	~겠으므로
	After a vowel	~므로	~았/었으므로	~겠으므로
	After "ㄹ"	~므로	~았/었으므로	~겠으므로

"~(으)므로" can be used to express that the situation in the preceding clause is the main reason for the situation in the following clause, which can be rendered as "and therefore." Due to its formality, however, it can only be used in written text and in formal speech.

앞으로 어떤 일이 일어날지 예측할 수 없<u>으므로</u> 항상 미리 대비해야 한다.
(=We cannot predict what is going to happen in the future, and therefore we must always get prepared for something beforehand.)

추석 명절에는 모든 고속도로가 다 막히<u>므로</u> 고향에 가려면 일찍 출발해야 한다.
(=All highways are going to be congested on Harvest Day, and therefore you must leave early if you want to visit your hometown.)

이 기계는 성능이 좋<u>으므로</u> 다른 기계보다 가격이 훨씬 비싸다.
(=This machine shows good performance, and therefore it is a lot more expensive than other machines.)

요즘 날씨가 쌀쌀하<u>므로</u> 감기에 걸리지 않도록 조심하세요.
(=The weather is chilly these days, and therefore you must be careful not to catch a cold.)

In addition, the preceding verb can take its own tense suffix which is independent of the tense of the main verb.

범인이 잡**혔으므로** 이제 안심해도 된다.

The suspect was captured, and therefore now you can have a piece of mind.)

요즘 물가가 많이 올**랐으므로** 이 돈으로 살기가 아주 빠듯하다.

(=The prices of commodities have gone up a lot, and therefore I can barely make ends meet with this money.)

갑작스런 폭염으로 인해 전기 사용량이 급증**했으므로** 전력 부족 현상이 일어났다.

(=The usage of electricity had rapidly increased due to a sudden heat wave, and therefore a power shortage problem occurred.)

내일은 장마전선의 영향으로 많은 비가 내리**겠으므로** 등산하실 때 조심하시기 바랍니다.

(=Tomorrow it must be raining due to the seasonal rain front, and therefore please be careful when you go hiking.)

Unlike "~아서/어서, ~기 때문에," "~(으)므로" can be freely used in all types of sentences including imperative and propositional sentences.

교통사고는 누구한테나 일어날 수 있**으므로** 항상 조심하십시오. (Imperative)

(=A traffic accident may occur to anyone, and therefore always be careful.)

다 지나간 일이**므로** 잊어버립시다. (Proposition)

(=That is all in the past now, and therefore let's forget about it.)

27. Expressing "Due to the reason that _": ~는/(으)ㄴ 관계로

"~는/(으)ㄴ 관계로" can be used to express that the situation in the following clause is somehow affected because of the reason in the preceding clause, which can be rendered as "due to the reason that _." It is commonly used to provide the justification for an unfavorable situation. Due to its formality, however, it is more likely to be used in written text and in formal speech, such as public announcements.

비가 오**는 관계로** 오늘 경기는 취소되었습니다.

(=Today's game was cancelled due to the reason that it is raining.)

여기는 멧돼지가 자주 출몰하**는 관계로** 산책로가 폐쇄되었음을 알려드립니다.

(=We are announcing that this trail is closed due to the reason that wild hogs frequently appear here.)

Function	Expressing "Due to the reason that _"		
Form	~는/(으)ㄴ 관계로		
Meaning	Due to the reason that _		
Distribution	Present	Past	Future
Action Verb Stem — After a consonant	~는 관계로[*1]		
Action Verb Stem — After a vowel	~는 관계로[*1]		
Action Verb Stem — After "ㄹ"	~는 관계로[*1,2]		
Stative Verb Stem — After a consonant	~은 관계로[*1]		
Stative Verb Stem — After a vowel	~ㄴ 관계로[*1]		
Stative Verb Stem — After "ㄹ"	~ㄴ 관계로[*1,3]		

[*1] The preceding verb cannot take its own tense suffix, and its tense is determined by the tense of the main verb.

[*2] If the verb stem ends with "ㄹ," "ㄹ" will be dropped before we attach "~는 관계로, ~ㄴ 관계로"" according to the rule of "ㄹ" deletion that says "the consonant "ㄹ" at the end of a verb stem is dropped before "ㄴ, ㅂ, ㅅ." (See Chapter 12 Verbs)
팔다 (to sell): 팔→파는 관계로, 멀다 (far): 멀→먼 관계로

건물이 낡**은 관계로** 안전을 보장할 수 없으니 출입을 삼가하시기 바랍니다.
(=We highly discourage you to go in and out of this building because we cannot guarantee your safety due to the reason that the building structure is too old.)

정부예산이 부족**한 관계로** 차세대 전투기 사업이 늦어지고 있다.
(=The next generation fighter jet project is being delayed due to the reason that the government budget is not enough to cover it.)

공사 중**인 관계로** 고객 여러분들께 불편을 끼쳐드려 대단히 죄송합니다.
(=We sincerely apologize to our highly-valued customers for the inconvenience that you are experiencing due to the reason that the construction work is ongoing.)

재판이 현재 진행 중**인 관계로** 재판과 관련된 것에 대해서는 말씀드릴 수 없습니다.
(=I cannot tell you anything related to the trial due to the reason that the trial is currently ongoing.)

28. Expressing the reason for one's busy schedule: ~(으)랴

Function	Expressing the reason for one's busy schedule		
Form	~(으)랴		
Meaning	Because one is busy doing things like _		
Distribution	Present	Past	Future
Action Verb Stem / After a consonant	~으랴*		
After a vowel	~랴*		
After "ㄹ"	~랴*		
Stative Verb Stem / After a consonant			
After a vowel			
After "ㄹ"			

* The preceding verb cannot take its own tense suffix, and its tense is determined by the tense of the main verb.

"~(으)랴" can be used to express that the situation in the following clause happens due to one's busy schedule carrying out the multiple tasks in the preceding clause, which can be rendered as "because one is busy doing things like _." It can be attached to the verb stem of each task listed in the preceding clause.

책 읽**으랴** 리포트 쓰**랴** 아주 피곤해 죽겠다.
(=I am dead tired because I am busy doing things like reading books and writing a report.)

빨래하**랴** 집안 청소하**랴** 힘들어 죽겠어요.
(=I am dead tired because I am busy doing things like laundry and house cleaning.)

회사일 하**랴** 아이들 돌보**랴** 눈 코 뜰 새 없이 바빠요.
(=I am extremely busy because I am doing things like my company work and child care.)

With regard to the tense rule, the preceding verb cannot take its own tense suffix, and its tense is determined by the tense of the main verb.

회사일 하**랴** 아이들 돌보**랴** 눈 코 뜰 새 없이 바<u>빴</u>다.
(=I was extremely busy because I was doing things like my company work and child care.)

회사일 **했으랴** 아이들 돌보**았으랴** 눈 코 뜰 새 없이 바**빴**다. (NOT OK)

29. Expressing "Even though": ~아도/어도

Function		Expressing "Even though"		
Form		~아도/어도		
Meaning		Even though		
Distribution		Present	Past	Future
Action Verb Stem	After "오" or "아"	~아도	~았어도[*]	
	Otherwise	~어도	~었어도[*]	
Stative Verb Stem	After "오" or "아"	~아도	~았/어도[*]	
	Otherwise	~어도	~었어도[*]	

[*] The preceding verb can take its own tense suffix, or its tense can be determined by the tense of the main verb.

"~아도/어도" can be used to express that the situation in the following clause occurs regardless of the situation in the preceding clause, which can be rendered as "even though."

메리는 밥을 많이 먹**어도** 살이 안 찐다.

(=Even though Mary eats a lot, she doesn't gain weight.)

약을 발**라도** 온 몸이 가렵다.

(=Even though I apply the medicine, I am itching all over my body.)

존은 학교에 가**도** 공부를 안 한다.

(=Even though John goes to school, he doesn't study.)

내일 비가 **와도** 소풍을 간다.

(=Even though it will rain tomorrow, we are going on a field trip.)

존은 부자가 아니**어도** 가난한 사람들을 도와준다.

(=Even though John is not a rich man, he helps poor people.)

존은 날씨가 추**워도** 항상 반바지만 입는다.

(=Even though the weather is cold, John always wears short pants.)

메리는 똑똑**해도** 남들한테 자랑을 하지 않는다.

(=Even though Mary is smart, she is not snobbish.)

With regard to the tense rule, the preceding verb does not normally take its own tense suffix, but if it does, the sentence will be only marginally acceptable.

밥을 먹었**어도** 배가 고팠다. (Marginally acceptable)

(=Even though I ate, I was hungry.)

밥을 먹었**어도** 배가 고프다. (Marginally acceptable)

(=Even though I ate, I am still hungry.)

약을 발랐**어도** 온 몸이 가려웠다. (Marginally acceptable)

(=Even though I applied the medicine, I was itching all over my body.)

약을 발랐**어도** 온 몸이 가렵다. (Marginally acceptable)

(=Even though I applied the medicine, I am itching all over my body.)

"~아도/어도" can be freely used in any type of sentences including imperative or propositional sentences.

배가 고**파도** 조금만 기다려라. (Imperative)

(=Even though you might be hungry, just wait a little more.)

화가 **나도** 참으세요. (Imperative)

(=Even though you might be angry, please hold your anger.)

배가 고**파도** 조금만 기다리자. (Proposition)

(=Even though you might be hungry, let's wait a little more.)

화가 **나도** 참읍시다. (Proposition)

(=Even though you might be angry, let's hold our anger.)

30. Expressing "In any circumstances": ~더라도, ~(으)ㄹ지라도

Function		Expressing "In any circumstances"					
Form		~더라도			~(으)ㄹ지라도		
Meaning		Even if					
Distribution		Present	Past	Future	Present	Past	Future
Action Verb Stem	After a consonant	~더라도	~았/었더라도			~았/었을지라도	~을지라도
	After a vowel	~더라도	~았/었더라도			~았/었을지라도	~ㄹ지라도
	After "ㄹ"	~더라도	~았/었더라도			~았/었을지라도	~지라도
Stative Verb Stem	After a consonant	~더라도	~았/었더라도			~았/었을지라도	~을지라도
	After a vowel	~더라도	~았/었더라도			~았/었을지라도	~ㄹ지라도
	After "ㄹ"	~더라도	~았/었더라도			~았/었을지라도	~지라도

"~더라도, ~(으)ㄹ지라도" can be used to express that the situation in the following clause occurs in any circumstances like the situation in the preceding clause, which can be rendered as "even if." Unlike "~아도/어도," however, they carry the implication that the situation in the preceding clause is less likely to occur.

지금 죽**더라도**/죽**을지라도** 후회는 없다.

(=I have no regret even if I die now.)

지금 떠나**더라도**/떠**날지라도** 이미 늦었다.

(=You are already late even if you leave now.)

메리는 화가 나**더라도**/**날지라도** 절대 화를 내지 않는다.

(=Mary never loses her temper even if she gets angry.)

With regard to the tense rule, the preceding verb can take its own tense suffix, which is independent of the tense of the main verb.

존이 여기 **왔더라도**/**왔을지라도** 할 수 있는 일이 아무 것도 없다.

(=There is nothing that John can do even if he came here.)

메리가 실수를 **했더라도**/**했을지라도** 용서해 주어야 한다.

(=You must forgive Mary even if Mary made a mistake.)

"~더라도, ~(으)ㄹ지라도" can be freely used in any type of sentences including imperative or propositional sentences.

배가 고프**더라도**/고플**지라도** 조금만 기다려라. (Imperative)

(=Even though you might be hungry, just wait a little more.)

화가 나**더라도**/날**지라도** 참으세요. (Imperative)

(=Even though you might get angry, please hold your anger.)

배가 고프**더라도**/고플**지라도** 조금만 기다리자. (Proposition)

(=Even though you might be hungry, let's wait a little more.)

화가 나**더라도**/날**지라도** 참읍시다. (Proposition)

(=Even though we might get angry, let's hold our anger.)

On the other hand, "~더라도, ~(으)ㄹ지라도" are frequently used with the optional adverb "아무리 (no matter)." In that case, it can be rendered as "No matter how."

(아무리) 친한 사이라 하**더라도**/할**지라도** 예의는 지켜야 한다.

(=No matter how close you are to each other, you must be courteous to the other party.)

(아무리) 피곤하**더라도**/피곤할**지라도** 이 일은 꼭 끝내야 합니다.

(=No matter how tired I am, I must get this done without fail.)

(아무리) 힘들**더라도**/힘들**지라도** 포기하지 마세요

(=No matter how much you suffer from it, please don't give up.)

(아무리) 가난하**더라도**/가난할**지라도** 남의 물건을 훔치는 것은 정당화 될 수 없죠.

(=No matter how poor a person is, stealing something from others cannot be justified.)

(아무리) 바**빴더라도**/바**빴을지라도** 나한테 전화 한 통은 했어야지.

(=No matter how busy you were, you should have called me at least once.)

31. Expressing the unexpected outcome of a given situation:

~는/(으)ㄴ데도 (불구하고)

Function	Expressing the unexpected outcome of a given situation		
Form	~는/(으)ㄴ데도 (불구하고)		
Meaning	But nevertheless		
Distribution	Present	Past	Future
Action Verb Stem / After a consonant	~는데도 (불구하고)	~았/었는데도 (불구하고)	
After a vowel	~는데도 (불구하고)	~았/었는데도 (불구하고)	
After "ㄹ"	~는데도 (불구하고)*	~았/었는데도 (불구하고)	
Stative Verb Stem / After a consonant	~은데도 (불구하고)	~았/었는데도 (불구하고)	
After a vowel	~ㄴ데도 (불구하고)	~았/었는데도 (불구하고)	
After "ㄹ"	~ㄴ데도 (불구하고)*	~았/었는데도 (불구하고)	

* If the verb stem ends with "ㄹ," "ㄹ" will be dropped before we attach "~는데도 (불구하고), ~ㄴ데도 (불구하고)" according to the rule of "ㄹ" deletion that says "the consonant "ㄹ" at the end of a verb stem is dropped before "ㄴ, ㅂ, ㅅ." (See Chapter 12 Verbs)
벌다 (to make money): 벌→버는데도 (불구하고), 멀다 (far): 멀→먼데도 (불구하고)

"~는/(으)ㄴ데도 (불구하고)" can be used to express that the situation in the following clause is the unexpected or undesirable outcome of a given situation in the preceding clause, which can be rendered as "but nevertheless."

존은 잘 먹**는데도 (불구하고)** 자꾸 살이 빠진다.

(=John eats well, but nevertheless he continues to lose weight.)

항상 공부를 열심히 하**는데도 (불구하고)** 시험성적이 별로 좋지 않다.

(=I always study hard, but nevertheless my test results are not that good.)

존은 키가 작**은데도 (불구하고)** 농구를 잘한다.

(=John is short, but nevertheless he is good at basketball.)

메리는 아프**ㄴ데도 (불구하고)** 그 일을 다 끝마쳤다.

(=Mary was sick, but nevertheless she finished the work.)

With regard to the tense rule, the preceding verb can take its own tense suffix, which is independent of the tense of the main verb.

저녁을 먹<u>었</u>**는데도 (불구하고)** 또 배가 고프다.

(=I already ate dinner, but nevertheless I am still hungry again.)

UN이 북한에 대해 전례 없는 경제제재 조치를 취<u>했</u>**는데도 불구하고** 김정은 정권은 핵개발에 박차를 가하고 있다.

(=The UN approved unprecedented economic sanctions against North Korea, but nevertheless the Kim Jong-un regime is spurring on nuclear development.)

"~는/(으)ㄴ데도 (불구하고)" cannot be used in imperative or propositional sentences.

배가 **고픈데도 (불구하고)** 조금만 기다려라. (Imperative: NOT OK)

(=You might be hungry, but nevertheless wait a little more.)

화가 **나는데도 (불구하고)** 참자. (Proposition: NOT OK)

(=You might get angry, but nevertheless let's hold our anger.)

32. Expressing an unexpected situation: ~(으)면서도

Function	Expressing an unexpected situation		
Form	~(으)면서도		
Meaning	Even when _/despite		
Distribution	Present	Past	Future
Action Verb Stem — After a consonant	~으면서도	~았/었으면서도	
Action Verb Stem — After a vowel	~면서도	~았/었으면서도	
Action Verb Stem — After "ㄹ"	~면서도	~았/었으면서도	
Stative Verb Stem — After a consonant	~으면서도	~았/었으면서도	
Stative Verb Stem — After a vowel	~면서도	~았/었으면서도	
Stative Verb Stem — After "ㄹ"	~면서도	~았/었으면서도	

"~(으)면서도" can be used to express that the situation in the following clause continues, which is not normally expected from the given situation in the preceding clause. It can be rendered as "even when _/despite."

존은 밥을 먹<u>으면서도</u> 공부를 한다.

(=John studies even when he is eating a meal.)

존은 혼이 나**면서도** 자기는 아무 잘못한 것이 없다고 했다.

(=John said that he didn't do anything wrong even when he was being scolded.)

메리는 그 사실을 알**면서도** 모르는 체한다.

(=Mary pretends that she doesn't know anything despite the fact that she knows the truth.)

존은 할 일이 많**으면서도** 컴퓨터 게임을 한다.

(=John plays computer games despite the tons of work he has to do.)

어머님은 몸이 아프시**면서도** 하루 종일 부엌에서 일하신다.

(=My mother continues to work in the kitchen all day long despite her illness.)

With regard to the tense rule, the preceding verb can take its own tense suffix, which is independent of the tense of the main verb.

존은 망했**으면서도** 돈이 많은 척하고 다닌다.

(=John pretends that he is rich despite his bankruptcy.)

존은 망했**으면서도** 돈이 많은 척하고 다녔다.

(=John pretended that he was rich despite his bankruptcy.)

존은 자기가 실수를 했**으면서도** 인정을 안 한다.

(=John does not admit his fault despite his mistake.)

존은 자기가 실수를 했**으면서도** 인정을 안 했다.

(=John did not admit his fault despite his mistake.)

메리는 진실을 알았**으면서도** 모르는 체한다.

(=Mary pretends that she doesn't know anything despite the fact that she knew the truth.)

메리는 진실을 알았**으면서도** 모르는 체했다.

(=Mary pretended that she didn't know anything despite the fact that she knew the truth.)

33. Expressing one's purpose in carrying out the intended action:

~(으)러, ~(으)려고, ~고자

Function		Expressing one's purpose in carrying out the intended action		
Form		~(으)러	~(으)려고	~고자
Meaning		(In order) to		
Distribution		Present	Present	Present
Action Verb Stem	After a consonant	~으러*	~으려고*	~고자*
	After a vowel	~러*	~려고*	~고자*
	After "ㄹ"	~러*	~려고*	~고자*
Stative Verb Stem	After a consonant			
	After a vowel			
	After "ㄹ"			

* The preceding verb cannot take its own tense suffix, and its tense is determined by the tense of the main verb.

"~(으)러, ~(으)려고, ~고자" can be used to express that the situation in the following clause happens in order to carry out the intended action in the preceding clause, which can be rendered as "(in order) to." "~(으)러" requires that the main verb in the following clause, but not the preceding verb, must be one of the verbs of locomotion.

Verbs of locomotion: 가다(to go), 오다(to come), 나가다(to go out), 나오다(to come out), 돌아오다(to come back), 돌아가다(to go back), 들어가다(to go in), 들어오다(to come in), 뛰어가다(to go running), 뛰어오다(to come running), 출발하다(to depart), 도착하다(to arrive), 이민 가다(to emigrate), 이민 오다(to immigrate), 들르다(to stop by), 다가가다(to approach), 다가오다(to come close), etc.

존은 점심을 먹**으러** 식당에 갔습니다.
(=John went to a restaurant to eat lunch.)

메리는 저녁을 준비하**러** 집에 돌아왔습니다.
(=Mary returned home to prepare dinner.)

숙제를 제출하**러** 선생님 사무실에 뛰어갔습니다.
(=I ran to the teacher's office to submit my homework.)

한국말을 배우**러** 한국에 <u>왔습니다</u>.

(=I came to Korea to learn Korean.)

친구를 만나**러** 스벅에 <u>갔습니다</u>.

(=I went to Starbucks to meet my friend.)

Unlike "~(으)러," however, "~(으)려고" can be used with any kind of main verb as long as it is an action verb including the verbs of locomotion.

존은 점심을 먹**으려고** 식당에 <u>갔습니다</u>.

존은 점심을 먹**으러** 식당에 <u>갔습니다</u>.

(=John went to a restaurant to eat lunch.)

메리는 저녁을 준비하**려고** 집에 <u>돌아왔습니다</u>.

메리는 저녁을 준비하**러** 집에 <u>돌아왔습니다</u>.

(=Mary returned home to prepare dinner.)

케이크를 나중에 먹**으려고** 냉장고에 <u>넣어</u> <u>두었습니다</u>.

(=I put the cake in the refrigerator to eat it later.)

케이크를 나중에 먹**으러** 냉장고에 <u>넣어</u> <u>두었습니다</u>. (NOT OK)

존은 돈을 벌**려고** 열심히 <u>일했습니다</u>.

(=John worked hard to make money.)

존은 돈을 벌**러** 열심히 <u>일했습니다</u>. (NOT OK)

메리는 옷을 사**려고** 백화점에서 <u>쇼핑했습니다</u>.

(=Mary was shopping at the department store to buy some clothes.)

메리는 옷을 사**러** 백화점에서 <u>쇼핑했습니다</u>. (NOT OK)

On the other hand, due to its formality, "~고자" is mainly used in written text or in formal speech.

존은 시험에 합격하**고자** 열심히 공부했습니다.

(=John studied hard to pass the test.)

오늘은 우리 정부의 최근 경제정책에 대해서 논의를 하**고자** 경제 전문가들을 모셨습니다.

(=Today we invited the economists to discuss our government's recent economic policy.)

With regard to the tense rule, the preceding verb of "~(으)러, ~(으)려고, ~고자" cannot take its own tense suffix, and its tense is determined by the tense of the main verb.

> 존은 점심을 먹<u>으러</u> 식당에 갔습니다.
>
> (=John went to a restaurant to eat lunch.)
>
> 존은 점심을 먹<u>었으러</u> 식당에 갔습니다. (NOT OK)
>
> 메리는 옷을 사<u>려고</u> 백화점에서 쇼핑했습니다.
>
> (=Mary was shopping at the department store to buy some clothes.)
>
> 메리는 옷을 샀<u>으려고</u> 백화점에서 쇼핑했습니다. (NOT OK)
>
> 존은 시험에 합격하<u>고자</u> 열심히 공부했습니다.
>
> (=John studied hard to pass the test.)
>
> 존은 시험에 합격<u>했고자</u> 열심히 공부했습니다. (NOT OK)

34. Expressing one's purpose in achieving his/her goal:
~기 위해(서)/위하여/위한

Function		Expressing one's purpose in achieving his/her goal		
Form		~기 위해(서)	~기 위하여	~기 위한
Meaning		In order to/For the sake of		
Distribution		Present	Present	Present
Action Verb Stem	After a consonant	~기 위해(서)*	~기 위하여*	~기 위한*
	After a vowel	~기 위해(서)*	~기 위하여*	~기 위한*
	After "ㄹ"	~기 위해(서)*	~기 위하여*	~기 위한*
Stative Verb Stem	After a consonant			
	After a vowel			
	After "ㄹ"			

* The preceding verb cannot take its own tense suffix, and its tense is determined by the tense of the main verb.

"~기 위해(서), ~기 위하여" can be used to express that one is carrying out the action in the following clause in order to achieve his/her goal in the preceding clause, which can be rendered as "in order to/for the sake of." Since "위해(서), 위하여" always require the preceding expression to be a noun or the noun equivalent, the preceding verb must be changed into a gerund form by attaching the gerundival suffix "~기."

존은 시험에 합격하**기 위해(서)**/합격하**기 위하여** 열심히 공부했다.

(=John studied hard in order to pass the exam.)

피해자의 정확한 사인을 밝히**기 위해(서)**/밝히**기 위하여** 경찰이 국립과학연구소에 부검을 의뢰했다.

(=The police requested that the National Forensic Center conduct an autopsy in order to find out the precise cause of the victim's death.)

먹**기 위해(서)**/먹**기 위하여** 사는 것이 아니라 살**기 위해(서)**/살**기 위하여** 먹는다.

(=I don't live to eat, but I eat to live.)

The preceding verb cannot take its own tense suffix, and its tense is determined by the tense of the main verb.

존은 시험에 합격했**기 위해(서)**/합격했**기 위하여** 열심히 공부했다. (NOT OK)

(=John studied hard in order to pass the exam.)

먹었**기 위하여** 사는 것이 아니라 살았**기 위해(서)** 먹는다. (NOT OK)

(=I don't live to eat, but I eat to live.)

On the other hand, "**~기 위한**," the modifying form of "**~기 위해(서), ~기 위하여**," can be used to modify the following noun.

메리는 한국에 유학 가**기 위한** 절차를 알아보고 있다.

(=Mary is trying to find out the procedures to follow in order to study in Korea.)

비겁하게 살**기 위한** 방법을 찾지 말고 용감하게 죽는 방법을 선택해라.

(=Don't look for the way to live as a coward, but choose to die as a hero.)

35. Expressing "To carry out a given task": ~는 데(에)

"~는 데(에)" can be used to express that the situation in the following clause happens in order to carry out the task in the preceding clause, which can be rendered as "to do something."

집을 구하**는 데(에)** 시간이 좀 더 필요합니다.

(=I need more time to find a place to live.)

Function	Expressing "To carry out a given task"		
Form	~는 데(에)		
Meaning	To do something		
Distribution	Present	Past	Future
Action Verb Stem — After a consonant	~는 데(에)*		
Action Verb Stem — After a vowel	~는 데(에)*		
Action Verb Stem — After "ㄹ"	~는 데(에)*		
Stative Verb Stem — After a consonant			
Stative Verb Stem — After a vowel			
Stative Verb Stem — After "ㄹ"			

* The preceding verb cannot take its own tense suffix, and its tense is determined by the tense of the main verb.

이 차는 고치는 데(에) 돈이 많이 듭니다.

(=It costs a lot of money to fix this car.)

이 일을 처리하는 데(에) 사람이 좀 더 필요합니다.

(=I need more manpower to take care of this job.)

한국에 가는 데(에) 비행기로 10시간 쯤 걸립니다.

(=It takes about ten hours to go to Korea by plane.)

한국을 방문하는 데(에) 여권과 비자가 필요합니다.

(=You need a passport and a visa to visit Korea.)

경제 난국을 극복하는 데(에) 다 함께 노력해야 합니다.

(=We must work together to overcome our economic crisis.)

With regard to the tense rule, the preceding verb cannot take its own tense suffix, and its tense is determined by the tense of the main verb.

집을 구하는 데(에) 시간이 많이 걸렸습니다.
(=It took me a long time to find a place to live.)
집을 구했는 데(에) 시간이 많이 걸렸습니다. (NOT OK)

이 차를 사는 데(에) 돈이 많이 들었습니다.
(=It cost me a lot of money to buy this car.)
이 차는 샀는 데(에) 돈이 많이 들었습니다. (NOT OK)

36. Expressing a conditional clause: ~(으)면

Function		Expressing a conditional clause		
Form		~(으)면		
Meaning		If		
Distribution		Present	Past	Future
Action Verb Stem	After a consonant	~으면	~았/었으면	
	After a vowel	~면	~았/었으면	
	After "ㄹ"	~면	~았/었으면	
Stative Verb Stem	After a consonant	~으면	~았/었으면	
	After a vowel	~면	~았/었으면	
	After "ㄹ"	~면	~았/었으면	

"~(으)면" can be used to express that the situation in the following clause happens if the condition in the preceding clause is to be met, which can be rendered as "If."

상한 음식을 먹<u>으면</u> 병에 걸려요.

(=If you eat spoiled food, you will get sick.)

시간 있<u>으면</u> 우리 집에 한번 놀러 와.

(=If you have time, just come over to my house once.)

한국에 가<u>면</u> 제일 먼저 뭐를 하고 싶어요?

(=If you go to Korea, what do you want to do first?)

날씨가 따뜻하<u>면</u> 집안일을 좀 해야겠다.

(=If the weather is warm, I need to take care of my household chores.)

피곤하시<u>면</u> 좀 쉬세요.

(=If you are tired, please take a rest.)

With regard to the tense rule, the preceding verb can take its own tense suffix, which is independent of the tense of the main verb.

숙제 다 **했으면** 밖에 나가 놀아라.

(=If you finished your homework, go out and play.)

날씨가 **좋았으면** 골프를 치려고 했다.

(=If the weather was good, I was going to play golf.)

"~(으)면" can be frequently used with the optional adverb "만약(에) (just in case)" if the condition in the preceding clause is less likely to be met, which can be rendered as "Just in case __." "만약" can be freely used in both written text and conversation, whereas "만약에" is more likely to be used in conversation. Another optional adverb "만일(에) (just in case)" can also be used for the same function, but it is only used in conversation.

만약(에)/만일(에) 내가 사무실에 없<u>으면</u> 이 번호로 연락해라.

(=Just in case I am not in my office, contact me at this number.)

만약(에)/만일(에) 존이 말을 안 들<u>으면</u> 저한테 말하세요.

(=Just in case John doesn't listen to you, please tell me.)

만약(에)/만일(에) 내 도움이 필요하<u>면</u> 언제든지 전화해.

(=Just in case you need some help from me, feel free to call me.)

만약(에)/만일(에) 존이 이번 시험에 합격하<u>면</u> 내 손에 장을 지져라.

(=Just in case John passes this upcoming test, I will eat my hat.)

On the other hand, if the preceding verb is the copula "~이다," then "~이라면/라면" can be used instead.

학생<u>이라면</u> 누구나 열심히 공부해야 한다.

(=If someone is to be a student, he/she must study hard.)

학자<u>라면</u> 남의 논문을 표절해서는 안 된다.

(=If someone is to be a scholar, he/she must not plagiarize other people's papers.)

Another variant form of the copula "~이다" is "~이면/면" which can be used to emphasize one's state of being as the preceding noun.

학생<u>이면</u> 누구나 열심히 공부해야 한다

(=If someone is truly a student, he/she must study hard.)

학자<u>면</u> 남의 논문을 표절해서는 안 된다.

(=If someone is truly a scholar, he/she must not plagiarize other people's papers.)

37. Expressing the speaker's response to a given condition: ~(는/ㄴ)다면

Function		Expressing the speaker's response to a given condition		
Form		~(는/ㄴ)다면		
Meaning		If _, then _		
Distribution		Present	Past	Future
Action Verb Stem	After a consonant	~는다면	~았/었다면	~겠다면
	After a vowel	~ㄴ다면	~았/었다면	~겠다면
	After "ㄹ"	~ㄴ다면*	~았/었다면	~겠다면
Stative Verb Stem	After a consonant	~다면	~았/었다면	
	After a vowel	~다면	~았/었다면	
	After "ㄹ"	~다면	~았/었다면	

*If the verb stem ends with "ㄹ," "ㄹ" will be dropped before we attach "~ㄴ다면" according to the rule of "ㄹ" deletion that says "the consonant "ㄹ" at the end of a verb stem is dropped before "ㄴ, ㅂ, ㅅ." (See Chapter 12 Verbs)
벌다 (to make money): 벌→번다면, 살다 (to live): 살→산다면

"~(는/ㄴ)다면" can be used to express the speaker's response to a given situation if the condition in the preceding clause is to be met, which can be rendered as "If _, then _."

존이 이 피자를 다 먹**는다면** 10불을 주겠다.

(=If John eats all of this pizza, then I will give him ten dollars.)

메리를 진심으로 사랑**한다면** 아무 말 없이 보내줘라.

(=If you truly love Mary, then just let her go without saying anything.)

존이 아프**다면** 집에서 쉬게 해라.

(=If John is sick, then let him take a rest at home.)

With regard to the tense rule, the preceding verb can take its own tense suffix, which is independent of the tense of the main verb.

메리가 그 것 때문에 상처를 받**았다면** 미안하다고 전해라.

(=If that hurt Mary's feelings, tell her that I am sorry about that.)

존이 안 하**겠다면** 그냥 내버려 두어라.

(=If John says he will not do it, just leave him alone.)

38. Expressing the speaker's response to a cited condition:

~(는/ㄴ)다고/냐고/(으)라고/자고 하면

Function			Expressing the speaker's response to a cited condition		
Form			~(는/ㄴ)다고/냐고/(으)라고/자고 하면		
Meaning			Just in case one says/asks/orders/suggests _		
Distribution			Present	Past	Future
Action Verb Stem	Statement	After a consonant	~는다고 하면	~았/었다고 하면	~겠다고 하면
		After a vowel	~ㄴ다고 하면	~았/었다고 하면	~겠다고 하면
		After "ㄹ"	~ㄴ다고 하면*	~았/었다고 하면	~겠다고 하면
	Question	Regardless of the ending	~냐고 하면*	~았/었냐고 하면	~겠냐고 하면
	Imperative	After a consonant	~으라고 하면		
		After a vowel or "ㄹ"	~라고 하면		
	Proposition	Regardless of the ending	~자고 하면		
Stative Verb Stem	Statement	Regardless of the ending	~다고 하면	~았/었다고 하면	~겠다고 하면
	Question	Regardless of the ending	~냐고 하면*	~았/었냐고 하면	~겠냐고 하면

* If the verb stem ends with "ㄹ," "ㄹ" will be dropped before we attach "~ㄴ다고 하면, ~냐고 하면" according to the rule of "ㄹ" deletion that says "the consonant "ㄹ" at the end of a verb stem is dropped before "ㄴ, ㅂ, ㅅ." (See Chapter 12 Verbs)
벌다 (to make money): 벌→번다고 하면/버냐고 하면, 살다 (to live): 살→산다고 하면/사냐고 하면,
멀다 (far): 멀→머냐고 하면

"~(는/ㄴ)다고하면, ~냐고 하면, ~(으)라고 하면, ~자고 하면" can be used to express the speaker's response to a cited condition just in case that the situation in the preceding clause actually occurs, which can be rendered as "Just in case one says/asks/orders/suggests _." These conditional citation forms can be frequently contracted into "~(는/ㄴ)다면, ~냐면, ~(으)라면, ~자면," respectively, in conversation.

존이 이 피자를 다 먹**는다고 하면**/먹**는다면** 그냥 먹게 해라.

(=Just in case John says he wants to eat all of this pizza, just let him eat it all.)

메리가 지금 떠**난다고 하면**/떠**난다면** 그냥 가게 해 줘라.

(=Just in case Mary says she wants to leave now, just let her go.)

존이 배고프**다고 하면**/배고프**다면** 저녁을 좀 차려 줘라.

(=Just in case John says he is hungry, just fix him dinner.)

메리가 그 모든 일을 혼자 **했다고 하면/했다면** 아무도 안 믿을 겁니다.

(=Just in case Mary says she did the work by herself, no one would believe it.)

존이 가**겠다고 하면/가겠다면** 그냥 보내줘라.

(=Just in case John says he wants to leave, just let him go.)

내가 왜 떠나**냐고 하면/떠나냐면** 일이 있어서 간다고 해라.

(=Just in case someone asks you why I am leaving, tell him/her that I have things to take care of.)

내가 왜 한국에 **갔냐고 하면/갔냐면** 출장 갔다고 해라.

(=Just in case someone asks you why I went to Korea, tell him/her I went there on a business trip.)

존한테 그 일을 하**겠냐고 하면/하겠냐면** 안 한다고 할 거다.

(=Just in case you ask John to do the work, he will say no.)

의사가 약물치료를 받**으라고 하면/받으라면** 안 받을 거라고 할 겁니다.

(=Just in case the doctor orders me to get chemotherapy, I will say no.)

그 일을 존한테 하**라고 하면/하라면** 시간 낭비일 겁니다.

(=Just in case you ask John to do the job, it will be a waste of time.)

메리한테 같이 일을 하**자고 하면/하자면** 안 한다고 할 겁니다.

(=Just in case you suggest to Mary to work with you, she will say no.)

39. Regretting not taking action or not being in a certain state:
~았/었더라면

"~았/었더라면" can be used to express the speaker's belated regret for not carrying out the necessary action or not being in a certain state in the preceding clause, which prevented the favorable situation in the following clause from having happened. It can be rendered as "If one had done so/If one had been so." Although the preceding and following clauses are positive in their grammatical forms, they both reflect the negative meanings that the opposite situations actually occurred.

Function	Regretting not taking action or not being in a certain state		
Form	~았/었더라면		
Meaning	If one had done so/If one had been so		
Distribution	Present	Past	Future
Action Verb Stem — After "오" or "아"		~았더라면	
Action Verb Stem — Otherwise		~었더라면	
Stative Verb Stem — After "오" or "아"		~았더라면	
Stative Verb Stem — Otherwise		~었더라면	

조금만 일찍 도착**했더라면** 범인을 체포할 수 있었다.

(=If we had arrived a little bit earlier, we could have arrested the suspect.)

조금만 더 열심히 공부**했더라면** 시험에 합격할 수 있었을 텐데.

(=If you had studied harder, you could have passed the exam.)

시간이 조금만 더 있**었더라면** 그 사람을 살릴 수 있었는데.

(=If I had had a little more time, I could have saved his/her life.)

존이 조금만 더 키가 **컸더라면** 농구선수가 될 수 있었을 텐데.

(=If John had been a little bit taller, he could have been a basketball player.)

메리가 얼굴이 예**뻤더라면** 영화배우가 될 수 있었다.

(=If Mary had been prettier, she could have been a movie star.)

40. Expressing the likeliness of the situation: ~는/(으)ㄴ/(으)ㄹ 것 같으면

"~는 것 같으면" can be used to express that the situation in the following clause applies if the condition in the preceding clause is likely to be met, which can be rendered as "If it seems that ＿." "~(으)ㄴ 것 같으면, ~(으)ㄹ 것 같으면" are used if the preceding clause is in the past tense, the future tense, respectively.

존은 돈이 되**는 것 같으면** 무엇이든 한다.

(=If it seems that something is related to making money, John will do whatever it is.)

닭고기가 안 익**은 것 같으면** 잘 익혀서 먹어야 한다.

(=If it seems that the chicken was not cooked well, you must thoroughly cook and then eat it.)

Function	Expressing the likeliness of the situation		
Form	~는/(으)ㄴ/(으)ㄹ 것 같으면		
Meaning	If it seems that _		
Distribution	Present	Past	Future
Action Verb Stem — After a consonant	~는 것 같으면	~은 것 같으면	~을 것 같으면
Action Verb Stem — After a vowel	~는 것 같으면	~ㄴ 것 같으면	~ㄹ 것 같으면
Action Verb Stem — After "ㄹ"	~는 것 같으면[*]	~ㄴ 것 같으면[*]	것 같으면
Stative Verb Stem — After a consonant	~은 것 같으면		~을 것 같으면
Stative Verb Stem — After a vowel	~ㄴ 것 같으면		~ㄹ 것 같으면
Stative Verb Stem — After "ㄹ"	~ㄴ 것 같으면[*]		것 같으면

[*] If the verb stem ends with "ㄹ," "ㄹ" will be dropped before we attach "~는 것 같으면, ~ㄴ 것 같으면" according to the rule of "ㄹ" deletion that says "the consonant "ㄹ" at the end of a verb stem is dropped before "ㄴ, ㅂ, ㅅ." (See Chapter 12 Verbs)
(ex) 벌다 (to make money): 벌→버는 것 같으면/번 것 같으면, 멀다 (far): 멀→먼 것 같으면

전문가가 만든 **것 같으면** 이렇게 형편 없을 리가 없죠.

(=If it seems that it was made by an expert, it would not be shoddy like this.)

나중에 먹을 **것 같으면** 냉장고에 넣어 두어라.

(=If it seems that you will eat it later, put it in the refrigerator.)

내일 아침에 떠날 **것 같으면** 일찍 자라.

(=If it seems that you will leave tomorrow morning, go to bed early.)

"~(으)ㄴ 것 같으면" can also be used with a present tense stative verb, and ~(으)ㄹ 것 같으면 with a future tense stative verb.

옷이 작은 **것 같으면** 한 치수 큰 걸로 사라.

(=If it seems that these clothes are too tight for you, buy them in the next size up.)

우유가 상한 **것 같으면** 마시지 말아라.

(=If it seems that the milk is spoiled, don't drink it.)

늦을 **것 같으면** 전화해라.

(=If it seems that you will be late, call me.)

너무 힘들 **것 같으면** 내가 대신 해줄 게.

(=If it seems that it will be too difficult for you, I will do it instead.)

41. Expressing the precondition for one's intended action:
~(으)려(고 하)면, ~(으)려거든

Function	Expressing the precondition for one's intended action					
Form	~(으)려(고 하)면			~(으)려거든		
Meaning	If one intends to _/If one wants to _					
Distribution		Present	Past	Future	Present	Past	Future
Action Verb Stem	After a consonant	~으려고 하면/ ~으려면*			~으려거든*		
	After a vowel	~려고 하면/ ~려면*			~려거든*		
	After "ㄹ"	~려고 하면/ ~려면*			~려거든*		
Stative Verb Stem	After a consonant						
	After a vowel						
	After "ㄹ"						

* The preceding verb cannot take its own tense suffix, and its tense is determined by the tense of the main verb.

"~(으)려고 하면" and its contraction form "~(으)려면" can be used to express that the situation in the following clause is the precondition for carrying out one's intended action in the preceding clause. "~(으)려고 하면" is actually the combination of "~(으)려고 하다 (intend to)" and "~(으)면 (If)." Therefore, it can be rendered as "If one intends to _/If one wants to_."

호랑이를 잡으려고 하면/잡으려면 호랑이 굴로 들어가야 한다.

(=If you intend to catch a tiger, you must go into the tiger's cave.)

(Implication: You must carry out a bold action to achieve your goal.)

집을 사려고 하면/사려면 돈을 많이 모아야 한다.

(=If you intend to buy a house, you must save a lot of money.)

시험에 합격하려고 하면/합격하려면 열심히 공부하세요.

(=If you intend to pass the exam, study hard.)

내일 아침 일찍 출발하시려고 하면/출발하시려면 지금 주무세요.

(=If you intend to leave early tomorrow morning, please get some sleep now.)

On the other hand, "~(으)려거든" can be used for the same function, but it is more likely to be used in conversation.

원하는 걸 얻**으려거든** 최선을 다 해라.

(=If you intend to get something that you want, you must do your best.)

잠을 자**려거든** 불을 꼭 끄고 자라.

(=If you intend to go to bed, turn the light off without fail.)

42. Expressing "The more _, the more _": (~(으)면) ~(으)ㄹ수록

Function		Expressing "The more _, the more _"		
Form		(~(으)면) ~(으)ㄹ수록		
Meaning		The more _, the more _		
Distribution		Present	Past	Future
Action Verb Stem	After a consonant	~으면 ~을수록*/~을수록*		
	After a vowel	~면 ~ㄹ수록*/~ㄹ수록*		
	After "ㄹ"	~면 ~수록*/~수록*		
Stative Verb Stem	After a consonant	~으면 ~을수록*/~을수록*		
	After a vowel	~면 ~ㄹ수록*/~ㄹ수록*		
	After "ㄹ"	~면 ~수록*/~수록*		

* The preceding verb cannot take its own tense suffix, and its tense is determined by the tense of the main verb.

"(~(으)면) ~(으)ㄹ수록" can be used to express that the situation in the following clause is more likely to happen if the action or state in the preceding clause repeatedly occurs, which can be rendered as "The more _, the more _." The conditional expression led by "~(으)면" is generally optional, and it can be used just for emphasis.

칭찬은 받**으면** 받**을수록** 기분이 좋아진다.
칭찬은 받**을수록** 기분이 좋아진다.

(=The more compliments you receive, the better you may feel.)

한국말은 배우**면** 배울**수록** 더 재미가 있다.
한국말은 배울**수록** 더 재미가 있다.

(=The more I study Korean, the more fun I have.)

메리는 보**면 볼수록** 아름답다.

메리는 **볼수록** 아름답다.

(=The more times I see Marry, the more beautiful she looks to me.)

집은 넓**으면** 넓**을수록** 좋다.

집은 넓**을수록** 좋다.

(=The more spacious the house is, the better it is.)

농구는 키가 크**면 클수록** 유리하다.

농구는 키가 **클수록** 유리하다.

(=The taller a person is, the more suited he/she is to play basketball.)

If the preceding verb of "~(으)면" is the so called "하다 verb" which contains the generic verbal suffix "~하다," then the repeated verb before "~(으)ㄹ수록" can be shortened into "하다."

한국말은 공부하**면** 공부**할수록** 더 재미가 있다.

한국말은 공부하**면 할수록** 더 재미가 있다.

(=The more I study Korean, the more fun I have.)

생각하**면** 생각**할수록** 화가 난다.

생각하**면 할수록** 화가 난다.

(=The more I think about it, the more I become angry.)

메리를 그리워하**면** 그리워**할수록** 아픔만 남는다.

메리를 그리워하**면 할수록** 아픔만 남는다.

(=The more I miss Mary, the more pain will remain in my heart.)

43. Expressing "In case": ~는/(으)ㄴ/(으)ㄹ 경우(에)

"~는/(으)ㄴ/(으)ㄹ 경우(에)" can be used to express that the situation in the following clause applies to the specific situation in the preceding clause, which can be rendered as "In case _."

이 제품에 문제가 있**는 경우(에)** 가까운 서비스센터에 연락하세요.

(=In case there is a problem with this product, please contact the nearest service center.)

Function		Expressing "In case"		
Form		~는/(으)ㄴ/(으)ㄹ 경우(에)		
Meaning		In case _		
Distribution		Present	Past	Future
Action Verb Stem	After a consonant	~는 경우(에)	~은 경우(에)	~을 경우(에)
	After a vowel	~는 경우(에)	~ㄴ 경우(에)	~ㄹ 경우(에)
	After "ㄹ"	~는 경우(에)*	~ㄴ 경우(에)*	경우(에)
Stative Verb Stem	After a consonant	~은 경우(에)		~을 경우(에)
	After a vowel	~ㄴ 경우(에)		~ㄹ 경우(에)
	After "ㄹ"	~ㄴ 경우(에)*		경우(에)

* If the verb stem ends with "ㄹ," "ㄹ" will be dropped before we attach "~는 경우(에), ~ㄴ 경우(에)" according to the rule of "ㄹ" deletion that says "the consonant "ㄹ" at the end of a verb□ stem is dropped before "ㄴ, ㅂ, ㅅ." (See Chapter 12 Verbs)

팔다 (to sell): 팔→파는 경우(에)/판 경우(에), 멀다 (far): 멀→먼 경우(에)

보이스피싱 전화를 받**은 경우(에)** 범죄신고센터에 바로 신고하세요.

(=In case you received a voice phishing call, please report it to the crime report center.)

뺑소니 차량을 목격**한 경우(에)** 112로 신고하시기 바랍니다.

(=In case you witnessed a vehicle involved in a hit and run accident, please report it by calling 112.)

혈압이 높**은 경우(에)** 뇌졸중이 올 확률이 높습니다.

(=In case you have a high blood pressure, you have a high risk of having a stroke.)

값이 너무 비**싼 경우(에)** 사지 마세요.

(=In case the price is too expensive, please don't buy it.)

앞차와의 안전거리를 확보하지 않**을 경우(에)** 사고가 날 가능성이 높습니다.

(=In case you won't keep a safe following distance, you will have a high risk of getting into an accident.)

내일 비가 **올 경우(에)** 야외 수업은 취소 될 겁니다.

(=In case it will rain tomorrow, the outdoor class will be cancelled.)

44. Expressing "In the case that _": ~거든, ~거들랑

Function		Expressing "In the case that _"					
Form		~거든			~거들랑		
Meaning		In the case that _					
Distribution		Present	Past	Future	Present	Past	Future
Action Verb Stem	After a consonant	~거든	~았/었거든		~거들랑	~았/었거들랑	
	After a vowel	~거든	~았/었거든		~거들랑	~았/었거들랑	
	After "ㄹ"	~거든	~았/었거든		~거들랑	~았/었거들랑	
Stative Verb Stem	After a consonant	~거든			~거들랑		
	After a vowel	~거든			~거들랑		
	After "ㄹ"	~거든			~거들랑		

"~거든" can be used in imperative and propositional sentences to express that the action in the following clause needs to be carried out if the condition in the preceding clause is met, which can be rendered as "In the case that _."

집에 가**거든** 꼭 샤워부터 해라.

(=In the case that you go home, you must take a shower first.)

사장님한테 전하실 말이 있으시**거든** 저한테 말씀하세요.

(=In the case that you need to deliver a message to the president, please tell me.)

신발이 너무 작**거든** 큰 걸로 바꿔라.

(=In the case that the shoes are too small for you, exchange them for bigger ones.)

일을 다 끝**냈거든** 빨리 퇴근하자.

(=In the case that you finish the work, let's call it a day quickly.)

On the other hand, "~거들랑" can also be used for the same function. But it is more likely to be used in casual conversation.

한국에 오**거들랑** 꼭 연락해라.

(=In the case that you come to Korea, contact me without fail.)

집에 도착하**거들랑** 먼저 전화부터 해라.

(=In the case that you get home, call me first.)

값이 너무 비싸**거들랑** 사지 말아라.

(=In the case that the price is too expensive, don't buy that.)

숙제를 다 **했거들랑** 나가 놀아라.

(=In the case that you finished your homework, go out and play.)

45. Enumerating the list of available options: ~거나/든지/든가

Function		Enumerating the list of available options		
Form		~거나	~든지	~든가
Meaning		Or		
Distribution		Present	Present	Present
Action Verb Stem	After a consonant	~거나*	~든지*	~든가*
	After a vowel	~거나*	~든지*	~든가*
	After "ㄹ"	~거나*	~든지*	~든가*
Stative Verb Stem	After a consonant	~거나*	~든지*	~든가*
	After a vowel	~거나*	~든지*	~든가*
	After "ㄹ"	~거나*	~든지*	~든가*

* The preceding verb cannot take its own tense suffix, and its tense is determined by the tense of the main verb.

"~거나, ~든지, ~든가" can be used to enumerate stereotypical examples that one can freely choose from the list of options available to respond to a question, which can be rendered as "or." If we want to indicate that the enumerated examples are the exhaustive list, they should be attached to all the examples, except for the last one. It implies that no other options are available related to the question.

저는 시간이 있으면 보통 영화를 보**거나**/보**든지**/보**든가** 테니스를 치**거나**/치**든지**/치**든가** 쇼핑을 합니다.

(=If I have time, I usually watch movies, play tennis, or go shopping.)

그 여자와 결혼하려면 얼굴이 잘생기**거나**/잘생기**든지**/잘생기**든가** 돈이 많**거나**/많**든지**/많**든가** 학력이 좋아야 합니다.

(=If someone wants to marry that woman, he should be handsome, rich, or well educated.)

On the other hand, if we want to indicate that the enumerated examples are only the partial list of options, and some other options are still available, they must be attached to all the enumerated examples including the last one. In this case, the generic verb "하다" must be added at the end of the sentence.

시간이 있으면 보통 영화를 보**거나**/보**든지**/보**든가** 테니스를 치**거나**/치**든지**/치**든가** 쇼핑을 하**거나**/하**든지**/하**든가** 합니다.
(=If I have time, I usually watch movies, play tennis, go shopping or the like.)

그 여자와 결혼하려면 얼굴이 잘생기**거나**/잘생기**든지**/잘생기**든가** 돈이 많**거나**/많**든지**/많**든가** 학력이 좋**거나**/좋**든지**/좋**든가** 해야 합니다.
(=If someone wants to marry that woman, he should be handsome, rich, have a good educational background or the like.)

"~거나, ~든지, ~든가" can also be used together with question words such as "무엇 (what)," "어디 (where)," "누구 (who)," "언제 (when)," "어떻게 (how)," etc., to express that the situation in the following clause always holds true regardless of the situation in the preceding clause. In this usage "~거" in "~거나" is more likely to be deleted in casual conversation.

메리는 **누구**를 보**(거)나**/보**든지**/보**든가** 인사를 잘합니다.
(=Mary greets other people well no matter who she sees.)

메리는 제가 **무엇**을 하**(거)나**/하**든지**/하**든가** 관심이 없어요.
(=Mary doesn't care about whatever I do.)

존은 **어디**를 가**(거)나**/가**든지**/가**든가** 찬밥 신세예요.
(=John has been left out in the cold wherever he goes.)

그 일은 아주 단순하기 때문에 **누가** 하**(거)나**/하**든지**/하**든가** 별 차이 없어요.
(=Because this is a very simple job, it will not make any difference who does it.)

존은 **언제** 보**(거)나**/보**든지**/보**든가** 항상 믿음직합니다.
(=John is always reliable whenever I see him.)

이 일은 **어떻게** 하**(거)나**/하**든지**/하**든가** 별 차이가 없어요.
(=It will not make any difference how you do this work.)

46. Providing concrete examples of one's action:
~(는/ㄴ)다/냐/라/자거나/든지/든가 하면서

Function			Providing concrete examples of one's action		
Form			~(는/ㄴ)다/냐/라/자거나/든지/든가 하면서		
Meaning			While saying/asking/ordering/suggesting _ or _		
Distribution			Present	Present	Present
Action Verb Stem	Statement	After a consonant	~는다거나 하면서[1]	~는다든지 하면서[1]	~는다든가 하면서[1]
		After a vowel	~ㄴ다거나 하면서[1]	~ㄴ다든지 하면서[1]	~ㄴ다든가 하면서[1]
		After "ㄹ"	~ㄴ다거나 하면서[1,2]	~ㄴ다든지 하면서[1,2]	~ㄴ다든가 하면서[1,2]
	Question	Regardless of the ending	~냐거나 하면서[1,2]	~냐든지 하면서[1,2]	~냐든가 하면서[1,2]
	Imperative	After a consonant	~으라거나 하면서[1]	~으라든지 하면서[1]	~으라든가 하면서[1]
		After a vowel or "ㄹ"	~라거나 하면서[1]	~라든지 하면서[1]	~라든가 하면서[*]
	Proposition	Regardless of the ending	~자거나 하면서[1]	~자든지 하면서[1]	~자든가 하면서[1]
Stative Verb Stem	Statement	Regardless of the ending	~다거나 하면서[1]	~다든지 하면서[1]	~다든가 하면서[1]
	Question	Regardless of the ending	~냐거나 하면서[1,2]	~냐든지 하면서[1,2]	~냐든가 하면서[1,2]

[1] The preceding verb cannot take its own tense suffix, and its tense is determined by the tense of the main verb.

[2] If the verb stem ends with "ㄹ," "ㄹ" will be dropped before we attach "~ㄴ다거나 하면서, ~ㄴ다든지 하면서, ~ㄴ다든가 하면서, ~냐거나 하면서, ~냐든지 하면서~냐든가 하면서" according to the rule of "ㄹ" deletion that says "the consonant "ㄹ" at the end of a verb stem is dropped before "ㄴ, ㅂ, ㅅ." (See Chapter 12 Verbs)
팔다 (to sell): 팔→판다거나 하면서/판다든지 하면서/판다든가 하면서/파냐거나 하면서/파냐든지 하면서/파냐든가 하면서
멀다 (far): 멀→머냐거나 하면서/머냐든지 하면서/머냐든가 하면서

"~ (는/ㄴ)다거나/든지/든가 하면서, ~냐거나/든지/든가 하면서, ~ (으)라거나/든지/든가 하면서, ~자거나/든지/든가 하면서" can be used to express that the speaker is reporting to the listener that another person is carrying out the action in the following clause by providing concrete examples of his/her action in the preceding clauses. They are actually the combination of three different grammar features plus the verb "하다 (do)": the citation endings "~(는/ㄴ)다/냐/(으)라/자" + "~거나/든지/든가 (or)" + "하다 (do)" + "~(으)면서

(while)." Therefore, they can be rendered as "while saying/asking/ordering/ suggesting _ or _." "~(는/ㄴ)다거나/든지/든가," "~냐거나/든지/든가," and "~(으)라거나/든지/든가" can be repeated more than once, typically twice, in a given sentence, but "하면서" must be attached only to the last one.

존은 요즘 닭가슴살만 먹**는다든지** 저칼로리 음식만 먹**는다든지 하면서** 다이어트를 한다.
(=John has been on a diet these days while saying that he eats only chicken breast or low-calorie food.)

존은 자기가 높은 사람들을 많이 **안다거나** 돈이 많**다거나 하면서** 항상 거짓말을 한다.
(=John always tells me a lie while saying that he is close to a lot of high-ranking officials or he is rich.)

메리는 나한테 왜 설거지를 안 하**냐든가** 왜 집이 더러우**냐든가 하면서** 잔소리를 한다.
(=Mary is nagging me while asking me why I don't do dishes or why the house is dirty.)

존은 나한테 빨리 돈을 갚**으라거나** 이자를 더 많이 내**라거나 하면서** 재촉하고 있다.
(=John is pushing me while ordering me to pay his money back quickly or to pay more interest on it.)

메리는 존한테 한국에 여행을 가**자든가** 유럽여행을 가**자든가 하면서** 조르고 있다.
(=Mary is twisting my arm while suggesting to me to take a trip to Korea or to Europe.)

47. Expressing "To get to the point of" or the main reason for a situation: ~는/(으)ㄴ/(으)ㄹ 만큼

"~는/(으)ㄴ/(으)ㄹ 만큼" can be used to express that the situation in the following clause can be taken to the point that the situation in the preceding clause describes, which can be rendered as "as _ as _/so _ that _."

존은 돈을 벌 수 있**는 만큼** 벌었다.
(=John made money as much as he could.)

제가 주위사람들에게서 도움을 받**은 만큼** 저도 다른 사람들을 돕고 싶어요.
(=I also want to help others as much help as I received from people around me.)

Function	Expressing "To get to the point of"			Expressing the main reason for a given situation		
Form	~는/(으)ㄴ/(으)ㄹ 만큼					
Meaning	As _ as _/So _ that _			(Mainly) because		
Distribution	Present	Past	Future	Present	Past	Future
Action Verb Stem — After a consonant	~는 만큼	~은 만큼/~았/었던 만큼	~을 만큼	~는 만큼	~은 만큼	
Action Verb Stem — After a vowel	~는 만큼	~ㄴ 만큼/~았/었던 만큼	~ㄹ 만큼	~는 만큼	~ㄴ 만큼	
Action Verb Stem — After "ㄹ"	~는 만큼*	~ㄴ 만큼*/~았/었던 만큼	만큼	~는 만큼*	~ㄴ 만큼*	
Stative Verb Stem — After a consonant				~은 만큼		
Stative Verb Stem — After a vowel				~ㄴ 만큼		
Stative Verb Stem — After "ㄹ"				~ㄴ 만큼*		

* If the verb stem ends with "ㄹ," "ㄹ" will be dropped before we attach "~는 만큼, ~ㄴ 만큼" according to the rule of "ㄹ" deletion that says "the consonant "ㄹ" at the end of a verb stem is dropped before "ㄴ, ㅂ, ㅅ." (See Chapter 12 Verbs)
(ex) 팔다 (to sell): 팔→파는 만큼,/판 만큼, 멀다 (far): 멀→먼 만큼

필요한 **만큼** 가져가세요.

(=You can take as much as you need.)

A380 비행기는 최대 525명이 탑승할 수 있을 **만큼** 세계에서 가장 큰 여객기다.

(=A380 is the world's largest passenger aircraft that can accommodate as many as 525 passengers maximum on board.)

나는 이제 **살 만큼** 살았다.

(=Now I have lived as long as I could.)

존은 더 이상 참을 수 없을 **만큼** 화가 많이 났다.

(=John got so angry that he could not tolerate it anymore.)

이 음식은 말로 표현할 수 없을 **만큼** 맛이 있다.

(=This food is so tasty that I cannot put it into words.)

Sometimes "~았/었던 만큼" which is a past tense variant form of "~(으)ㄴ 만큼" can be used to express that the situation in the following clause actually happened contrary to one's previous belief.

기대**했던 만큼** 주식투자로 재미를 못 봤다.

(=I did not make as much money from my stock investment as I previously expected.)

생각**했던 만큼** 이번 지진으로 인한 피해는 심하지 않았다.

(=The earthquake damage was not as serious as I previously thought.)

On the other hand, "~는/(으)ㄴ 만큼" can also be used to express that the situation in the following clause applies mainly because the situation in the preceding clause holds true, which can be rendered as "(mainly) because." But this usage is not the main function of "~는/(으)ㄴ 만큼", but rather it originally belongs to "~(으)니만큼, ~(느)니만큼," which will be discussed below.

모든 국민이 염원하**는 만큼**/염원하**느니만큼** 남북통일은 반드시 이루어야 한다.
(=Mainly because all citizens have been longing for unification between South and North Korea, we must accomplish it without fail.)

여러분들로부터 많은 성원을 받**은 만큼**/받**았으니만큼** 최선을 다하도록 하겠습니다.
(=Mainly because I have received a lot of support from you, I will do our best.)

이미 이 프로젝트를 시작**한 만큼**/시작**했으니만큼** 꼭 성공해야겠다.
(=Mainly because I already started this project, I need to make it a success.)

이 스포츠카는 성능이 아주 좋**은 만큼**/좋**으니만큼** 값이 아주 비싸다.
(=Mainly because the performance of this sports car is excellent, it is very expensive.)

이 향수는 값이 아주 비**싼 만큼**/비**싸니만큼** 아껴 써야 한다.
(=Mainly because this perfume is very expensive, you must use it sparingly.)

48. Expressing "As much as/As many as": ~(으)ㄹ 만치, ~(으)리만치

"~(으)ㄹ 만치, ~(으)리만치" can be used to express that the situation in the following clause can be taken to the point that the preceding clause describes, which can be rendered as "as much as/as many as." They are generally limited to use in conversation, unlike their equivalent grammar feature "~(으)ㄹ 만큼" which can be freely used in both written text and conversation. In addition, "~(으)리만치" is now on the verge of becoming an archaic expression other than being used in some frozen expressions, such as "놀라우리만치 (surprisingly) and 무서우리만치 (as scary as possible)."

Function		Expressing "As much as/As many as"					
Form		~(으)ㄹ 만치			~(으)리만치		
Meaning		As much as/As many as					
Distribution		Present	Past	Future	Present	Past	Future
Action Verb Stem	After a consonant			~을 만치			~으리만치
	After a vowel			~ㄹ 만치			~리만치
	After "ㄹ"			만치			~리만치
Stative Verb Stem	After a consonant						
	After a vowel						
	After "ㄹ"						

음식은 먹**을 만치**/먹**으리만치** 가져와라.

(=Bring as much food as you can eat.)

(Implication: Don't bring more food than you can eat.)

한국말을 잘하는 외국인들이 놀라**울 만치**/놀라우**리만치** 증가하고 있다.

(=The number of foreigners who are fluent in Korean has been surprisingly increasing by a whopping number.)

49. Expressing "As long as": ~는 한

Function		Expressing "As long as"		
Form		~는 한		
Meaning		As long as		
Distribution		Present	Past	Future
Action Verb Stem	After a consonant	~는 한[*]		
	After a vowel	~는 한[*]		
	After "ㄹ"	~는 한[*]		
Stative Verb Stem	After a consonant			
	After a vowel			
	After "ㄹ"			

[*] If the verb stem ends with "ㄹ," "ㄹ" will be dropped before we attach "~는 한" according to the rule of "ㄹ" deletion that says "the consonant "ㄹ" at the end of a verb stem is dropped before "ㄴ, ㅂ, ㅅ." (See Chapter 12 Verbs)
벌다 (to make money): 벌다→버는 한

"~는 한" can be used to express that the situation in the following clause can be ensured if the condition in the preceding clause is met, which can be rendered as "as long as."

제가 여기 있**는 한** 앞으로 다시는 그런 일이 일어나지 않도록 하겠습니다.
(=I will make sure that such a thing won't happen again as long as I am here.)

제가 도울 수 있**는 한** 최대한 돕도록 하겠습니다.
(=I will help you out to the best of my ability as long as I can.)

제 목숨이 붙어 있**는 한** 반드시 그 범인을 찾아서 복수할 겁니다.
(=I will find the criminal and get back at him as long as I am alive.)

내가 옆에 있**는 한** 아무 일도 없을 거야.
(=Nothing is going to happen to you as long as I stay next to you.)

제 힘이 닿**는 한** 최선을 다 하겠습니다.
(=I will do my best as long as I can do it.)
(=I will do it to the best of my ability.)

내가 돈을 버**는 한** 돈 걱정할 필요는 없다.
(=You don't have to worry about money as long as I make money.)

"~ㄴ 한" which is a variant form of "~는 한" can be used with the verb "가능하다 (to be possible)" in a conversational idiom.

가능**한 한** 빨리 해 주세요.
(=Please get it done quickly as long as it is possible.)
(=Please get it done as quickly as possible.)

50. Expressing "Because of the given situation": ~는/(으)ㄴ 이상

"~는/(으)ㄴ 이상" can be used to express that the situation in the following clause applies because the situation in the preceding clause already occurred, which can be rendered as "Now that _."

팀장이 그 프로젝트를 반대하**는 이상** 더 이상 밀어붙일 수 없다.
(=Now that the team leader is disapproving the project, we cannot push it forward anymore.)

Function	Expressing "Because of the given situation"		
Form	~는/(으)ㄴ 이상		
Meaning	Now that _		
Distribution	Present	Past	Future
Action Verb Stem — After a consonant	~는 이상	~은 이상	
Action Verb Stem — After a vowel	~는 이상	~ㄴ 이상	
Action Verb Stem — After "ㄹ"	~는 이상*	~ㄴ 이상*	
Stative Verb Stem — After a consonant	~은 이상		
Stative Verb Stem — After a vowel	~ㄴ 이상		
Stative Verb Stem — After "ㄹ"	~ㄴ 이상*		

* If the verb stem ends with "ㄹ," "ㄹ" will be dropped before we attach "~는 이상, ~ㄴ 이상" according to the rule of "ㄹ" deletion that says "the consonant "ㄹ" at the end of a verb stem is dropped before "ㄴ, ㅂ, ㅅ." (See Chapter 12 Verbs)
살다 (to live): 살→사는 이상/산 이상, 멀다 (far): 멀→먼 이상

적의 허점을 잡**은 이상** 더 이상 공격을 늦출 수 없다.

(=Now that we found the weak spot of the enemy forces, we cannot delay our attack any longer.)

일이 이렇게 **된 이상** 어쩔 도리가 없다.

(=Now that things turned out to be like this, there is nothing we can do about it.)

한번 약속**한 이상** 꼭 지켜야 합니다.

(=Now that you made the promise, you must keep it.)

사람을 다치게 **한 이상** 처벌을 받아야 한다.

(=Now that he/she injured the person, he/she must get punished.)

중상자가 많**은 이상** 사망자 수가 늘어날 것 같다.

(=Now that we have so many seriously injured people, the number of dead people is likely to rise.)

존의 증상이 이렇게 심각**한 이상** 더 이상 방치할 수 없다.

(=Now that John's symptoms are so serious like this, we cannot neglect it.)

상황이 이렇게 급박**한 이상** 우리의 계획을 더 이상 늦출 수 없다.

(=Now that the situation is urgent like this, we can no longer delay our plan.)

51. Expressing the main reason for taking action: ~(으)니만큼, ~느니만큼

Function		Expressing the main reason for taking action					
Form		~(으)니만큼			~느니만큼		
Meaning		(Mainly) because					
Distribution		Present	Past	Future	Present	Past	Future
Action Verb Stem	After a consonant	~으니만큼	~았/었으니만큼		~느니만큼	~았/었느니만큼	
	After a vowel	~니만큼	~았/었으니만큼		~니만큼	~았/었느니만큼	
	After "ㄹ"	~니만큼*	~았/었으니만큼		~니만큼*	~았/었느니만큼	
Stative Verb Stem	After a consonant	~으니만큼	~았/었으니만큼				
	After a vowel	~니만큼	~았/었으니만큼				
	After "ㄹ"	~니만큼*	~았/었으니만큼				

* If the verb stem ends with "ㄹ," "ㄹ" will be dropped before we attach "~니만큼" according to the rule of "ㄹ" deletion that says "the consonant "ㄹ" at the end of a verb stem is dropped before "ㄴ, ㅂ, ㅅ."" (See Chapter 12 Verbs)
살다 (to live): 살→사니만큼/사느니만큼, 멀다 (far): 멀→머니만큼

"~(으)니만큼, ~느니만큼" can be used to express that the action in the following clause must be carried out mainly because of the reason in the preceding clause, which can be rendered as "(mainly) because." They are more or less interchangeable, but "~느니만큼" brings a more dramatic effect to the description of the reason.

이 문제는 국가의 안보가 걸려 **있으니만큼**/**있느니만큼** 단호하게 대처해야 합니다.
(=Mainly because our national security depends on this issue, we must take a decisive measure.)

올해는 심한 가뭄이 예상되**니만큼**/예상되**느니만큼** 물을 아껴 써야 합니다.
(=Mainly because we are expecting a severe drought this year, we must conserve water.)

시간을 다투는 일이**니만큼**/일이**느니만큼** 어서 서두르세요.
(=Mainly because it is time-sensitive work, please hurry up.)

한 나라의 대통령은 그 나라를 대표하**니만큼**/대표하**니만큼** 품위를 지켜야 한다.
(=Mainly because the president of a country represents the nation, he/she must maintain decency.)

남들보다 늦게 시작**했으니만큼**/시작**했느니만큼** 배로 노력해야 한다.

(=Mainly because you started working on it later than others, you must double your efforts.)

Unlike "~(으)니만큼, "~느니만큼" cannot be used with a stative verb.

돈이 적**으니만큼** 아껴 써야 한다.

(=Mainly because it's not enough money, we must use it sparingly.)

돈이 적**느니만큼** 아껴 써야 한다. (NOT OK)

예산이 부족**했으니만큼** 그 공사를 마무리하는 것이 불가능했다.

(=Mainly because the budget was insufficient, it was impossible to finish the construction.)

예산이 부족**했느니만큼** 그 공사를 마무리하는 것이 불가능했다. (NOT OK)

52. Expressing "To the extent that": ~(으)ㄹ 정도로

Function		Expressing "To the extent that"		
Form		~(으)ㄹ 정도로		
Meaning		So _ that _		
Distribution		Present	Past	Future
Action Verb Stem	After a consonant		~았/었을 정도로[*]	~을 정도로
	After a vowel		~았/었을 정도로[*]	~ㄹ 정도로
	After "ㄹ"		~았/었을 정도로[*]	정도로
Stative Verb Stem	After a consonant		~았/었을 정도로[*]	~을 정도로
	After a vowel		~았/었을 정도로[*]	~ㄹ 정도로
	After "ㄹ"		~았/었을 정도로[*]	정도로

[*] The preceding verb can take its own tense suffix or its tense can be determined by the tense of the main verb.

"~(으)ㄹ 정도로" can be used to express that the action or state in the following clause is taken to the extent of the situation in the preceding clause, which can be rendered as "so _ that _."

이 일은 초보자도 쉽게 할 수 있**을 정도로** 아주 단순하다.

(=This task is so simple that even a beginner can easily handle it.)

뼈가 부숴**질 정도로** 정말 열심히 일했다.

(=I worked so hard that my bones might be crushed.)

이 식당은 접시가 작**을 정도로** 일 인분의 양이 아주 많다.

(=The amount of one serving at this restaurant is so much that a dish is too small to hold it.)

이번 일은 머리가 아**플 정도로** 아주 복잡하다.

(=This job is so complicated that I might get a headache.)

요즘 미세먼지 때문에 숨쉬기가 힘**들 정도로** 공기가 나쁘다.

(=These days the air quality is so bad due to micro dust that it is difficult to breathe.)

With regard to the tense rule, the tense of the preceding verb is determined by the tense of the main verb. But sometimes the past-tense suffix can be optionally used to emphasize the completion of the situation in the preceding clause.

존은 모두 A학점을 받**을 정도로** 아주 공부를 잘했다.
존은 모두 A학점을 받**았을 정도로** 아주 공부를 잘했다.

(=John studied so well that he received all A's.)

존은 인사불성이 **될 정도로** 술을 너무 많이 마셨다.
존은 인사불성이 **됐을 정도로** 술을 너무 많이 마셨다.

(=John drank so much that he passed out.)

53. Expressing "Not only _ but also _": ~(으)ㄹ 뿐(만) 아니라, ~(으)ㄹ뿐더러

"~(으)ㄹ 뿐(만) 아니라" can be used to express that the situation in the following clause holds true in addition to the situation in the preceding clause, which can be rendered as "not only _ but also _." It puts more emphasis on the situation in the following clause.

존은 3점슛을 잘 넣**을 뿐(만) 아니라** 리바운드도 잘한다.

(=John is not only good at making three-point shots but also good at catching rebound balls.)

Function	Expressing "Not only _ but also _"					
Form	~(으)ㄹ 뿐(만) 아니라			~(으)ㄹ뿐더러		
Meaning	Not only _ but also _					
Distribution		Present	Past	Future	Present	Past	Future
Action Verb Stem	After a consonant	~을 뿐(만) 아니라	~았/었을 뿐(만) 아니라		~을뿐더러	~았/었을 뿐더러	
	After a vowel	~ㄹ 뿐(만) 아니라	~았/었을 뿐(만) 아니라		~ㄹ뿐더러	~았/었을 뿐더러	
	After "ㄹ"	뿐(만) 아니라	~았/었을 뿐(만) 아니라		~뿐더러	~았/었을 뿐더러	
Stative Verb Stem	After a consonant	~을 뿐(만) 아니라	~았/었을 뿐(만) 아니라		~을뿐더러	~았/었을 뿐더러	
	After a vowel	~ㄹ 뿐(만) 아니라	~았/었을 뿐(만) 아니라		~ㄹ뿐더러	~았/었을 뿐더러	
	After "ㄹ"	뿐(만) 아니라	~았/었을 뿐(만) 아니라		~뿐더러	~았/었을 뿐더러	

메리는 공부를 잘**할 뿐(만) 아니라** 봉사활동도 열심히 한다.

(=Mary not only studies well but also works hard for her community service.)

존은 돈이 많**을 뿐(만) 아니라** 집안 배경도 아주 좋다.

(=John not only has a lot of money but he also has a good family background.)

그 집은 값이 비**쌀 뿐(만) 아니라** 너무 오래 됐다.

(=That house is not only pricey but also too old.)

메리는 예**쁠 뿐(만) 아니라** 몸매도 날씬하다.

(=Mary is not only pretty but also slender.)

With regard to the tense rule, the preceding verb can take its own tense suffix, which is independent of the tense of the main verb.

지난번 총격사건은 정전협정을 위반**했을 뿐(만) 아니라** 남북 간의 긴장을 고조시키고 있다.

(=The last shooting incident not only violated the truce treaty but also continues to heighten the tension between South and North Korea.)

On the other hand, "~(으)ㄹ뿐더러" can also be used for the same function, but it is less likely to be used these days in favor of "~(으)ㄹ 뿐(만) 아니라."

그 집은 값이 비쌀**뿐더러** 너무 오래 됐다.

(=That house is not only pricey but also too old.)

메리의 결혼식에 많은 사람들이 **왔을뿐더러** 부조금도 많이 냈다.

(=Not only many people came to Mary's wedding ceremony but they also gave her a lot of gift money.)

54. Expressing "Not going beyond the given situation":

~(으)ㄹ 뿐(이지), ~(는/ㄴ)다 뿐이지

Function		Expressing "Not going beyond the given situation"					
Form		~(으)ㄹ 뿐(이지)			~(는/ㄴ)다 뿐이지		
Meaning		Other than just					
Distribution		Present	Past	Future	Present	Past	Future
Action Verb Stem	After a consonant	~을 뿐(이지)	~았/었을 뿐(이지)		~는다 뿐이지	~았/었다 뿐이지	
	After a vowel	~ㄹ 뿐(이지)	~았/었을 뿐(이지)		~ㄴ다 뿐이지	~았/었다 뿐이지	
	After "ㄹ"	뿐(이지)	~았/었을 뿐(이지)		~다 뿐이지	~았/었다 뿐이지	
Stative Verb Stem	After a consonant	~을 뿐(이지)	~았/었을 뿐(이지)		~는다 뿐이지	~았/었다 뿐이지	
	After a vowel	~ㄹ 뿐(이지)	~았/었을 뿐(이지)		~ㄴ다 뿐이지	~았/었다 뿐이지	
	After "ㄹ"	뿐(이지)	~았/었을 뿐(이지)		~다 뿐이지	~았/었다 뿐이지	

"~(으)ㄹ 뿐(이지)" can be used to express that the situation in the following clause holds true in that the situation in the preceding clause does not go beyond what is being described, which can be rendered as "other than just _."

그저 존만 믿을 **뿐(이지)** 별다른 해결책이 없습니다.

(=There is no other solution other than just trusting John.)

메리는 존을 그냥 쳐다볼 **뿐(이지)** 아무 말도 하지 않았다.

(=Mary didn't even say a word to John other than just looking at him.)

이 휴대폰은 화면만 조금 작을 **뿐(이지)** 성능은 아주 좋다.

(=The performance of this cell phone is excellent other than just its small screen size.)

메리는 얼굴만 예**쁠 뿐(이지)** 스스로 할 줄 아는 게 아무것도 없다.

(=There is nothing that Mary can do by herself other than just having a pretty face.)

그 사람과 한 번 전화통화만 **했을 뿐(이지)** 일면식도 없습니다.

(=I have never met him/her before other than just having one telephone conversation.)

With regard to the tense rule, the preceding verb can take its own tense suffix, which is independent of the tense of the main verb.

범퍼에 살짝 기스만 **났을 뿐(이지)** 심각한 문제는 없습니다.

(=There are no serious problems other than a light scratch on the bumper.)

On the other hand, "~(는/ㄴ)다 뿐이지" carries the same function, but it can be used to make a more definitive statement.

그저 존만 믿**는다 뿐이지** 별다른 방법이 없습니다.

(=There is no other solution other than just trusting John.)

남들보다 좀 더 열심히 일**한다 뿐이지** 특별한 성공의 비결은 없습니다.

(=There is no special secret to my success other than just working harder than others.)

존은 키가 조금 작**다 뿐이지** 아주 훌륭한 남편감이다.

(=John will make a great husband other than just his short height.)

메리는 얼굴만 예쁘**다 뿐이지** 스스로 할 줄 아는 게 아무것도 없다.

(=There is nothing that Mary can do by herself other than just having a pretty face.)

저는 그저 다친 사람을 도와 주**었다 뿐이지** 이번 사건과 아무 관련이 없습니다.

(=I have nothing to with this case other than just helping the injured person.)

55. Expressing "Like (the way in which)": ~는/(으)ㄴ/(으)ㄹ 것같이/처럼

"~는/(으)ㄴ/(으)ㄹ 것같이/처럼" can be used to create "simile" expressions by comparing the situation in the following clause with another comparable situation in the preceding clause, which can be rendered as "like (the way in which)."

Function		Expressing "Like (the way in which)"		
Form		~는/(으)ㄴ/(으)ㄹ 것같이/처럼		
Meaning		Like (the way in which)		
Distribution		Present	Past	Future
Action Verb Stem	After a consonant	~는 것같이/처럼	~은 것같이/처럼	~을 것같이/처럼
	After a vowel	~는 것같이/처럼	~ㄴ 것같이/처럼	~ㄹ 것같이/처럼
	After "ㄹ"	~는 것같이/처럼*	~ㄴ 것같이/처럼*	것같이/처럼
Stative Verb Stem	After a consonant	~은 것같이/처럼		~을 것같이/처럼
	After a vowel	~ㄴ 것같이/처럼		~ㄹ 것같이/처럼
	After "ㄹ"	~ㄴ 것같이/처럼*		것같이/처럼

* If the verb stem ends with "ㄹ," "ㄹ" will be dropped before we attach "~는 것같이/처럼, ~ㄴ 것같이/처럼" according to the rule of "ㄹ" deletion that says "the consonant "ㄹ" at the end of a verb stem is dropped before "ㄴ, ㅂ, ㅅ."" (See Chapter 12 Verbs)

살다 (to live): 살→사는 것같이/처럼, 멀다 (far): 멀→먼 것같이/처럼

평소에 하**는 것같이/처럼** 하면 돼.

(=It's ok to act like you normally do in your daily routine.)

창문을 한 번도 안 닦**은 것같이/처럼** 지저분하게 보인다.

(=The window looks dirty, like it has never been cleaned.)

메리는 그 일을 자기 혼자 다 **한 것같이/처럼** 말한다.

(=Mary talks like she did all the work by herself.)

옷이 작**은 것같이/처럼** 보인다.

(=Your clothes look like they are too tight for you.)

이 패딩을 입으면 뚱뚱**한 것같이/처럼** 보인다.

(=If I wear this padding jumper, I look like I am fat.)

구조작업이 늦어지면 모두 얼어 죽**을 것같이/처럼** 보인다.

(=If the rescue operation is going to be delayed, it looks like all of them will be frozen to death.)

모든 것을 삼**킬 것같이/처럼** 태풍이 도시 전체를 휩쓸었다.

(=The typhoon swept the entire city like it was swallowing everything.)

56. Expressing "Like (the way in which)": ~는/(으)ㄴ/(으)ㄹ 듯(이)

Function		Expressing "Like (the way in which)"		
Form		~는/(으)ㄴ/(으)ㄹ 듯(이)		
Meaning		Like (the way in which)		
Distribution		Present	Past	Future
Action Verb Stem	After a consonant	~는 듯(이)	~은 듯(이)	~을 듯(이)
	After a vowel	~는 듯(이)	~ㄴ 듯(이)	~ㄹ 듯(이)
	After "ㄹ"	~는 듯(이)*	~ㄴ 듯(이)*	듯(이)
Stative Verb Stem	After a consonant			
	After a vowel			
	After "ㄹ"			

* If the verb stem ends with "ㄹ," "ㄹ" will be dropped before we attach "~는 듯(이), ~ㄴ 듯(이)" according to the rule of "ㄹ" deletion that says "the consonant "ㄹ" at the end of a verb stem is dropped before "ㄴ, ㅂ, ㅅ." (See Chapter 12 Verbs)
살다 (to live): 살→사는 듯(이), 벌다 (to make money): 벌→번 듯(이)

"~는/(으)ㄴ/(으)ㄹ 듯(이)" can be used to create "simile" expressions by comparing the situation in the main clause with another comparable situation in the preceding clause, which can be rendered as "like (the way in which)." Unlike its equivalent expression "~는/(으)ㄴ/(으)ㄹ 것같이/처럼," however, it provides a more figurative effect on the comparison of the situations.

존은 실수를 매일 밥 먹(**는) 듯(이)** 한다.
(=John makes mistakes like he eats meals every day.)
(=John is always making mistakes.)

땀이 비 오(**는) 듯(이)** 흘러내린다.
(=I am sweating like rain.)
(=I am sweating a lot.)

메리는 돈을 물 쓰(**는) 듯(이)** 쓴다.
(=Mary is spending money like she is using water.)
(=Mary is going on a spending spree.)

도시 전체가 쥐 죽**은 듯(이)** 아주 조용했다.
(=The entire city was so quiet like a dead rat.)
(=The entire city was extremely quiet.)

메리는 존을 못 **본 듯(이)** 지나쳤다.

(=Mary walked away from John like she didn't see him.)

존은 마치 나를 잡아먹**을 듯(이)** 달려듭니다.

(=John is pouncing on me like he is trying to butcher me.)

경찰은 실타래를 **풀 듯(이)** 그 사건을 조심스럽게 조사하고 있다.

(=The police are carefully investigating the case like they are handling entangled knots.)

57. Expressing "As the situation warrants": ~는/(으)ㄴ/(았/었)던 대로

Function		Expressing "As the situation warrants"		
Form		~는/(으)ㄴ/(았/었)던 대로		
Meaning		As		
Distribution		Present	Past	Future
Action Verb Stem	After a consonant	~는 대로	~은 대로 ~(았/었)던 대로	
	After a vowel	~는 대로	~ㄴ 대로 ~(았/었)던 대로	
	After "ㄹ"	~는 대로*	~ㄴ 대로* ~(았/었)던 대로	
Stative Verb Stem	After a consonant			
	After a vowel			
	After "ㄹ"			

* If the verb stem ends with "ㄹ," "ㄹ" will be dropped before we attach "~는 대로, ~ㄴ 대로" according to the rule of "ㄹ" deletion that says "the consonant "ㄹ" at the end of a verb stem is dropped before "ㄴ, ㅂ, ㅅ." (See Chapter 12 Verbs)
팔다 (to live): 팔→파는 대로, 벌다 (to make money): 벌→번 대로

"~는/(으)ㄴ 대로" can be used to express that the action in the following clause can be carried out as the situation in the preceding clause warrants, which can be rendered as "as." It is frequently used in conversational idioms.

서울에 도착하**는 대로** 전화할 게.

(=I will give you a call as I arrive in Seoul.)

저는 그냥 시키**는 대로** 했을 뿐입니다.

(=I just did as I was ordered to do.)

생각나**는 대로** 말씀해 주세요.

(=Please tell me as you can recall.)

시간 나**는 대로** 연락 주세요.

(=Please contact me as you may have time.)

존한테서 들**은 대로** 말해 봐.

(=Just tell me as you heard it from John.)

본 **대로** 자세히 얘기 해.

(=Tell me in detail as you saw.)

"~았던/었던 대로, ~던 대로" which are the past tense variant forms of "~(으)ㄴ 대로" can be used to express that the action in the following clause can be carried out the way in which it used to be done in the past.

그냥 평상시 하**던 대로/했던 대로** 해.

(=Just act as you normally do.)

존이 나에게 하**던 대로/했던 대로** 되갚아 주었습니다.

(=I got back at John as he did to me.)

58. Expressing "As _ as you can": ~(으)ㄹ 수 있는 대로

"~(으)ㄹ 수 있는 대로" can be used to express that the action in the main clause can be carried out as much as the situation in the preceding clause allows. This grammar feature is actually the combination of "~(으)ㄹ 수 있다 (can/be able to)" and "~는 대로 (as)." Therefore, it can be rendered as "as _ as you can."

물건들을 제 차에 실**을 수 있는 대로** 실어 주세요.

(=Please load as many items as you can in my car.)

구급차를 될 **수 있는 대로** 빨리 보내 주세요.

(=Please dispatch an ambulance as quickly as you can.)

Function	Expressing "As _ as you can"		
Form	~(으)ㄹ 수 있는 대로		
Meaning	As _ as you can		
Distribution	Present	Past	Future
Action Verb Stem — After a consonant			~을 수 있는 대로[*]
Action Verb Stem — After a vowel			~ㄹ 수 있는 대로[*]
Action Verb Stem — After "ㄹ"			수 있는 대로[*]
Stative Verb Stem — After a consonant			
Stative Verb Stem — After a vowel			
Stative Verb Stem — After "ㄹ"			

[*] The preceding verb cannot take its own tense suffix, and its tense is determined by the tense of the main verb.

될 수 있는 대로 기름진 음식은 드시지 마세요.

(=Try to avoid any kind of oily food as much as you can.)

오실 수 있는 대로 빨리 와 주세요.

(=Please come as quickly as you can.)

59. Expressing "In accordance with": ~(는/ㄴ)다는/(으)라는/자는 대로

"~는/ㄴ다는/(으)라는/자는 대로" can be used to express that the speaker is responding to the listener that the action in the main clause is to be carried out in accordance with the situation in the preceding clause. This grammar feature is actually the combination of the citation endings "~는/ㄴ다/(으)라/자" and "~는 대로 (as)." Therefore, they can be rendered as "as (one says/asks/suggests _)," respectively.

존이 먹는다는 대로 다 주세요.

(=Just give John as much food as he says he wants to eat.)

메리가 간다는 대로 따라가 보세요.

(=Try to go after Mary in the direction (as she says) she wants to go.)

존이 했다는 대로 그대로 따라했습니다.

(=I repeated exactly the same way as John said he did it.)

Function	Expressing "In accordance with"		
Form	~(는/ㄴ)다는/(으)라는/자는 대로		
Meaning	As (one says/asks/suggests _)		

Distribution			Present	Past	Future
Action Verb Stem	Statement	After a consonant	~는다는 대로	~았/었다는 대로	~겠다는 대로
		After a vowel	~ㄴ다는 대로	~았/었다는 대로	~겠다는 대로
		After "ㄹ"	~ㄴ다는 대로*	~았/었다는 대로	~겠다는 대로
	Imperative	After a consonant	~으라는 대로		
		After a vowel or "ㄹ"	~라는 대로		
	Proposition	Regardless of the ending	~자는 대로		
Stative Verb Stem	Statement	Regardless of the ending			
	Question	Regardless of the ending			

* If the verb stem ends with "ㄹ," "ㄹ" will be dropped before we attach "~ㄴ다는 대로" according to the rule of "ㄹ" deletion that says "the consonant "ㄹ" at the end of a verb stem is dropped before "ㄴ, ㅂ, ㅅ." (See Chapter 12 Verbs)

팔다 (to live): 팔→판다는 대로

존이 하**겠다는 대로** 내 버려 두세요.

(=Just leave John alone as he says he would do it in his own way.)

적**으라는 대로** 쓰세요.

(=Just write as you are asked to do.)

선생님이 하**라는 대로** 그냥 하세요.

(=Just do it as your teacher asks you to do.)

메리가 달**라는 대로** 주세요.

(=Just give Mary as much as she asks/wants.)

존은 여자친구가 하**자는 대로** 합니다.

(=John does things as his girlfriend suggests to him to do.)

60. Expressing "On one's way to the destination": ~는 길에

Function		Expressing "On one's way to the destination"		
Form		~는 길에		
Meaning		On one's way to _		
Distribution		Present	Past	Future
Action Verb Stem	After a consonant	~는 길에[*]		
	After a vowel	~는 길에[*]		
	After "ㄹ"	~는 길에[*]		
Stative Verb Stem	After a consonant			
	After a vowel			
	After "ㄹ"			

[*] The preceding verb cannot take its own tense suffix, and its tense is determined by the tense of the main verb.

"~는 길에" can be used to express that the action in the following clause is to be carried out on one's way to his/her destination in the preceding clause, which can be rendered as "on one's way to _."

존은 학교에 가는 **길에** 친구 집에 들렀다.

(=John stopped by his friend's house on his way to school.)

메리는 제주도에 출장 가는 **길에** 부산에 들러서 해운대를 구경했다.

(=Mary stopped by Busan and looked around Haeundae Beach on her business trip to Jeju Island.)

집에 오는 **길에** 편의점에서 우유 좀 사오세요.

(=Please buy some milk at a convenience store on your way back home.)

61. Expressing "While you are at it": ~는/(으)ㄴ 김에

Function	Expressing "While you are at it"		
Form	~는/(으)ㄴ 김에		
Meaning	While you are at it		Speaking of which
Distribution	Present	Past	Future
Action Verb Stem — After a consonant	~는 김에*	~은 김에	
Action Verb Stem — After a vowel	~는 김에*	~ㄴ 김에	
Action Verb Stem — After "ㄹ"	~는 김에*	~ㄴ 김에*	
Stative Verb Stem — After a consonant			
Stative Verb Stem — After a vowel			
Stative Verb Stem — After "ㄹ"			

* If the verb stem ends with "ㄹ," "ㄹ" will be dropped before we attach "~는 김에, ~ㄴ 김에" according to the rule of "ㄹ" deletion that says "the consonant "ㄹ" at the end of a verb stem is dropped before "ㄴ, ㅂ, ㅅ." (See Chapter 12 Verbs)
팔다 (to sell): 팔→파는 김에/판 김에

"~는/(으)ㄴ 김에" can be used to express that the action in the following clause is to be carried out as a free ride given the situation that the action in the preceding clause is being carried out, which can be rendered as "While you are at it."

이왕 쓰시는 **김에** 조금만 더 쓰세요.

(=While you are at it, why don't you spend a little more money on it?)

드시는 **김에** 이 것도 한 번 드셔 보세요.

(=While you are at it, just try this one, too.)

옷을 입은 **김에** 밖에 나가서 아이스크림 좀 사와라.

(=While you are wearing your clothes, go out and buy some ice cream.)

It can also be used as part of a conversational idiom to express that the speaker wants to talk about the topic that happened to be mentioned in the conversation, which can be rendered as "Speaking of which."

말이 나온 **김에** 누가 잘못 했는지 한번 따져 봅시다.

(=Speaking of which, let's find out whose fault it is.)

62. Talking about something that has been just said or you just remembered:

~아서/어서 말인데

Function		Talking about something that has been just said	Talking about something that you just remembered	
Form		~아서/어서 말인데		
Meaning		Speaking of which	Come to think of it	
Distribution		Present	Past	Future
Action Verb Stem	After "오" or "아"	~아서 말인데[*]		
	Otherwise	~어서 말인데[*]		
Stative Verb Stem	After "오" or "아"			
	Otherwise			

[*] The preceding verb cannot take its own tense suffix, and its tense is determined by the tense of the main verb.

"~아서/어서 말인데" can be used to express that the speaker is trying to initiate a conversation about the topic that has been just mentioned during the conversation to ensure the situation in the following clause, which can be rendered as "Speaking of which." It can also be used to express that the speaker is trying to initiate a conversation about the topic that he/she just remembered, which can be rendered as "Come to think of it." It is generally interchangeable with "~는/(으)ㄴ 김에" in both cases.

말이 나**와서 말인데** 누가 잘못 했는지 한번 따져 봅시다.

말이 나**온 김에** 누가 잘못 했는지 한번 따져 봅시다.

(=Speaking of which, let's find out whose fault it is.)

(갑자기) 생각**나서 말인데** 우리 한 번 허심탄회하게 이야기해 봅시다.

(갑자기) 생각**난 김에** 우리 한 번 허심탄회하게 이야기해 봅시다.

(=Come to think of it, why don't we have a heart to heart talk with each other?)

63. Expressing an ongoing state: ~(으)ㄴ 채(로), ~(으)ㄴ 상태로/상태에서

Function		Expressing an ongoing state					
Form		~(으)ㄴ 채(로)			~(으)ㄴ 상태로/상태에서		
Meaning		While					
Distribution		Present	Past	Future	Present	Past	Future
Action Verb Stem	After a consonant		~은 채(로)			~은 상태로/ ~은 상태에서	
	After a vowel		~ㄴ 채(로)			~ㄴ 상태로/ ~ㄴ 상태에서	
	After "ㄹ"		~ㄴ 채(로)*			~ㄴ 상태로/ ~ㄴ 상태에서*	
Stative Verb Stem	After a consonant				~은 상태로/ ~은 상태에서		
	After a vowel				~ㄴ 상태로/ ~ㄴ 상태에서		
	After "ㄹ"				~ㄴ 상태로/ ~ㄴ 상태에서*		

* If the verb stem ends with "ㄹ," "ㄹ" will be dropped before we attach "~ㄴ 채(로), ~ㄴ 상태로/~ㄴ 상태에서" according to the rule of "ㄹ" deletion that says "the consonant "ㄹ" at the end of a verb stem is dropped before "ㄴ, ㅂ, ㅅ." (See Chapter 12 Verbs)
매달다 (to hang): 매달→매단 채(로)/매단 상태로/매단 상태에서, 길다 (long): 길→긴 상태로/긴 상태에서

"~(으)ㄴ 채(로), ~(으)ㄴ 상태로, ~(으)ㄴ 상태에서" can be used to express that the action in the following clause is being carried out while the situation in the preceding clause is ongoing, which can be rendered as "while."

존은 옷을 입은 **채(로)/입은 상태로/입은 상태에서** 수영을 한다.

(=John is swimming while wearing clothes.)

메리는 신발을 벗은 **채(로)/벗은 상태로/벗은 상태에서** 길거리를 돌아다녔다.

(=Mary walked around the street while not wearing her shoes.)

(=Mary walked around the street without wearing her shoes.)

존은 자동차에 시동을 **건 채(로)/건 상태로/건 상태에서** 차 안에서 잠이 들었습니다.

(=John fell asleep inside the car while the engine was running.)

그 음주운전자는 경찰관을 매**단 채(로)/매단 상태로/매단 상태에서** 도망가려고 했다.

(=The drunk driver was trying to escape while the police officer was still hanging on to the car.)

그 살인사건의 용의자는 굳게 입을 다문 **채(로)**/다문 **상태로**/다문 **상태에서** 꼼짝도 하지
않았습니다.

(=The suspect in the homicide case did not even move an inch while having closed
his mouth firmly.)

Unlike "~(으)ㄴ 채(로)," "~(으)ㄴ 상태로/상태에서" can also be used with a stative verb.

존은 기분이 **좋은 상태로**/좋은 **상태에서** 여행을 떠났다.

(=John took a trip while he was in good mood.)

존은 기분이 **좋은 채(로)** 여행을 떠났다. (NOT OK)

메리는 아픈 **상태로**/아픈 **상태에서** 학교에 왔다.

(=Mary came to school while she was sick.)

메리는 아픈 **채(로)** 학교에 왔다. (NOT OK)

64. Expressing "On top of that": ~는/(으)ㄴ데다(가)

Function	Expressing "On top of that"		
Form	~는/(으)ㄴ 데다(가)		
Meaning	On top of that		
Distribution	Present	Past	Future
Action Verb Stem — After a consonant	~는 데다(가)	~은 데다(가)	
Action Verb Stem — After a vowel	~는 데다(가)	~ㄴ 데다(가)	
Action Verb Stem — After "ㄹ"	~는 데다(가)*	~ㄴ 데다(가)*	
Stative Verb Stem — After a consonant	~은 데다(가)		
Stative Verb Stem — After a vowel	~ㄴ 데다(가)		
Stative Verb Stem — After "ㄹ"	~ㄴ 데다(가)*		

* If the verb stem ends with "ㄹ," "ㄹ" will be dropped before we attach "~는 데다(가), ~ㄴ 데다(가)" according
to the rule of "ㄹ" deletion that says "the consonant "ㄹ" at the end of a verb stem is dropped before "ㄴ, ㅂ,
ㅅ." (See Chapter 12 Verbs)
팔다 (to live): 팔→파는 데다(가)/판 데다(가)

"~는/(으)ㄴ 데다(가)" can be used to express that the situation in the following clause
happens on top of the situation in the preceding clause, which can be rendered as "on

top of that."

이 프로젝트는 돈이 많이 드**는 데다(가)** 끝내는데 시간도 많이 걸린다.
(=This project costs a lot of money, and on top of that it also takes a long time to finish it.)

비가 오**는 데다(가)** 밖이 어두워서 구조작업이 중단됐습니다.
(=Because it was raining, and on top of that it was dark outside, the rescue operation has been halted.)

그 남자는 총상을 입**은 데다(가)** 뇌를 다쳐서 금방 죽을 것 같다.
(=Because he received a gunshot wound, and on top of that he has a brain damage, he may die soon.)

이 의자는 부러**진 데다(가)** 너무 오래됐다.
(=This chair is broken, and on top of that it's too old.)

존은 돈이 많**은 데다(가)** 얼굴도 잘생겼다.
(=John is rich, and on top of that he is also handsome.)

메리는 얼굴이 예**쁜 데다(가)** 공부도 잘한다.
(=Mary has a pretty face, and on top of that she also studies well.)

65. Carrying out an alternative action/In compensation for:
~는/(으)ㄴ 대신(에)

"~는 대신(에)" can be used with an action verb to express that one prefers to carry out the alternative action in the following clause instead of the originally purported action in the preceding clause, which can be rendered as "instead of."

외식을 하**는 대신(에)** 집에서 시켜 먹자.
(=Let's order some food at home instead of eating out.)

메리는 영화를 보**는 대신(에)** 연극을 보고 싶다고 했다.
(=Mary said that she wants to watch a theatrical play instead of watching a movie.)

고속버스를 타**는 대신(에)** 기차를 타고 부산에 갔다.
(=I went to Busan by train instead of taking an express bus.)

Function	Carrying out an alternative action			Expressing "In compensation for"		
Form	~는/(으)ㄴ 대신(에)					
Meaning	Instead of			In compensation for/In return for		
Distribution	Present	Past	Future	Present	Past	Future
Action Verb Stem — After a consonant	~는 대신(에)			~는 대신(에)		
Action Verb Stem — After a vowel	~는 대신(에)			~는 대신(에)		
Action Verb Stem — After "ㄹ"	~는 대신(에)[*]			~는 대신(에)[*]		
Stative Verb Stem — After a consonant				~은 대신(에)		
Stative Verb Stem — After a vowel				~ㄴ 대신(에)		
Stative Verb Stem — After "ㄹ"				~ㄴ 대신(에)*		

[*] If the verb stem ends with "ㄹ," "ㄹ" will be dropped before we attach "~는 대신(에), ~ㄴ 대신(에)" according to the rule of "ㄹ" deletion that says "the consonant "ㄹ" at the end of a verb stem is dropped before "ㄴ, ㅂ, ㅅ." (See Chapter 12 Verbs)
팔다 (to live): 팔→파는 대신(에)/판 대신(에), 멀다 (far): 멀→먼 대신(에)

"~는 대신(에)" can also be used with an action verb to express that the situation in the following clause occurs in compensation for the situation in the preceding clause, which can be rendered as "in compensation for."

존은 노래를 못하<u>는 대신(에)</u> 춤을 아주 잘 춘다.

(=John is good at dancing in compensation for being bad at singing.)

나는 존의 점퍼를 빌려 입<u>는 대신(에)</u> 저녁을 사 줬다.

(=I treated John to dinner in compensation for borrowing his jumper.)

오늘 일찍 퇴근하<u>는 대신(에)</u> 내일 아침 일찍 출근하겠습니다.

(=I will come to work early tomorrow morning in compensation for leaving work early today.)

On the other hand, "~(으)ㄴ 대신(에)" can be used with a stative verb to express that the situation in the following clause applies in compensation for/in return for the situation in the preceding clause.

존은 키가 작<u>은 대신(에)</u> 아주 빨라서 농구를 잘한다.

(=John is good at basketball because he is so fast in compensation for his short height.)

이 TV는 값이 **비싼 대신(에)** 화질이 아주 좋아요.

(=The picture quality of this TV is very good in compensation for its high price tag.)

이 차는 성능이 **좋은 대신(에)** 값이 비싸다.

(=The price of this car is expensive in return for its good performance.)

이 지역은 교통이 편리**한 대신(에)** 집값이 아주 비싸다.

(=Home prices in this area are very expensive in return for its convenient transportation.)

66. Expressing the outcome of the past action/the subsequent change on the situation: ~더니(만)

Function	The outcome of the past action			The subsequent change on the situation		
Form	~더니(만)					
Meaning	As a result of			Used to _, but _		
Distribution	Present	Past	Future	Present	Past	Future
Action Verb Stem — After a consonant		~더니(만) ~았/었더니(만)			~더니(만)	
Action Verb Stem — After a vowel		~더니(만) ~았/었더니(만)			~더니(만)	
Action Verb Stem — After "ㄹ"		~더니(만) ~았/었더니(만)			~더니(만)	
Stative Verb Stem — After a consonant					~더니(만)	
Stative Verb Stem — After a vowel					~더니(만)	
Stative Verb Stem — After "ㄹ"					~더니(만)	

"~더니(만)" can be used to express that the situation in the following clause is the direct outcome of one's taking action in the preceding clause according to the speaker's observation, which can be rendered as "as a result of." The subject of the preceding clause must be in the second person or the third person.

존은 열심히 공부하**더니(만)** 드디어 시험에 합격했다.

(=John finally passed the exam as a result of his having studied hard.)

내가 열심히 공부하**더니(만)** 드디어 시험에 합격했다. (The 1st person subject: NOT OK)

메리는 무리하게 사업을 확장하**더니(만)** 지난달에 파산 신청했다.

(=Mary filed a bankruptcy claim last month as a result of the excessive expansion of her business.)

내가 무리하게 사업을 확장하더니(만) 지난달에 파산 신청했다. (The 1st person subject: NOT OK)

너 다이어트를 하**더니(만)** 훨씬 날씬해졌다.

(=You became much slender as a result of your diet.)

내가 다이어트를 하**더니(만)** 날씬해졌다. (The 1st person subject: NOT OK)

Another past tense form "~았/었더니(만)" can be used to express the speaker's own experience of the situation in the following clause, which is the direct outcome of taking action in the preceding clause. It can also be rendered as "as a result of." The subject of the preceding clause must be in the first person.

내가 어제 과식을 **했더니(만)** 심하게 체했다.

(=My stomach hurts badly as a result of eating too much food yesterday.)

내가 어제 밤늦게까지 일**했더니(만)** 너무 피곤하다.

(=I am so tired as a result of working till late at night yesterday.)

내가 열심히 공부**했더니(만)** 드디어 시험에 합격했다.

(=I finally passed the exam as a result of having studied hard.)

존이 열심히 공부**했더니(만)** 드디어 시험에 합격했다. (The 3rd person subject: NOT OK)

내가 다이어트를 **했더니(만)** 훨씬 날씬해졌다.

(=I became much slender as a result of my diet.)

네가 다이어트를 **했더니(만)** 훨씬 날씬해졌다. (The 2nd person subject: NOT OK)

On the other hand, "~더니(만)" can also be used to express that the subsequent change in the following clause has been made since the speaker's last observation in the preceding clause, which can be rendered as "used to _, but _." It can be freely used with both action verbs and stative verbs, and there is no restriction on the subject of the preceding clause.

존은 고등학교 때 열심히 공부하**더니(만)** 지금은 전혀 공부를 안 한다.

(=John used to study hard when he was at high school, but now he doesn't study at all.)

조금 전까지 아프**더니(만)** 지금은 괜찮다.

(=I used to have a pain until a moment ago, but now I am fine.)

너 어렸을 때 말썽만 부리**더니(만)** 지금은 아주 점잖아졌다.

(=You used to be a trouble maker when you were a kid, but now you became very gentle.)

이 곳은 전에는 황량한 벌판이**더니(만)** 지금은 여기에 고층빌딩이 많이 들어서고 있다.

(=This place used to be a barren field before, but now many high-rise buildings are being built here.)

조금 전까지 복도가 아주 시끄럽**더니(만)** 갑자기 조용해졌다.

(=The hallway used to be very loud until a moment ago, but it suddenly became quiet.)

메리는 어렸을 때는 예쁘**더니(만)** 지금은 별로 예쁘지 않다.

(=Mary used be pretty when she was a kid, but now she is not that pretty.)

67. Expressing a change in the course of action: ~다(가) (말고)

Function		Expressing a change in the course of action					
Form		~다(가)			~다(가) 말고		
Meaning		While			After one stopped -ing		
Distribution		Present	Past	Future	Present	Past	Future
Action Verb Stem	After a consonant	~다(가)	~았/었다(가)		~다(가) 말고/ ~다(가)		
	After a vowel	~다(가)	~았/었다(가)		~다(가) 말고/ ~다(가)		
	After "ㄹ"	~다(가)	~았/었다(가)		~다(가) 말고/ ~다(가)		
Stative Verb Stem	After a consonant						
	After a vowel						
	After "ㄹ"						

"~다(가)" can be used to express that the ongoing action in the preceding clause undergoes a sudden change into the action in the following clause, which can be rendered as "while."

존은 TV를 보**다(가)** 졸았다.

(=John dozed off while watching TV.)

메리는 비틀거리**다(가)** 땅바닥에 쓰러졌다.

(=Mary fell down on the ground while staggering.)

존은 노래를 부르**다(가)** 춤을 추기 시작했다.

(=John started dancing while singing a song.)

메리는 슬픈 영화를 보**다(가)** 자주 운다.

(=Mary often cries while watching sad movies.)

어머님께 편지를 쓰**다(가)** 갑자기 눈물이 났다.

(=I shed tears while writing a letter to my mother.)

존은 주식에 투자**했다(가)** 망했다.

(=John went into bankruptcy while having invested in stocks.)

On the other hand, "~다(가) 말고" can be used to emphasize that the ongoing action in the preceding clause is completely halted before it is changed into the action in the following clause, which can be rendered as "after one stopped -ing." The subject has the control over whether or not to stop the ongoing action in the preceding clause.

존은 밥을 먹**다(가) 말고** 밖으로 나갔다.

(=John went outside after he stopped eating his meal.)

메리는 숙제하**다(가) 말고** 밖에서 친구하고 놀았다.

(=Mary played outside with her friends after she stopped doing her homework.)

68. Expressing the discovery of a new fact:

~아/어 보니(까), ~고 보니(까), ~다(가) 보니(까)

"~아/어 보니(까)" can be used to express that the speaker has discovered a new fact in the following clause that has gone previously unnoticed when he/she tried to carry out the action in the preceding clause. This grammar feature is actually the combination of "~아/어 보다 (try to)" and "~(으)니까 (because)," which can be rendered as "When I did so, I found out that _."

Function		Expressing the discovery of a new fact		
Form		~아/어 보니(까)	~고 보니(까)	~다(가) 보니(까)
Meaning		When I did so, I found out that _	After I did so, I found out that _	While I was doing so, I found out that _
Distribution		Present	Present	Present
Action Verb Stem	After "오" or "아"	~아 보니(까)*	~고 보니(까)*	~다(가) 보니(까)*
	Otherwise	~어 보니(까)*	~고 보니(까)*	~다(가) 보니(까)*
Stative Verb Stem	After "오" or "아"			
	Otherwise			

* The preceding verb cannot take its own tense suffix, and its tense is determined by the tense of the main verb.

한국 음식을 먹**어 보니(까)** 맛이 아주 괜찮았다.

(=When I tried Korean food, I found out that it was very tasty.)

"~고 보니(까)" and "~다(가) 보니(까)" can be basically used for the same function, which can be rendered as "After I did so, I found out that _," "While I was doing so, I found out that _," respectively.

존하고 이야기를 하**고 보니(까)** 괜찮은 사람인 것 같다.

(=After I talked to John, I found out that he seems to be a good person.)

메리하고 이야기를 하**다(가) 보니(까)** 시간 가는 줄 몰랐다.

(=While I was talking with Mary, I found out that I didn't realize how much time had passed.)

한국에 오래 살**다(가) 보니(까)** 한국사람이 다 된 것 같다.

(=While I had been living in Korea for a long time, I found out that I almost became a Korean.)

69. Expressing the natural outcome of a continuing action: ~다(가) 보면

Function		Expressing the natural outcome of a continuing action		
Form		~다(가) 보면		
Meaning		If one keeps -ing, (it is natural that) _		
Distribution		Present	Past	Future
Action Verb Stem	After a consonant	~다(가) 보면[*]		
	After a vowel	~다(가) 보면[*]		
	After "ㄹ"	~다(가) 보면[*]		
Stative Verb Stem	After a consonant			
	After a vowel			
	After "ㄹ"			

[*] The preceding verb cannot take its own tense suffix, and its tense is determined by the tense of the main verb.

"~다(가) 보면" can be used to express that the situation in the following clause is the natural outcome of the continuing action in the preceding clause. This grammar feature is actually the combination of "~다(가) 보다 (while one was doing something)" and "~(으)면 (If)," which can be rendered as "If one keeps -ing, it is natural that _."

일을 하**다(가) 보면** 누구나 다 실수할 때가 있다.

(=If one keeps working for a while, (it is natural that) he/she is liable to make mistakes.)

열심히 일하**다(가) 보면** 언젠가는 크게 성공할 겁니다.

(=If you keep working hard, (it is natural that) someday you will make a great success.)

혼자 살**다(가) 보면** 가끔 제 생각날 때가 있을 겁니다.

(=If you keep living alone, (it is natural that) sometimes you will miss me.)

70. Expressing worry about facing an unwanted situation:

~(으)ㄹ까 봐(서), ~(으)ㄹ까 싶어(서)

Function		Expressing worry about facing an unwanted situation					
Form		~(으)ㄹ까 봐(서)			~(으)ㄹ까 싶어(서)		
Meaning		Because one is worried that _					
Distribution		Present	Past	Future	Present	Past	Future
Action Verb Stem	After a consonant			~을까 봐(서)			~을까 싶어(서)
	After a vowel			~ㄹ까 봐(서)			~ㄹ까 싶어(서)
	After "ㄹ"			~까 봐(서)			~까 싶어(서)
Stative Verb Stem	After a consonant			~을까 봐(서)			~을까 싶어(서)
	After a vowel			~ㄹ까 봐(서)			~ㄹ까 싶어(서)
	After "ㄹ"			~까 봐(서)			~까 싶어(서)

"~(으)ㄹ까 봐(서), ~(으)ㄹ까 싶어(서)" can be used to express that the action in the following clause is to be carried out because one is worried about the possibility of facing the unwanted situation in the preceding clause, which can be rendered as "Because one is worried that _."

존이 내 돈을 **뺏을 까 봐(서)** 몰래 감춰 놓았다.
존이 내 돈을 **뺏을 까 싶어(서)** 몰래 감춰 놓았다.
(=Because I was worried that John might take away my money, I hid the money secretly.)

시험에 떨어**질까 봐(서)** 열심히 공부했습니다.
시험에 떨어**질까 싶어(서)** 열심히 공부했습니다.
(=Because I was worried that I might fail the test, I studied hard.)

수업시간에 늦**을까 봐(서)** 서둘렀다.
수업시간에 늦**을까 싶어(서)** 서둘렀다.
(=Because I was worried that I might be late for class, I hurried up.)

"~(으)ㄹ까 봐(서), ~(으)ㄹ까 싶어(서)" are frequently used with the optional adverb "혹시 (probably/possibly)."

(혹시) 범인이 도망**갈까 봐**(서) 수갑을 채웠습니다.

(혹시) 범인이 도망**갈까 싶어**(서) 수갑을 채웠습니다.

(=Because I was worried that the suspect might possibly run away, I handcuffed him/her.)

Sometimes "~(으)ㄹ까 봐 싶어(서)" which is the combination of "~(으)ㄹ까 봐(서)" and "~(으)ㄹ까 싶어(서)" can be used instead.

존이 다 **먹을까 봐 싶어**(서) 미리 피자 한 조각을 먹었다.

(=Because I was worried that John might eat all of the pizza, I already ate one slice of it.)

지붕이 바람에 날아**갈까 봐 싶어**(서) 무거운 것을 올려놓았다.

(=Because I was worried that the roof might be blown away by the wind, I put something heavy on it.)

71. Getting prepared for an uncertain situation: ~(으)ㄹ 지(도) 몰라(서)

Function		Getting prepared for an uncertain situation		
Form		~(으)ㄹ 지(도) 몰라(서)		
Meaning		Just in case		
Distribution		Present	Past	Future
Action Verb Stem	After a consonant			~을 지(도) 몰라(서)
	After a vowel			~ㄹ 지(도) 몰라(서)
	After "ㄹ"			지(도) 몰라(서)
Stative Verb Stem	After a consonant			~을 지(도) 몰라(서)
	After a vowel			~ㄹ 지(도) 몰라(서)
	After "ㄹ"			지(도) 몰라(서)

"~(으)ㄹ 지(도) 몰라(서)" can be used to express that the action in the following clause is to be carried out because one wants to get prepared for the uncertain situation in the preceding clause, which can be rendered as "just in case." It is frequently used with the optional adverb "혹시 (probably/possibly)."

(혹시) 사장님이 찾**을 지(도) 몰라(서)** 대기하고 있습니다.

(=I have been standing by, just in case my company president might page me at any minute.)

(혹시) 나중에 필요**할 지(도) 몰라(서)** 잘 보관해 두었습니다.

(=I kept it in a safe place, just in case we might need it later.)

(혹시) 갑자기 이곳을 떠**날 지(도) 몰라(서)** 미리 인사를 드립니다.

(=I have to say goodbye to you beforehand, just in case I might have to leave this place without notice.)

(혹시) 늦**을 지(도) 몰라(서)** 전화를 드립니다.

(=I am calling you, just in case I might be late.)

72. Expressing the contrastive situations: ~는/(으)ㄴ가 하면, ~나 하면

Function	Expressing the contrastive situations		
Form	~는/(으)ㄴ가 하면, ~나 하면		
Meaning	I wondered if _, but _	On the one hand _, but on the other hand _	If you wonder _, I can tell you _
Distribution	Present	Past	Future
Action Verb Stem — After a consonant	~는가 하면 ~나 하면	~았/었는가 하면 ~았/었나 하면	
Action Verb Stem — After a vowel	~는가 하면 ~나 하면	~았/었는가 하면 ~았/었나 하면	
Action Verb Stem — After "ㄹ"	~는가 하면* ~나 하면*	~았/었는가 하면 ~았/었나 하면	
Stative Verb Stem — After a consonant	~은가 하면 ~나 하면		
Stative Verb Stem — After a vowel	~ㄴ가 하면 ~나 하면		
Stative Verb Stem — After "ㄹ"	~ㄴ가 하면* ~나 하면*		

* If the verb stem ends with "ㄹ," "ㄹ" will be dropped before we attach "~는가 하면, ~ㄴ가 하면, ~나 하면" according to the rule of "ㄹ" deletion that says "the consonant "ㄹ" at the end of a verb stem is dropped before "ㄴ, ㅂ, ㅅ." (See Chapter 12 Verbs)
팔다 (to sell): 팔→파는가 하면, 파나 하면, 둥글다 (round): 둥글→둥근가 하면, 둥그나 하면

"~는/(으)ㄴ가 하면, ~나 하면" can be used to express that the situation in the following clause actually happens contrary to the speaker's expectation from a given situation in the preceding clause, which can be rendered as "I wondered if _, but _." "~는/(으)ㄴ가 하면" can be freely used in both written text and conversation, whereas "~나 하면" is more likely to be used in conversation.

경제가 살아나**는가 하면**/살아나**나 하면** 또 다시 불황이 닥쳐온다.
(=I wondered if economic conditions are getting better, but the recession strikes again.)

이제 고생이 다 끝**났는가 하면**/끝**났나 하면** 또 다른 시련들이 기다리고 있었다.
(=I wondered if all the hardships were over, but another round of hardships was waiting for me.)

집값이 좀 내**렸는가 하면**/내**렸나 하면** 또 다시 오르기 시작한다.
(=I wondered if home prices went down a little, but they are starting to go up again.)

존은 잠이 들**었는가 하면**/들**었나 하면** 다시 깨서 울기 시작했다.
(=I wondered if John fell asleep, but he woke up again and started crying.)

이제 좀 괜찮**은가 하면**/괜찮**나 하면** 다시 아프기 시작한다.
(=I wondered if I got better, but I start having pains again.)

품질이 좀 좋**은가 하면**/좋**나 하면** 값이 터무니 없이 비싸다.
(=I wondered if the quality is kind of good, but the price is ridiculously expensive.)

값이 좀 **싼가 하면**/싸**나 하면** 품질이 형편없다.
(=I wondered if the price is inexpensive, but the quality is terrible.)

On the other hand, "~는/(으)ㄴ가 하면, ~나 하면" can also be used to express that the situation in the preceding clause is in contrast to the situation in the following clause, and they both hold true, which can be rendered as "On the one hand _, but on the other hand _."

세상에는 좋은 사람들이 있**는가 하면**/있**나 하면** 나쁜 사람들도 많아요.
(=On the one hand there are some good people living in the world, but on the other hand there are also some bad people.)

저는 지하철을 탈 때가 있**는가 하면**/있**나 하면** 택시를 타고 갈 때도 있어요.
(=On the one hand there are times I take the subway, but on the other hand there are also times that I take a taxi.)

메리랑 살면서 행복했던 때가 있**었는가 하면**/있**었나 하면** 괴로웠던 때도 있었어요.
(=On the one hand there were times that I was happy while living with Mary, but on the other hand there were also times that I got frustrated.)

Unlike "~는/(으)ㄴ가 하면," "~나 하면" in this usage cannot be used with a stative verb.

인삼이 어떤 사람에게는 몸에 좋**은가 하면** 혈압이 높은 사람에게는 해로울 수도 있다.
(=On the one hand ginseng may be good for health for some people, but on the other hand it may be harmful for people with high blood pressure.)
인삼이 어떤 사람에게는 몸에 좋**나 하면** 혈압이 높은 사람에게는 해로울 수도 있다. (NOT OK)

혼자 살다 보면 어떤 때는 편**한가 하면** 아주 외로울 때도 있어요.
(=On the one hand there are times that I feel comfortable while living alone, but on the other hand there are also times that I feel very lonely.)
혼자 살다 보면 어떤 때는 편하**나 하면** 아주 외로울 때도 있어요. (NOT OK)

Lastly, "~는/(으)ㄴ가 하면, ~나 하면" can also be used with a question word to draw the listener's attention to what the speaker is about to say in the following clause regarding his/her previous question in the preceding clause, which can be rendered as "If you wonder _, I can tell you _."

존이 어디에 있**는가 하면** 메리의 집에 숨어 있다.
(=If you wonder where John is, I can tell you that he is hiding in Mary's house.)

우리가 어디서 만나**는가 하면** 세종대왕 동상 앞에서다.
(=If you wonder where we are going meet, I can tell you that we are going to meet in front of the statue of King Sejong.)

이 알약이 얼마나 좋은가 하면 거의 만병통치약이다.
(=If you wonder how good this pill is, I can tell you that it's almost like a panacea.)

날씨가 얼마나 더**운가 하면** 아스팔트조차도 녹아 버릴 정도다.
(=If you wonder how hot the weather is, I can tell you that it can even melt asphalt.)

73. Providing the primary reason for the given situation:

왜 ~는/(으)ㄴ가 하면, 왜 ~(으)냐 하면

Function		Providing the primary reason for the given situation			
Form		왜 ~는/(으)ㄴ가 하면		왜 ~으냐 하면	
Meaning		The reason why _ is that _			
Distribution		Present	Past	Present	Past
Action Verb Stem	After a consonant	왜 ~는가 하면	왜 ~았/었는가 하면	왜 ~으냐 하면	왜 ~았/었냐 하면
	After a vowel	왜 ~는가 하면	왜 ~았/었는가 하면	왜 ~냐 하면	왜 ~았/었냐 하면
	After "ㄹ"	왜 ~는가 하면*	왜 ~았/었는가 하면	왜 ~냐 하면*	왜 ~았/었냐 하면
Stative Verb Stem	After a consonant	왜 ~은가 하면	왜 ~았/었는가 하면	왜 ~으냐 하면	
	After a vowel	왜 ~ㄴ가 하면	왜 ~았/었는가 하면	왜 ~냐 하면	
	After "ㄹ"	왜 ~ㄴ가 하면*	왜 ~았/었는가 하면	왜 ~냐 하면*	

* If the verb stem ends with "ㄹ," "ㄹ" will be dropped before we attach "~는가 하면, ~냐 하면, ~ㄴ가 하면" according to the rule of "ㄹ" deletion that says "the consonant "ㄹ" at the end of a verb stem is dropped before "ㄴ, ㅂ, ㅅ." (See Chapter 12 Verbs)
(ex) 팔다 (to sell): 팔→파는가 하면, 파냐 하면 , 멀다 (far): 멀→먼가 하면, 머냐 하면

"왜 ~는/(으)ㄴ가 하면, 왜 ~(으)냐 하면" can be used to express that the situation in the following clause is the reason for the situation in the preceding clause, which can be rendered as "The reason why _ is that _." They are typically used with the sentence endings "때문이다, ~거든(요)." The vowel "으" in "왜 ~(으)냐 하면" can be often deleted in casual conservation even after a consonant.

내가 **왜** 이 문법책을 쓰**는가 하면** 한국말을 공부하는 외국인을 도와주고 싶기 **때문입니다**.
내가 **왜** 이 문법책을 쓰**냐 하면** 한국말을 공부하는 외국인을 도와주고 싶**거든요**.
(=The reason why I am writing this grammar book is that I want to help foreigners who are studying Korean.)

왜 이 TV가 좋**은가 하면** 화질이 뛰어나기 **때문이죠**.
왜 이 TV가 좋**(으)냐 하면** 화질이 뛰어나**거든요**.
(=The reason why this TV is good is that the picture quality is excellent.)

왜 이게 그렇게 비**싼가 하면** 명품 핸드백이**기 때문이에요**.
왜 이게 그렇게 비싸**냐 하면** 명품 핸드백이**거든요**.
(=The reason why this is so expensive is that it is a famous-brand handbag)

제가 **왜** 미팅에 늦었**는가 하면** 집에 일이 좀 생겼**기 때문입니다**.

제가 **왜** 미팅에 늦었**냐 하면** 집에 일이 좀 생겼**거든요**.

(The reason why I was late for the meeting is that I had something to take care of at my house.)

74. Expressing "Before carrying out an action": ~기에 앞서

Function		Expressing "Before carrying out an action"		
Form		~기에 앞서		
Meaning		Before		
Distribution		Present	Past	Future
Action Verb Stem	After a consonant	~기에 앞서[*]		
	After a vowel	~기에 앞서[*]		
	After "ㄹ"	~기에 앞서[*]		
Stative Verb Stem	After a consonant			
	After a vowel			
	After "ㄹ"			

[*] The preceding verb cannot take its own tense suffix, and its tense is determined by the tense of the main verb.

"~기에 앞서" can be used to express that the situation in the following clause needs to be taken care of before carrying out the action in the preceding clause, which can be rendered as "before."

적을 공격하**기에 앞서** 적의 전력을 정확히 분석해야 한다.

(=We must precisely analyze the enemy's military power before we attack the enemy.)

일을 시작하**기에 앞서** 철저한 계획을 세우는 것이 필요하다.

(=We need to make a thorough plan before we start working on something.)

남을 탓하**기에 앞서** 먼저 자신을 돌아봐야 한다.

(=We must look back at ourselves before we blame others.)

75. Expressing a gratitude: ~(으)ㄴ 덕(분)에

Function	Expressing a gratitude		
Form	~(으)ㄴ 덕(분)에		
Meaning	Thanks to		
Distribution	Present	Past	Future
Action Verb Stem — After a consonant		~은 덕(분)에	
After a vowel		~ㄴ 덕(분)에	
After "ㄹ"		~ㄴ 덕(분)에[*]	
Stative Verb Stem — After a consonant	~은 덕(분)에		
After a vowel	~ㄴ 덕(분)에		
After "ㄹ"	~ㄴ 덕(분)에[*]		

[*] If the verb stem ends with "ㄹ," "ㄹ" will be dropped before we attach "~ㄴ 덕(분)에" according to the rule of "ㄹ" deletion that says "the consonant "ㄹ" at the end of a verb stem is dropped before "ㄴ, ㅂ, ㅅ." (See Chapter 12 Verbs)
팔다 (to sell): 팔→판 덕(분)에, 멀다 (far): 멀→먼 덕(분)에

"~(으)ㄴ 덕(분)에" can be used to express that the situation in the following clause happened thanks to the situation in the preceding clause, which can be rendered as "Thanks to."

장학금을 받**은 덕(분)에** 대학을 마칠 수 있었다.
(=I could finish my college education thanks to my scholarship.)

존이 도와 **준 덕(분)에** 이 일을 끝낼 수 있었다.
(=I could finish the work thanks to John's help.)

모든 선수들이 잘 싸워 **준 덕(분)에** 우리 팀이 결승전에 진출했다.
(=Our team advanced to the finals thanks to all the players who fought well.)

존은 부모님이 돈이 많**은 덕(분)에** 경제적 어려움을 겪지 않았다.
(=John has not gone through any financial difficulties thanks to his rich parents.)

메리는 얼굴이 예**쁜 덕(분)에** 모델이 될 수 있었다.
(=Mary could become a model thanks to her pretty face.)

76. Expressing "In contrast": ~는/(으)ㄴ 반면(에)

Function	Expressing "In contrast"		
Form	~는/(으)ㄴ 반면(에)		
Meaning	But in contrast		
Distribution		Present	Past	Future
Action Verb Stem	After a consonant	~는 반면(에)	~은 반면(에)	
	After a vowel	~는 반면(에)	~ㄴ 반면(에)	
	After "ㄹ"	~는 반면(에)*	~ㄴ 반면(에)*	
Stative Verb Stem	After a consonant	~은 반면(에)		
	After a vowel	~ㄴ 반면(에)		
	After "ㄹ"	~ㄴ 반면(에)*		

* If the verb stem ends with "ㄹ," "ㄹ" will be dropped before we attach "~는 반면(에), ㄴ 반면(에)" according to the rule of "ㄹ" deletion that says "the consonant "ㄹ" at the end of a verb stem is dropped before "ㄴ, ㅂ, ㅅ." (See Chapter 12 Verbs)
팔다 (to sell): 팔→판 반면(에), 멀다 (far): 멀→먼 반면(에)

"~는/(으)ㄴ 반면(에)" can be used to express that the situation in the following clause is directly in contrast to the situation in the preceding clause, which can be rendered as "but in contrast."

존은 공부를 잘하**는 반면(에)** 운동은 잘 못한다.

(=John studies very well, but in contrast, he is not good at sports.)

승진하면 봉급이 올라가**는 반면(에)** 책임감도 더 무거워져요.

(=When you get promoted, you will get a pay raise, but in contrast, you need to take more responsibility.)

메리는 카지노에서 돈을 잃**은 반면에** 존은 많이 땄다.

(=Mary lost her money at the casino, but in contrast, John won a lot of money.)

존은 시험을 망**친 반면(에)** 메리는 잘 봤다.

(=John screwed up on the test, but in contrast, Mary did well on the test.)

존은 키가 작**은 반면(에)** 점프력이 아주 좋아요.

(=John is short, but in contrast, he has good jumping ability.)

메리는 얼굴이 예**쁜 반면(에)** 성격이 좀 까다로워요.

(=Mary is pretty, but in contrast, she is hard to please.)

77. Taking two different paths at the same time/Contrasting two different situation: ~는 한편

Function		Taking two different paths at the same time	Contrasting two different situation	
Form		~는 한편		
Meaning		On the one hand, and _ also	But on the other hand	
Distribution		Present	Past	Future
Action Verb Stem	After a consonant	~는 한편		
	After a vowel	~는 한편		
	After "ㄹ"	~는 한편*		
Stative Verb Stem	After a consonant			
	After a vowel			
	After "ㄹ"			

* If the verb stem ends with "ㄹ," "ㄹ" will be dropped before we attach "~는 한편" according to the rule of "ㄹ" deletion that says "the consonant "ㄹ" at the end of a verb stem is dropped before "ㄴ, ㅂ, ㅅ." (See Chapter 12 Verbs)
(ex) 팔다 (to sell): 팔→파는 한편

"~는 한편" can be used to express that one is carrying out the action in the preceding clause, and at the same time he/she is also carrying out another action in the following clause, which can be rendered as "On the one hand, and _ also."

존은 K-드라마를 즐겨 보**는 한편** K-팝도 듣는다.
(=John enjoys watching Korean dramas on the one hand, and he also listens to K-pop music.)

메리는 오프라인 매장을 운영하**는 한편** 온라인 쇼핑몰 창업을 준비하고 있다.
(=Mary is running an offline store on the one hand, and she is also preparing to open an online shopping mall.)

북한은 최근 여러 차례 핵실험을 강행하**는 한편** 장거리탄도미사일 개발을 서두르고 있다.
(=Recently North Korea has boldly carried out a series of nuclear tests on the one hand, and it is also spurring on the development of long range ballistic missiles.)

On the other hand, "~는 한편" can also be used to express that the situation in the following clause occurs in contrast to the situation in the preceding clause. It can be rendered as "but on the other hand."

메리는 열심히 공부하고 있<u>는 **한편**</u> 존은 밖에서 놀기만 한다.

(=Mary is studying hard, but on the other hand John is just playing outside.)

세계경제는 지난 수년 동안 침체하고 있<u>는 **한편**</u> 한국경제는 꾸준히 성장을 지속하고 있다.

(=The world economy has fallen into recession for the last several years, but on the other hand the Korean economy has continued to grow steadily.)

CHAPTER 2 Clausal Conjunctions II (구절 접속사 II)

1. Soliciting the listener's acceptance of a given situation: ~(으)나마

Function	Soliciting the listener's acceptance of a given situation		
Form	~(으)나마		
Meaning	Even though		
Distribution	Present	Past	Future
Action Verb Stem — After a consonant			
Action Verb Stem — After a vowel			
Action Verb Stem — After "ㄹ"			
Stative Verb Stem — After a consonant	~으나마[*1]		
Stative Verb Stem — After a vowel	~나마[*1]		
Stative Verb Stem — After "ㄹ"	~나마[*1,2]		

[*1] The preceding verb cannot take its own tense suffix, and its tense is determined by the tense of the main verb.

[*2] If the verb stem ends with "ㄹ," "ㄹ" will be dropped before we attach "~나마" according to the rule of "ㄹ" deletion that says "the consonant "ㄹ" at the end of a verb stem is dropped before "ㄴ, ㅂ, ㅅ." (See Chapter 12 Verbs)
멀다 (far): 멀→머나마

"~(으)나마" can be used to express that the speaker is soliciting the listener's acceptance of the situation in the following clause even though it may not be good enough to meet the listener's expectation in the preceding clause, which can be rendered as "Even though." It is likely to be used in formal speech when you need to humble yourself in order to show respect to the listener.

액수는 적<u>으나마</u> 살림에 보탬이 되었으면 합니다.

(=Even though this is just a small amount of money, I hope it can be of some help to run your household.)

보잘 것 없**으나마** 한번 봐 주시기 바랍니다.

(=Even though this is not that good, I hope you can take a look at it.)

능력은 좀 부족하**나마** 열심히 하겠습니다.

(=Even though I am not that capable, I will do my best.)

집이 좀 누추하**나마** 쉬어가시기 바랍니다.

(=Even though this is a humble place, I hope you can take a rest before you leave.)

In most cases, it can be replaced by the more frequently-used grammar feature "~지만 (even though)" without changing the meaning.

액수는 적**지만** 살림에 보탬이 되었으면 합니다.

(=Even though this is just a small amount of money, I hope it can be of some help to run your household.)

보잘 것 없**지만** 한번 봐 주시기 바랍니다.

(=Even though this is not that good, I hope you can take a look at it.)

능력은 좀 부족하**지만** 열심히 하겠습니다.

(=Even though I am not that capable, I will do my best.)

집이 좀 누추하**지만** 쉬어가시기 바랍니다.

(=Even though this is a humble place, I hope you can take a rest before you leave.)

2. Expressing "Like the way in which": ~는/(으)ㄴ 양

"~는/(으)ㄴ 양" can be used to express that one is carrying out the action in the following clause the way in which the situation in the preceding clause is granted, which can be rendered as "as if." It is mainly used with a preceding clause that has a negative connotation. Its usage is generally limited to written text and formal speech.

존은 자기가 마치 뭐라도 되**는 양** 행세한다.

(=John acts as if he were someone important.)

메리는 자기는 아무렇지도 않**은 양** 행동하고 있다.

(=Mary behaves as if nothing had happened to her.)

Function	Expressing "Like the way in which"		
Form	~는/(으)ㄴ 양		
Meaning	As if		
Distribution	Present	Past	Future
Action Verb Stem — After a consonant	~는 양*	~은 양	
Action Verb Stem — After a vowel	~는 양	~ㄴ 양	
Action Verb Stem — After "ㄹ"	~는 양*	~ㄴ 양*	
Stative Verb Stem — After a consonant			
Stative Verb Stem — After a vowel			
Stative Verb Stem — After "ㄹ"			

* If the verb stem ends with "ㄹ," "ㄹ" will be dropped before we attach "~는 양, ~ㄴ 양" according to the rule of "ㄹ" deletion that says "the consonant "ㄹ" at the end of a verb stem is dropped before "ㄴ, ㅂ, ㅅ." (See Chapter 12 Verbs)
살다 (to live): 살→사는 양/산 양

존은 마치 제 세상을 만**난 양** 모든 걸 제멋대로 하고 있다.

(=John does everything in his own way as if the whole world were under his control.)

메리는 사실이 아닌 것을 사실**인 양** 꾸미고 있다.

(=Mary is fabricating something as if it were true.)

In most cases, it can be replaced by the more frequently used grammar features "~는/(으)ㄴ 듯(이) (like)" or "~는/(으)ㄴ 것처럼 (like)."

존은 자기가 마치 뭐라도 되**는 듯(이)**/되**는 것처럼** 행세한다.

(=John acts like he is someone important.)

메리는 자기는 아무렇지도 않**은 듯(이)**/않**은 것처럼** 행동하고 있다.

(=Mary behaves like nothing has happened to her.)

존은 마치 제 세상을 만**난 듯(이)**/만**난 것처럼** 모든 걸 제멋대로 하고 있다.

(=John does everything in his own way like the whole world is under his control.)

메리는 사실이 아닌 것을 사실**인 듯(이)**/사실**인 것처럼** 꾸미고 있다.

(=Mary is fabricating something like it is a fact.)

3. Carrying out an action to ensure a certain situation: ~(으)ㄹ 양으로

Function		Carrying out an action to ensure a certain situation		
Form		~(으)ㄹ 양으로		
Meaning		In order to make sure that _		
Distribution		Present	Past	Future
Action Verb Stem	After a consonant			~을 양으로
	After a vowel			~ㄹ 양으로
	After "ㄹ"			양으로
Stative Verb Stem	After a consonant			
	After a vowel			
	After "ㄹ"			

"~(으)ㄹ 양으로" can be used to express that the action in the following clause is being carried out to ensure that the situation in the preceding clause occurs, which can be rendered as "in order to make sure that _." The usage of this grammar feature, however, is generally limited to written text.

존은 피자를 혼자 먹**을 양으로** 자기 방으로 가지고 갔다.

(=John took the pizza to his room in order to make sure that he can eat it all by himself.)

정부는 공직사회의 부정부패를 척결**할 양으로** 칼을 빼들었다.

(=The government unsheathed a sword in order to make sure that it can rid the bureaucracy of injustice and corruption.)

In most cases, it can be replaced by the more frequently-used grammar feature "~(으)려고 (in order to)."

존은 피자를 혼자 먹**으려고** 자기 방으로 가지고 갔다.

(=John took the pizza to his room in order to eat it all by himself.)

정부는 공직사회의 부정부패를 척결하**려고** 칼을 빼들었다.

(=The government unsheathed a sword in order to get rid of injustice and corruption from the bureaucracy.)

4. Expressing a probable cause: ~아서/어서 (그런지)

Function	Expressing a probable cause		
Form	~아서/어서 (그런지)		
Meaning	Probably because		
Distribution	Present	Past	Future
Action Verb Stem — After "오" or "아"	~아서 (그런지)*		
Action Verb Stem — Otherwise	~어서 (그런지)*		
Stative Verb Stem — After "오" or "아"	~아서 (그런지)*		
Stative Verb Stem — Otherwise	~어서 (그런지)*		

* The preceding verb cannot take its own tense suffix, and its tense is determined by the tense of the main verb.

"~아/어서 (그런지)" can be used to express that the situation in the following clause occurs probably because of the situation in the preceding clause, which can be rendered as "probably because."

점심을 늦게 먹**어서 (그런지)** 아직 배가 안 고파요.

(=I am not hungry yet probably because I had a late lunch.)

어제 밤 늦게까지 일을 **해서 (그런지)** 아주 피곤하네요.

(=I am very tired probably because I worked until late at night yesterday.)

존은 몸이 아주 약**해서 (그런지)** 감기에 자주 걸려요.

(=John often catches a cold probably because he is so weak.)

메리는 아직 어**려서 (그런지)** 이 상황을 잘 이해 못 하네요.

(=Mary cannot understand this situation well probably because she is too young.)

너무 피곤**해서 (그런지)** 자꾸 잠이 쏟아지네요.

(=I feel so drowsy probably because I am too tired.)

시험이 너무 어려워**서 (그런지)** 성적이 별로 좋지 않네요.

(=The test scores are not that good probably because the test was too difficult.)

5. Expressing the aftermath of an action:
~고 나서야/나서도/났는데도/나면/나니(까)

Function		Expressing the aftermath of an action			
Form		~고 나서야	~고 나서도 ~고 났는데도	~고 나면	~고 나니(까)
Meaning		Only after	Even after	Upon doing something	Since having done something
Distribution		Present	Present	Present	Present
Action Verb Stem	After a consonant	~고 나서야[*]	~고 나서도[*] ~고 났는데도[*]	~고 나면[*]	~고 나니(까)[*]
	After a vowel	~고 나서야[*]	~고 나서도[*] ~고 났는데도[*]	~고 나면[*]	~고 나니(까)[*]
	After "ㄹ"	~고 나서야[*]	~고 나서도[*] ~고 났는데도[*]	~고 나면[*]	~고 나니(까)[*]
Stative Verb Stem	After a consonant				
	After a vowel				
	After "ㄹ"				

[*] The preceding verb cannot take its own tense suffix, and its tense is determined by the tense of the main verb.

"~고 나" can be combined with a variety of other conjunctions to generate the following new clausal conjunctions to express the various aspects of the aftermath of an action.

 ~고 나 + ~아서/어서 → ~고 나서 (after)
 ~고 나 + ~아서/어서 + ~아야/어야 → ~고 나서야
 ~고 나 + ~아서/어서 + ~아도/어도 → ~고 나서도
 ~고 나 + ~았/었는데 + ~아/어도 → ~고 났는데도
 ~고 나 + ~ (으)면 → ~고 나면
 ~고 나 + ~ (으)니(까) → ~고 나니(까)

"~고 나서야" can be used to express that the situation in the following clause occurs only after the situation in the preceding clause happens, which can be rendered as "Only after."

신원조회를 하고 **나서야** 인터뷰 스캐줄을 알려 주었다.

(=Only after my background check was done, they let me know my interview schedule.)

On the other hand, "~고 나서도, ~고 났는데도" can be used to express that the existing situation in the following clause continues even after the situation in the preceding clause, which can be rendered as "Even after." They are more or less interchangeable, but "~고 났는데도" is used to emphasize the completion of the situation in the preceding clause.

존은 취직하고 **나서도** 부모님께 돈을 달라고 한다.

(=Even after he got a job, John is still asking his parents for money.)

잠을 충분히 자고 **났는데도** 아직 피로가 풀리지 않아요.

(=Even after I had a good night's sleep, I still cannot recover from fatigue.)

In addition, "~고 나면, ~고 나니(까)" can be used to express that the situation in the following clause applies after the completion of the action in the preceding clause, which can be rendered as "Upon doing something," "Since having done something," respectively.

저녁을 먹고 **나면** 설거지를 좀 하세요.

(=Upon finishing dinner, please do the dishes.)

목욕을 하고 **나니(까)** 개운하네요.

(=Since I have taken a bath, I feel much better now.)

6. Carrying out an action immediately: ~기가 무섭게

"~기가 무섭게" can be used to express that the action in the following clause is to be carried out immediately after the situation in the preceding clause happens, which can be rendered as "immediately after."

존은 보스 말이 떨어지**기가 무섭게** 행동을 취했습니다.

(=John took action immediately after the boss finished talking.)

메리는 해가 뜨**기가 무섭게** 일하러 갔습니다.

(=Mary went to work immediately after sunrise.)

종이 울리**기가 무섭게** 화장실로 달려 갔습니다.

(=I rushed to the restroom immediately after the bell rang.)

7. Expressing "During the short period of time": ~는/(으)ㄴ/(으)ㄹ 사이(에)

Function		Expressing "During the short period of time"		
Form		~는/(으)ㄴ/(으)ㄹ 사이(에)		
Meaning		Just at the moment that _		
Distribution		Present	Past	Future
Action Verb Stem	After a consonant	~는 사이(에)	~은 사이(에)	~을 사이(에)
	After a vowel	~는 사이(에)	~ㄴ 사이(에)	~ㄹ 사이(에)
	After "ㄹ"	~는 사이(에)*	~ㄴ 사이(에)*	사이(에)
Stative Verb Stem	After a consonant			
	After a vowel			
	After "ㄹ"			

* If the verb stem ends with "ㄹ," "ㄹ" will be dropped before we attach "~는 사이(에), ~ㄴ 사이(에)" according to the rule of "ㄹ" deletion that says "the consonant "ㄹ" at the end of a verb stem is dropped before "ㄴ, ㅂ, ㅅ." (See Chapter 12 Verbs)
만들다 (to make): 만들→만드는 사이(에)/만든 사이(에)

"~는/(으)ㄴ/(으)ㄹ 사이(에)" can be used to express that the situation in the following clause happens just at the moment that the situation in the preceding clause occurs, which can be rendered as "just at the moment that _." It is more or less interchangeable with "~는/(으)ㄴ/(으)ㄹ 순간(에) (right at the moment that _)."

경찰이 잠깐 한눈파**는 사이(에)/파는 순간(에)** 범인이 도망갔다.

(=The suspect ran away just at the moment that the police officer looked away from him.)

벤치에 앉아서 잠깐 눈을 감**은 사이(에)/감은 순간(에)** 누군가가 내 가방을 훔쳐 갔다.

(=Somebody stole my bag just at the moment that I sat on the bench and closed my eyes.)

납치범이 잠깐 잠<u>든 사이(에)/잠든 순간(에)</u> 몰래 빠져 나왔다.

(=I escaped from the kidnapper secretly just at the moment that he fell asleep.)

적이 방심하고 있<u>을 사이(에)/있을 순간(에)</u> 기습공격을 해야 한다.

(=We must make a surprise attack just at the moment that the enemy forces are off guard.)

눈 깜짝<u>할 사이(에)/깜짝할 순간(에)</u> 모든 일이 한꺼번에 일어났다.

(=All the things happened at once just at the moment that I blinked my eyes.)

(=All the things happened at once in the blink of an eye.)

8. Expressing "At the end of": ~(으)ㄴ/던 끝에

Function		Expressing "At the end of"					
Form		~(으)ㄴ 끝에			~던 끝에		
Meaning		At the end of					
Distribution		Present	Past	Future	Present	Past	Future
Action Verb Stem	After a consonant		~은 끝에			~던 끝에	
	After a vowel		~ㄴ 끝에			~던 끝에	
	After "ㄹ"		~ㄴ 끝에*			~던 끝에	
Stative Verb Stem	After a consonant						
	After a vowel						
	After "ㄹ"						

* If the verb stem ends with "ㄹ," "ㄹ" will be dropped before we attach "~ㄴ 끝에" according to the rule of "ㄹ" deletion that says "the consonant "ㄹ" at the end of a verb stem is dropped before "ㄴ, ㅂ, ㅅ." (See Chapter 12 Verbs)
만들다 (to make): 만들→만든 끝에

"~(으)ㄴ 끝에" can be used to express that the situation in the following clause finally happened at the cost of one's previous effort in the preceding clause, which can be rendered as "at the end of."

오랫동안 항암치료를 받<u>은 끝에</u> 암이 완치됐다.

(=I got fully recovered from cancer at the end of having received chemotherapy for a long time.)

한참을 찾아다**닌 끝에** 드디어 범인이 숨은 곳을 찾아냈다.

(=I finally found the place where the suspect is hiding at the end of a long search for it.)

"~던 끝에" can be used for the same function, but it focuses more on one's repetitive actions in the past.

한참을 찾아다니**던 끝에** 마침내 동굴 입구를 발견했다.

(=I finally found the entrance of the cave at the end of a long search.)

오랫동안 망설이**던 끝에** 이번 선거에 출마하기로 결심했다.

(=I decided to run for this election at the end of a long hesitation.)

9. Expressing "Throughout the period of time": ~는 내내

Function	Expressing "Throughout the period of time"		
Form	~는 내내		
Meaning	Throughout the period of time		
Distribution		Present	Past	Future
Action Verb Stem	After a consonant	~는 내내[1]		
	After a vowel	~는 내내[1]		
	After "ㄹ"	~는 내내[1,2]		
Stative Verb Stem	After a consonant			
	After a vowel			
	After "ㄹ"			

[1] The preceding verb cannot take its own tense suffix, and its tense is determined by the tense of the main verb.

[2] If the verb stem ends with "ㄹ," "ㄹ" will be dropped before we attach "~는 내내" according to the rule of "ㄹ" deletion that says "the consonant "ㄹ" at the end of a verb stem is dropped before "ㄴ, ㅂ, ㅅ." (See Chapter 12 Verbs)
살다 (to live): 살→사는 내내

"~는 내내" can be used to express that the situation in the following clause continues to happen during the entire period of time while the action in the preceding clause is being carried out, which can be rendered as "throughout the period of time."

존은 일을 하**는 내내** 항상 불평만 한다.

(=John always complains throughout the period of time while he is working.)

메리는 운동하**는 내내** 음악을 듣는다.

(=Mary listens to music throughout the period of time while she is working out.)

10. Expressing "Rather than accepting the given situation: ~느니(보다)

Function	Expressing "Rather than accepting the given situation		
Form	~느니(보다)		
Meaning	Would rather _ than _		
Distribution	Present	Past	Future
Action Verb Stem — After a consonant	~느니(보다)[1]		
Action Verb Stem — After a vowel	~느니(보다)[1]		
Action Verb Stem — After "ㄹ"	~느니(보다)[1,2]		
Stative Verb Stem — After a consonant			
Stative Verb Stem — After a vowel			
Stative Verb Stem — After "ㄹ"			

[1] The preceding verb cannot take its own tense suffix and its tense is determined by the tense of the main verb.

[2] If the verb stem ends with "ㄹ," "ㄹ" will be dropped before we attach "~느니(보다)" according to the rule of "ㄹ" deletion that says "the consonant "ㄹ" at the end of a verb stem is dropped before "ㄴ, ㅂ, ㅅ." (See Chapter 12 Verbs)

살다 (to live): 살→사느니(보다)

"~느니(보다)" can be used with an action verb to express that the speaker prefers to carry out the action in the following clause rather than accepting the unpleasant situation in the preceding clause, which can be rendered as "would rather _ than _." It is often used with the optional adverb "차라리 (rather)."

너를 시키**느니(보다)** (차라리) 내가 하겠다.

(=I would rather do it by myself than ask you to do it.)

여기서 한 없이 기다리**느니(보다)** (차라리) 내가 혼자 가 보겠다.

(=I would rather try to go by myself than wait here endlessly.)

여기서 개 죽음을 당하<u>느니(보다)</u> (차라리) 전선에서 용감히 싸우다 죽겠습니다.

(=I would rather fight bravely and die on the front lines than die here for nothing.)

이런 수모를 당하<u>느니(보다)</u> (차라리) 다른 직장을 알아보겠다.

(=I would rather find another job than get humiliated like this.)

11. Taking the better option in a given situation:

~는/(으)ㄴ/(으)ㄹ 바에야/바에는

Function	Taking the better option in a given situation		
Form	~는/(으)ㄴ/(으)ㄹ 바에야/바에는		
Meaning	Given the situation that _		
Distribution	Present	Past	Future
Action Verb Stem — After a consonant	~는 바에야 ~는 바에는	~은 바에야 ~은 바에는	~을 바에야 ~을 바에는
Action Verb Stem — After a vowel	~는 바에야 ~는 바에는	~ㄴ 바에야 ~ㄴ 바에는	~ㄹ 바에야 ~ㄹ 바에는
Action Verb Stem — After "ㄹ"	~는 바에야 ~는 바에는*	~ㄴ 바에야* ~ㄴ 바에는*	바에야 바에는
Stative Verb Stem — After a consonant	~은 바에야 ~은 바에는		
Stative Verb Stem — After a vowel	~ㄴ 바에야 ~ㄴ 바에는		
Stative Verb Stem — After "ㄹ"	~ㄴ 바에야* ~ㄴ 바에는*		

* If the verb stem ends with "ㄹ," "ㄹ" will be dropped before we attach "~는 바에야/바에는, ~ㄴ 바에야/ 바에는" according to the rule of "ㄹ" deletion that says "the consonant "ㄹ" at the end of a verb stem is dropped before "ㄴ, ㅂ, ㅅ." (See Chapter 12 Verbs)
살다 (to live): 살→사는 바에는/바에야, 산 바에는/바에야

"~는/(으)ㄴ/(으)ㄹ 바에야" can be used to express that it would be better to take the option in the following clause given the unpleasant situation in the preceding clause, which can be rendered as "Given the situation that _." "~는/(으)ㄴ/(으)ㄹ바에는" can be used for the same function, but it expresses a stronger negative feeling about the given situation in the preceding clause.

이렇게 사**는 바에야/바에는** 차라리 죽는 게 낫다.

(=Given the situation that I have to live like this, it would be better to die.)

이왕 욕을 먹**은 바에야/바에는** 처음 계획대로 밀어붙이겠다.

(=Given the situation that they already blamed me, I will push for the original plan.)

일이 이렇게 **된 바에야/바에는** 포기하는게 낫겠다.

(=Given the situation that things turned out like this, it would be better to give up.)

이왕 늦**은 바에야** 좀 쉬었다 갑시다.

(=Given the situation that we are already late like this, let's take a rest and then go.)

전세값이 이렇게 비**싼 바에야/바에는** 차라리 집을 사는 게 낫다.

(=Given the situation that the one-time deposit lease is this expensive, it would be better to buy a house.)

햄버거를 먹**을 바에야/바에는** 대신 피자를 먹읍시다

(=Given the situation that we will eat hamburgers, let's eat pizza instead.)

이왕 그 일을 **할 바에야/바에는** 처음부터 다시 시작하는 것이 좋겠다.

(=Given the situation that we will do the work anyway, it would be better to start from the beginning.)

너를 시**킬 바에야/바에는** 차라리 내가 하는 것이 낫겠다.

(=Given the situation that I will end up asking you to do it, it would be better to do it by myself.)

너와 결혼**할 바에야/바에는** 차라리 혼자 사는 편이 낫겠다.

(=Given the situation that I will end up marrying you, it would be better to live alone.)

12. Expressing "Would rather _ than": ~(으)ㄹ지언정, ~(으)ㄹ망정

"~(으)ㄹ지언정, ~(으)ㄹ망정" can be used to express that the speaker is strongly refusing to carry out the action in the following clause even at the cost of facing the unpleasant situation in the preceding clause, which can be rendered as "would rather _ than." "~(으)ㄹ지언정" can be freely used in both written text and conversation, whereas "~(으)ㄹ망정" is more likely to be used in conversation. They are often used with the optional adverb "차라리 (rather)" in the preceding clause. In addition, the following clause must be in negative form.

Function		Expressing "Would rather _ than"					
Form		~(으)ㄹ지언정			~(으)ㄹ망정		
Meaning		Would rather _ than					
Distribution		Present	Past	Future	Present	Past	Future
Action Verb Stem	After a consonant			~을지언정			~을망정
	After a vowel			~ㄹ지언정			~ㄹ망정
	After "ㄹ"			~지언정			~망정
Stative Verb Stem	After a consonant						
	After a vowel						
	After "ㄹ"						

(**차라리**) 굶어 죽**을지언정**/굶어 죽**을망정** 존한테는 절대 돈을 빌리지 않을 겁니다.

(=I would rather starve to death than borrow money from John.)

(**차라리**) 쓰레기통에 갖다 버**릴지언정**/버**릴망정** 그 가격에는 안 팔겠습니다.

(=I would rather dump it into a trash can than sell it at that price.)

(**차라리**) 길거리에서 **잘지언정**/**잘망정** 그 사람 집에 들어가 살고 싶지 않습니다.

(=I would rather sleep on a street than live in his/her house.)

(**차라리**) 평생 독신으로 **살지언정**/**살망정** 그 사람과는 절대 결혼하지 않겠습니다.

(=I would rather live as a confirmed bachelor than marry the person).

13. Expressing "Lucky to avoid the worst situation":

~(으)니(까) 망정이지, ~기에/길래 망정이지

"~(으)니(까) 망정이지, ~기에 망정이지" can be used to express that one is lucky enough to avoid the worst-case scenario in the following clause thanks to the situation in the preceding clause, which can be rendered as "Be lucky to _. Otherwise, _." "~길래 망정이지" carries the same function, but it is more likely to be used in casual conversation.

빵이라도 있**으니(까)**/있**기에**/있**길래 망정이지** 굶어 죽을 뻔했다.

(=We are lucky to have some bread. Otherwise, we might have starved to death.)

Function	Expressing "Lucky to avoid the worst situation"					
Form	~(으)니(까) 망정이지			~기에/길래 망정이지		
Meaning	Be lucky to _. Otherwise, _					
Distribution		Present	Past	Future	Present	Past	Future

		Present	Past	Future	Present	Past	Future
Action Verb Stem	After a consonant	~으니까 망정이지	~았/었으니(까) 망정이지		~기에/길래 망정이지	~았/었기에/ 길래 망정이지	
	After a vowel	~니까 망정이지	~았/었으니(까) 망정이지		~기에/길래 망정이지	~았/었기에/ 길래 망정이지	
	After "ㄹ"	~니까 망정이지*	~았/었으니(까) 망정이지		~기에/길래 망정이지	~았/었기에/ 길래 망정이지	
Stative Verb Stem	After a consonant	~으니까 망정이지	~았/었으니(까) 망정이지		~기에/길래 망정이지	~았/었기에/ 길래 망정이지	
	After a vowel	~니까 망정이지	~았/었으니(까) 망정이지		~기에/길래 망정이지	~았/었기에/ 길래 망정이지	
	After "ㄹ"	~니까 망정이지*	~았/었으니(까) 망정이지		~기에/길래 망정이지	~았/었기에/ 길래 망정이지	

* If the verb stem ends with "ㄹ," "ㄹ" will be dropped before we attach "~니까 망정이지" according to the rule of "ㄹ" deletion that says "the consonant "ㄹ" at the end of a verb stem is dropped before "ㄴ, ㅂ, ㅅ." (See Chapter 12 Verbs)
살다 (to live): 살→사니까 망정이지, 길다 (long): 길→기니까 망정이지

메리가 도와주**니(까)**/도와주**기에**/도와주**길래 망정이지** 일을 시작도 못할 뻔했다.
(=I am lucky to get some help from Mary. Otherwise, I could not have even started working on it.)

컴퓨터를 찾았**으니(까)**/찾았**기에**/찾았**길래 망정이지** 일한 거 다 날라갈 뻔했다.
(=I was lucky to find my computer. Otherwise, I might have lost all the work I had done.)

아이들이 무사히 집에 돌아**왔으니(까)**/돌아**왔기에**/돌아**왔길래 망정이지** 큰일 날 뻔했다.
(=I was lucky to have my children back home safely. Otherwise, I was going to be in big trouble.)

차가 좋**으니(까)**/좋**기에**/좋**길래 망정이지** 많이 다칠 뻔했다.
(=You are lucky to have a good car. Otherwise, you were going to get seriously injured.)

무사하**니(까)**/무사하**기에**/무사하**길래 망정이지** 큰일 날 뻔했다.
(=You are lucky to be safe. Otherwise, you were going to be in big trouble.)

14. Expressing an effort that will be in vain:

~아/어 봐야/보았자/봤자/보았댔자/봤댔자

Function		Expressing an effort that will be in vain		
Form		~아/어 봐야	~아/어 보았자 ~아/어 봤자	~아/어 보았댔자 ~아/어 봤댔자
Meaning		Even though one tries to do something		Even though one has kept trying to do something
Distribution		Present	Present	Present
Action Verb Stem	After "오" or "아"	~아 봐야[*]	~아 보았자[*] ~아 봤자[*]	~아 보았댔자[*] ~아 봤댔자[*]
	Otherwise	~어 봐야[*]	~어 보았자[*] ~어 봤자[*]	~어 보았댔자[*] ~어 봤댔자[*]
Stative Verb Stem	After "오" or "아"			
	Otherwise			

[*] The preceding verb cannot take its own tense suffix, and its tense is determined by the tense of the main verb.

"~(아/어) 봐야, ~(아/어) 보았자/봤자" can be used to express that one's effort in the preceding clause will be in vain, which can be rendered as "Even though one tries to do something."

존은 얘기**해 봐야**/얘기해 **보았자**/얘기해 **봤자** 말을 듣지 않을 겁니다.

(=Even though you try to talk to John, he won't listen to you.)

사정사정**해 봐야**/사정사정해 **보았자**/사정사정해 **봤자** 메리는 전혀 꿈쩍도 안 할 겁니다.

(=Even though you try to beg Mary for mercy, she won't budge at all.)

뛰**어 봐야**/뛰**어 보았자**/뛰**어 봤자** 벼룩이지.

(=Even though you try to run, you are such a flea.)

(Implication: You can run, but you cannot hide.)

"~(아/어) 보았댔자/봤댔자" is the combination of "~(아/어) 보았자/봤자" and "~아/어 대다 (keep -ing)," which can be rendered as "Even though one has kept trying to do something."

열심히 일해 **보았댔자/봤댔자** 요즘 먹고 살기가 빠듯합니다.

(=Even though I have kept working hard, it is still difficult to make ends meet these days.)

On the other hand, "~(아/어) 봐야, ~(아/어) 보았자/봤자, ~(아/어) 보았댔자/봤댔자" can also be used with the optional adverb "아무리 (No matter how)," which can be rendered as "No matter how _ one tries/tried/has kept trying to do."

존은 아무리 얘기**해 봐야** 말을 듣지 않을 겁니다.

(=No matter how many times you try to talk to John, he won't listen to you.)

아무리 애원**해 보았자/봤자** 메리는 전혀 꿈쩍도 안 했습니다.

(=No matter how many times I tried to beg Mary for mercy, she didn't budge at all.)

아무리 열심히 일**해 보았댔자/봤댔자** 요즘 먹고 살기가 빠듯합니다.

(=No matter how hard I have kept working, it is still difficult to make ends meet these days.)

15. Expressing "Just for doing something": ~는 데야

Function		Expressing "Just for doing something"		
Form		~는 데야		
Meaning		Just for doing something		
Distribution		Present	Past	Future
Action Verb Stem	After a consonant	~는 데야[*1]		
	After a vowel	~는 데야[*1]		
	After "ㄹ"	~는 데야[*1,2]		
Stative Verb Stem	After a consonant			
	After a vowel			
	After "ㄹ"			

[*1] The preceding verb cannot take its own tense suffix, and its tense is determined by the tense of the main verb.

[*2] If the verb stem ends with "ㄹ," "ㄹ" will be dropped before we attach "~는 데야" according to the rule of "ㄹ" deletion that says "the consonant "ㄹ" at the end of a verb stem is dropped before "ㄴ, ㅂ, ㅅ." (See Chapter 12 Verbs)

살다 (to live): 살→사는 데야

"~는 데야" can be used to express that the situation in the following clause is just good enough for carrying out the action in the preceding clause, which can be rendered as "Just for doing something."

고작 범인 한 명을 잡**는 데야** 이 정도 인력이 필요없죠.
(=Just for catching one suspect, we don't need this much man power.)

출퇴근하**는 데야** 이 차 정도면 충분하지.
(=Just for commuting, this car is good enough.)

이 문제를 푸**는 데야** 뭐 5분이면 됩니다.
(=Just for solving the problem, five minutes is good enough.)

이 물건을 옮기**는 데야** 저 혼자면 충분하죠.
(=Just for moving this item, I can handle it by myself.)

16. Expressing "Just because of one's claim":
~(는/ㄴ)다고/냐고/(으)라고/자고 하는데야

"~(는/ㄴ)다고 하는데야, ~냐고 하는데야, ~(으)라고 하는데야, ~자고 하는데야" and their contraction forms "~(는/ㄴ)다는데야, ~냐는데야, ~(으)라는데야, ~자는데야" can be used to express that the speaker is reporting to the listener that he/she has no choice but to accept the situation in the following clause just because of another person's claim in the preceding clause. They can be rendered as "Just because another person is saying/asking/ordering/ suggesting _."

존이 자기 아버지 원수를 갚**는다(고 하)는데야** 말릴 수가 없었죠.
(=Just because John is saying that he will take his father's revenge, I had no choice but to let it happen.)

메리가 자기 인생은 자기가 책임**진다(고 하)는데야** 그냥 놔둘 수 밖에 없죠.
(=Just because Mary is saying that she will take full responsibility for her life, I have no choice but to leave her alone.)

메리가 자기는 아무 것도 **몰랐다고 하는데야** 야단을 칠 수가 없었습니다.
(=Just because Mary is saying that she didn't know anything, I could not scold her.)

Function	Expressing "Just because of one's claim"		
Form	~(는/ㄴ)다고/냐고/(으)라고/자고 하는데야		
Meaning	Just because another person is saying/asking/ordering/suggesting _		

Distribution			Present	Past	Future
Action Verb Stem	Statement	After a consonant	~는다고 하는데야 ~는다는데야	~았/었다고 하는데야 ~았/었다는데야	~겠다고 하는데야 ~겠다는데야
		After a vowel	~ㄴ다고 하는데야 ~ㄴ다는데야	~았/었다고 하는데야 ~았/었다는데야	~겠다고 하는데야 ~겠다는데야
		After "ㄹ"	~ㄴ다고 하는데야* ~ㄴ다는데야*	~았/었다고 하는데야 ~았/었다는데야	~겠다고 하는데야 ~겠다는데야
	Question	Regardless of the ending	~냐고 하는데야* ~냐는데야*	~았/었냐고 하는데야 ~았/었냐는데야	~겠냐고 하는데야 ~겠냐는데야
	Imperative	After a consonant	~으라고 하는데야 ~으라는데야		
		After a vowel or "ㄹ"	~라고 하는데야 ~라는데야		
	Proposition	Regardless of the ending	~자고 하는데야 ~자는데야		
Stative Verb Stem	Statement	Regardless of the ending	~다고 하는데야 ~다는데야	~았/었다고 하는데야 ~았/었다는데야	~겠다고 하는데야 ~겠다는데야
	Question	Regardless of the ending	~냐고 하는데야* ~냐는데야*	았/었냐고 하는데야 ~았/었냐는데야	~겠냐고 하는데야 ~겠냐는데야

* If the verb stem ends with "ㄹ," it will be dropped before we attach "~ㄴ다(고 하)는데야, ~냐(고 하)는데야" according to the rule of "ㄹ" deletion that says "the consonant "ㄹ" at the end of a verb stem is dropped before "ㄴ, ㅂ, ㅅ." (See Chapter 12 Verbs)
팔다 (to sell): 팔→판다(고 하)는데야, 파냐(고 한)는데야, 멀다 (far): 멀→머냐(고 하)는데야

집주인이 갑자기 집을 안 **팔겠다(고 하)는데야** 제가 할 수 있는 게 아무 것도 없죠.
(=Just because the home owner is suddenly saying that he/she is not going to sell the house, there's nothing I can do about it.)

존이 자기한테 해 준 게 뭐 있**냐(고 하)는데야** 화가 날 수 밖에 없었죠.
(=Just because John was asking me what I had done for him, I had no choice but to lose my temper.)

메리가 나한테 그동안 뭐 **했냐(고 하)는데야** 정말 화가 끝까지 치밀었죠.
(=Just because Mary asked me what I had done in the meantime, I really got upset.)

갑자기 이 문제를 어떻게 처리하**겠냐(고 하)는데야** 아무 할 말이 없었죠.

(=Just because all of a sudden I was asked how I could handle the case, I had nothing to say about it.)

존이 나한테 상한 음식을 먹**으라(고 하)는데야** 어처구니가 없었죠.

(=Just because John ordered me to eat the spoiled food, I became speechless.)

메리가 저한테 그 일을 하**라(고 하)는데야** 어쩔 도리가 없죠.

(=Just because Mary is ordering me to do it, I have no choice but to do it.)

존이 지금 당장 떠나**자(고 하)는데야** 어처구니가 없죠.

(=Just because John is suggesting to me to leave now, I became speechless.)

농구를 하기에는 키가 너무 작**다(고 하)는데야** 포기할 수 밖에 없죠.

(=Just because he/she is saying that I am too short for playing basketball, I have no choice but to give it up.)

메리가 싫**다(고 하)는데야** 더 강요할 수는 없죠.

(=Just because Mary is saying that she doesn't want to do it, I cannot push her anymore.)

그 돈이 모자**랐다(고 하)는데야** 기가 막히죠.

(=Just because he/she said it was not enough money, I became speechless.)

17. Expressing the unacceptability of the given situation: ~는/ㄴ대서야

"~는/ㄴ대서야" can be used to express that the situation in the following clause applies once the unacceptable situation in the preceding clause happens, which can be rendered as "Once it happens that _/If _." The following clause is typically a negative statement carrying the meaning of unacceptability.

공직자가 뇌물을 받**는대서야** 말이 **안** 됩니다.

(=Once it happens that government officials receive any bribe, it is ridiculous.)
(=If government officials receive any bribe, it is ridiculous.)

친구를 배신**한대서야** 사람의 도리가 **아닙니다**.

(=Once it happens that one betrays his/her friend, it is unethical.)
(=If one betrays his/her friend, it is unethical.)

Function		Expressing the unacceptability of the given situation		
Form		~는/ㄴ대서야		
Meaning		Once it happens that _/If _		
Distribution		Present	Past	Future
Action Verb Stem	After a consonant	~는대서야[1]		
	After a vowel	~ㄴ대서야[1]		
	After "ㄹ"	~ㄴ대서야[1,2]		
Stative Verb Stem	After a consonant			
	After a vowel			
	After "ㄹ"			

[1] The preceding verb cannot take its own tense suffix, and its tense is determined by the tense of the main verb.

[2] If the verb stem ends with "ㄹ," "ㄹ" will be dropped before we attach "~는대서야, ~ㄴ대서야" according to the rule of "ㄹ" deletion that says "the consonant "ㄹ" at the end of a verb stem is dropped before "ㄴ, ㅂ, ㅅ." (See Chapter 12 Verbs)
팔다 (to sell): 팔→판대서야

이 쉬운 것을 **모른대서야** 전문가라고 **할 수 없지**.
(=Once it happens that someone doesn't know this simple thing, we cannot say that he/she is an expert.)
(=If someone doesn't know this simple thing, we cannot say that he/she is an expert.)

귀순병의 목숨을 구해 준 의사한테 욕을 **한대서야** 이건 **아니죠**.
(=Once we blame the doctor who saved the defector's life, that's not right.)
(=If we blame the doctor who saved the defector's life, that's not right.)

It can also be used in a positive rhetorical question with the optional adverb "어떻게 (how)" in the following clause, which can be rephrased as its corresponding negative statement.

검사가 뇌물을 **받는대서야** (**어떻게**) 법을 공정하게 집행할 수 있겠습니까?
(=Once it happens that prosecutors receive any bribes, how can they faithfully execute the law?)
(=If prosecutors receive any bribes, how can they faithfully execute the law?)

검사가 뇌물을 **받는대서야** 법을 공정하게 집행할 수 **없습니다**.
(=Once it happens that prosecutors receive any bribes, they cannot faithfully execute the laws.)
(=If prosecutors receive any bribes, they cannot faithfully execute the laws.)

이 중대한 시국에 여야가 서로 싸움만 하고 있**는대서야 (어떻게)** 이 경제위기를 극복할 수 있겠습니까?

(=Once it happens that the ruling party and the opposition party are just fighting against each other at this critical juncture, how can we overcome this economic crisis?)
(=If the ruling party and the opposition party are just fighting against each other at this critical juncture, how can we overcome this economic crisis?)

이 중대한 시국에 여야가 서로 싸움만 하고 있**는대서야** 경제위기를 극복**할 수 없습니다**.

(=Once it happens that the ruling party and the opposition party are just fighting against each other at this critical juncture, we cannot overcome this economic crisis.)
(=If the ruling party and the opposition party are just fighting against each other at this critical juncture, we cannot overcome this economic crisis.)

그만한 일로 모든 걸 포기**한대서야 (어떻게)** 큰 일을 할 수 있겠어요?

(=Once it happens that you give up on everything because of such a trivial matter, how can you carry out a major task?)
(=If you give up on everything because of such a trivial matter, how can you carry out a major task?)

그만한 일로 모든 걸 포기**한대서야** 큰 일을 **할 수 없어요**.

(=Once it happens that you give up on everything because of such a trivial matter, you cannot carry out a major task.)
(=If you give up on everything because of such a trivial matter, you cannot carry out a major task.)

18. Expressing "Given that the condition is met": ~(으)면야

"~(으)면야" can be used to express that the situation in the following clause applies if the situation in the preceding clause happens to be the case, which can be rendered as "If that happens to be the case that _."

제가 그 일을 할 수 있**으면야** 벌써 해 드렸지요.

(=If it happened to be the case that I am able to do it, I could have already done it for you.)

Function	Expressing "Given that the condition is met"		
Form	~(으)면야		
Meaning	If that happens to be the case that _		
Distribution	Present	Past	Future
Action Verb Stem / After a consonant	~으면야[*]		
Action Verb Stem / After a vowel	~면야[*]		
Action Verb Stem / After "ㄹ"	~면야[*]		
Stative Verb Stem / After a consonant	~으면야[*]		
Stative Verb Stem / After a vowel	~면야[*]		
Stative Verb Stem / After "ㄹ"	~면야[*]		

[*] The preceding verb cannot take its own tense suffix, and its tense is determined by the tense of the main verb.

그렇게 해 주시**면야** 더할 나위가 없죠.

(=If it happens to be the case that you are going to do so, it leaves nothing more to be desired.)

저 대신 그 일을 해 주시**면야** 저는 더할 나위 없이 좋죠.

(=If it happens to be the case that you will do it instead of me, it couldn't be better for me.)

돈이 많**으면야** 저도 존을 도와주고 싶죠.

(=If it happens to be the case that I have a lot of money, I also want to help John.)

사람이 모자라**면야** 더 채용할 수 있습니다.

(=If it happens to be the case that we are short of manpower, we can hire more people.)

19. Reporting the reason for a given situation:

~(는/ㄴ)다는/냐는/(으)라는/자는 이유로

"~는/ㄴ다는/냐는/(으)라는/자는 이유로" are the combination of the citation endings and "~는 이유로." They can be used to express that the speaker is reporting to the listener that one is going through the situation in the following clause because of the situation in the preceding clause, which can be rendered as "because of the reason that (one says/asks/orders/suggests) _."

Function	Reporting the reason for a given situation		
Form	~(는/ㄴ)다는/냐는/(으)라는/자는 이유로		
Meaning	Because of the reason that (one says/asks/orders/suggests) _		

Distribution			Present	Past	Future
Action Verb Stem	Statement	After a consonant	~는다는 이유로	~았/었다는 이유로	~겠다는 이유로
		After a vowel	~ㄴ다는 이유로	~았/었다는 이유로	~겠다는 이유로
		After "ㄹ"	~ㄴ다는 이유로[*]	~았/었다는 이유로	~겠다는 이유로
	Question	Regardless of the ending	~냐는 이유로[*]	~았/었냐는 이유로	
	Imperative	After a consonant	~으라는 이유로		
		After a vowel or "ㄹ"	~라는 이유로		
	Proposition	Regardless of the ending	~자는 이유로		
Stative Verb Stem	Statement	Regardless of the ending	~다는 이유로	~았/었다는 이유로	
	Question	Regardless of the ending	~다는 이유로	~았/었다는 이유로	

[*] If the verb stem ends with "ㄹ," "ㄹ" will be dropped before we attach "~ㄴ다는 이유로, ~냐는 이유로" according to the rule of "ㄹ" deletion that says "the consonant "ㄹ" at the end of a verb stem is dropped before "ㄴ, ㅂ, ㅅ." (See Chapter 12 Verbs)
살다 (to live): 살→산다는 이유로, 사냐는 이유로

돈을 안 갚**는다는 이유로** 존이 메리를 고소했습니다.
(=John filed a lawsuit against Mary because of the reason that she didn't pay his money back.)

상사에게 대**든다는 이유로** 징계를 받았습니다.
(=I received a reprimand because of the reason that I argued with my boss.)

주정차금지구역에 주차**했다는 이유로** 제 차를 견인해 갔습니다.
(=My car was towed away because of the reason that it was parked in the no parking/no stopping zone.)

존이 집을 사**겠다는 이유로** 메리에게 돈을 빌려달라고 했다.
(=John asked Mary to lend him some money because of the reason that he wants to buy a house.)

존은 왜 자기를 처다보**냐는 이유로** 나한테 시비를 걸었습니다.
(=John picked a fight with me because of the reason that I was looking at him.)

왜 자기 돈을 훔쳤**냐는 이유로** 존은 친구를 마구 때렸습니다.
(=John beat up his friend because of the reason that his friend stole his money.)

존은 돈을 갚**으라는 이유로** 저를 협박했습니다.

(=John threatened me because of the reason that he wants me to pay his money back.)

더 열심히 일하**라는 이유로** 보너스를 주었습니다.

(=He/she gave me a bonus because of the reason that he/she wants me to work harder.)

노숙자들을 도와주**자는 이유로** 돈을 걷었습니다.

(He/she collected money because of the reason that he wants us to help homeless people.)

존은 집이 멀**다는 이유로** 항상 회사에 지각한다.

(=John is always late for work because of the reason that he lives far from the workplace.)

단지 뚱뚱하**다는 이유로** 면접시험에서 떨어졌습니다.

(=I failed the interview test because of the reason that I am overweight.)

20. Expressing an unacceptable justification: ~기로서니

Function	Expressing an unacceptable justification		
Form	~기로서니		
Meaning	Although/No matter how		
Distribution		Present	Past	Future
Action Verb Stem	After a consonant	~기로서니	~았/었기로서니	
	After a vowel	~기로서니	~았/었기로서니	
	After "ㄹ"	~기로서니	~았/었기로서니	
Stative Verb Stem	After a consonant	~기로서니	~았/었기로서니	
	After a vowel	~기로서니	~았/었기로서니	
	After "ㄹ"	~기로서니	~았/었기로서니	

"~기로서니" can be used to express that the situation in the following clause is not acceptable even when the situation in the preceding clause holds true, which can be rendered as "Although." It is often used together with the optional adverb "아무리 (no matter)," which can be rendered as "No matter how."

내가 비록 자기 밑에서 일하**기로서니** 이렇게 대하면 안 되죠.

(=Although I work under his/her supervision, he/she is not supposed to treat me like this.)

아무리 내가 잘못**했기로서니** 그만한 일로 해고 시키는 게 말이 됩니까?

(=No matter how critical my fault was, do you think it makes sense to fire me over that trivial matter?)

아무리 먹고 살기가 힘들**기로서니** 남의 물건을 훔치면 안 되죠.

(=No matter how difficult it is to make ends meet, it is not acceptable to steal things from others.)

존이 아무리 무식하**기로서니** 이 쉬운 것을 모른단 말입니까?

(=No matter how ignorant John is, are you saying that he doesn't know this simple thing?)

아무리 바쁘**기로서니** 같이 저녁 먹을 시간도 없단 말이에요?

(=No matter how busy you are, don't you have time to have dinner with me?)

아무리 화가 **났기로서니** 다른 사람한테 화풀이를 하면 어떻게 합니까?

(=No matter how angry you were, how come you took your anger out on someone else?)

21. Expressing the speaker's warning against one's unacceptable action:
~다가는

Function	Expressing the speaker's warning against one's unacceptable action		
Form	~다가는		
Meaning	If one keeps doing something like that		
Distribution		Present	Past	Future

		Present	Past	Future
Action Verb Stem	After a consonant	~다가는	~았/었다가는	
	After a vowel	~다가는	~았/었다가는	
	After "ㄹ"	~다가는	~았/었다가는	
Stative Verb Stem	After a consonant			
	After a vowel			
	After "ㄹ"			

"~다가는" can be used to express that the speaker is issuing a warning against one's unacceptable ongoing action in the preceding clause which may result in an unpleasant situation in the following sentence. It can be rendered as "If one keeps doing something like that."

그렇게 까불**다가는** 선생님한테 혼난다.

(=If you keep acting up like that, you may get scolded by your teacher.)

이렇게 시간을 지체하**다가는** 비행기를 놓칠 수도 있어.

(=If we keep wasting our time like this, we may miss the flight.)

그렇게 잘난척하**다가는** 큰 코 다친다.

(=If you keep bragging about youself like that, you may run into big trouble.)

The past-tense suffix can be optionally used to emphasize the completion of the action in the preceding clause.

그렇게 까불었**다가는** 선생님한테 혼난다.

(=If you keep acting up like that, you may get scolded by your teacher.)

이렇게 시간을 지체했**다가는** 비행기를 놓칠 수도 있어.

(=If we keep wasting our time like this, we may miss the flight.)

그렇게 잘난척했**다가는** 큰 코 다친다.

(=If you keep bragging about youself like that, you may run into big trouble.)

그렇게 폭발물을 함부로 다루었**다가는** 죽을 수도 있다.

(=If you keep handling the explosives recklessly like that, you may kill yourself.)

존이 이렇게 비밀을 누설했**다가는** 우리의 모든 계획이 수포로 돌아갈 수 있다.

(=If John keeps leaking the secret like this, all of our plans may be in vain.)

22. Expressing a sudden change from a continuing situation: ~다가도

"~다가도" can be used to express that the situation in the preceding clause continues for a while, and then it undergoes a sudden change into the situation in the following clause, which can be rendered as "even when _." It is typically used with the adverb "갑자기 (suddenly)" in the following clause.

Function	Expressing a sudden change from a continuing situation		
Form	~다가도		
Meaning	Even when _		
Distribution	Present	Past	Future
Action Verb Stem — After a consonant	~다가도	~았/었다가도	
Action Verb Stem — After a vowel	~다가도	~았/었다가도	
Action Verb Stem — After "ㄹ"	~다가도	~았/었다가도	
Stative Verb Stem — After a consonant	~다가도	~았/었다가도	
Stative Verb Stem — After a vowel	~다가도	~았/었다가도	
Stative Verb Stem — After "ㄹ"	~다가도	~았/었다가도	

존은 밥을 먹**다가도** 메리가 부르면 뛰쳐나간다.

(=Even when John is eating, he runs out when Mary calls him.)

메리는 일을 열심히 하**다가도** 갑자기 엉뚱한 짓을 해요.

(=Even when Mary is working hard, she suddenly does a weird thing.)

존은 멀쩡하**다가도** 갑자기 미친 사람처럼 행동해요.

(=Even when John is clear minded, he suddenly acts like a crazy person.)

장마철에는 날씨가 좋**다가도** 갑자기 소나기가 쏟아져요.

(=During the monsoon season, even when the weather is good, a shower suddenly pours down.)

존은 돈을 모**았다가도** 한꺼번에 다 써버린다.

(=Even when John saves money, he uses up all the money at once.)

메리는 기분이 좋**았다가도** 갑자기 아무한테나 화를 낸다.

(=Even when Mary is in a good mood, she suddenly takes her anger out on someone.)

"~다가도" can sometimes be used in the idiomatic expression like "알다가도 모르겠다 (seem to know, but actually don't know =to have no idea)."

존이 갑자기 왜 그러는지 알**다가도** 모르겠어요.

(=I have no idea why John suddenly behaves like that.)

23. Being unable to keep the situation under control: ~다(가) 못해(서)

Function		Being unable to keep the situation under control					
Form		~다(가) 못해(서)					
Meaning		Because one could not keep –ing			After having kept –ing, _ even _		
Distribution		Present	Past	Future	Present	Past	Future
Action Verb Stem	After a consonant	~다(가) 못해(서)*			~다(가) 못해(서)*		
	After a vowel	~다(가) 못해(서)*			~다(가) 못해(서)*		
	After "ㄹ"	~다(가) 못해(서)*			~다(가) 못해(서)*		
Stative Verb Stem	After a consonant				~다(가) 못해(서)*		
	After a vowel				~다(가) 못해(서)*		
	After "ㄹ"				~다(가) 못해(서)*		

* The preceding verb cannot take its own tense suffix, and its tense is determined by the tense of the main verb.

"~다가 못해서" and its contraction forms "~다가 못해, ~다 못해서, ~다 못해" can be used to express that the situation in the following clause happened because one could not keep the situation in the preceding clause under control, which can be rendered as "Because one could not keep -ing." It is actually derived from the combination of "~다가 (while)" + "못하다 (unable to do)" + "~아/어서 (because)."

더 이상 참**다가 못해서**/참**다가 못해**/참**다 못해서**/참**다 못해** 문을 박차고 나왔다.
(=Because I could not keep tolerating it, I kicked the door open and came out.)

지켜보**다가 못해서**/지켜보**다가 못해**/지켜보**다 못해서**/지켜보**다 못해** 이젠 내가 나서기로 했다.
(=Because I could not keep sitting on the fence, I decided to take the lead from now on.)

하다 하**다가 못해서**/하**다가 못해**/하**다 못해서**/하**다 못해** 포기해 버렸다.
(=Because I could not keep doing it, I completely gave up.)

보**다가 못해서**/보**다가 못해**/보**다 못해서**/보**다 못해** 내가 나서기로 했다.
(=Because I could not keep sitting on the fence, I decided to take the lead.)

극심한 고통을 견디**다가 못해서**/견디**다가 못해**/견디**다 못해서**/견디**다 못해** 의사에게 존엄사를 시켜달라고 요구했다.

(=Because I could not keep suffering from the extreme pain, I asked my doctor for euthanasia.)

On the other hand, it can also be used to express that the ongoing situation in the preceding clause gets out of control and takes one step further to an extreme situation in the following clause, which can be rendered as "After having kept -ing, _ even _."

존은 거짓말을 하**다가 못해서**/하**다가 못해**/하**다 못해서**/하**다 못해** 이젠 나를 갖고 놀기까지 한다.

(=After having kept lying to me, John is now even making fun of me.)

너무 배 고프**다가 못해서**/고프**다가 못해**/고프**다 못해서**/고프**다 못해** 이젠 말할 기력조차도 없다.

(=After having kept being hungry, now I don't have any energy left even to speak a word.)

24. Expressing the worst-case scenario: ~는 날에는

Function	Expressing the worst-case scenario		
Form	~는 날에는		
Meaning	If it happens that _		
Distribution		Present	Past	Future
Action Verb Stem	After a consonant	~는 날에는[1]		
	After a vowel	~는 날에는[1]		
	After "ㄹ"	~는 날에는[1,2]		
Stative Verb Stem	After a consonant			
	After a vowel			
	After "ㄹ"			

[1] The preceding verb cannot take its own tense suffix, and its tense is determined by the tense of the main verb.

[2] If the verb stem ends with "ㄹ," "ㄹ" will be dropped before we attach "~는 날에는" according to the rule of "ㄹ" deletion that says "the consonant "ㄹ" at the end of a verb stem is dropped before "ㄴ, ㅂ, ㅅ." (See Chapter 12 Verbs)
(ex) 팔다 (to sell): 팔→파는 날에는

"~는 날에는" can be used to express that the situation in the following clause which is the purportedly worst-case scenario may occur if the situation in the preceding clause happens, which can be rendered as "If it happens that _."

그러다가 쓰러지기라도 하**는 날에는** 다시 회복하기가 불가능합니다.
(=If it happens that you collapse while you are doing so, it will be impossible to recover from it.)

이번 선거에서 지**는 날에는** 우리 모두 끝장이다.
(=If it happens that we lose the upcoming election, it will be the end of the world for us.)

한반도에서 핵전쟁이 일어나**는 날에는** 남한 인구의 절반 정도가 살아남기 힘들 겁니다.
(=If it happens that a nuclear war breaks out on the Korean peninsula, half of the South Korean population could not survive.)

25. Expressing "Whenever one is about to do something": ~(으)ㄹ라치면

Function	Expressing "Whenever one is about to do something"		
Form	~(으)ㄹ라치면		
Meaning	Whenever one is about to do something		
Distribution	Present	Past	Future
Action Verb Stem — After a consonant			~을라치면
Action Verb Stem — After a vowel			~ㄹ라치면
Action Verb Stem — After "ㄹ"			~라치면
Stative Verb Stem — After a consonant			
Stative Verb Stem — After a vowel			
Stative Verb Stem — After "ㄹ"			

"~(으)ㄹ라치면" can be used to express that the unpleasant situation in the following clause occurs whenever the situation in the preceding clause is about to happen, which can be rendered as "Whenever one is about to do something." It is now on the verge of becoming an archaic expression in favor of its equivalent grammar feature "~(으)려고 하면 (If one intends to _/If one wants to _)."

이제 그 악몽을 거의 잊**을라치면** 다시 생각나게 만들어요.

(=Whenever I am about to erase the nightmare from my memory, he/she reminds me of it again.)

제가 무슨 일을 **할라치면** 꼭 방해를 해요.

(=Whenever I am about to start working on something, he/she always disturbs me.)

꼭 일을 할**라치면** 무슨 일이 생겨요

(=Whenever I am about to start working, something always happens.)

잠이 좀 **들라치면** 와서 깨워요.

(=Whenever I am about to fall asleep, he/she comes in and wakes me up.)

26. Expressing "Contrary to the speaker's wish":

~(으)련마는/만, ~았/었으련마는/만

Function		Expressing "Whenever one is about to do something"		
Form		~(으)련마는/만		~았/었으련마는/만
Meaning		Can/Might _, but _		Could have verb + pp, but _
Distribution		Present	Past	Future
Action Verb Stem	After a consonant	~으련마는/만	~았/었으련마는/만	
	After a vowel	~련마는/만	~았/었으련마는/만	
	After "ㄹ"	~련마는/만	~았/었으련마는/만	
Stative Verb Stem	After a consonant	~으련마는/만	~았/었으련마는/만	
	After a vowel	~련마는/만	~았/었으련마는/만	
	After "ㄹ"	~련마는/만	~았/었으련마는/만	

"~(으)련마는" and its contraction form "~(으)련만" can be used to express that the situation in the following clause actually happens contrary to the speaker's wish in the preceding clause, which can be rendered as "can/might _, but _." They are typically used with a conditional clause.

존은 열심히 공부하면 시험에 합격할 수 있**으련마는**/있**으련만** 도무지 노력을 안 하네요.
(=If John studies harder, he can pass the exam, but he doesn't put any effort into his studies.)

가만히 놔두면 제가 어련히 알아서 **하련마는**/하**련만** 어머니는 항상 잔소리만 하세요.
(=If my mother leaves me alone, I can take good care of it by myself, but she always keeps nagging me.)

메리가 거기에 같이 가면 좋**으련마는**/좋**으련만** 안 간다고 하네요.
(=If Mary goes there with me, it might be good, but she says she won't go.)

존은 하루 종일 집에 있으면 심심하**련마는**/심심하**련만** 밖에 나갈 생각을 안 하네요.
(=John might get bored if he stays at home all day long, but he doesn't think about going out at all.)

Their corresponding past forms "~았/었으련마는" and its contraction form "~았/었으련만" can be used for a similar function, which can be rendered as "could have+pp, but _."

메리는 조금만 더 기다렸으면 헤어진 가족을 만날 수 있**었으련마는**/있**었으련만** 이미 떠나 버렸네.
(=If Mary had waited a little longer, she could have met her separated family, but she already left.)

서로를 이해하려고 노력했으면 좋**았으련마는**/좋**았으련만** 결국 이혼 신청을 했다.
(=If they had tried to understand each other, it could have been better, but they ended up filing for divorce.)

27. Expressing the benefit of the doubt:
~(으)랴마는, ~겠냐마는, ~(으)ㄹ까마는

"~ (으)랴마는, ~겠냐마는, ~ (으)ㄹ까마는" can be used to express that the situation in the following clause applies even though the speaker doubts that the situation in the preceding clause will actually occur, which can be rendered as "I doubt that _, but _." They differ in terms of the degree of doubtfulness.

~ (으)랴마는	>	~겠냐마는	>	~ (으)ㄹ까마는
Strongly doubt that				Less strongly doubt that

설마 그럴리가 있**으랴마는**/있**겠냐마는**/있**을까마는** 다시 한 번 확인해 보자.
(=I doubt that it is/will be true, but let's double check.)

Function	Expressing the benefit of the doubt		
Form	~(으)랴마는	~겠냐마는	~(으)ㄹ까마는
Meaning	I doubt that _, but _		
Distribution	Future	Future	Future
Action Verb Stem / After a consonant	~으랴마는	~겠냐마는	~을까마는
Action Verb Stem / After a vowel	~랴마는	~겠냐마는	~ㄹ까마는
Action Verb Stem / After "ㄹ"	~랴마는	~겠냐마는	~까마는
Stative Verb Stem / After a consonant			
Stative Verb Stem / After a vowel			
Stative Verb Stem / After "ㄹ"			

뭐 크게 달라질 게 있**으랴마는**/있**겠냐마는**/있**을까마는** 그래도 한 번 존을 믿어 보자.

(=I doubt that there will be a big change, but let's trust John just once.)

굶어 죽기야 하**랴마는**/하**겠냐마는**/할**까마는** 요즘 먹고 살기가 힘들다.

(=I doubt that we are going to starve to death, but it is hard to make ends meet these days.)

On the other hand, they can also be used as a conversational strategy to express the speaker's doubt indirectly. In this case, the speaker actually has some doubt about the situation in the preceding clause, but says the opposite: that he/she has no doubt about the situation. This is what is called "an ironic conversational strategy" in that what is meant is the opposite to what is said.

어련히 알아서 하**랴마는**/하**겠냐마는**/할**까마는** 그래도 혹시 같이 한 번 살펴보자.

(=I have no doubt that you can surely take care of it by yourself, but let's take a look at it together just in case.)

(Implication: I have some doubt that that you can take care of it by yourself.)

28. Expressing "Because of the expected outcome": ~(으)ㄹ진대

"~(으)ㄹ진대" can be used to express that the situation in the following clause is the speaker's response to a given situation because of the expected outcome in the preceding clause, which can be rendered as "because of the reason that _."

Function	Expressing "Because of the expected outcome"		
Form	~(으)ㄹ진대		
Meaning	Because of the reason that _		
Distribution	Present	Past	Future
Action Verb Stem — After a consonant			~을진대
Action Verb Stem — After a vowel			~ㄹ진대
Action Verb Stem — After "ㄹ"			~진대
Stative Verb Stem — After a consonant			~을진대
Stative Verb Stem — After a vowel			~ㄹ진대
Stative Verb Stem — After "ㄹ"			~진대

군사쿠데타에 실패하면 사형을 받**을진대** 누가 쉽게 가담하겠습니까?

(=Who can readily join a military coup because of the reason that one can receive the death penalty if it fails?)

자칫하면 모두의 생명이 위험**할진대** 조심하세요.

(=Please be careful because of the reason that it may jeopardize everyone's life if something goes wrong.)

나라의 앞날이 위험**할진대** 가만히 책상 앞에 앉아 공부만 할 수 없어요.

(=I cannot just study sitting in front of a desk because of the reason that our country's future is in danger.)

누가 그랬는지 불 보듯 뻔**할진대** 왜 아직도 안 잡아들이는지 모르겠네요.

(=I don't know why they don't arrest the person yet because of the reason that it is so clear who did it.)

"~(으)ㄹ진대" is only used in written text and is now becoming an archaic expression in favor of the more frequently used grammar feature "~는/(으)ㄴ데 (Given that _)."

군사쿠데타에 실패하면 사형을 받**는데** 누가 쉽게 가담하겠습니까?

(=Given that one can receive the death penalty if a military coup fails, who can readily join it?)

자칫하면 모두의 생명이 위험**한데** 조심하세요.

(=Given that it may jeopardize everyone's life if something goes wrong, please be careful.)

나라의 앞날이 위험**한데** 가만히 책상 앞에 앉아 공부만 할 수 없어요.

(=Given that our country's future is in danger, I cannot just study sitting in front of a desk.)

누가 그랬는지 불 보듯 뻔**한데** 왜 아직도 안 잡아들이는지 모르겠네요.

(=Given that it is so clear who did it, I don't know why they don't arrest the person yet.)

29. Expressing "Even after considering the situation":

~(는/ㄴ)다(고) 하더라도, ~(는/ㄴ)다(손) 치더라도

Function		Expressing "Even after considering the situation"		
Form		~(는/ㄴ)다(고) 하더라도, ~(는/ㄴ)다(손) 치더라도		
Meaning		Even after considering that _		
Distribution		Present	Past	Future
Action Verb Stem	After a consonant	~는다(고) 하더라도 ~는다(손) 치더라도	~았/었다(고) 하더라도 ~았/었다(손) 치더라도	
	After a vowel	~ㄴ다(고) 하더라도 ~ㄴ다(손) 치더라도	~았/었다(고) 하더라도 ~았/었다(손) 치더라도	
	After "ㄹ"	~ㄴ다(고) 하더라도* ~ㄴ다(손) 치더라도*	~았/었다(고) 하더라도 ~았/었다(손) 치더라도	
Stative Verb Stem	After a consonant	~다(고) 하더라도 ~다(손) 치더라도	~았/었다(고) 하더라도 ~았/었다(손) 치더라도	
	After a vowel	~다(고) 하더라도 ~다(손) 치더라도	~았/었다(고) 하더라도 ~았/었다(손) 치더라도	
	After "ㄹ"	~다(고) 하더라도 ~다(손) 치더라도	~았/었다(고)) 하더라도 ~았/었다(손) 치더라도	

* If the verb stem ends with "ㄹ," "ㄹ" will be dropped before we attach "~ㄴ다(고) 하더라도, ~ㄴ다(손) 치더라도" according to the rule of "ㄹ" deletion that says "the consonant "ㄹ" at the end of a verb stem is dropped before "ㄴ, ㅂ, ㅅ." (See Chapter 12 Verbs)
팔다 (to sell): 팔→판다(고) 하더라도/판다(손) 치더라도

"~(는/ㄴ)다(고) 하더라도, ~(는/ㄴ)다(손) 치더라도" can be used to express that the situation in the following clause is the speaker's response to the given situation even after considering the situation in the preceding clause, which can be rendered as "Even after considering that _." "~(는/ㄴ)다(고) 하더라도" can be freely used in both written text and conversation, whereas "~(는/ㄴ)다(손) 치더라도" is more likely to be used in conversation.

보너스를 받**는다(고) 하더라도**/받**는다(손) 치더라도** 생활이 빠듯하다.
(=Even after considering that I get a bonus, it is hard to make ends meet.)

지금 거기 **간다(고) 하더라도**/**간다(손) 치더라도** 메리를 만날 수 없을 겁니다.
(=Even after considering that you go there now, you cannot see Mary.)

버르장머리가 **없다(고) 하더라도**/**없다(손) 치더라도** 어른들한테 어떻게 이럴 수 있어요?
(=Even after considering that you have no manners, how dare you treat the elderly like this?)

품질이 아무리 **좋다(고) 하더라도**/**좋다(손) 치더라도** 값이 터무니 없이 비싸요.
(=Even after considering that its quality is so good, the price is ridiculously expensive.)

회사가 어렵**다(고) 하더라도**/어렵**다(손) 치더라도** 봉급을 깎으면 어떻게 먹고살라는 말입니까?
(=Even after considering that the company is facing a financial difficulty, how can I make ends meet if you take a pay cut?)

내가 좀 잘못**했다(고) 하더라도**/잘못**했다(손) 치더라도** 니가 나한테 어떻게 이럴 수 있니?
(=Even after considering that I did something wrong, how come you treat me like this?)

30. Describing an action which is not to be fully carried out:
~는/(으)ㄴ/(으)ㄹ 듯 마는/만/말 듯

"~는 듯 마는 듯, ~(으)ㄴ 듯 만 듯, ~(으)ㄹ 듯 말 듯" can be used to express that the situation in the following clause happens because the action in the preceding clause has not been fully carried out, which brings a pending emotion to the speaker. It can be rendered as "making me wonder if _." "듯" can sometimes be replaced with "둥" in casual speech.

Function	Describing an action which is not to be fully carried out		
Form	~는/(으)ㄴ/(으)ㄹ 듯 마는/만/말 듯		
Meaning	Making me wonder if _		
Distribution		Present	Past	Future

	Distribution	Present	Past	Future
Action Verb Stem	After a consonant	~는 듯 마는 듯	~은 듯 만 듯	~을 듯 말 듯
	After a vowel	~는 듯 마는 듯	~ㄴ 듯 만 듯	~ㄹ 듯 말 듯
	After "ㄹ"	~는 듯 마는 듯*	~ㄴ 듯 만 듯*	듯 말 듯
Stative Verb Stem	After a consonant			
	After a vowel			
	After "ㄹ"			

* If the verb stem ends with "ㄹ," "ㄹ" will be dropped before we attach "~는 듯 마는 듯, ~ㄴ 듯 만 듯" according to the rule of "ㄹ" deletion that says "the consonant "ㄹ" at the end of a verb stem is dropped before "ㄴ, ㅂ, ㅅ." (See Chapter 12 Verbs)
벌다 (to make money): 벌→버는 듯 마는 듯/번 듯 만 듯

존은 일을 <u>하는 듯 마는 듯</u>/하는 둥 마는 둥 대충대충 합니다.

(=John does his work in a clumsy way, making me wonder if he is working on it or not.)

메리는 제 의견을 <u>들은 듯 만 듯</u>/들은 둥 만 둥 무시하네요.

(=Mary is ignoring my opinion, making me wonder if she heard it or not.)

잠을 <u>잔 듯 만 듯</u>/잔 둥 만 둥 피곤해 죽겠어요.

(=I am dead tired, making me wonder if I had enough sleep.)

비행접시가 땅에 내려앉<u>을 듯 말 듯</u>/내려앉을 둥 말 둥 빙빙 돌고 있네요.

(=The flying saucer is circling around, making me wonder if it is going to land on the ground or not.)

범인이 잡<u>힐 듯 말 듯</u>/잡힐 둥 말 둥 경찰을 피해 숨어 다니고 있다.

(=The suspect is hiding to escape from the police, making me wonder if he/she can be caught or not.)

31. Reporting one's main justification for an action:
~(는/ㄴ)다고/냐고/(으)라고/자고 (하면서)

Function			Reporting one's main justification for an action		
Form			~(는/ㄴ)다고/냐고/(으)라고/자(고 하)면서		
Meaning			While saying/asking/suggesting that _		
Distribution			Present	Past	Future
Action Verb Stem	Statement	After a consonant	~는다고 (하면서) ~는다면서	~았/었다고 (하면서) ~았/었다면서	~겠다고 (하면서) ~겠다면서
		After a vowel	~ㄴ다고 (하면서) ~ㄴ다면서	~았/었다고 (하면서) ~았/었다면서	~겠다고 (하면서) ~겠다면서
		After "ㄹ"	~ㄴ다고 (하면서)* ~ㄴ다면서*	~았/었다고 (하면서) ~았/었다면서	~겠다고 (하면서) ~겠다면서
	Question	Regardless of the ending	~냐고 (하면서)* ~냐면서*	~았/었냐고 (하면서) ~았/었냐면서	~겠냐고 (하면서) ~겠냐면서
	Imperative	After a consonant	~으라고 (하면서) ~으라면서		
		After a vowel or "ㄹ"	~라고 (하면서) ~라면서		
	Proposition	Regardless of the ending	~자고 (하면서) ~자면서		
Stative Verb Stem	Statement	Regardless of the ending	~다고 (하면서) ~다면서	~았/었다고 (하면서) ~았/었다면서	~겠다고 (하면서) ~겠다면서
	Question	Regardless of the ending	~냐고 (하면서)* ~냐면서*	~았/었냐고 (하면서) ~았/었냐면서	~겠냐고 (하면서) ~겠냐면서

* If the verb stem ends with "ㄹ," "ㄹ" will be dropped before we attach "~ㄴ다고 (하면서), ~ㄴ다면서, ~냐고 (하면서), ~냐면서" according to the rule of "ㄹ" deletion that says "the consonant "ㄹ" at the end of a verb stem is dropped before "ㄴ, ㅂ, ㅅ." (See Chapter 12 Verbs)
살다 (to live): 살→산다고 (하면서)/산다면서/사냐고 (하면서)/사냐면서, 멀다(far): 멀→머냐고 (하면서)/머냐면서

"~(는/ㄴ)다고 (하면서), ~냐고 (하면서), ~(으)라고 (하면서), ~자고 (하면서)" can be used to express that the speaker is reporting to the listener that one is carrying out the action in the following clause while providing his/her main justification in the preceding clause, which can be rendered as "while saying/asking/suggesting that _." "하면서" can be freely deleted in conversation or can be contracted into the following forms "~(는/ㄴ)다면서,

~냐면서, ~(으)라면서, ~자면서." In addition, "하면서" can be frequently replaced by "하며" in written text and formal speech.

존은 돈을 찾**는다고 (하면서)**/찾**는다면서**/찾**는다고 (하며)**/찾**는다며** 은행에 갔다.
(=John went to the bank while saying that he was going to withdraw some money.)

메리는 그 일을 자기 스스로 **한다고 (하면서)**/**한다면서**/**한다고 (하며)**/**한다며** 방해하지 말라고 했다.
(=Mary asked me not to disturb her while saying that she was going to do it by herself.)

존은 전에 살던 아파트가 전세값이 비싸**다고 (하면서)**/비싸**다면서**/비싸**다고 (하며)**/비싸**다며** 다른 아파트로 이사했다.
(=John moved into another apartment while saying that the one-time deposit lease on the previous apartment was too expensive.)

존은 잃어버린 가방을 찾**겠다고 (하면서)**/찾**겠다면서**/찾**겠다고 (하며)**/찾**겠다며** 밖으로 나갔다.
(=John went out while saying that he is going to find the bag that he lost.)

메리는 존과 살면서 한 번도 행복했던 적이 없**었다고 (하면서)**/없**었다면서** 없**었다고 (하며)**/ 없**었다며** 이혼 신청을 했다.
(=Mary filed for a divorce suit while saying that she had never been happy while having lived with John.)

존은 왜 자기만 고생해야 하**냐고 (하면서)**/하**냐면서**/하**냐고 (하며)**/하**냐며** 나한테 따지고 들었다.
(=John was splitting hairs with me while asking me why he is the only one who has to suffer.)

메리는 누가 이 일을 하**겠냐고 (하면서)**/하**겠냐면서**/하**겠냐고 (하며)**/하**겠냐며** 불평을 한다.
(=Mary is complaining while asking me who is going to do such a thing.)

메리는 왜 허락 없이 자기 방에 들어**왔냐고 (하면서)**/들어**왔냐면서**/들어**왔냐고 (하며)**/들어**왔냐며** 나에게 불평을 했다.
(=Mary complained against me while asking me why I entered her room without her permission.)

존은 자기 말만 들**으라고 (하면서)**/들**으라면서**/들**으라고 (하며)**/들**으라며** 메리를 속이고 있다.

(=John is deceiving Mary while asking her just to listen to him.)

메리는 모두들 조용히 하**라고 (하면서)**/하**라면서**/하**라고 (하며)**/하**라며** 소리를 질렀다.
(=Mary shouted while asking everyone to be quiet.)

존은 한국에 같이 가**자고 (하면서)**/가**자면서**/가**자고 (하며)**/가**자며** 비행기표 예약을 부탁했다.
(=John asked me to reserve an airplane ticket while suggesting to me to go to Korea together.)

32. Reporting the examples for one's justification:
~(는/ㄴ)다/냐/(으)라/자는 둥 (하면서)

"~(는/ㄴ)다/냐/(으)라/자는 둥 (하면서)" can be used to express that the speaker is reporting to the listener that one is carrying out the action in the following clause while providing one or more concrete examples for his/her justification in the preceding clause, which can be rendered as "while saying/asking/suggesting that _." This grammar feature is more likely to be used in casual conversation.

존은 중요한 서류를 찾**는다는 둥 (하면서)** 내 방을 막 뒤지고 있다.
(=John is rummaging in my room while saying that he is searching for an important document.)

메리는 피곤해서 자야 **된다는 둥 (하면서)** 자꾸만 나를 피하고 있다.
(=Mary is repeatedly avoiding me while saying that she has to get some sleep because she is tired.)

존은 허리가 아프**다는 둥 (하면서)** 자주 병가를 낸다.
(=John often submits sick leave requests while saying that he has back pain.)

메리는 시간이 없**다는 둥 (하면서)** 집안일을 하나도 안 하고 있다.
(=Mary doesn't do any household chores while saying that she doesn't have time.)

메리는 나중에 하**겠다는 둥 (하면서)** 자기 할 일을 미루고 있다.
(=Mary has been procrastnating doing her work while saying that she is going to do it later.)

Function	Reporting the examples for one's justification		
Form	~(는/ㄴ)다/냐/(으)라/자는 둥 (하면서)		
Meaning	While saying/asking/suggesting that _		

Distribution			Present	Past	Future
Action Verb Stem	Statement	After a consonant	~는다는 둥 (하면서)	~았/었다는 둥 (하면서)	~겠다는 둥 (하면서)
		After a vowel	~ㄴ다는 둥 (하면서)	~았/었다는 둥 (하면서)	~겠다는 둥 (하면서)
		After "ㄹ"	~ㄴ다는 둥 (하면서)*	~았/었다는 둥 (하면서)	~겠다는 둥 (하면서)
	Question	Regardless of the ending	~냐는 둥 (하면서)*	~았/었냐는 둥 (하면서)	~겠냐는 둥 (하면서)
	Imperative	After a consonant	~으라는 둥 (하면서)		
		After a vowel or "ㄹ"	~라는 둥 (하면서)		
	Proposition	Regardless of the ending	~자는 둥 (하면서)		
Stative Verb Stem	Statement	Regardless of the ending	~다는 둥 (하면서)	~았/었다는 둥 (하면서)	~겠다는 둥 (하면서)
	Question	Regardless of the ending	~냐는 둥 (하면서)*	~았/었냐는 둥 (하면서)	~겠냐는 둥 (하면서)

*If the verb stem ends with "ㄹ," "ㄹ" will be dropped before we attach "~ㄴ다는 둥 (하면서), ~냐는 둥 (하면서)" according to the rule of "ㄹ" deletion that says "the consonant "ㄹ" at the end of a verb stem is dropped before "ㄴ, ㅂ, ㅅ." (See Chapter 12 Verbs)
살다 (to live): 살→산다는 둥 (하면서)/사냐는 둥 (하면서), 멀다(far): 멀→머냐는 둥 (하면서)

존은 자기는 아무것도 몰**랐다는 둥 (하면서)** 말도 안 되는 소리만 하고 있다.
(=John is just talking ridiculously while saying that he didn't know anything.)

메리는 존이 어떻게 다른 여자와 바람을 피울 수 있**냐는 둥 (하면서)** 절대 용서할 수 없다고 한다.
(=Mary said that she would never forgive John while asking me how he could have an affair with another woman.)

존은 누가 이 일을 하**겠냐는 둥 (하면서)** 불평만 늘어놓고 있다.
(=John keeps complaining while asking me who on earth is going to do this work.)

메리는 왜 허락 없이 자기 방에 들어**왔냐는 둥 (하면서)** 존에게 화를 내고 있다.
(=Mary takes her anger out on John while asking John why he entered her room without her permission.)

존은 메리가 싫어하는 것을 먹**으라는 둥 (하면서)** 괴롭히고 있다.

(=John is harassing Mary while asking her to eat the food that she dislikes.)

김 과장은 근무시간에 자기 개인적인 일을 나한테 하**라는 둥 (하면서)** 지위를 남용하고 있다.

(=Section chief Kim has been abusing his position while asking me to take care of his personal matters during work hours.)

존은 자기와 같이 일을 하**자는 둥 (하면서)** 계속 화해의 손길을 보내고 있다.

(=John continues to hold out an olive branch to me while suggesting to me to work together with him.)

Unlike "~(는/ㄴ)다고/냐고/(으)라고/자고 하면서" which can specify only one main justification, however, "~(는/ㄴ)다/냐/(으)라/자는 둥" can list more than one justification in a given sentence. In that case, "하면서" can be optionally attached only to the last one.

존은 몸이 아프**다는 둥** 스케줄이 바쁘**다는 둥 (하면서)** 자기 할 일을 차일피일 미루고 있다.

(=John is putting off his work while saying that he is sick, or he has a busy schedule.)

존은 몸이 아프**다고** 스케줄이 바쁘**다고 (하면서)** 자기 할 일을 차일피일 미루고 있다.

(NOT OK)

33. Providing supporting examples for a given situation:
~(는/ㄴ)다/냐/(으)라/자느니 (하면서)

"~(는/ㄴ)다/냐/(으)라/자느니 (하면서)" can be used to express that the speaker is reporting to the listener that the situation in the following clause happens by providing one or more supporting examples in the preceding clauses, which can be rendered as "while saying/asking/suggesting that _."

존은 탄수화물은 안 먹**는다느니** 단백질 보충제를 먹어야 **한다느니 (하면서)** 근육을 키우는 데에만 관심이 있다.

(=John is only concerned about building up his muscles while saying that he doesn't want to eat carbohydrates, or he must take protein supplements.)

Function	Providing supporting examples for a given situation		
Form	~(는/ㄴ)다/냐/(으)라/자느니 (하면서)		
Meaning	While saying/asking/suggesting that _		

Distribution			Present	Past	Future
Action Verb Stem	Statement	After a consonant	~는다느니 (하면서)	~았/었다느니 (하면서)	~겠다느니 (하면서)
		After a vowel	~ㄴ다느니 (하면서)	~았/었다느니 (하면서)	~겠다느니 (하면서)
		After "ㄹ"	~ㄴ다느니 (하면서)*	~았/었다느니 (하면서)	~겠다느니 (하면서)
	Question	Regardless of the ending	~냐느니 (하면서)*	~았/었냐느니 (하면서)	~겠냐느니 (하면서)
	Imperative	After a consonant	~으라느니 (하면서)		
		After a vowel or "ㄹ"	~라느니 (하면서)		
	Proposition	Regardless of the ending	~자느니 (하면서)		
Stative Verb Stem	Statement	Regardless of the ending	~다느니 (하면서)	~았/었다느니 (하면서)	~겠다느니 (하면서)
	Question	Regardless of the ending	~냐느니 (하면서)*	~았/었냐느니 (하면서)	~겠냐느니 (하면서)

* If the verb stem ends with "ㄹ," "ㄹ" will be dropped before we attach "~ㄴ다느니 (하면서), ~냐느니 (하면서)" according to the rule of "ㄹ" deletion that says "the consonant "ㄹ" at the end of a verb stem is dropped before "ㄴ, ㅂ, ㅅ." (See Chapter 12 Verbs)
살다 (to live): 살→산다느니 (하면서)/사냐느니 (하면서), 멀다(far): 멀→머냐느니 (하면서)

존은 바쁘**다느니** 몸이 아프**다느니 (하면서)** 핑계만 대고 있다.

(=John is making excuses while saying that he has been busy, or he has been sick.)

이 사건의 용의자는 자신은 아무 것도 **모르겠다느니** 피해자의 얼굴을 한 번도 본 적이 **없었다느니 (하면서)** 같은 말만 되풀이하고 있어요.

(=The suspect in this case repeats the same thing over and over again while saying that he/she doesn't know anything about the crime or has never seen the victim's face.)

메리는 나한테 왜 쓸데 없는 데 돈을 쓰**냐느니** 왜 또 소주를 마**셨냐느니 (하면서)** 항상 바가지를 긁는다.

(=Mary keeps nagging me while asking me why I am spending money on unnecessary things, or why I drank soju again.)

김과장은 자기 옆에 있는 창문을 닫**으라느니** 스벅에서 커피를 사오**라느니 (하면서)** 마치 나를 노예처럼 부려 먹는다.

(=Section chief Kim treats me like dirt while asking me to close the window next to him or to get his coffee from Starbucks.)

이번 휴가 때 몇 사람은 부산에 가**자느니** 또 다른 사람은 제주도에 가**자느니 (하면서)** 아직 여행목적지에 대해 결정을 못 내리고 있다.

(=We haven't reached a decision yet regarding the destination for the upcoming vacation trip while some people are suggesting we go to Busan, and others to Jeju Island.)

34. Expressing "Killing two birds with one stone": ~(으)ㄹ 겸

Function	Expressing "Killing two birds with one stone"		
Form	~(으)ㄹ 겸		
Meaning	And at the same time		
Distribution	Present	Past	Future
Action Verb Stem — After a consonant			~을 겸
Action Verb Stem — After a vowel			~ㄹ 겸
Action Verb Stem — After "ㄹ"			겸
Stative Verb Stem — After a consonant			
Stative Verb Stem — After a vowel			
Stative Verb Stem — After "ㄹ"			

"~(으)ㄹ 겸" can be used to express that one is to carry out the action in the following clause for multiple purposes in the preceding clauses, which can be rendered as "and at the same time." It can be freely repeated to enumerate any number of purposes, typically two, in a given sentence.

가족들도 만**날 겸** 여행도 **할 겸** 한국에 갔다 왔습니다.

(=I visited Korea to meet my family and at the same time to travel around the country.)

필요한 자료를 얻**을 겸** 앞으로의 계획도 세**울 겸** 존과 여러 가지 문제를 상의했다.

(=I discussed various kinds of issues with John to get some data that I need and at the same time to make our future plans.)

On the other hand, the optional adverbial expressions "해서" or "겸사겸사해서 (taking care of many matters)" can also be used together after specifying the last one in a given list of purposes.

책도 **살 겸** 장도 **볼 겸** (**해서/겸사겸사해서**) 시내에 갔습니다.

(=I went to downtown to buy some books and at the same time to do grocery shopping.)

기분전환도 **할 겸** 머리도 식힐 **겸** (**해서/겸사겸사해서**) 노래방에나 가자.

(=Let's go to a karaoke room to change our mood and at the same time to blow off some steam.)

35. Expressing "Even in the middle of another situation":

~는/(으)ㄴ 가운데도/중에도/와중에도

Function		Even in the middle of another situation		Even in the middle of the turmoil
Form		~는/(으)ㄴ 가운데도	~는/(으)ㄴ 중에도	~는/(으)ㄴ 와중에도
Meaning		Even while _		
Distribution		Present	Present	Present
Action Verb Stem	After a consonant	~는 가운데도[1]	~는 중에도[1]	~는 와중에도[1]
	After a vowel	~는 가운데도[1]	~는 중에도[1]	~는 와중에도[1]
	After "ㄹ"	~는 가운데도[1,2]	~는 중에도[1,2]	~는 와중에도[1,2]
Stative Verb Stem	After a consonant	~은 가운데도[1]	~은 중에도[1]	~은 와중에도[1]
	After a vowel	~ㄴ 가운데도[1]	~ㄴ 중에도[1]	~ㄴ 와중에도[1]
	After "ㄹ"	~ㄴ 가운데도[1,2]	~ㄴ 중에도[1,2]	~ㄴ 와중에도[1,2]

[1] The preceding verb cannot take its own tense suffix, and its tense is determined by the tense of the main verb.

[2] If the verb stem ends with "ㄹ," "ㄹ" will be dropped before we attach "~는 가운데도/중에도/와중에도, ~ㄴ 가운데도/중에도/와중에도" according to the rule of "ㄹ" deletion that says "the consonant "ㄹ" at the end of a verb stem is dropped before "ㄴ, ㅂ, ㅅ." (See Chapter 12 Verbs)

살다 (to live): 살→사는 가운데도/중에도/와중에도, 멀다(far): 멀→갈길이 먼 가운데도/갈길이 먼 중에도

"~는/(으)ㄴ 가운데도, ~는/(으)ㄴ 중에도" can be used to express that the situation in the following clause occurs even in the middle of another situation in the preceding clause, which can be rendered as "even while _."

어머님은 식사를 하시**는 가운데도**/하시**는 중에도** 항상 저를 걱정하신다.

(=My mother is always worried about me even while she is eating her meal.)

여름에는 날씨가 맑**은 가운데도**/맑**은 중에도** 갑자기 소나기가 내린다.

(=In summer, a shower pours down even while there is sunny weather.)

존은 어려**운 가운데도**/어려**운 중에도** 희망을 잃지 않았다.

(=John did not give up his hope even while he was going through difficult times.)

On the other hand, "~는/(으)ㄴ 와중에도" can be used to express that the situation in the following clause occurs even during the turmoil in the preceding clause, which can be rendered as "even while."

존은 암과 투병하**는 와중에도** 자기 임무를 완수했다.

(=John had accomplished his mission even while he was fighting cancer.)

존은 몸이 아**픈 와중에도** 자기 할 일을 다 했다.

(=John completed his work even while he was sick.)

Without regard to the tense rule, the tense of the preceding verb is determined by the tense of the main verb.

어머님은 식사를 하시**는 가운데도**/하시**는 중에도** 항상 저를 걱정하셨다.

(=My mother was always worried about me even while she was eating her meal.)

어머님은 식사를 하셨**는 가운데도**/하셨**는 중에도** 항상 저를 걱정하셨다. (NOT OK)

존은 암과 투병하**는 와중에도** 모든 것에 아주 낙천적이었다.

(=John was very optimistic about everything even while he was fighting cancer.)

존은 암과 투병했**는 와중에도** 모든 것에 아주 낙천적이었다. (NOT OK)

"~ㄴ 가운데도, ~ㄴ 중에도, ~ㄴ 와중에도" are often used with the stative verb "바쁘다 (busy)" as part of courtesy expression used to greet the audience gathered at an important social event, such as a wedding ceremony. However, "바쁘신 와중에도" is not an appropriate expression because one's busy schedule is not normally considered a turmoil. Therefore, many Korean grammarians highly discourage people from using it, but rather they recommend using "바쁘**신 가운데도**" or "바쁘**신 중에도**" instead.

바쁘**신 가운데도**/바쁘**신 중에도** 이렇게 방문해 주시니 대단히 고맙습니다.

(=I express my sincere gratitude to all of you for visiting us even while you are busy.)

바쁘**신 와중에도** 이렇게 방문해 주시니 대단히 고맙습니다. (NOT Recommended)

36. Considering a critical situation: ~는/(으)ㄴ 마당에/터에/판에

Function		Considering a critical situation		
Form		~는/(으)ㄴ 마당에	~는/(으)ㄴ 터에	~는/(으)ㄴ 판에
Meaning		Given the situation that _		
Distribution		Present	Present	Present
Action Verb Stem	After a consonant	~는 마당에[1]	~는 터에[1]	~는 판에[1]
	After a vowel	~는 마당에[1]	~는 터에[1]	~는 판에[1]
	After "ㄹ"	~는 마당에[1,2]	~는 터에[1,2]	~는 판에[1,2]
Stative Verb Stem	After a consonant	~은 마당에[1]	~은 터에[1]	~은 판에[1]
	After a vowel	~ㄴ 마당에[1]	~ㄴ 터에[1]	~ㄴ 판에[1]
	After "ㄹ"	~ㄴ 마당에[1,2]	~ㄴ 터에[1,2]	~ㄴ 판에[1,2]

[1] The preceding verb cannot take its own tense suffix, and its tense is determined by the tense of the main verb.

[2] If the verb stem ends with "ㄹ," "ㄹ" will be dropped before we attach "~는 마당에/터에/판에, ~ㄴ 마당에/터에/판에 " according to the rule of "ㄹ" deletion that says "the consonant "ㄹ" at the end of a verb stem is dropped before "ㄴ, ㅂ, ㅅ." (See Chapter 12 Verbs)

살다 (to live): 살→사는 마당에/터에/판에, 산 마당에/터에/판에, 멀다(far): 멀→먼 마당에/터에/판에

"~는/(으)ㄴ 마당에/터에/판에" can be used to express that the situation in the following clause is the speaker's negative response to the listener in consideration of the critical situation in the preceding clause, which can be rendered as "Given the situation that _." "~는/(으)ㄴ 마당에" is the most commonly used one in both written text and conversation. "~는/(으)ㄴ 터에" is now on the verge of becoming an archaic expression, and "~는/(으)ㄴ 판에" is more likely to be used in casual speech.

지금 죽느냐 사느냐 하**는 마당에/터에/판에** 쓸 데 없는 얘기는 하지 말아라.

(=Given the situation that we are facing life or death, don't talk about foolish things.)

나 자신도 못 믿**는 마당에/터에/판에** 지금은 아무도 못 믿습니다.

(=Given the situation that I cannot even trust myself, I cannot trust anyone now.)

회사가 망해가는 **마당에/터에/판에** 어떻게 봉급을 올려달라고 합니까?
(=Given the situation that our company is on the verge of going bankrupt, how can I ask for a pay raise?)

이미 늦은 **마당에/터에/판에** 천천히 합시다
(=Given the situation that we are already late, please hold your horses.)

제 입에 풀칠하기도 어려운 **마당에/터에/판에** 지금 남을 도와 줄 형편이 안 됩니다.
(=Given the situation that I am having a hard time making ends meet, I don't think I can help others now.)

37. Showing the speaker's frustration with an intended action:
~(으)려고 하니(까), ~(으)려니(까)

Function		Showing the speaker's frustration with an intended action		
Form		~(으)려고 하니(까)		~(으)려니(까)
Meaning		Because I intend to do something		
Distribution		Present	Past	Future
Action Verb Stem	After a consonant	~으려고 하니(까)[*] ~으려니(까)[*]		
	After a vowel	~려고 하니(까)[*] ~려니(까)[*]		
	After "ㄹ"	~려고 하니(까)[*] ~려니(까)[*]		
Stative Verb Stem	After a consonant			
	After a vowel			
	After "ㄹ"			

[*] The preceding verb cannot take its own tense suffix, and its tense is determined by the tense of the main verb.

"~(으)려고 하니(까)" can be used to express that the speaker is showing frustration in the following clause because he/she intends to carry out the action in the preceding clause, which can be rendered as "Because I intend to do something." Its contaction form "~(으)려니(까)" is more likely to be used in casual speech.

다른 사람의 기회를 빼앗**으려고 하니(까)**/빼앗**으려니(까)** 좀 마음에 걸린다.

(=It has been weighing on my mind because I intend to deprive another person of his/her opportunity.)

혼자 일을 다 **하려고 하니(까)**/하**려니(까)** 생각한 것보다 시간이 많이 걸리네요.

(=It takes more time than I thought because I intend to do all the work by myself.)

마지막 결과를 기다리**려고 하니(까)**/기다리**려니(까)** 가슴이 조마조마하네요.

(=I have butterflies in my stomach because I intend to wait for the final result.)

38. Showing the speaker's frustration with a planned action:
~고자 하니(까), ~자니(까)

Function	Showing the speaker's frustration with a planned action		
Form	~고자 하니(까)		~자니(까)
Meaning	Because I am planning to do something		
Distribution	Present	Past	Future
Action Verb Stem / After a consonant	~고자 하니(까)[*] ~자니(까)[*]		
Action Verb Stem / After a vowel	~고자 하니(까)[*] ~자니(까)[*]		
Action Verb Stem / After "ㄹ"	~고자 하니(까)[*] ~자니(까)[*]		
Stative Verb Stem / After a consonant			
Stative Verb Stem / After a vowel			
Stative Verb Stem / After "ㄹ"			

[*] The preceding verb cannot take its own tense suffix, and its tense is determined by the tense of the main verb.

"~고자 하니(까)" can be used to express that the speaker is showing frustration in the following clause because he/she is planning to carry out the action in the preceding clause, which can be rendered as "Because I am planning to do something." Its contaction form "~자니(까)" is more likely to be used in casual speech.

존한테 승진 기회를 주**고자 하니(까)**/주**자니(까)** 메리가 샘을 낼 것 같아서 신경이 쓰입니다.

(=It's getting on my nerves that Mary may become jealous of John because I am planning to give him the promotion opportunity.)

집을 수리하**고자 하니(까)**/수리하**자니(까)** 돈이 너무 많이 들까봐 걱정입니다.

(=I am worried that it may cost too much money because I am planning to remodel my house.)

내년에 이 회사를 그만두**고자 하니(까)**/그만두**자니(까)** 노후대책이 걱정이다.

(=I am worried about my plan after retirement because I am planning to quit my job at this company next year.)

39. Expressing "Be about to carry out an intended action":

~(으)려던 차에/참에

Function	Expressing "Be about to carry out an intended action"		
Form	~(으)려던 차에		~(으)려던 참에
Meaning	When one was about to do something		
Distribution		Present	Past	Future
Action Verb Stem	After a consonant	~으려던 차에[*] ~으려던 참에[*]		
	After a vowel	~려던 차에[*] ~려던 참에[*]		
	After "ㄹ"	~려던 차에[*] ~려던 참에[*]		
Stative Verb Stem	After a consonant			
	After a vowel			
	After "ㄹ"			

[*] The preceding verb cannot take its own tense suffix, and its tense is determined by the tense of the main verb.

"~(으)려던 차에/참에" can be used to express that the situation in the following clause just occured when one was about to carry out the intended action in the preceding clause, which can be rendered as "When one was about to do something." "~(으)려던

차에" can be freely used in both written text and conversation, whereas "~(으)려던 참에"
is more likely to be used in casual speech.

가게 문을 닫**으려던 차에** 손님들이 막 들이닥쳤다.

(=Customers just rushed in when I was about to close the store.)

막 퇴근하**려던 차에/참에** 팀장님이 전화를 걸었다.

(=My team leader called me when I was about to get off work.)

밥 먹고 공부하**려던 차에/참에** 전기가 나갔다.

(=The power went out when I was about to study after eating.)

지금 막 공항으로 떠나려던 **차에/참에** 존이 집에 찾아왔다.

(=John came to my house when I was about to leave for the airport.)

40. Expressing "Because of an extreme situation":
얼마나/어찌나 ~(았/었)던지

Function		Expressing "Because of an extreme situation"		
Form		얼마나/어찌나 ~(았/었)던지		
Meaning		Because _ extremely _		
Distribution		Present	Past	Future
Action Verb Stem	After a consonant		얼마나/어찌나 ~던지 얼마나/어찌나 ~았/었던지	
	After a vowel		얼마나/어찌나 ~던지 얼마나/어찌나 ~았/었던지	
	After "ㄹ"		얼마나/어찌나 ~던지 얼마나/어찌나 ~았/었던지	
Stative Verb Stem	After a consonant		얼마나/어찌나 ~던지 얼마나/어찌나 ~았/었던지	
	After a vowel		얼마나/어찌나 ~던지 얼마나/어찌나 ~았/었던지	
	After "ㄹ"		얼마나/어찌나 ~던지 얼마나/어찌나 ~았/었던지	

"얼마나/어찌나 ~던지" can be used to express that the situation in the following clause
is the direct result of the situation in the preceding clause that went to the extreme,

which can be rendered as "because _ extremely _." The adverb "얼마나 (how)" is a gender neutral term and can be used by both males and females, whereas "어찌나 (how)" is more likely to be used by females.

애기가 **얼마나/어찌나** 울**던지** 정말 보기 힘들었어요.

(=Because the baby cried badly, I really had a hard time taking care of him/her.)

날씨가 **얼마나/어찌나** 춥**던지** 얼어 죽는 줄 알았어요.

(=Because the weather was extremely cold, I thought that I was going to die.)

얼굴이 **얼마나/어찌나** 예쁘**던지** 첫눈에 반해 버렸어요.

(=Because she was extremely beautiful, I fell in love with her at first sight.)

"얼마나/어찌나 ~았/었던지" can be used to emphasize the completion of the situation in the preceding clause.

어제 술을 **얼마나/어찌나** 마**셨던지** 아무것도 기억이 안 나요.

(=Because I was completely drunk yesterday, I cannot remember anything.)

얼마나/어찌나 울**었던지** 얼굴이 퉁퉁 부었어요.

(=Because I cried badly, my face got very swollen.)

41. Judging from one's personal observation:

~는/(으)ㄴ 걸 보니(까), ~는/(으)ㄴ 걸로 봐서

"~는/(으)ㄴ 걸 보니(까), ~는/(으)ㄴ 걸로 봐서" can be used to express that the situation in the following clause is the speaker's response to a given situation based on his/her personal observation of the situation in the preceding clause, which can be rendered as "judging from the fact that _."

존이 아직까지 일을 하**는 걸 보니(까)**/하**는 걸로 봐서** 오늘 끝내기가 어려울 것 같다.
(=Judging from the fact that John is still working on it, it seems unlikely that he can finish it today.)

얼음이 녹**은 걸 보니(까)**/녹**은 걸로 봐서** 봄이 벌써 온 것 같다.
(=Judging from the fact that the ice has melted, it seems that spring has already come.)

Function	Judging from one's personal observation		
Form	~는/(으)ㄴ 걸 보니(까)	~는/(으)ㄴ 걸로 봐서	
Meaning	Judging from the fact that _		
Distribution	Present	Past	Future
Action Verb Stem — After a consonant	~는 걸 보니(까) ~는 걸로 봐서	~은 걸 보니(까) ~은 걸로 봐서	
Action Verb Stem — After a vowel	~는 걸 보니(까) ~는 걸로 봐서	~ㄴ 걸 보니(까) ~ㄴ 걸로 봐서	
Action Verb Stem — After "ㄹ"	~는 걸 보니(까)* ~는 걸로 봐서*	~ㄴ 걸 보니(까)* ~ㄴ 걸로 봐서*	
Stative Verb Stem — After a consonant	~은 걸 보니(까) ~은 걸로 봐서		
Stative Verb Stem — After a vowel	~ㄴ 걸 보니(까) ~ㄴ 걸로 봐서		
Stative Verb Stem — After "ㄹ"	~ㄴ 걸 보니(까)* ~ㄴ 걸로 봐서*		

* If the verb stem ends with "ㄹ," "ㄹ" will be dropped before we attach "~는 걸 보니(까), ~ㄴ 걸 보니(까), ~는 걸로 봐서, ~ㄴ 걸로 봐서" according to the rule of "ㄹ" deletion that says "the consonant "ㄹ" at the end of a verb stem is dropped before "ㄴ, ㅂ, ㅅ." (See Chapter 12 Verbs)
살다 (to live): 살→사는 걸 보니(까)/사는 걸로 봐서, 팔다 (to sell): 팔→판 걸 보니(까), 판 걸로 봐서
멀다(far): 멀→먼 걸 보니(까), 먼 걸로 봐서

이 어려운 문제를 해결**한 걸 보니(까)**/해결**한 걸로 봐서** 존의 리더십이 훌륭한 것 같다.
(=Judging from the fact that John resolved this difficult issue, he seems to have excellent leadership.)

가게에 손님이 많**은 걸 보니(까)**/많은 **걸로 봐서** 장사가 잘 되는 것 같다.
(=Judging from the fact that there are so many customers at this store, its business seems to be going well.)

몸이 삐쩍 마른 **걸 보니(까)**/마른 **걸로 봐서** 적어도 며칠은 굶은 것 같다.
(=Judging from the fact that he is so skinny, it seems that he has been starving at least for several days.)

42. Expressing the cause of a negative outcome: ~는/(으)ㄴ 탓에

Function	Expressing the cause of a negative outcome		
Form	~는/(으)ㄴ 탓에		
Meaning	Due to the reason that _		
Distribution	Present	Past	Future
Action Verb Stem — After a consonant	~는 탓에	~은 탓에	
Action Verb Stem — After a vowel	~는 탓에	~ㄴ 탓에	
Action Verb Stem — After "ㄹ"	~는 탓에*	~ㄴ 탓에*	
Stative Verb Stem — After a consonant	~은 탓에		
Stative Verb Stem — After a vowel	~ㄴ 탓에		
Stative Verb Stem — After "ㄹ"	~ㄴ 탓에*		

* If the verb stem ends with "ㄹ," "ㄹ" will be dropped before we attach "~는 탓에~ㄴ 탓에" according to the rule of "ㄹ" deletion that says "the consonant "ㄹ" at the end of a verb stem is dropped before "ㄴ, ㅂ, ㅅ." (See Chapter 12 Verbs)

살다 (to live): 살→사는 탓에, 산 탓에, 멀다(far): 멀→먼 탓에

"~는/(으)ㄴ 탓에" can be used to express that the negative outcome in the following clause can be directly attributed to the situation in the preceding clause, which can be rendered as "due to the reason that _."

존은 편식을 하**는 탓에** 건강이 안 좋다.

(=John is not healthy due to the reason that he is a picky eater.)

점심을 굶**은 탓에** 배고파 죽겠다.

(=I am starving to death due to the reason that I skipped lunch.)

급히 서두**른 탓에** 중요한 서류를 집에 두고 왔습니다.

(=I left the important document at home due to the reason that I was in a rush.)

존은 전과자**인 탓에** 취직을 하는데 어려움을 겪고 있다.

(=John is having a hard time getting a job due to the reason that he is an ex-convict.)

존은 키가 작**은 탓에** 농구선수가 될 수 없었다.

(=John could not become a basketball player due to the reason that he is short.)

메리는 가난**한 탓에** 여기 저기 서너 개의 알바를 뛰고 있다.

(=Mary has three or four part-time jobs here and there due to the reason that she is poor.)

"~는/(으)ㄴ 탓에" cannot be used in imperative or propositional sentences. In this case, the more general cause and effect relationship conjunction "~(으)니까" can be used instead.

밖에 비가 **오니까** 창문을 닫아라. (Imperative: OK)

(=Close the window because it's raining outside.)

밖에 비가 **오는 탓에** 창문을 닫아라. (Imperative: NOT OK)

지금 시간이 없**으니까** 나중에 이야기하자. (Imperative: OK)

(=Let's talk about it later because I don't have time now.)

지금 시간이 없는 **탓에** 나중에 이야기하자. (Imperative: NOT OK)

43. Expressing the probable cause of a negative outcome: ~는/(으)ㄴ 탓인지

Function		Expressing the probable cause of a negative outcome		
Form		~는/(으)ㄴ 탓인지		
Meaning		Probably because _		
Distribution		Present	Past	Future
Action Verb Stem	After a consonant	~는 탓인지	~은 탓인지	
	After a vowel	~는 탓인지	~ㄴ 탓인지	
	After "ㄹ"	~는 탓인지*	~ㄴ 탓인지*	
Stative Verb Stem	After a consonant	~은 탓인지		
	After a vowel	~ㄴ 탓인지		
	After "ㄹ"	~ㄴ 탓인지*		

* If the verb stem ends with "ㄹ," "ㄹ" will be dropped before we attach "~는 탓인지~ㄴ 탓인지" according to the rule of "ㄹ" deletion that says "the consonant "ㄹ" at the end of a verb stem is dropped before "ㄴ, ㅂ, ㅅ." (See Chapter 12 Verbs)
살다 (to live): 살→사는 탓인지, 산 탓인지, 멀다(far): 멀→먼 탓인지

"~는/(으)ㄴ 탓인지" can be used to express that the situation in the following clause is the negative outcome which is probably caused by the situation in the preceding clause. It can be rendered as "probably because _."

존은 혼자 사**는 탓인지** 외로워 보이네요.

(=John looks lonely probably because he has been living alone.)

메리는 친구가 없**는 탓인지** 항상 혼자 있어요.

(=Mary has always been alone probably because she doesn't have friends.)

너무 많이 먹**은 탓인지** 심하게 체했어요.

(=My stomach hurts badly probably because I ate too much.)

소리를 계속 너무 많이 지른 **탓인지** 목이 쉬었어요.

(=My voice became hoarse probably because I kept shouting a lot.)

음식 양이 적**은 탓인지** 2인분을 먹어도 배가 고프네요.

(=I am hungry even though I ate two servings of food probably because the serving size is too small.)

날씨가 더**운 탓인지** 식욕이 하나도 없어요.

(=I have no appetite probably because the weather is too hot.)

44. Expressing the direct cause of a negative outcome: ~(으)ㄴ 나머지

Function	Expressing the direct cause of a negative outcome		
Form	~(으)ㄴ 나머지		
Meaning	As a result of		
Distribution	Present	Past	Future
Action Verb Stem — After a consonant		~은 나머지	
Action Verb Stem — After a vowel		~ㄴ 나머지	
Action Verb Stem — After "ㄹ"		~ㄴ 나머지*	
Stative Verb Stem — After a consonant	~은 나머지		
Stative Verb Stem — After a vowel	~ㄴ 나머지		
Stative Verb Stem — After "ㄹ"	~ㄴ 나머지*		

* If the verb stem ends with "ㄹ," "ㄹ" will be dropped before we attach "~ㄴ 나머지" according to the rule of "ㄹ" deletion that says "the consonant "ㄹ" at the end of a verb stem is dropped before "ㄴ, ㅂ, ㅅ." (See Chapter 12 Verbs)
살다 (to sell): 팔→판 나머지, 멀다(far): 멀→먼 나머지

"~(으)ㄴ 나머지" can be used to express that the situation in the following clause was directly caused by the situation in the preceding clause, which can be rendered as "As a result of."

메리는 직장에서 지나치게 스트레스를 받<u>**은 나머지**</u> 결국 회사를 그만뒀다.

(=Mary ended up quitting her job as a result of having received tremondous amount of stress at her workplace.)

존은 사업을 무리하게 확장<u>**한 나머지**</u> 빚더미에 올라 앉았다.

(=John became indebted up to his eyeballs as a result of having expanded his business beyond his control.)

그 영화배우는 오랫동안 우울증으로 고생<u>**한 나머지**</u> 결국 자살을 했다.

(=The movie actor ended up committing suicide as a result of having suffered from mental depression for a long time.)

그 물건은 단가가 터무니 없이 낮<u>**은 나머지**</u> 팔 때마다 오히려 손해를 본다.

(=We lose money whenever we sell the product as a result of the ridiculously low unit price.)

존은 너무 피곤<u>**한 나머지**</u> 저녁도 안 먹도 자고 있다.

(=John is sleeping without having dinner as a result of his extreme tiredness.)

45. Expressing "Because of a pre-existing condition": ~는/(으)ㄴ/던 터라(서)

Function		Expressing "Because of a pre-existing condition"		
Form		~는/(으)ㄴ/던 터라(서)		
Meaning		Because of the situation that _		
Distribution		Present	Past	Future
Action Verb Stem	After a consonant	~는 터라(서)	~은 터라(서)	
	After a vowel	~는 터라(서)	~ㄴ 터라(서)	
	After "ㄹ"	~는 터라(서)*	~ㄴ 터라(서)*	
Stative Verb Stem	After a consonant	~은 터라(서)		
	After a vowel	~ㄴ 터라(서)		
	After "ㄹ"	~ㄴ 터라(서)*		

* If the verb stem ends with "ㄹ," "ㄹ" will be dropped before we attach "~는 터라(서), ~ㄴ 터라(서)" according to the rule of "ㄹ" deletion that says "the consonant "ㄹ" at the end of a verb stem is dropped before "ㄴ, ㅂ, ㅅ." (See Chapter 12 Verbs)

살다 (to live): 살→사는 터라(서), 풀다 (to solve): 풀→푼 터라(서), 멀다(far): 멀→먼 터라(서)

"~는/(으)ㄴ/던 터라(서)" can be used to express that the situation in the following clause happens because of the pre-existing condition in the preceding clause, which can be rendered as "Because of the situation that _."

지금은 저 혼자 가족을 부양하고 있**는 터라(서)** 군입대를 연기해야만 합니다.
(=Because of the situation that I have been financially supporting my family all by myself now, I must postpone my military enlistment.)

이미 돈을 선불로 받**은 터라(서)** 지금 이 공사에서 손떼기가 불가능합니다.
(=Because of the situation that I have already received the money in advance, it is impossible to take my hands off this construction project.)

이미 그 프로젝트에 많은 돈을 투자**한 터라(서)** 쉽게 포기할 수 없습니다.
(=Because of the situation that we have already invested a large sum of money on that project, we cannot easily give it up.)

요즘 회사 사정이 안 좋**은 터라(서)** 올해는 신입사원을 채용할 수가 없습니다.
(=Because of the situation that our company's financial situation has not been good these days, we cannot recruit new employees this year.)

집이 좀 비좁**은 터라(서)** 집들이를 하기가 힘듭니다.
(=Because of the situation that my house is too small, it is difficult to host a house-warming party.)

마침 저도 그쪽으로 가려**던 터라(서)** 제가 댁에 모셔다 드릴게요.
(=Because of the situation that I also happen to be going in that direction, I will give you a ride home.)

어려서부터 온갖 역경을 극복해 **왔던 터라(서)** 이 정도 어려움은 아무 것도 아닙니다.
(=Because of the situation that I have overcome all kinds of hardships since I was young, this kind of ordeal is nothing to me.)

46. Expressing "Because of one's specific personal characteristics":
~아/어 가지고(서)

"~아/어 가지고(서)" can be used to express that the situation in the following clause happens because one has the specific personal characteristics in the preceding clause, which can be rendered as "because one is _."

Function	Expressing "Because of one's specific personal characteristics"		
Form	~아/어 가지고(서)		
Meaning	Because one is _		
Distribution	Present	Past	Future
Action Verb Stem — After "오" or "아"			
Action Verb Stem — Otherwise			
Stative Verb Stem — After "오" or "아"	~아 가지고(서)[*]		
Stative Verb Stem — Otherwise	~어 가지고(서)[*]		

* The preceding verb cannot take its own tense suffix, and its tense is determined by the tense of the main verb.

존은 욕심은 많**아 가지고(서)** 자기 혼자 다 가지려고 한다.

(=John wants to take it all because he is so greedy.)

메리는 항상 성격이 급**해 가지고(서)** 모든 일을 빨리만 하려고 한다.

(=Mary wants to just get everything done quickly because she is always in a rush.)

그렇게 게을**러 가지고(서)** 오늘 중으로 일을 끝낼 수가 없어요.

(=You cannot finish the work by today because you are so lazy.)

47. Expressing "As a result of an uncontrollable ongoing situation":

~는 통에

"~는 통에" can be used to express that the negative outcome in the following clause occurs due to the uncontrollable, undesirable, or unfavorable ongoing situation in the preceding clause, which can be rendered as "because."

중부지방에 폭설이 쏟아지**는 통에** 모든 비행기가 결항되었다.

(=All the flights were cancelled because a snow storm hit the central region.)

존은 쓸데없이 고집부리**는 통에** 신세를 망쳤습니다.

(=John's life was ruined because he was so stubborn without any reasonable cause.)

배가 뒤집히**는 통에** 사상자가 급속도로 늘고 있다.

(=The number of casualties has been rapidly increasing because the boat capsized.)

Function	Expressing "As a result of an uncontrollable ongoing situation"		
Form	~는 통에		
Meaning	Because		
Distribution	Present	Past	Future
Action Verb Stem — After a consonant	~는 통에[1]		
Action Verb Stem — After a vowel	~는 통에[1]		
Action Verb Stem — After "ㄹ"	~는 통에[1,2]		
Stative Verb Stem — After a consonant			
Stative Verb Stem — After a vowel			
Stative Verb Stem — After "ㄹ"			

[1] The preceding verb cannot take its own tense suffix, and its tense is determined by the tense of the main verb.

[2] If the verb stem ends with "ㄹ," "ㄹ" will be dropped before we attach "~는 통에" according to the rule of "ㄹ" deletion that says "the consonant "ㄹ" at the end of a verb stem is dropped before "ㄴ, ㅂ, ㅅ." (See Chapter 12 Verbs)
(ex) 살다 (to live): 살→사는 통에

"~는 통에" is more or less interchangeable with "~는 바람에."

중부지방에 폭설이 쏟아지**는 바람에** 모든 비행기가 결항되었다.

(=All the flights were cancelled because a snow storm hit the central region.)

존은 쓸데 없이 고집부리**는 바람에** 신세를 망쳤습니다.

(=John's life was ruined because he was so stubborn without any reasonable cause.)

배가 뒤집히**는 바람에** 사상자가 급속도로 늘고 있다.

(=The number of casualties has been rapidly increasing because the boat capsized.)

Unlike "~는 바람에," however, it cannot be used if the outcome in the following clause is a positive one.

존은 복권에 당첨되**는 바람에** 갑자기 부자가 되었다.

(=Because John won the lottery, he suddenly became rich.)

존은 복권에 당첨되**는 통에** 갑자기 부자가 되었다. (Positive outcome: NOT OK)

On the other hand, "~는 통에" cannot be used in imperative or propositional sentences. In this case, the more general cause and effect relationship conjunction "~(으)니까" can be used instead.

지금 폭설이 내리는 **통에** 가게문을 닫아라. (Imperative: NOT OK)

지금 폭설이 내리**니까** 가게문을 닫아라. (OK)

(=Close the store because a heavy snow is falling now.)

오늘은 바쁜 **통에** 나중에 이야기하자. (Proposition: NOT OK)

오늘은 바쁘**니까** 나중에 이야기하자. (OK)

(=Let's talk about it later because I am busy today.

48. Expressing the reason for a given situation: ~는/(으)ㄴ 까닭에

Function	Expressing the reason for a given situation		
Form	~는/(으)ㄴ 까닭에		
Meaning	Because of the reason that _		
Distribution		Present	Past	Future
Action Verb Stem	After a consonant	~는 까닭에	~은 까닭에 ~았/었던 까닭에	
	After a vowel	~는 까닭에	~ㄴ 까닭에 ~았/었던 까닭에	
	After "ㄹ"	~는 까닭에*	~ㄴ 까닭에* ~았/었던 까닭에	
Stative Verb Stem	After a consonant	~은 까닭에	~았/었던 까닭에	
	After a vowel	~ㄴ 까닭에	~았/었던 까닭에	
	After "ㄹ"	~ㄴ 까닭에*	~았/었던 까닭에	

* If the verb stem ends with "ㄹ," "ㄹ" will be dropped before we attach "~는 까닭에, ~ㄴ 까닭에" according to the rule of "ㄹ" deletion that says "the consonant "ㄹ" at the end of a verb stem is dropped before "ㄴ, ㅂ, ㅅ." (See Chapter 12 Verbs)
살다 (to live): 살→사는 까닭에, 산 까닭에, 멀다 (far): 멀→먼 까닭에

"~는/(으)ㄴ 까닭에" can be used to express that the situation in the preceding clause is the main reason for the situation in the following clause, which can be rendered as "because of the reason that _."

커피를 마시면 잠을 못자**는 까닭에** 저는 커피를 안 마십니다.

(=I don't drink coffee because of the reason that I cannot sleep if I drink it.)

부모님한테서 재산을 좀 물려받**은 까닭에** 집을 장만할 수 있었습니다.

(=I was able to buy a house because of the reason that I inherited some properities from my parents.)

비행기표를 몇 달 전에 구입**한 까닭에** 아주 싸게 살 수 있었습니다.

(=I was able to buy the airplane ticket at a very low price because of the reason that I purchased it several months ago.)

존이 회의에 참석 중**인 까닭에** 회의실 밖에서 기다렸습니다.

(=I was waiting for John outside the conference room because of the reason that he was attending the meeting.)

메리는 성격이 좋**은 까닭에** 주위에 친구가 많습니다.

(=Mary has many friends around her because of the reason that she has a good personality.)

서울은 물가가 비**싼 까닭에** 생활비가 아주 많이 듭니다.

(=The cost of living in Seoul is very high because of the reason that the prices of commodities are expensive.)

To emphasize the completion of the action or the state in the preceding clause, the past tense form "~았/었던 까닭에" can be used instead.

부모님한테서 재산을 좀 물려받**았던 까닭에** 집을 장만할 수 있었습니다.

(=I was able to buy a house because of the reason that I had inherited some properities from my parents.)

비행기표를 몇 달 전에 구입**했던 까닭에** 아주 싸게 살 수 있었습니다.

(=I was able to buy the airplane ticket at a very low price because of the reason that I had purchased it several months ago.)

돈이 별로 없**었던 까닭에** 치료를 받지 못했다.

(=I could not receive medical treatment because of the reason that I did not have enough money.)

키가 너무 작**았던 까닭에** 프로농구선수가 되지 못했습니다.

(=I could not become a professional basketball player because of the reason that I was too short.)

49. Expressing a situation that went to the extreme: ~(으)ㄹ 대로 ~아서/어서

Function	Expressing a situation that went to the extreme		
Form	~(으)ㄹ 대로 ~아서/어서		
Meaning	Because _ as much as one/it can		
Distribution		Present	Past	Future
Action Verb Stem / After a consonant		~을 대로 ~아서/어서*		
Action Verb Stem / After a vowel		~ㄹ 대로 ~아서/어서*		
Action Verb Stem / After "ㄹ"		대로 ~아서/어서*		
Stative Verb Stem / After a consonant		~을 대로 ~아서/어서*		
Stative Verb Stem / After a vowel		~ㄹ 대로 ~아서/어서*		
Stative Verb Stem / After "ㄹ"		대로 ~아서/어서*		

* The preceding verb cannot take its own tense suffix, and its tense is determined by the tense of the main verb.

"~(으)ㄹ 대로 ~아서/어서" can be used to express that the negative situation in the following clause happens because the situation in the preceding clause went to the extreme, which can be rendered as "Because _ as much as one/it can."

참을 대로 참아서 더 이상 참을 수가 없어요.

(=I cannot bear it any more because I have tolearated it as much as I could.)

차값이 오를 대로 올라서 차를 사기가 힘들다.

(=It is hard to buy a car because car prices went up as much as they can go.)

이 청바지는 낡을 대로 낡아서 입을 수가 없다.

(=I cannot wear this blue jean because it is worn out as much as it can go.)

(=I cannot wear this blue jean because it is completely worn out.)

지칠 대로 지쳐서 아무 것도 할 수 없어요.

(=I cannot do anything because I am exhausted as much as I can handle.)

(=I cannot do anything because I am completely exhausted.)

50. Expressing "Matching with one's experience": ~다시피

Function		Expressing "Matching with one's experience"		
Form		~다시피		
Meaning		As you know/As you can see/As you have heard		
Distribution		Present	Past	Future
Action Verb Stem	After a consonant	~다시피	~았/었다시피	
	After a vowel	~다시피	~았/었다시피	
	After "ㄹ"	~다시피	~았/었다시피	
Stative Verb Stem	After a consonant			
	After a vowel			
	After "ㄹ"			

"~다시피" can be used to express that the speaker assumes that the situation in the following clause matches with the listener's personal experience in the preceding clause. It is typically combined with the verbs "알다/보다/듣다," which can be subsequently rendered as "As you know/As you can see/As you have heard," respectively.

아시**다시피** 저는 대학에서 언어학을 공부했어요.

(=As you know, I studied linguistics at college.)

보시**다시피** 지금 일이 밀려서 눈코 뜰새 없이 바쁩니다.

(=As you can see, I am extremely busy because I am behind on my work schedule.)

들으**셨다시피** 이번 홍수 때문에 많은 사람이 죽었어요.

(As you have heard, many people died because of this flood.)

51. Expressing a contradictory situation: ~(는/ㄴ)다/냐/(으)라/자더니

"~(는/ㄴ)다/냐/(으)라/자더니" are actually the combination of the citation endings and "~더니 (used to _, but _)." They can be used to express that the situation in the following clause actually happens, which contradicts one's original claim in the preceding clause, which can be rendered as "One said/asked/suggested that _, but _."

Function	Expressing a contradictory situation		
Form	~(는/ㄴ)다/냐/(으)라/자더니		
Meaning	One said/asked/suggested that _, but _		

Distribution			Present	Past	Future
Action Verb Stem	Statement	After a consonant	~는다더니	~았/었다더니	~겠다더니
		After a vowel	~ㄴ다더니	~았/었다더니	~겠다더니
		After "ㄹ"	~ㄴ다더니*	~았/었다더니	~겠다더니
	Question	Regardless of the ending	~냐더니*	~았/었냐더니	~겠냐더니
	Imperative	After a consonant	~으라더니		
		After a vowel or "ㄹ"	~라더니		
	Proposition	Regardless of the ending	~자더니		
Stative Verb Stem	Statement	Regardless of the ending	~다더니	~았/었다더니	~겠다더니
	Question	Regardless of the ending	~냐더니*	~았/었냐더니	~겠냐더니

* If the verb stem ends with "ㄹ," "ㄹ" will be dropped before we attach "~ㄴ다더니, ~냐더니" according to the rule of "ㄹ" deletion that says "the consonant "ㄹ" at the end of a verb stem is dropped before "ㄴ, ㅂ, ㅅ." (See Chapter 12 Verbs)
살다 (to live): 살→산다더니/사냐더니, 멀다(far): 멀→머냐더니

존은 메리와 같이 피자를 먹**는다더니** 혼자 다 먹어 버렸다.

(=John said that he was going to share the pizza with Mary, but he already ate it all.)

존은 그 일을 자기가 **한다더니** 갑자기 나한테 하라고 한다.

(=John said that he was going to do the work, but suddenly he is asking me to do it.)

존은 자기 여자친구가 예쁘**다더니** 내가 만나보니까 영 아니다.

(=John said his girlfriend is pretty, but she was not pretty at all when I met her.)

메리는 존이 돈을 훔**쳤다더니** 지금은 모른다고 한다.

(=Mary said that John stole the money, but now she is saying that she doesn't know about it.)

정부는 법인세를 올리**겠다더니** 결국 포기하고 말았다.

(=The government said that it would raise the corporate tax rate, but it gave up the plan in the end.)

존은 나한테 왜 한국말을 공부하**냐더니** 자기도 지금 한국말을 배우고 있다.

(=John asked me why I was studying Korean, but now he is studying Korean, too.)

메리는 나한테 왜 다른 여자를 만**났냐더니** 자기도 지금 다른 남자를 만나고 있다.

(=Mary asked me why I was dating another girl, but now she is also dating another guy.)

메리는 나한테 아이를 그렇게 키워 뭐 하**겠냐더니** 자기도 똑 같이 하고 있다.

(=Mary asked me why I was raising my kid like that, but she is doing exactly the same thing.)

존은 메리한테서 돈을 받**으라더니** 이미 자기가 받아 써 버렸다.

(=John asked me to get the money from Mary, but he had already gotten the money from Mary and spent it.)

존은 나한테 그 일을 하**라더니** 지금은 메리한테 하라고 한다.

(=John asked me to do the work, but now he is asking Mary to do it.)

메리는 한국에 같이 가**자더니** 혼자 가버렸다.

(=Mary suggested to me to go to Korea together, but she went there alone.)

52. Making no difference to a given situation: ~(으)나 마나

Function	Making no difference to a given situation		
Form	~(으)나 마나		
Meaning	Regardless of whether one does something or not		
Distribution	Present	Past	Future
Action Verb Stem · After a consonant	~으나 마나[*]		
Action Verb Stem · After a vowel	~나 마나[*]		
Action Verb Stem · After "ㄹ"	~나 마나[*]		
Stative Verb Stem · After a consonant			
Stative Verb Stem · After a vowel			
Stative Verb Stem · After "ㄹ"			

[*] The preceding verb cannot take its own tense suffix, and its tense is determined by the tense of the main verb.

"~(으)나 마나" can be used to express that the situation in the following clause applies regardless of whether one carries out the action in the preceding clause or not, which can be rendered as "Regardless of whether one does something or not."

이 약은 먹<u>으나 마나</u> 아무런 효과가 없습니다.

(=This medicine has no effect at all regardless of whether you take it or not.)

보<u>나 마나</u> 뻔하죠.

(=It is so obvious regardless of whether I take a look at it or not.)

하<u>나 마나</u> 마찬가지일 겁니다.

(=It will be all the same regardless of whether you do it or not.)

물어 보<u>나 마나</u> 대답을 안 해 줄 거예요.

(=He/she will not give you the answer regardless of whether you ask him/her about it or not.)

53. Expressing "Even by taking the less preferred option":
~고(서)라도, ~아서/어서라도

Function	Even by taking the less preferred option		
Form	~고(서)라도	~아서/어서라도	
Meaning	Even by doing so	Even by doing so as a last resort	
Distribution	Present	Past	Future
Action Verb Stem — After "오" or "아"	~고(서)라도[*] ~아서라도[*]		
Action Verb Stem — Otherwise	~고(서)라도[*] ~어서라도[*]		
Stative Verb Stem — After "오" or "아"			
Stative Verb Stem — Otherwise			

[*] The preceding verb cannot take its own tense suffix, and its tense is determined by the tense of the main verb.

"~고서라도" and its contraction form "~고라도" can be used to express that the action in the preceding clause is not the preferred option, but it needs to be taken anyway to carry out the action in the following clause, which can be rendered as "Even by doing so."

그 사람들에게 돈을 더 주**고(서)라도** 빨리 그 작업을 끝내야겠다.

(=I need to get the job done quickly even by paying more money to them.)

수면제를 먹**고(서)라도** 잠을 좀 자야겠다.

(=I need to get some sleep even by taking sleeping pills.)

On the other hand, "~아서/어서라도" can be used to express that the action in the preceding clause is the least preferred option, but it needs to be taken anyway as a last resort to carry out the action in the following clause, which can be rendered as "Even by doing so as a last resort."

목숨을 바**쳐서라도** 이번 작전을 성공시켜야 합니다.

(=We must successfully carry out this operation even by sacrificing our lives as a last resort.)

집을 팔**아서라도** 유학을 보내 줄 게.

(=I will send you to study abroad even by selling my house as a last resort.)

선제공격을 **해서라도** 북한의 핵무기를 파괴해야 한다.

(=We must destroy North Korea's nuclear weapons even by taking a preemptive strike as a last resort.)

54. Expressing one's simple response to a given situation: ~기에, ~길래

"~기에, ~길래" can be used to express that the situation in the following clause is one's simple response to a given situation in the preceding clause, which can be rendered as "Just because _." "~기에" can be freely used in both written text and conversation, whereas "~길래" is more likely to be used in conversation.

존이 나한테 물어보**기에**/물어보**길래** 나는 그것에 대해서 아무 것도 모른다고 했다.

(=Just because John asked me about it, I told him that I don't know anything about it.)

그 남자가 아는 척을 하**기에**/하**길래** 그냥 인사만 했다.

(=Just because the man pretended to know me, I just said hello to him.)

Function	Expressing one's simple response to a given situation		
Form	~기에		~길래
Meaning	Just because _		
Distribution	Present	Past	Future
Action Verb Stem — After a consonant	~기에 ~길래	~았/었기에[*] ~았/었길래[*]	~겠기에 ~겠길래
Action Verb Stem — After a vowel	~기에 ~길래	~았/었기에[*] ~았/었길래[*]	~겠기에 ~겠길래
Action Verb Stem — After "ㄹ"	~기에 ~길래	~았/었기에[*] ~았/었길래[*]	~겠기에 ~겠길래
Stative Verb Stem — After a consonant	~기에 ~길래	~았/었기에[*] ~았/었길래[*]	~겠기에 ~겠길래
Stative Verb Stem — After a vowel	~기에 ~길래	~았/었기에[*] ~았/었길래[*]	~겠기에 ~겠길래
Stative Verb Stem — After "ㄹ"	~기에 ~길래	~았/었기에[*] ~았/었길래[*]	~겠기에 ~겠길래

[*] The preceding verb can take its own tense suffix or its tense can be determined by the tense of the main verb.

날씨가 하도 덥**기에**/덥**길래** 바닷가에 놀러 갔다.

(=Just because the weather was so hot, we went out to the beach.)

값이 하도 싸**기에**/싸**길래** 두 개를 샀다.

(=Just because the price was so cheap, I bought two of them.)

존이 돈이 하나도 없**기에**/없**길래** 메리가 좀 빌려줬다.

(=Just because John did not have any money at all, Mary lent him some money.)

With regard to the tense rule, the preceding verb can take its own tense suffix, which is independent of the tense of the main verb.

옆집에 누가 이사 **왔기에**/이사 **왔길래** 인사를 하러 갔다.

(=Just because someone moved in next door, I went there to say hello to him/her.)

메리가 젊었을 때 하도 예**뻤기에**/예**뻤길래** 영화배우였냐고 물어봤다.

(=Just because Mary was so pretty when she was young, I asked her whether she was a movie star.)

혼자 있으면 심심하**겠기에**/심심하**겠길래** 메리한테 우리집에 놀러오라고 했다.

(=Just because I must be getting bored if I am alone, I asked Mary to come over to my house.)

55. Expressing one's simple response to a given situation:
~(는/ㄴ)다/냐/(으)라/자기에/길래

Function	Expressing one's simple response to a given situation		
Form	~(는/ㄴ)다/냐/(으)라/자기에/길래		
Meaning	Just because one said/asked/suggested that _		

Distribution			Present	Past	Future
Action Verb Stem	Statement	After a consonant	~는다기에 ~는다길래	~았/었다기에 ~았/었다길래	~겠다기에 ~겠다길래
		After a vowel	~ㄴ다기에 ~ㄴ다길래	~았/었다기에 ~았/었다길래	~겠다기에 ~겠다길래
		After "ㄹ"	~ㄴ다기에* ~ㄴ다길래*	~았/었다기에 ~았/었다길래	~겠다기에 ~겠다길래
	Question	Regardless of the ending	~냐기에* ~냐길래*	~았/었냐기에 ~았/었냐길래	~겠냐기에 ~겠냐길래
	Imperative	After a consonant	~으라기에 ~으라길래		
		After a vowel or "ㄹ"	~라기에 ~라길래		
	Proposition	Regardless of the ending	~자기에 ~자길래		
Stative Verb Stem	Statement	Regardless of the ending	~다기에 ~다길래	~았/었다기에 ~았/었다길래	~겠다기에 ~겠다길래
	Question	Regardless of the ending	~냐기에* ~냐길래*	~았/었냐기에 ~았/었냐길래	~겠냐기에 ~겠냐길래

* If the verb stem ends with "ㄹ," "ㄹ" will be dropped before we attach "~ㄴ다기에/길래, ~냐기에/길래" according to the rule of "ㄹ" deletion that says "the consonant "ㄹ" at the end of a verb stem is dropped before "ㄴ, ㅂ, ㅅ." (See Chapter 12 Verbs)
살다 (to live): 살→산다기에/산다길래, 사냐기에/사냐길래, 멀다(far): 멀→머냐기에/머냐길래

"~(는/ㄴ)다/냐/(으)라/자기에, ~(는/ㄴ)다/냐/(으)라/자길래" are actually the combination of the citation endings and "~기에, ~길래 (Just because _)." They can be used to express that the situation in the following clause is one's simple response to the given situation in the preceding clause, which can be rendered as "Just because one said/asked/suggested that _."

존이 약속시간에 좀 **늦는다기에**/**늦는다길래** 괜찮다고 했어요.
(=Just because John said that he was going to be late for the appointment, I told him it's ok.)

메리가 그 일을 **한다기에**/**한다길래** 하라고 했어요.
(=Just because Mary said she wanted to do the work, I let her do it.)

존이 메리의 집이 아주 **좋다기에**/**좋다길래** 한 번 보러 갔다.
(=Just because John said Mary's house is so nice, I went to see her house.)

존이 옆 집에 사람이 이사 **왔다기에**/이사 **왔다길래** 인사를 하러 갔다.
(=Just because John said my next-door neighbor moved in, I went there to say hello to them.)

메리가 나중에 저녁을 **먹겠다기에**/**먹겠다길래** 알아서 하라고 했어요.
(=Just because Mary said she was going to eat dinner later, I told her it's up to her.)

존이 나한테 왜 일을 그렇게 하**냐기에**/하**냐길래** 상관하지 말라고 했다.
(=Just because John asked me why I was doing things like that, I told him it's none of his business.)

메리가 나한테 한국에 왜 **왔냐기에**/**왔냐길래** 공부하러 왔다고 했다.
(=Just because Mary asked me why I came to Korea, I told her I came here to study.)

존이 나한테 그 프로젝트를 맡**겠냐기에**/맡**겠냐길래** 시간이 없다고 했어요.
(=Just because John asked me to take charge of the project, I told him I have no time to do it.)

메리가 존을 믿**으라기에**/믿**으라길래** 주식에 투자했더니 모두 날려버렸다.
(=Just because Mary asked me to trust John, I invested my money in stocks, but I lost it all.)

제 상사가 저보고 집에 **가라기에**/**가라길래** 아무말하지 않고 집에 갔습니다.
(=Just because my supervisor asked me to go home, I went home without saying a word.)

메리가 영화를 같이 보**자기에**/**보자길래** 싫다고 했다.

(=Just because Mary suggested to me to watch a movie together, I told her I don't want to.)

56. Expressing the speaker's own assessment of a given situation: ~기(가)

Function		Expressing the speaker's own assessment of a given situation		
Form		~기(가)		
Meaning		I think that it is _		
Distribution		Present	Past	Future
Action Verb Stem	After a consonant	~기(가)*		
	After a vowel	~기(가)*		
	After "ㄹ"	~기(가)*		
Stative Verb Stem	After a consonant	~기(가)*		
	After a vowel	~기(가)*		
	After "ㄹ"	~기(가)*		

* The preceding verb cannot take its own tense suffix, and its tense is determined by the tense of the main verb.

"~기(가)" can be used to express that the speaker is making his/her own assessment of a given situation as in the preceding clause and reaches his/her conclusion in the following clause, which can be rendered as "I think that it is _."

이 문제는 너무 복잡해서 풀**기(가)** 힘들다.

(=I think that it is difficult to solve the problem because it is too complicated.)

이 일은 시간이 많이 걸리기 때문에 내일까지 끝내**기(가)** 불가능하다.

(=I think that it is impossible to finish the work by tomorrow because it takes so much time to do it.)

존은 성격이 급하**기(가)** 이루 말할 수 없다.

(=I think that it is hard to describe how short tempered John is.)
(=John is extremely short tempered.)

With regard to the tense rule, the tense of the preceding verb can be determined by the tense of the main verb.

그 지역은 너무 위험해서 밤에 돌아다니**기(가)** 아주 무서웠다.

(=I thought it was too scary to walk around the area at night because it was so dangerous.)

그 지역은 너무 위험해서 밤에 돌아다<u>녔</u><u>기</u>(가) 아주 무서<u>웠</u>다. (NOT OK)

57. Expressing a worry about facing an unwanted situation: ~(으)ㄹ세라

Function		Expressing a worry about facing an unwanted situation		
Form		~(으)ㄹ세라		
Meaning		Because one is worried that _		
Distribution		Present	Past	Future
Action Verb Stem	After a consonant			~을세라
	After a vowel			~ㄹ세라
	After "ㄹ"			~세라
Stative Verb Stem	After a consonant			
	After a vowel			
	After "ㄹ"			

"~(으)ㄹ세라" can be used to express that the action in the following clause is being carried out because one is worried about the possibility of facing the unwanted situation in the preceding clause, which can be rendered as "because one is worried that _." It is frequently used with the optional adverb "혹시 (probably/possibly)." It is now on the verge of becoming an archaic expression in favor of the more commonly used expression "~(으)ㄹ까 봐(서) (because one is worried that _)."

존은 (혹시) 누가 자기 초코렛을 뺏어 먹<u>을세라</u>/뺏어 먹<u>을까 봐(서)</u> 몰래 감춰놓고 먹고 있다.

(=John is eating his chocolate after hiding it because he is worried that others might steal it.)

존은 (혹시) 평생 한 번 있을까 말까한 기회를 <u>놓칠세라</u>/<u>놓칠까 봐(서)</u> 즉각 행동에 나섰다.

(=John took action immediately because he is worried that he might lose his once-in-a-lifetime opportunity.)

교도관들은 (혹시) 죄수들이 탈옥**할세라**/탈옥**할까 봐(서)** 모든 신경을 곤두세우고 있다.
(=The prison guards are paying all their attention to the prisoners because they are worried that prisoners might escape from the prison.)

58. Expressing the undesirable condition for achieving one's goal:
~아/어서는, ~아/어서야

Function		Expressing the undesirable condition for achieving one's goal		
Form		~아/어서는		~아/어서야
Meaning		Given that _		
Distribution		Present	Past	Future
Action Verb Stem	After "오" or "아"	~아서는[*] ~아서야[*]		
	Otherwise	~어서는[*] ~어서야[*]		
Stative Verb Stem	After "오" or "아"	~아서는[*] ~아서야[*]		
	Otherwise	~어서는[*] ~어서야[*]		

[*] The preceding verb cannot take its own tense suffix, and its tense is determined by the tense of the main verb.

"~아/어서는" can be used to express that one cannot achieve his/her goal from the undesirable condition in the preceding clause, which can be rendered as "Given that _." The following clause must be a negative statement.

그렇게 공부**해서는** 시험에 합격할 수 없다.

(=Given that you study like that, it is not possible to pass the test.)

그렇게 게을**러서는** 성공할 수 없다.

(=Given that you are lazy like that, it is not possible to become a successful person.)

"~아/어서야" can be used instead if the following clause is a question, more specially a rhetorical question. In this case, the question can be rephrased into its corresponding negative statement with "~아/어서는" like the sentences above.

그렇게 공부**해서야** 시험에 합격할 수 있겠어요?

(=Given that you study like that, is it possible to pass the test?)

그렇게 게을**러서야** 성공할 수 있겠어요?

(=Given that you are lazy like that, is it possible to become a successful person?)

On the other hand, "~아/어서는, ~아/어서야" can be frequently used with the demonstrative verbs "이렇다, 그렇다, 저렇다," which results in "이래서는/이래서야, 그래서는/그래서야, 저래서는/ 저래서야," respectively.

음식 맛이 **이래서는** 손님들에게 내놓을 수 없다.

(=Given that the taste of food is like this, it is not possible to serve it to our customers.)

몸이 **그래서는** 패션모델이 되는 것은 불가능하다.

(=Given that your body shape is like that, it is not possible to become a fashion model.)

가게 주인이 **저래서는** 장사가 안 될 수 밖에 없다.

(=Given that the store owner behaves like that, it is not possible to run his/her business well.)

음식 맛이 **이래서야** 손님들에게 내놓을 수 있겠어요?

(=Given that the taste of food is like this, is it possible to serve it to our customers?)

몸이 **그래서야** 패션모델이 되는 것이 가능하겠어요?

(=Given that your body shape is like that, is it possible to become a fashion model?)

가게 주인이 **저래서야** 장사가 잘 되겠어요?

(=Given that the store owner behaves like that, is it possible to run his/her business well?)

59. Carrying out a necessary action instead of a less desirable one: ~아/어야지

"~아/어야지" can be used to express that the action in the preceding clause must be carried out instead of the undesirable action in the following clause, which can be rendered as "must do something instead of another one." The following clause is typically in negative form.

Function	Carrying out a necessary action instead of a less desirable one		
Form	~아/어야지	~았/었어야지	
Meaning	Must do something instead of another one	Must have done something	
Distribution	Present	Past	Future
Action Verb Stem — After "오" or "아"	~아야지	~았어야지	
Action Verb Stem — Otherwise	~어야지	~었어야지	
Stative Verb Stem — After "오" or "아"			
Stative Verb Stem — Otherwise			

학생이면 공부를 **해야지** 그렇게 시간을 낭비하면 안 된다.

(=If you are a student, you must study instead of wasting time like that.)

한번 시작했으면 끝장을 **봐야지** 도중에 포기하면 안 된다.

(=Once you start, you must see it through to the end instead of giving up in the middle of it.)

무슨 수를 쓰던가 **해야지** 이대로 마냥 기다릴 수만은 없다.

(=I must come up with something instead of just waiting like this without an end.)

Its past tense form "~았/었어야지" can be used to express that the necessary action in the preceding clause was not carried out beforehand, which resulted in the undesirable situation in the following clause. It can be rendered as "must have done something."

나한테 미리 말**했어야지** 갑자기 떠난다고 하면 어떡하니?

(=You must have told me so. What am I supposed to do if you are saying that you are going to leave all of a sudden?)

진작 그렇게 **했어야지** 지금 한들 아무 소용이 없다.

(=You must have done so already. It is of no use to do it now.)

60. Expressing one of the reasons for carrying out an action: ~고 해서

"~고 해서" can be used to express that the situation in the preceding clause is one of the main reasons for carrying out the action in the following clause, which can be rendered as "mainly because."

Function		Expressing one of the reasons for carrying out an action		
Form		~고 해서		
Meaning		Mainly because		
Distribution		Present	Past	Future
Action Verb Stem	After a consonant	~고해서[*]		
	After a vowel	~고해서[*]		
	After "ㄹ"	~고해서[*]		
Stative Verb Stem	After a consonant	~고해서[*]		
	After a vowel	~고해서[*]		
	After "ㄹ"	~고해서[*]		

[*] The preceding verb cannot take its own tense suffix, and its tense is determined by the tense of the main verb.

존이 하도 열심히 일하**고 해서** 봉급을 올려 주었습니다.

(=I gave John a pay raise mainly because he had worked so hard.)

메리가 리더십도 좋**고 해서** 팀장으로 승진시켰습니다.

(=I promoted Mary to become team leader mainly because she has good leadership.)

머리도 아프**고 해서** 집에 있었습니다.

(=I stayed home mainly because I had a headache.)

61. Expressing the main reason for carrying out an action:
~(는/ㄴ)다고/냐고/(으)라고/자고 해서

"~(는/ㄴ)다고/냐고/(으)라고/자고 해서" are the combination of the citation endings and "~고 해서 (mainly because)." They can be used to express that the situation in the preceding clause cited from what another person said/asked/ordered/suggested is the main reason for the situation in the following clause, which can be rendered as "mainly because one said/asked/ordered/suggested _."

직원들이 상사로부터 여러 가지 부당한 대우를 받**는다고 해서** 노조가 나섰습니다.

(The labor union came forward mainly because the employees said they have been receiving various kinds of improper treatment from their supervisors.)

Function	Expressing the main reason for carrying out an action		
Form	~(는/ㄴ)다고/냐고/(으)라고/자고 해서		
Meaning	Mainly because one said/asked/ordered/ suggested _		

Distribution			Present	Past	Future
Action Verb Stem	Statement	After a consonant	~는다고 해서	~았/었다고 해서	~겠다고 해서
		After a vowel	~ㄴ다고 해서	~았/었다고 해서	~겠다고 해서
		After "ㄹ"	~ㄴ다고 해서*	~았/었다고 해서	~겠다고 해서
	Question	Regardless of the ending	~냐고 해서*	~았/었냐고 해서	~겠냐고 해서
	Imperative	After a consonant	~으라고 해서		
		After a vowel or "ㄹ"	~라고 해서		
	Proposition	Regardless of the ending	~자고 해서		
Stative Verb Stem	Statement	Regardless of the ending	~다고 해서	~았/었다고 해서	~겠다고 해서
	Question	Regardless of the ending	~냐고 해서*	~았/었냐고 해서	~겠냐고 해서

* If the verb stem ends with "ㄹ," "ㄹ" will be dropped before we attach "~ㄴ다고 해서, ~냐고 해서" according to the rule of "ㄹ" deletion that says "the consonant "ㄹ" at the end of a verb stem is dropped before "ㄴ, ㅂ, ㅅ." (See Chapter 12 Verbs)
살다 (to live): 살→산다고 해서, 사냐고 해서, 멀다(far): 멀→머냐고 해서

돈을 더 준**다고 해서** 일을 예정보다 빨리 끝냈습니다.
(=I finished the work earlier than scheduled mainly because he/she said he/she will give me more money.)

이 맛집이 아주 유명하**다고 해서** 한 번 와 봤습니다.
(=I just came here mainly because people say that this restaurant is so famous.)

모든 일이 다 수포로 돌아**갔다고 해서** 너무나 실망했습니다.
(=I was very disappointed mainly because he/she said that everything was in vain.)

존이 도와주**겠다고 해서** 그 일을 맡기로 했습니다.
(=I decided to take charge of the work mainly because John said he would help me.)

메리가 어디 가**냐고 해서** 서울에 간다고 말했습니다.
(=I told Mary that I was going to Seoul mainly because she asked me where I was going.)

존이 메리가 어디 **갔냐고 해서** 서울에 갔다고 했습니다.
(=I told John that Mary went to Seoul mainly because he asked me where Mary went.)

메리가 저한테 그 일을 맡**겠냐고 해서** 정중히 거절했습니다.

(=I politely rejected Mary's offer to put me in charge of the job mainly because she asked me to do so.)

과장님이 메리한테서 서류를 받**으라고 해서** 달라고 했습니다.

(=I asked Mary to give me the document mainly because my section chief ordered me to get the document from her.)

팀장님이 여기 **오라고 해서** 왔습니다.

(=I came here mainly because my team leader ordered me to come.)

존이 같이 가**자고 해서** 하와이로 여행을 갔습니다.

(=I took a trip to Hawaii mainly because John suggested to me to go there with him.)

62. Discovering the fact by carrying out an ongoing action:

~고 보면/봐야/봐도

Function	Discovering the fact by carrying out an ongoing action		
Form	~고 보면	~고 봐야	~고 봐도
Meaning	If one is doing something	Only after one is doing something	Even after one have been doing something
Distribution	Present	Present	Present
Action Verb Stem — After a consonant	~고 보면[*]	~고 봐야[*]	~고 봐도[*]
Action Verb Stem — After a vowel	~고 보면[*]	~고 봐야[*]	~고 봐도[*]
Action Verb Stem — After "ㄹ"	~고 보면[*]	~고 봐야[*]	~고 봐도[*]
Stative Verb Stem — After a consonant			
Stative Verb Stem — After a vowel			
Stative Verb Stem — After "ㄹ"			

[*] The preceding verb cannot take its own tense suffix, and its tense is determined by the tense of the main verb.

"~고 보면, ~고 봐야, ~고 봐도" can be used to express that one can discover the situation in the following clause by carrying out the ongoing action in the preceding clause, which can be rendered as "if one is doing something/only after one is doing something/even after one has been doing something," respectively.

존은 알고 **보면** 착한 사람이다.

(=John is a kind-hearted person if you are getting to know him.)

이번 실험의 최종 결과는 두고 **봐야** 알 수 있다.

(=We can find the final result of this experiment only after waiting for a while.)

존은 오랫동안 두고 **봐도** 정말 부지런한 사람이다.

(=John is a very diligent person even after I have been watching him over for a long time.)

63. Discovering the fact at the final stage of an action:

~아/어 보면/봐야/봐도

Function		Discovering the fact at the final stage of an action		
Form		~아/어 보면	~아/어 봐야	~아/어 봐도
Meaning		If one has done something	Only after one has done something	Even after one has done something
Distribution		Present	Present	Present
Action Verb Stem	After "오" or "아"	~아 보면*	~아 봐야*	~아 봐도*
	Otherwise	~어 보면*	~어 봐야*	~어 봐도*
Stative Verb Stem	After "오" or "아"			
	Otherwise			

* The preceding verb cannot take its own tense suffix and its tense is determined by the tense of the main verb.

"~아/어 보면, ~아/어 봐야, ~아/어 봐도" can be used to express that one can discover the situation in the following clause at the final stage of carrying out the action in the preceding clause, which can be rendered as "if one has done something/only after one has done something/even after one has done something," respectively.

문제를 잘 살**펴 보면** 해결책을 찾을 수 있을 겁니다.

(=You can find the solution if you have taken a close look at the problem.)

사람은 같이 일을 **해 봐야** 그 속을 알 수 있다.

(=You can read someone's mind only after you have worked together with the person.)

그동안 지**켜 봐도** 존이 그 일에 적임자일 것 같습니다.

(=It seems that John will be the right person for the job even after I have kept an eye on him.)

64. Expressing "Regardless of the situation":
~(는/ㄴ)다고/냐고/(으)라고/자고 해도

Function	Expressing "Regardless of the situation"		
Form	~(는/ㄴ)다고/냐고/(으)라고/자고 해도		
Meaning	Even though one says/asks/orders/suggests _		
Distribution		Present	Past	Future

			Present	Past	Future
Action Verb Stem	Statement	After a consonant	~는다고 해도	~았/었다고 해도	~겠다고 해도
		After a vowel	~ㄴ다고 해도	~았/었다고 해도	~겠다고 해도
		After "ㄹ"	~ㄴ다고 해도*	~았/었다고 해도	~겠다고 해도
	Question	Regardless of the ending	~냐고 해도*	~았/었냐고 해도	~겠냐고 해도
	Imperative	After a consonant	~으라고 해도		
		After a vowel or "ㄹ"	~라고 해도		
	Proposition	Regardless of the ending	~자고 해도		
Stative Verb Stem	Statement	Regardless of the ending	~다고 해도	~았/었다고 해도	~겠다고 해도
	Question	Regardless of the ending	~냐고 해도*	~았/었냐고 해도	~겠냐고 해도

* If the verb stem ends with "ㄹ," "ㄹ" will be dropped before we attach "~ㄴ다고 해도, ~냐고 해도" according to the rule of "ㄹ" deletion that says "the consonant "ㄹ" at the end of a verb stem is dropped before "ㄴ, ㅂ, ㅅ." (See Chapter 12 Verbs)
살다 (to live): 살→산다고 해도/사냐고 해도, 멀다(far): 멀→머냐고 해도

"~는/ㄴ다고/냐고/(으)라고/자고 해도" are the combination of the citation endings and "~아/어도 (even though)." They can be used to express that the situation in the following clause happens regardless of the situation in the preceding clause, which can be rendered as "even though one says/asks/orders/suggests _."

메리가 고기를 안 먹**는다고 해도** 존이 자꾸 스테이크집에 가자고 한다.
(=Even though Mary says she doesn't eat meat, John repeatedly asks her to go to a steak restaurant.)

지금 출발**한다고 해도** 이미 늦었다.
(=Even though you say you are going to leave now, it is already late.)

존이 똑똑하**다고 해도** 이 문제는 풀 수 없다.
(=Even though they say John is smart, he cannot solve this problem.)

메리는 내가 안 **했다고 해도** 믿지 않는다.
(=Even though I said I didn't do it, Mary doesn't believe me.)

메리가 존과 결혼하**겠다고 해도** 부모님이 허락하지 않으셨다.
(=Even though Mary said she wants to marry John, her parents did not allow her to marry him.)

존은 왜 공부를 안 하**냐고 해도** 들은 척도 하지 않는다.
(=Even though I asked John why he doesn't study, he pretends that he didn't hear anything.)

메리는 왜 존과 헤어**졌냐고 해도** 아무 말도 하지 않았다.
(=Even though I asked Mary why she broke up with John, she didn't say anything.)

존한테 언제 이 프로젝트를 끝낼 수 있**겠냐고 해도** 잘 모른다고 했다.
(=Even though I asked John when he could finish this project, he said he didn't know.)

메리한테 돈을 갚**으라고 해도** 아무 반응이 없다.
(=Even though I asked Mary to pay the money back to me, she doesn't respond to me.)

존은 자**라고 해도** 계속 게임만 한다.
(=Even though I asked John to go to bed, he continues to play the game.)

메리는 같이 여행을 가**자고 해도** 항상 바쁘다고 한다.
(=Even though I suggested to Mary to take a trip together with me, she always says she is busy.)

65. Expressing "Not a game changer": ~(으)ㄴ들

Function		Expressing "Not a game changer"		
Form		~(으)ㄴ들		
Meaning		No matter wh-words (how/what/where, etc)		
Distribution		Present	Past	Future
Action Verb Stem	After a consonant		~은들	
	After a vowel		~ㄴ들	
	After "ㄹ"		~ㄴ들	
Stative Verb Stem	After a consonant	~은들		
	After a vowel	~ㄴ들		
	After "ㄹ"	~ㄴ들		

"~(으)ㄴ들" can be used to express that the situation in the following clause applies anyway regardless of the situation in the preceding clause, which can be rendered as "No matter wh-words."

범인이 어디 **숨은들** 이제 독 안에 든 쥐입니다.

(=Now the suspect is like a rat in a trap no matter where he/she is hiding.)

이제 와서 **후회한들** 무슨 소용이 있어요?

(=There is no point no matter how much you regret it at this moment.)

존은 아무리 얘기**한들** 말을 듣지 않아요.

(=John doesn't listen to me no matter how many times I talked to him.)

다른 사람이 너에게 뭐라고 **한들** 신경 쓰지 마.

(=Don't let it get to you no matter what other people say about you.)

건강을 잃으면 아무리 돈이 **많은들** 다 필요 없습니다.

(=If you lose your health, nothing is good for you no matter how rich you are.)

존이 아무리 똑똑**한들** 이 문제는 풀 수 없다.

(=John cannot solve this problem no matter how smart he is.)

66. Expressing a negative outcome against the speaker's wish: ~았/었던들

Function	Expressing a negative outcome against the speaker's wish		
Form	~았/었던들		
Meaning	If one had V + pp		
Distribution	Present	Past	Future
Action Verb Stem — After "오" or "아"		~았던들	
Action Verb Stem — Otherwise		~었던들	
Stative Verb Stem — After "오" or "아"		~았던들	
Stative Verb Stem — Otherwise		~었던들	

"~았/었던들" can be used to express that the condition in the preceding clause was not met against the speaker's wish, which resulted in the negative outcome in the following clause, which can be rendered as "If one had V + pp." The following clause has the implication that the opposite negative situation actually happened.

한 문제만 더 맞**았던들** 시험에 합격할 수 있었을텐데.
(=If I had had one more correct answer, I might have passed the exam.)

시간이 조금만 더 있**었던들** 그 경기를 이길 수 있었는데.
(=If we had had a little more time, we might have won the game.)

존이 조심해서 운전을 **했던들** 이런 사고는 안 일어났을 거야.
(=If John had driven his car more carefully, this kind of accident might not have occurred.)

부모님이 살아계**셨던들** 그렇게 고생하지는 않았을텐데.
(=If my parents had been alive, I might not have suffered from such hardships.)

메리가 조금만 더 조심**했던들** 그런 사고는 일어나지 않았을 거다.
(=If Mary had been a little more careful, that kind of accident might not have happened.)

67. Getting the unintended outcome of an action: ~는/ㄴ다는 것이 (그만)

Function		Getting the unintended outcome of an action		
Form		~는/ㄴ다는 것이 (그만)		
Meaning		Was going to do something, but _ ended up -ing		
Distribution		Present	Past	Future
Action Verb Stem	After a consonant	~는다는 것이 (그만)		
	After a vowel	~ㄴ다는 것이 (그만)		
	After "ㄹ"	~ㄴ다는 것이 (그만)*		
Stative Verb Stem	After a consonant			
	After a vowel			
	After "ㄹ"			

* The preceding verb cannot take its own tense suffix, and its tense is determined by the tense of the main verb.

"~는/ㄴ다는 것이 (그만)" can be used to express that the situation in the following clause accidently happened because the intended action in the preceding clause was not appropriately carried out, which can be rendered as "was going to do something, but _ ended up -ing."

커피에 설탕을 넣**는다는 것이 (그만)** 소금을 넣어 버렸네요.

(=I was going to put some sugar in the coffee, but I ended up putting salt in it.)

뉴욕에 소포를 보**낸다는 것이 (그만)** 시카고로 보내고 말았어요.

(=I was going to send the package to New York, but I ended up sending it to Chicago.)

도와 드**린다는 것이 (그만)** 방해만 되었네요.

(=I was going to help you, but I ended up only disturbing you.)

"그만 (in the end)" can be sometimes replaced with another optional adverb "도리어 (on the contrary)" in the case that the resulting situation in the following clause is directly opposite to one's intention in the preceding clause.

도와 드**린다는 것이 (도리어)** 방해만 되었네요.

(=I was going to help you, but on the contrary it only disturbed you.)

경제 활성화를 위**한다는 것이** (도리어) 경제불황을 일으켰어요.

(=It was going to stimulate our economy, but on the contrary it brought economic recession.)

68. Supposing that something is taken for granted:

~는/(으)ㄴ셈 치고, ~는/ㄴ다고 치고

Function		Supposing that something is taken for granted					
Form		~는/(으)ㄴ셈 치고			~는/ㄴ다고 치고		
Meaning		Supposing that _					
Distribution		Present	Past	Future	Present	Past	Future
Action Verb Stem	After a consonant	~는 셈 치고	~은 셈 치고		~는다고 치고	~았/었다고 치고	
	After a vowel	~는 셈 치고	~ㄴ 셈 치고		~ㄴ다고 치고	~았/었다고 치고	
	After "ㄹ"	~는 셈 치고*	~ㄴ 셈 치고*		~ㄴ다고 치고*	~았/었다고 치고	
Stative Verb Stem	After a consonant						
	After a vowel						
	After "ㄹ"						

* If the verb stem ends with "ㄹ," "ㄹ" will be dropped before we attach "~는 셈 치고, ~ ㄴ 셈 치고, ~ㄴ다고 치고" according to the rule of "ㄹ" deletion that says "the consonant "ㄹ" at the end of a verb stem is dropped before "ㄴ, ㅂ, ㅅ." (See Chapter 12 Verbs)
팔다 (to sell): 팔→파는 셈 치고/판 셈 치고, 판다고 치고

"~는/(으)ㄴ 셈 치고, ~는/ㄴ다고 치고" can be used to express that the situation in the following clause happens by supposing that the situation in the preceding clause is taken for granted, which can be rendered as "supposing that _."

속는 셈치고/속는다고 치고 이번 한 번만 봐 주세요.

(=Supposing that you give me the benefit of the doubt, let me off the hook just this once please.)

불쌍한 사람 도와주**는 셈 치고/도와준다고 치고** 이번 한 번만 용서해 주겠다.

(=Supposing that I am helping the person in need, I will forgive you just this once.)

지금까지 빚은 갚은 셈 치고/갚았다고 치고 이 돈은 제 날짜에 갚도록 해라.

(=Supposing that I waived your previous debt, you must pay this money back to me in time.)

이번에는 실수한 셈 치고/실수했다고 치고 앞으로는 잘해라.

(=Supposing that it was a mistake this time, you must do well from now on.)

69. Describing a given situation more appropriately:
~(는/ㄴ)다(라)기 보다(는)

Function	Describing a given situation more appropriately		
Form	~(는/ㄴ)다(라)기 보다(는)		
Meaning	Rather than saying _		
Distribution		Present	Past	Future

	Distribution	Present	Past	Future
Action Verb Stem	After a consonant	~는다라기 보다(는) ~는다기 보다(는)	~았/었다라기 보다(는) ~았/었다기 보다(는)	
	After a vowel	~ㄴ다라기 보다(는) ~ㄴ다기 보다(는)	~았/었다라기 보다(는) ~았/었다기 보다(는)	
	After "ㄹ"	~ㄴ다라기 보다(는) ~ㄴ다기 보다(는)	~았/었다라기 보다(는) ~았/었다기 보다(는)	
Stative Verb Stem	After a consonant	~다라기 보다(는) ~다기 보다(는)	~았/었다라기 보다(는) ~았/었다기 보다(는)	
	After a vowel	~다라기 보다(는) ~다기 보다(는)	~았/었다라기 보다(는) ~았/었다기 보다(는)	
	After "ㄹ"	~다라기 보다(는) ~다기 보다(는)	~았/었다라기 보다(는) ~았/었다기 보다(는)	

"~(는/ㄴ)다라기 보다는" and its contraction forms "~(는/ㄴ)다라기 보다, ~(는/ㄴ)다기 보다는, ~(는/ㄴ)다기 보다" can be used to express that the description of a given situation in the following clause is more appropriate than the one in the preceding clause, which can be rendered as "rather than saying _."

존은 살기 위해 먹는다라기 보다는/먹는다라기 보다 /먹는다기 보다는/먹는다기 보다 먹기 위해 사는 것 같다.

(=John seems to be living to eat rather than saying he is eating to live.)

등산을 좋아**한다라기 보다는**/좋아**한다라기 보다**/좋아**한다기 보다는**/좋아**한다기 보다** 건강을 위해서 등산을 합니다.

(=I go hiking for my health rather than saying I like hiking.)

메리는 예쁘**다라기 보다는**/예쁘**다라기 보다**/예쁘**다기 보다는**/예쁘**다기 보다** 귀여운 편이죠.

(=Mary is kind of cute rather than saying she is pretty.)

존은 열심히 공부**했다라기 보다는**/공부**했다라기 보다**/공부**했다기 보다는**/공부**했다기 보다** 운이 좋아서 시험에 합격했다.

(=John was lucky to pass the test rather than we can say that he studied hard for it.)

If the verb is the copula "이다," "~라기 보다(는)" is used instead.

이건 문제의 해결책**이라기 보다는**/해결책**이라기 보다** 상황만 더 악화시킬 뿐이다.

(=This will only aggravate the situation rather than saying it is the solution for the problem.)

메리는 천재**라기 보다는**/천재**라기 보다** 열심히 노력하는 편입니다.

(=Mary is kind of a hard worker rather than saying she is a genius.)

70. Acknowledging the truth value of multiple statements:
~(으)려니와, ~거니와, ~기도 하려니와

"~(으)려니와, ~거니와, ~기도 하려니와" can be used to express that the situation in the following clause holds true on top of the situation in the preceding clause, which can be rendered as "on top of that." They are generally interchangeable, but differ only in terms of the degree of conclusiveness.

~(으)려니와	〉	~거니와	〉	~기도 하려니와
More conclusive				Less conclusive

이 돈이면 빚을 충분히 갚**으려니와**/갚**거니와**/갚**기도 하려니와** 집도 살 수 있다.

(=This money is good enough to pay off your debt, and on top of that you can also buy a house.)

Function		Acknowledging the truth value of multiple statements					
Form		~(으)려니와		~거니와		~기도 하려니와	
Meaning		On top of that					
Distribution		Present	Past	Present	Past	Present	Past
Action Verb Stem	After a consonant	~으려니와	~았/었으려니와	~거니와	~았/었거니와	~기도 하려니와	~았/었기도 하려니와
	After a vowel	~려니와	~았/었으려니와	~거니와	~았/었거니와	~기도 하려니와	~았/었기도 하려니와
	After "ㄹ"	~려니와	~았/었으려니와	~거니와	~았/었거니와	~기도 하려니와	~았/었기도 하려니와
Stative Verb Stem	After a consonant	~으려니와	~았/었으려니와	~거니와	~았/었거니와	~기도 하려니와	~았/었기도 하려니와
	After a vowel	~려니와	~았/었으려니와	~거니와	~았/었거니와	~기도 하려니와	~았/었기도 하려니와
	After "ㄹ"	~려니와	~았/었으려니와	~거니와	~았/었거니와	~기도 하려니와	~았/었기도 하려니와

그 사람을 만난 적도 없**으려니와**/없**거니와**/없**기도 하려니와** 얼굴조차도 모른다.

(=I haven't met the person, and on top of that I don't know his face either.)

지금은 날씨도 몹시 더우**려니와**/덥**거니와**/덥**기도 하려니와** 비가 와서 공사를 계속 할 수 없다.

(=We cannot continue the construction now because the weather is so hot, and on top of that it's raining)

배도 고프**려니와**/고프**거니와**/고프**기도 하려니와** 피곤해서 더 이상은 일을 못하겠어요.

(=I cannot work anymore because I am hungry, and on top of that I am so tired.)

그 때는 돈도 없**었으려니와**/없**었거니와**/없**었기도 하려니와** 값이 너무 비싸서 집을 살 수 없었다.

(=At that time, I could not buy a house because I had no money, and on top of that home prices were so expensive.)

71. Expressing the speaker's response to one's change of mind over a done deal: ~(으)면 그만이지

Function		Expressing the speaker's response to one's change of mind over a done deal		
Form		~(으)면 그만이지		
Meaning		Once _, that's it		
Distribution		Present	Past	Future
Action Verb Stem	After a consonant	~으면 그만이지	~았/었으면 그만이지	
	After a vowel	~면 그만이지	~았/었으면 그만이지	
	After "ㄹ"	~면 그만이지	~았/었으면 그만이지	
Stative Verb Stem	After a consonant	~으면 그만이지	~았/었으면 그만이지	
	After a vowel	~면 그만이지	~았/었으면 그만이지	
	After "ㄹ"	~면 그만이지	~았/었으면 그만이지	

"~(으)면 그만이지" can be used to express that the situation in the following clause is the speaker's negative reaction to one's change of mind over the done deal in the preceding clause, which can be rendered as "Once _, that's it."

소설책은 한번 읽<u>으면 그만이지</u> 다시 볼 필요가 없습니다.
(=Once you read a novel, that's it. You don't need to read it again.)

한 번 주<u>면 그만이지</u> 왜 다시 달라고 합니까?
(=Once you gave it to me, that's it. Why are you asking me to give it back to you?)

일단 계약을 하<u>면 그만이지</u> 이제와서 취소하겠다면 어떻게 합니까?
(=Once you signed the contract, that's it. What am I supposed to do if you say you want to cancel it now?)

자기들만 좋<u>으면 그만이지</u> 그냥 결혼 시키세요.
(=Once they love each other, that's it. Just let them marry each other.)

아이가 똑똑<u>하면 그만이지</u> 뭘 더 바랍니까?
(=Once your child is smart, that's it. What more do you want from him/her?)

The preceding verb can optionally take the past-tense suffix to emphasize the completion of the situation in the preceding clause.

소설책은 한번 읽었**으면 그만이지** 다시 볼 필요가 없습니다.

(=Once you read a novel, that's it. You don't need to read it again.)

한 번 줬**으면 그만이지** 왜 다시 달라고 합니까?

(=Once you gave it to me, that's it. Why are you asking me to give it back to you?)

일단 계약을 했**으면 그만이지** 이제와서 취소하겠다면 어떻게 합니까?

(=Once you signed the contract, that's it. What am I supposed to do if you say you want to cancel it now?)

72. Expressing the speaker's response to one's excessive request/behavior: ~(으)면 됐지

Function		Expressing the speaker's response to one's excessive request/behavior		
Form		~(으)면 됐지		
Meaning		Once _, that's enough of it		
Distribution		Present	Past	Future
Action Verb Stem	After a consonant	~으면 됐지	~았/었으면 됐지	
	After a vowel	~면 됐지	~았/었으면 됐지	
	After "ㄹ"	~면 됐지	~았/었으면 됐지	
Stative Verb Stem	After a consonant	~으면 됐지	~았/었으면 됐지	
	After a vowel	~면 됐지	~았/었으면 됐지	
	After "ㄹ"	~면 됐지	~았/었으면 됐지	

"~(으)면 됐지" can be used to express that the situation in the following clause is the speaker's negative reaction to one's excessive request/behavior that went beyond the situation in the preceding clause, which can be rendered as "Once _, that's enough of it."

돈만 받**으면 됐지** 왜 사람을 그렇게 팹니까?

(=Once you got your money back, that's enough of it. Why are you beating him/her up like that?

이 정도 하**면 됐지** 날보고 어떻게 더 하란 말입니까?

(=Once I have done this much, that's enough of it. How come you ask me to do more?)

한 번 봐 **주면 됐지** 또 봐 달라면 어떻게 합니까?
(=Once I had let it slide, that's enough of it. What am I supposed to do if you ask me to do it again?)

집이 이 정도 넓**으면 됐지** 뭘 더 바랍니까?
(=Once the house is this spacious, that's enough of it. What more do you want from it?)

The preceding verb can optionally take the past-tense suffix to emphasize the completion of the action in the preceding clause.

돈만 받**으면 됐지** 왜 사람을 그렇게 팹니까?
(=Once you got your money back, that's enough of it. Why are you beating him/her up like that?

이 정도 했**으면 됐지** 날보고 어떻게 더 하란 말입니까?
(=Once I have done this much, that's enough of it. How come you ask me to do more?)

한 번 봐 **줬으면 됐지** 또 봐 달라면 어떻게 합니까?
(=Once I had let it slide, that's enough of it. What am I supposed to do if you ask me to do it again?)

73. Expressing "Whatever the situation is": ~(으)나 ~(으)나

"~(으)나 ~(으)나" can be to used to express that the situation in the following clause always happens regardless of the situations in the preceding clause, which can be rendered as "always _ whether one is doing one thing or another." It must be repeated more than once, typically twice, by juxtaposing two or more contrasting situations.

앉**으나** 서**나** 당신 생각뿐이에요.
(=I always think of you whether I am sitting or standing.)

존은 자**나** 깨**나** 술타령만 하네요.
(=John is always drinking alcohol whether he is awake or asleep.)

Function	Expressing "Whatever the situation is"		
Form	~(으)나 ~(으)나		
Meaning	Always _ whether one is doing one thing or another		
Distribution		Present	Past	Future
Action Verb Stem	After a consonant	~으나 ~(으)나[1]		
	After a vowel	~나 ~(으)나[1]		
	After "ㄹ"	~나 ~(으)나[1,2]		
Stative Verb Stem	After a consonant	~으나 ~(으)나[1]		
	After a vowel	~나 ~(으)나[1]		
	After "ㄹ"	~나 ~(으)나[1,2]		

[1] The preceding verb cannot take its own tense suffix, and its tense is determined by the tense of the main verb.

[2] If the verb stem ends with "ㄹ," "ㄹ" will be dropped before we attach "~나 (으)나, ~(으)나 ~나" according to the rule of "ㄹ" deletion that says "the consonant "ㄹ" at the end of a verb stem is dropped before "ㄴ, ㅂ, ㅅ." (See Chapter 12 Verbs)
알다 (to know): 알→아나 모르나, 멀다 (far): 멀→머나 가깝나, 가깝나 머나

즐거우**나** 괴로우**나** 항상 함께 하세요.

(=You should always get together whether you are happy or unhappy.)

어머니는 비가 오**나** 눈이 오**나** 바람이 부**나** 항상 자식 걱정뿐이다.

(=My mother is always worried about her children whether it rains, it snows, or it's windy.)

74. Expressing "Regardless of the situation":

~거나/든(지)/든(가)/건 ~거나/든(지)/든(가)/건 (간에)

"~거나 ~거나 (간에), ~든(지) ~든(지) (간에), ~든(가) ~든(가) (간에), ~건 ~건 (간에)" can be used by juxtaposing two directly contrasting situations to express that the situation in the following clause always applies regardless of the situations in the preceding clauses, which can be rendered as "regardless of whether _ or not." "~거나 ~거나 (간에)" can be freely used in written text and conversation, whereas all others are more likely to be used in conversation.

Function	Expressing "Regardless of the situation"			
Form	~거나 ~거나 (간에)	~든(지) ~든(지) (간에)	~든(가) ~든(가) (간에)	~건 ~건 (간에)
Meaning	Regardless of whether _ or not			
Distribution	Present	Present	Present	Present
Action Verb Stem After a consonant	~거나 ~거나 (간에)*	~든(지) ~든(지) (간에)*	~든(가) ~든(가) (간에)*	~건 ~건 (간에)*
After a vowel	~거나 ~거나 (간에)*	~든(지) ~든(지) (간에)*	~든(가) ~든(가) (간에)*	~건 ~건 (간에)*
After "ㄹ"	~거나 ~거나 (간에)*	~든(지) ~든(지) (간에)*	~든(가) ~든(가) (간에)*	~건 ~건 (간에)*
Stative Verb Stem After a consonant	~거나 ~거나 (간에)*	~든(지) ~든(지) (간에)*	~든(가) ~든(가) (간에)*	~건 ~건 (간에)*
After a vowel	~거나 ~거나 (간에)*	~든(지) ~든(지) (간에)*	~든(가) ~든(가) (간에)*	~건 ~건 (간에)*
After "ㄹ"	~거나 ~거나 (간에)*	~든(지) ~든(지) (간에)*	~든(가) ~든(가) (간에)*	~건 ~건 (간에)*

* The preceding verb cannot take its own tense suffix, and its tense is determined by the tense of the main verb.

비가 **오거나** 안 **오거나 (간에)** 모든 경기는 스케줄대로 진행됩니다.

(=All games will be played as scheduled regardless of whether it will rain or not.)

좋든(지) 싫**든(지) (간에)** 할 일은 해야지요.

(=I must do what I have to do regardless of whether I like it or not.)

시험이 있**건** 없**건 (간에)** 항상 열심해 공부해야 한다.

(=You must always study hard regardless of whether you have a test or not.)

75. Expressing the speaker's readiness to accept a challenging situation: ~(으)ㄹ 테면

Function	Expressing the speaker's readiness to accept a challenging situation		
Form	~(으)ㄹ 테면		
Meaning	If you want to do something, just do it		
Distribution	Present	Past	Future
Action Verb Stem After a consonant			~을 테면
After a vowel			~ㄹ 테면
After "ㄹ"			테면
Stative Verb Stem After a consonant			
After a vowel			
After "ㄹ"			

"~(으)ㄹ 테면" can be used to express that the speaker is ready to accept the challenging situation in the following clause by assuming that the listener wants to carry out the action in the preceding clause, which can be rendered as "If you want to do something, just do it." It is typically used in casual speech.

잡을 **테면** 잡아 봐.

(=If you want to catch me, catch me.)

떠날 **테면** 주저하지 말고 떠나라.

(=If you want to leave, leave without hesitation.)

덤빌 **테면** 덤벼 봐.

(=If you want to fight, go ahead.)

때릴 **테면** 때려 봐.

(=If you want to hit me, go ahead.)

갈 **테면** 가라지 뭐.

(=If he/she wants to go, let him/her go.)

76. Expressing the speaker's strong intention or a strong possibility of a situation: ~(으)ㄹ 테니(까)

Function		Expressing the speaker's strong intention			Expressing a strong possibility of a situation		
Form		~(으)ㄹ 테니(까)					
Meaning		Because I will _			Because _ might _		
Distribution		Present	Past	Future	Present	Past	Future
Action Verb Stem	After a consonant			~을 테니까			~을 테니까
	After a vowel			~ㄹ 테니까			~ㄹ 테니까
	After "ㄹ"			테니까			테니까
Stative Verb Stem	After a consonant						~을 테니까
	After a vowel						~ㄹ 테니까
	After "ㄹ"						테니까

"~(으)ㄹ 테니(까)" carries two different functions depending on the subject of the preceding clause. It can be used with the first person subject to express that the speaker asks the listener to carry out the action in the following clause because the speaker has the strong intention to carry out the action in the preceding clause, which can be rendered as "because I will _."

저는 나중에 먹**을 테니(까)** 먼저 드세요.

(=Because I will eat later, please help yourself first.)

제가 대신 **할 테니(까)** 좀 쉬세요.

(=Because I will do it instead of you, please get some rest.)

제가 한 번 이야기 해 **볼 테니(까)** 걱정하지 마세요.

(=Because I will try to talk to him/her about it, don't worry.)

On the other hand, if the subject of the preceding clause is not in the first person, "~(으)ㄹ 테니(까)" can be used to express that the speaker asks the listener to carry out the action in the following clause because there is a strong possibility of the situation in the preceding clause, which can be rendered as "Because _ might _."

아드님이 상을 받**을 테니(까)** 시상식에 참석하세요.

(=Because your son might/will receive an award, please attend the awards ceremony.)

지금은 길이 많이 막힐 **테니(까)** 내일 떠나세요.

(=Because the traffic might be bumper to bumper now, why don't you leave tomorrow?)

피곤하**실 테니(까)** 어서 주무세요.

(=Please get some sleep because you might be tired.)

77. Expressing the speaker's strong suggestion for a better option: ~(으)ㄹ 것이/게 아니라

Function	Expressing the speaker's strong suggestion for a better option		
Form	~(으)ㄹ 것이/게 아니라		
Meaning	Be not supposed to _, but rather _		
Distribution		Present	Past	Future
Action Verb Stem	After a consonant			~을 것이 아니라 ~을 게 아니라
	After a vowel			~ㄹ 것이 아니라 ~ㄹ 게 아니라
	After "ㄹ"			것이 아니라 게 아니라
Stative Verb Stem	After a consonant			
	After a vowel			
	After "ㄹ"			

"~(으)ㄹ 것이 아니라" and its contraction form "~(으)ㄹ 게 아니라" can be used to express that the speaker strongly suggests that the listener take the better option in the following clause rather than taking the less preferred option in the preceding clause, which can be rendered as "be not supposed to _, but rather _."

지금 이러고 있을 **것이 아니라**/있을 **게 아니라** 나가서 적과 싸워야 한다.

(=We are not supposed to stay here like this, but rather we must go out and fight against the enemy.)

잠자코 있을 **것이 아니라**/있을 **게 아니라** 뭔가 해야 한다.

(=We are not supposed to remain silent, but rather we must do something.)

구경만 **할 것이 아니라**/**할 게 아니라** 빨리 싸움을 말려야 한다.

(=We are not supposed to watch the fight, but rather you should quickly stop it.)

78. Taking advantage of a given situation: ~(는/ㄴ)답시고

Function		Taking advantage of a given situation		
Form		~(는/ㄴ)답시고		
Meaning		By making an excuse that _/By abusing _/By bragging about		
Distribution		Present	Past	Future
Action Verb Stem	After a consonant	~는답시고	~았/었답시고	
	After a vowel	~ㄴ답시고	~았/었답시고	
	After "ㄹ"	~ㄴ답시고*	~았/었답시고	
Stative Verb Stem	After a consonant	~답시고	~았/었답시고	
	After a vowel	~답시고	~았/었답시고	
	After "ㄹ"	~답시고	~았/었답시고	

* If the verb stem ends with "ㄹ," "ㄹ" will be dropped before we attach "~ㄴ답시고" according to the rule of "ㄹ" deletion that says "the consonant "ㄹ" at the end of a verb stem is dropped before "ㄴ, ㅂ, ㅅ." (See Chapter 12 Verbs)
알다 (to know): 알→안답시고

"~(는/ㄴ)답시고" can be used to express that one is to carry out the action in the following clause while taking advantage of the given situation in the preceding clause. Depending on the context, it can be rendered as "by making an excuse that _/by abusing _/by bragging about," etc.

경찰은 범인을 잡**는답시고** 선량한 시민들을 폭행했다.
(=The police violently assaulted innocent citizens by making an excuse that they were catching the suspect.)

존은 힘 좀 **쓴답시고** 다른 학생들을 괴롭힌다.
(=John is picking on other students by abusing his physical strength.)

메리는 얼굴이 예쁘**답시고** 다른 사람들을 무시한다.
(=Mary looks down on others by bragging about her pretty face.)

존은 좀 배**웠답시고** 온갖 잘난 체만 한다.
(=John is so condescending by bragging about his educational background.)

79. Drawing the listener's attention: ~건대, ~옵건대

Function		Drawing the listener's attention					
Form		~건대			~옵건대		
Meaning		As I _					
Distribution		Present	Past	Future	Present	Past	Future
Action Verb Stem	After a consonant	~건대*			~옵건대*		
	After a vowel	~건대*			~옵건대*		
	After "ㄹ"	~건대*			~옵건대*		
Stative Verb Stem	After a consonant						
	After a vowel						
	After "ㄹ"						

* The preceding verb cannot take its own tense suffix, and its tense is determined by the tense of the main verb.

"~건대" can be used to to draw the listener's attention to the situation in the following clause by expressing the speaker's hope, warning, prediction, and so on in the preceding clause, which can be rendered as "As I hope, As I say that again, etc." depending on the context.

바라**건대**, 앞으로 다시는 그러지 마라.

(=As I hope, don't ever do it again from now on.)

다시 말하**건대**, 앞으로 절대 마약에 손대지 마라.

(=As I say that again, don't even think of touching illegal drugs from now on.)

내가 듣**건대**, 너 요즘 뒤에서 나를 욕하고 다닌다며?

(=As far as I heard, you are cussing me out behind my back, aren't you?)

경고하**건대**, 앞으로 내 얘기 다른 사람한테 하고 다니지 마라.

(=As I am warning you, don't talk about me to others.)

내가 보**건대**, 이번 일은 제 시간에 끝내기 어려울 것 같다.

(=As far as I can tell, it might be hard to get this job done on time.)

짐작하**건대**, 북한에서 군사쿠데타가 일어날 것 같다.

(=As I can make a guess, a military coup seems likely to occur in North Korea.)

내가 장담하**건대**, 북한은 가까운 시일 내에 무너질 거다.

(=As I can guarantee, North Korea will collapse in the very near future.)

On the other hand, "~옵건대" which is the super honorific form of "~건대" can be used to express one's wish to a political or religious figure with extremely high status, such as a king or God. Now its usage is generally limited to biblical, historical, or literary text.

신이시여, 바라**옵건대**, 저에게 자비를 베풀어 주시옵소서.

(=May almighty God have mercy on me as I humbly wish.)

전하, 원하**옵건대**, 소인을 굽어 살펴 주시옵소서.

(=My Lord, please forgive this humble servant as I humbly wish.)

80. Expressing an unexpected situation from the speaker's point of view: ~건마는/건만

Function	Expressing an unexpected situation from the speaker's point of view		
Form	~건마는, ~건만		
Meaning	Even though		
Distribution	Present	Past	Future
Action Verb Stem / After a consonant	~건마는 ~건만	~았/었건마는 ~았/었건만	
Action Verb Stem / After a vowel	~건마는 ~건만	~았/었건마는 ~았/었건만	
Action Verb Stem / After "ㄹ"	~건마는 ~건만	~았/었건마는 ~았/었건만	
Stative Verb Stem / After a consonant	~건마는 ~건만	~았/었건마는 ~았/었건만	
Stative Verb Stem / After a vowel	~건마는 ~건만	~았/었건마는 ~았/었건만	
Stative Verb Stem / After "ㄹ"	~건마는 ~건만	~았/었건마는 ~았/었건만	

"~건마는" and its contraction form "~건만" can be used to express that the situation in the following clause cannot be expected from the given condition in the preceding clause according to the speaker's point of view, which can be rendered as "even though."

아직 쓸만하**건마는**/하**건만** 왜 새 걸로 바꾸는 지 모르겠어요.
(=I don't understand why they are replacing this with a new one even though it is still quite usable.)

내가 보기엔 괜찮**건마는**/괜찮**건만** 메리가 존을 왜 싫어하는 지 알다가도 모르겠다.
(=I cannot truly understand why Mary dislikes John even though he looks good to me.)

오랜 시간을 같이 보**냈건마는**/보**냈건만** 그 사람에 대해 아는 것이 별로 없다.
(=I don't know much about him/her even though we have spent time together for a long time.)

최선을 다**했건마는**/다**했건만** 경기에 져서 실망스럽다.
(=I am disappointed because we lost the game even though we did our best.)

존은 나이는 먹을 만큼 먹**었건마는**/먹**었건만** 아직 철이 들지 않았다.
(=John is still not mature even though he is old enough.)

81. Expressing "Not going beyond a given situation": ~기만 할 뿐, ~기만 하지

"~기만 할 뿐, ~기만 하지" can be used to express that one is just to carry out the action in the preceding clause, but will not go beyond that as in the situation in the following clause, which can be rendered as "just doing something, but _." The following clause is typically in negative form. "~기만 할 뿐" can be freely used in boh written text and conversation, whereas "~기만 하지" is more likely to be used in conversation.

존은 그저 웃**기만 할 뿐**/웃**기만 하지** 아무 말도 안 하고 있다.
(=John is just smiling, but he is not saying a word.)
(=John is just smiling without saying a word.)

존은 내가 말하는 것을 듣**기만 할 뿐**/듣**기만 하지** 아무런 변명도 하지 않았다.
(=John was just listening to what I said to him, but he did not make any excuses.)

Function	Expressing "Not going beyond a given situation"			
Form	~기만 할 뿐		~기만 하지	
Meaning	Just doing something, but _			
Distribution	Present	Past	Future	

		Present	Past	Future
Action Verb Stem	After a consonant	~기만 할 뿐 ~기만 하지	~기만 했을 뿐[*] ~기만 했지[*]	
	After a vowel	~기만 할 뿐 ~기만 하지	~기만 했을 뿐[*] ~기만 했지[*]	
	After "ㄹ"	~기만 할 뿐 ~기만 하지	~기만 했을 뿐[*] ~기만 했지[*]	
Stative Verb Stem	After a consonant			
	After a vowel			
	After "ㄹ"			

[*] The preceding verb cannot take its own tense suffix, and the tense is determined by the following verb "하다."

메리는 묻는 말에 대답하**기만 할 뿐**/대답하**기만 하지** 자기 생각이 뭔지 이야기를 안 한다.
(=Mary is just answering the questions that I ask her, but she is not talking about what she is thinking.)

화가 나서 째려 보**기만 했을 뿐**/보**기만 했지** 때리지는 않았다.
(=I just stared at him/her because I got angry, but did not hit him/her.)

메리는 존을 쳐다보**기만 했을 뿐**/쳐다보**기만 했지** 아무 말도 하지 않았습니다.
(=Mary was just looking at John, but she didn't say a word to him.)

나는 조용히 앉아 있**기만 했을 뿐**/있**기만 했지** 아무 짓도 하지 않았다.
(=I was just sitting quietly, but I didn't do anything wrong.)

나는 그저 시키는 대로 하**기만 했을 뿐**/하**기만 했지** 그게 불법이라는 것을 전혀 몰랐다.
(=I just did what I was asked to do, but I absolutely didn't know that it was illegal.)

82. Expressing the acknowledgment of a given situation:

~기는/긴 하지만, ~기야 하지만

"~기는/긴 하지만, ~기야 하지만" can be used to express that the situation in the following clause applies even though the speaker is acknowledging the situation in the preceding clause, which can be rendered as "even though." They are generally interchangeable, but differ slightly in terms of the degree of acknowledgment. For example, "~기는/긴 하지만" indicates the speaker's acknowledgment with some reservation, whereas "~기야 하지만" expresses the speaker's full acknowledgment.

Function		Expressing the acknowledgment of a given situation		
Form		~기는/긴 하지만		~기야 하지만
Meaning		Even though		
Distribution		Present	Past	Future
Action Verb Stem	After a consonant	~기는 하지만 ~긴 하지만 ~기야 하지만	~기는 했지만[*] ~긴 했지만[*] ~기야 했지만[*]	~기는 하겠지만[*] ~긴 하겠지만[*] ~기야 하겠지만[*]
	After a vowel	~기는 하지만 ~긴 하지만 ~기야 하지만	~기는 했지만[*] ~긴 했지만[*] ~기야 했지만[*]	~기는 하겠지만[*] ~긴 하겠지만[*] ~기야 하겠지만[*]
	After "ㄹ"	~기는 하지만 ~긴 하지만 ~기야 하지만	~기는 했지만[*] ~긴 했지만[*] ~기야 했지만[*]	~기는 하겠지만[*] ~긴 하겠지만[*] ~기야 하겠지만[*]
Stative Verb Stem	After a consonant	~기는 하지만 ~긴 하지만 ~기야 하지만	~기는 했지만[*] ~긴 했지만[*] ~기야 했지만[*]	~기는 하겠지만[*] ~긴 하겠지만[*] ~기야 하겠지만[*]
	After a vowel	~기는 하지만 ~긴 하지만 ~기야 하지만	~기는 했지만[*] ~긴 했지만[*] ~기야 했지만[*]	~기는 하겠지만[*] ~긴 하겠지만[*] ~기야 하겠지만[*]
	After "ㄹ"	~기는 하지만 ~긴 하지만 ~기야 하지만	~기는 했지만[*] ~긴 했지만[*] ~기야 했지만[*]	~기는 하겠지만[*] ~긴 하겠지만[*] ~기야 하겠지만[*]

[*] The preceding verb cannot take its own tense suffix, and the tense is determined by the following verb "하다."

메리는 얼굴이 예쁘**기는/긴 하지만** 성질이 있다.

(=Even though Mary has a pretty face, she has a bad temper.)

메리는 얼굴이 예쁘**기야 하지만** 성질이 있다.

(=Even though Mary has a pretty face, she has a bad temper.)

누가 했는지 알**기는/긴 하지만** 말씀 드릴 수가 없습니다.

(=Even though I know who did it, I cannot tell you.)

누가 했는지 알**기야 하지만** 말씀 드릴 수가 없습니다.

(=Even though I really know who did it, I cannot tell you.)

이 TV는 화질이 좋**기는/긴 하지만** 너무 비싸서 살 수가 없네요.

(=Even though the picture quality of this TV is good, I cannot buy it because it's too expensive.)

이 TV는 화질이 **좋기야 하지만** 너무 비싸서 살 수가 없네요.

(=Even though the picture quality of this TV is really good, I cannot buy it because it's too expensive.)

팀장이 시켜서 하**기는/긴 하지만** 이건 아닌 것 같다.

(=Even though I am doing it because my team leader asked me to do it, this doesn't seem right.)

팀장이 시켜서 **하기야 하지만** 이건 아닌 것 같다.

(=Even though I am really doing it because my team leader asked me to do it, this doesn't seem right.)

나름대로 열심히 하**기는/긴 했지만** 시험 결과가 어떻게 나올 지 걱정이 된다.

(=Even though I worked hard to the best of my ability, I am worried about the test result.)

나름대로 열심히 하**기야 했지만** 시험 결과가 어떻게 나올 지 걱정이 된다.

(=Even though I really worked hard to the best of my ability, I am worried about the test result.)

존한테 이야기를 해 보**기는/긴 하겠지만** 내 말을 들을 것 같지가 않다.

(=Even though I will talk to John, he doesn't seem to listen to me.)

존한테 이야기를 해 보**기야 하겠지만** 내 말을 들을 것 같지가 않다.

(=Even though I will really talk to John, he doesn't seem to listen to me.)

On the other hand, the generic verb "하다" in "~기는/긴 하지만, ~기야 하지만" can be sometimes replaced by more specific verbs such as "쉽다 (easy)," "힘들다 (hard)," etc., depending on the context.

말하**기는/긴 쉽지만** 행동으로 옮기기는 어렵습니다.

(=Even though it is easy to say it, it is difficult to actually do it.)

말하**기야** 쉽**지만** 행동으로 옮기기는 어렵습니다.

(=Even though it is really easy to say it, it is difficult to actually do it.)

내일까지 끝내**기는**/**긴** 힘들**지만** 최선을 다 하겠습니다.

(=Even though it is hard to get it done by tomorrow, I will do my best.)

내일까지 끝내**기야** 힘들**지만** 최선을 다 하겠습니다.

(=Even though it is really hard to get it done by tomorrow, I will do my best.)

83. Disapproving of the original expectation: ~기는/긴 커녕

Function	Disapproving of the original expectation		
Form	~기는 커녕, ~긴 커녕		
Meaning	Not _ at all, but _		
Distribution		Present	Past	Future
Action Verb Stem	After a consonant	~기는 커녕[*] ~긴 커녕[*]		
	After a vowel	~기는 커녕[*] ~긴 커녕[*]		
	After "ㄹ"	~기는 커녕[*] ~긴 커녕[*]		
Stative Verb Stem	After a consonant	~기는 커녕[*] ~긴 커녕[*]		
	After a vowel	~기는 커녕[*] ~긴 커녕[*]		
	After "ㄹ"	~기는 커녕[*] ~긴 커녕[*]		

[*] The preceding verb cannot take its own tense suffix, and its tense is determined by the tense of the main verb.

"~기는 커녕" and its contraction form "~긴 커녕" can be used to express that the originally expected outcome in the preceding clause did not come out at all, but instead the unexpected situation in the following clause actually happened, which can be rendered as "not _ at all, but _."

그 약을 먹고 낫**기는/긴 커녕** 오히려 증상이 더 악화되었다.

(=I didn't get any better at all after taking the medicine, but rather the symptoms got worse.)

메리와 데이트하**기는/긴 커녕** 말 한마디조차 못 건네 봤다.

(=I didn't go on a date with Mary at all, but I did not even have a chance to talk to her.)

도박장에서 돈을 따**기는/긴 커녕** 있는 돈까지 몽땅 날려 버렸어요.

(=I did not win any money at all at the casino, but I even lost all the money that I had.)

이 TV는 화질이 좋**기는/긴 커녕** 아주 형편 없다.

(=The picture quality of this TV is not good at all, but it is horrible.)

84. Expressing the condition for an immediate outcome: ~기만 하면

Function		Expressing the condition for an immediate outcome					
Form		~기만 하면					
Meaning		Once			Only if		
Distribution		Present	Past	Future	Present	Past	Future
Action Verb Stem	After a consonant	~기만 하면*			~기만 하면	~기만 했으면	
	After a vowel	~기만 하면*			~기만 하면	~기만 했으면	
	After "ㄹ"	~기만 하면*			~기만 하면	~기만 했으면	
Stative Verb Stem	After a consonant				~기만 하면	~기만 했으면	
	After a vowel				~기만 하면	~기만 했으면	
	After "ㄹ"				~기만 하면	~기만 했으면	

* The preceding verb cannot take its own tense suffix, and its tense is determined by the tense of the main verb.

"~기만 하면" can be used to express that the situation in the following clause immediately follows whenever one carries out the action in the preceding clause, which can be rendered as "once."

존은 입을 열**기만 하면** 항상 거짓말을 한다.

(=Once John opens his mouth, he always tells a lie.)

메리는 나를 보**기만 하면** 화를 낸다.

(=Once Mary sees me, she takes her anger out on me.)

존은 돈을 벌**기만 하면** 다 써버린다.

(=Once John makes money, he uses up all the money.)

이 약은 먹**기만 하면** 병이 금방 나아요.

(=Once you take this medicine, your illness can be cured immediately.)

이 주식에 투자하**기만 하면** 돈을 많이 벌 수 있다.

(=Once you invest your money in this stock, you can make a lot of money.)

공부를 열심히 하**기만 하면** 원하는 대학에 갈 수 있다.

(=Once you study hard, you can enter the good college that you want.)

On the other hand, "~기만 하면" can also be used to express that the situation in the following clause will happen if the condition in the preceding clause is to be met because all other necessary conditions are already met, which can be rendered as "only if."

모든 음식은 적당히 먹**기만 하면** 몸에 좋다.

(=Any kind of food is good for your body only if you eat the adequate amount.)

존이 공부를 열심히 하**기만 하면** 다 좋은데.

(=Everything is good about John only if he studies hard.)

집안이 좀 좋**기만 하면** 괜찮은 신랑감인데.

(=He will make a good bridegroom only if he has a good family background.)

값이 좀 싸**기만 하면** 이 가방을 사고 싶은데.

(=I want to buy this bag only if it is a little cheaper.)

주인이 월급을 올려주**기만 했으면** 거기서 계속 일했을텐데.

(=I could have kept working there only if the owner had given me a pay raise.)

집이 좀 넓**기만 했었으면** 아주 좋았을텐데.

(=It could not have been better only if the house had been a little more spacious.)

85. Enumerating a list of supporting examples: ~기도 하고 ~기도 하고/해서

Function		Enumerating a list of supporting examples	
Form		~기도 하고 ~기도 하고	~기도 하고 ~기도 해서
Meaning		For example, _ not only _ but also _	Because _ not only _ but also _
Distribution		Present	Present
Action Verb Stem	After a consonant	~기도 하고 ~기도 하고*	~기도 하고 ~기도 해서*
	After a vowel	~기도 하고 ~기도 하고*	~기도 하고 ~기도 해서*
	After "ㄹ"	~기도 하고 ~기도 하고*	~기도 하고 ~기도 해서*
Stative Verb Stem	After a consonant	~기도 하고 ~기도 하고*	~기도 하고 ~기도 해서*
	After a vowel	~기도 하고 ~기도 하고*	~기도 하고 ~기도 해서*
	After "ㄹ"	~기도 하고 ~기도 하고*	~기도 하고 ~기도 해서*

*The preceding verb cannot take its own tense suffix, and its tense is determined by the tense of the main verb.

"~기도 하고" can be used to provide a concrete example in the preceding clause to support the situation in the following clause. It is typically repeated twice in a given sentence, which can be rendered as "for example, _ not only _ but also _."

이 약은 씹어서 먹**기도 하고** 물에 타서 마시**기도 하고** 아주 편해요.
(=It is very convenient to take this medicine. For example, you can take it not only by chewing it but also by mixing it with water.)

존은 매일 산책을 하**기도 하고** 헬스클럽에서 운동을 하**기도 하고** 아주 건강해요.
(=John is very healthy. For example, he not only takes a walk every day but also exercises at a health club.)

메리는 얼굴이 예쁘**기도 하고** 친절하**기도 하고** 아주 괜찮은 아이예요.
(=Mary is a very good girl. For example, she is not only pretty but also kind.)

On the other hand, the last occurrence of "~기도 하고" can be optionally replaced with "~기도 해서" to indicate that the preceding examples are the reason for the situation in the following clause, which can be rendered as "because _ not only _ but also _."

이 약은 씹어서 먹**기도 하고** 물에 타서 마시**기도 해서** 아주 편해요.
(=It is very convenient to take this medicine because you can take it not only by chewing it but also by mixing it with water.)

존은 매일 산책을 하**기도 하고** 헬스클럽에서 운동을 하**기도 해서** 아주 건강해요.

(=John is very healthy because he not only takes a walk everyday but also exercises at a health club.)

메리는 얼굴이 예쁘**기도 하고** 친절하**기도 해서** 아주 괜찮은 아이예요.

(=Mary is a very good girl because she is not only pretty but also kind.)

86. Expressing the only exception for a situation:

~(으)면 모르(겠)지만, ~(으)면 몰라도

Function		Expressing the only exception for a situation					
Form		~(으)면 모르(겠)지만			~(으)면 몰라도		
Meaning		Unless					
Distribution		Present	Past	Future	Present	Past	Future
Action Verb Stem	After a consonant	~으면 모르(겠)지만	~았/었으면 모르(겠)지만		~으면 몰라도	~았/었으면 몰라도	
	After a vowel	~면 모르(겠)지만	~았/었으면 모르(겠)지만		~면 몰라도	~았/었으면 몰라도	
	After "ㄹ"	~면 모르(겠)지만	~았/었으면 모르(겠)지만		~면 몰라도	~았/었으면 몰라도	
Stative Verb Stem	After a consonant	~으면 모르(겠)지만	~았/었으면 모르(겠)지만		~으면 몰라도	~았/었으면 몰라도	
	After a vowel	~면 모르(겠)지만	~았/었으면 모르(겠)지만		~면 몰라도	~았/었으면 몰라도	
	After "ㄹ"	~면 모르(겠)지만	~았/었으면 모르(겠)지만		~면 몰라도	~았/었으면 몰라도	

"~(으)면 모르지만" can be used to express that the situation in the following clause holds true unless the situation in the preceding clause happens, which can be rendered as "unless." The probability suffix "~겠" can be optionally attached to the verb stem.

진통제를 먹**으면 모르(겠)지만** 통증이 너무 심하다.

(=Unless I take painkillers, I have severe pain.)

돈을 더 주**면 모르(겠)지만** 아무도 그 일을 하지 않을 거다.

(=Unless you give more money, no one is going to do that.)

대체에너지에 대한 대책이 있**으면 모르(겠)지만** 그냥 원전을 폐쇄하는 것은 올바른 정책이 아니다.

(=Unless we have a countermeasure for alternative energy, it is not the right policy to simply shut down nuclear power plants.)

성능이 아주 좋**으면 모르(겠)지만** 이 차는 값이 터무니 없이 비싸다.

(=Unless it really performs well, the price of this car is ridiculously expensive.)

내가 뭘 잘못**했으면 모르(겠)지만** 왜 나를 이런 취급하는 지 모르겠다.

(=Unless I did something wrong, I cannot understand why he/she treats me like this.)

조기에 발견**했으면 모르(겠)지만** 치료가 불가능하다.

(=Unless you discovered it at the early stage, it is impossible to cure it.)

"~(으)면 몰라도" carries the same function, but it is more likely to be used in conversation, whereas "~(으)면 모르(겠)지만" can be freely used in both written text and conversation.

대체에너지에 대한 대책이 있**으면 몰라도** 그냥 원전을 폐쇄하는 것은 올바른 정책이 아니다.

(=Unless we have a countermeasure for alternative energy, it is not the right policy to simply shut down nuclear power plants.)

돈을 더 주**면 몰라도** 아무도 그 일을 하지 않을 거다.

(=Unless you give more money, no one is going to do that.)

성능이 아주 좋**으면 몰라도** 이 차는 값이 터무니 없이 비싸다.

(=Unless it really performs well, the price of this car is ridiculously expensive.)

내가 뭘 잘못**했으면 몰라도** 왜 나를 이런 취급하는 지 모르겠다.

(=Unless I did something wrong, I cannot understand why he/she treats me like this.)

87. Expressing the only exception:

~(는/ㄴ)다면/(으)라면/자면 모르(겠)지만/몰라도

Function			Expressing the only exception for a given situation					
Form			~(는/ㄴ)다면/(으)라면/자면 모르(겠)지만			~(는/ㄴ)다면/(으)라면/자면 몰라도		
Meaning			Unless (one says/asks/suggests that _)					
Distribution			Present	Past	Future	Present	Past	Future
Action Verb Stem	Statement	After a consonant	~는다면 모르(겠)지만	~았/었다면 모르(겠)지만	~겠다면 모르(겠)지만	~는다면 몰라도	~았/었다면 몰라도	~겠다면 몰라도
		After a vowel	~ㄴ다면 모르(겠)지만	~았/었다면 모르(겠)지만	~겠다면 모르(겠)지만	~ㄴ다면 몰라도	~았/었다면 몰라도	~겠다면 몰라도
		After "ㄹ"	~ㄴ다면 모르(겠)지만*	~았/었다면 모르(겠)지만	~겠다면 모르(겠)지만	~ㄴ다면 몰라도*	~았/었다면 몰라도	~겠다면 몰라도
	Imperative	After a consonant	~으라면 모르(겠)지만			~으라면 몰라도		
		After a vowel or "ㄹ"	~라면 모르(겠)지만			~라면 몰라도		
	Proposition	Regardless of the ending	~자면 모르(겠)지만			~자면 몰라도		
Stative Verb Stem	Statement	Regardless of the ending	~다면 모르(겠)지만	~았/었다면 모르(겠)지만	~겠다면 모르(겠)지만	~다면 몰라도	~았/었다면 몰라도	~겠다면 몰라도

* If the verb stem ends with "ㄹ," "ㄹ" will be dropped before we attach "~ㄴ다면 모르(겠)지만, ~ㄴ다면 몰라도" according to the rule of "ㄹ" deletion that says "the consonant "ㄹ" at the end of a verb stem is dropped before "ㄴ, ㅂ, ㅅ." (See Chapter 12 Verbs)
팔다 (to sell): 팔→판다면 모르(겠)지만, 판다면 몰라도

"~(는/ㄴ)다면/(으)라면/자면 모르(겠)지만" are the combination of the citation endings for statement, imperative, and proposition with "~(으)면 모르(겠)지만 (unless)." They can be used to express that the situation in the following clause holds true unless the situation in the preceding clause happens, which can be rendered as "Unless one says/asks/suggests that _." "~(는/ㄴ)다면/(으)라면/자면 몰라도" carries more or less the same function.

존이 진통제를 먹**는다면 모르(겠)지만**/먹**는다면 몰라도** 통증이 아주 심한 것 같다.

(=Unless John is taking painkillers, he seems to have severe pains.)

돈을 더 **준다면 모르(겠)지만/준다면 몰라도** 아무도 그 일을 하지 않을 거다.
(=Unless you give more money, no one is going to do that.)

대체에너지에 대한 대책이 **있다면 모르(겠)지만/있다면 몰라도** 그냥 원전을 폐쇄하는 것은 올바른 정책이 아니다.
(=Unless they have a countermeasure for alternative energy, it is not the right policy to simply shut down nuclear power plants.)

성능이 아주 **좋다면 모르(겠)지만/좋다면 몰라도** 이 차는 값이 터무니 없이 비싸다.
(=Unless it really performs well, the price of this car is ridiculously expensive.)

내가 뭘 잘못**했다면 모르(겠)지만/잘못했다면 몰라도** 왜 나를 이런 취급하는 지 모르겠다.
(=Unless I did something wrong, I cannot understand why he/she treats me like this.)

메리가 하**겠다면 모르(겠)지만/하겠다면 몰라도** 강제로 시킬 수는 없다.
(=Unless Mary wants to do it, I cannot force her to do it.)

다른 사람을 믿**으라면 모르(겠)지만/믿으라면 몰라도** 존을 믿으라는 건 말도 안 된다.
(=Unless you ask me to trust other people, it is ridiculous to ask me to trust John.)

내일까지 하**라면 모르(겠)지만/하라면 몰라도** 오늘 끝내기는 불가능하다.
(=Unless you ask me to finish it by tomorrow, it is impossible to get it done by today.)

메리와 같이 가**자면 모르(겠)지만/가자면 몰라도** 저는 안 갈 거예요.
(=Unless you suggest to me to go with Mary, I am not going.)

88. Expressing "From that time on": ~(으)ㄴ 이래(로)

"~(으)ㄴ 이래(로)" can be used to express that the situation in the following clause happens since the important event or the historic moment in the preceding clause occurred, which can be rendered as "Since." It is typically used in written text and formal speech.

IMF 시절 최악의 경제위기를 맞**은 이래(로)** 한국 경제는 눈부시게 발전해 왔다.
(=Since Korea's economy faced the worst economic crisis during the IMF, it has developed remarkably.)

새 대통령이 당선**된 이래(로)** 국가 정책에 여러 가지 변화가 있었다.
(=Since the new president got elected, there have been various kinds of changes on national policies.)

Function	Expressing "From that time on"		
Form	~(으)ㄴ 이래(로)		
Meaning	Since		
Distribution	Present	Past	Future
Action Verb Stem — After a consonant		~은 이래(로)	
Action Verb Stem — After a vowel		~ㄴ 이래(로)	
Action Verb Stem — After "ㄹ"		~ㄴ 이래(로)[*]	
Stative Verb Stem — After a consonant			
Stative Verb Stem — After a vowel			
Stative Verb Stem — After "ㄹ"			

[*] If the verb stem ends with "ㄹ," "ㄹ" will be dropped before we attach "~ㄴ 이래(로)" according to the rule of "ㄹ" deletion that says "the consonant "ㄹ" at the end of a verb stem is dropped before "ㄴ, ㅂ, ㅅ." (See Chapter 12 Verbs)
(ex) 만들다 (to make): 만들→만든 이래(로)

삼성은 지금 회사가 창립**된 이래(로)** 최고의 호황을 누리고 있다.

(=Since the foundation of the company, Samsung is now enjoying the most favorable business condition.)

89. Judging from a common-sense statement: ~거늘 (하물며)

Function	Judging from a common-sense statement		
Form	~거늘 (하물며)		
Meaning	Granted that _ /Granting that_		
Distribution	Present	Past	Future
Action Verb Stem — After "오" or "아"	~거늘 (하물며)	~았거늘 (하물며)	
Action Verb Stem — Otherwise	~거늘 (하물며)	~었거늘 (하물며)	
Stative Verb Stem — After "오" or "아"			
Stative Verb Stem — Otherwise			

"~거늘" can be used to express that the situation in the following clause is the speaker's legimate reaction to the given situation judging from a common-sense statement in the preceding clause, which can be rendered as "Granted that _/Granting that _." It is often used with the optional adverb "하물며 (It is needless to say)." However, it is now on the verge of becoming an archaic expression in favor of the more frequently-used grammar feature "~는/(으)ㄴ데 (Given that)."

누구나 한번 쯤은 실수를 하**거늘**/하**는데** (**하물며**) 왜 나만 갖고 그러는지 모르겠다.
(=Granted that everyone is liable to make mistakes at least once, (it is needless to say that) I don't understand why he/she is just picking on me.)

짚신도 짝이 있**거늘**/있**는데** (**하물며**) 제 신부감이라고 없겠습니까?
(=Granted that every Jack has his Jill, (it is needless to say that) I can find my bride.)
(=Granted that every Jack has his Jill, isn't it possible that I can find my bride?)

짐승도 자기 새끼를 거두**거늘**/거두**는데** (**하물며**) 인간으로서 자기 자식을 죽인다는 것은 말이 안 됩니다.
(=Granted that even animals take care of their own babies, (it is needless to say that) it is ridiculous to kill one's own child if he/she is a human being.)

너만 믿고 모든 일을 **했거늘**/**했는데** 이제 와서 뒷통수를 쳐.
(=Granting that I did everything just because I trusted you, how dare you backstab me?)

90. Granting permission with some restrictions: ~되

Function		Granting permission with some restrictions		
Form		~되		
Meaning		Can do something, but _		
Distribution		Present	Past	Future
Action Verb Stem	After a consonant	~되		
	After a vowel	~되		
	After "ㄹ"	~되		
Stative Verb Stem	After a consonant			
	After a vowel			
	After "ㄹ"			

"~되" can be used to express that the speaker is granting permission to the listener in the preceding clause with the restriction in the following clause, which can be rendered as "can do something, but _"

야단은 치**되** 때리지는 마세요.

(=You can scold him/her, but please don't hit him/her.)

외출은 하시**되** 반드시 다섯까지는 병원에 돌아오셔야 합니다.

(=You can go out, but you must return to the hospital by five o'clcok.)

술은 마시**되** 과음하시면 안 됩니다.

(=You can drink, but don't drink too much.)

이번에는 니가 하자는 대로 하**되** 다음번에는 내가 하자는 대로 해야 해.

(=This time we will do it the way you want, but next time we must do it the way I want.)

CHAPTER 3 Sentence Connectors I (문장 접속사 I)

A sentence connector is a word or phrase that serves as a transition between two adjoining sentences. When two sentences are linked together in Korean, a sentence connector grammatically belongs to the second sentence, and it is placed at the beginning of the sentence. Depending on the syntactic, semantic, and pragmatic relationships between the preceding and following sentences, different types of sentence connectors can be used with certain restrictions on their usage. In the next two chapters, we will explore a variety of sentence connectors that are commonly used in Korean.

1. Expressing "And": 그리고

Function	Expressing "And"
Form	그리고
Meaning	And

"그리고" can be used to link two adjoining sentences, which can be rendered as "and." The following sentence is simply added to provide more information in addition to the preceding sentence.

존이 체육관에서 운동을 합니다. **그리고** 메리가 수영장에서 수영을 합니다.
(=John is doing exercise at the gym, and Mary is swimming at the swimming pool.)

존이 그 프로젝트를 한 달 전에 시작했습니다. **그리고** 메리가 어제 마무리를 했습니다.
(=John started that project a month ago, and Mary put a final touch on it yesterday.)

존이 머리가 좋습니다. **그리고** 메리도 똑똑합니다.
(=John is smart, and Mary is also smart.)

존이 아주 튼튼합니다. **그리고** 운동을 잘 합니다.

(=John is physically strong, and he is good at sports.)

메리는 키가 큽니다. **그리고** 날씬합니다. **그리고** 얼굴이 아주 예쁩니다.

(=Mary is tall, and she is slender, and she has a pretty face.)

Since "그리고" does not impose any sequence or order on the connected sentences, the speaker B's response below reflects that the three different listed actions can actually take place in any order.

A: 주말에 보통 뭐 하세요? (=What do you usually do on the weekends?)

B: 저는 보통 집에서 가까운 극장에 가서 영화를 봅니다. **그리고** 백화점에서 쇼핑을 합니다. **그리고** 친구와 같이 커피를 마시면서 여러 가지 이야기를 합니다.

(=I usually go to the movie theater near my house and watch a movie, I do shopping at a department store, and I talk with my friend about various things while drinking coffee.)

On the other hand, "그리고" can also be used to express the sequence of immediate actions, which can be rendered as "After that." But this is not the inherent function of "그리고," but rather it is the grammatical function of "그리고 (나서), 그리고(서) (After that)."

존이 도서관에서 공부를 했습니다. **그리고 나서/그리고서/그리고** 집에 갔습니다.

(=John studied at the library. After that, he went home.)

메리가 옷을 갈아입었습니다. **그리고 나서/그리고서/그리고** 운동을 했습니다.

(=Mary changed her clothes. After that, she did exercise.)

There is one syntactic restriction on the usage of "그리고." It can only be used to link the same sentence types.

(1) Linking the same sentence types

메리가 다음 달에 한국에 갑니다. **그리고** 한국어 어학당에서 한국말을 공부할 겁니다.

(=Mary will go to Korea next month, and she is going to study Korean at a Korean Language Institute.)

존이 결혼했습니까? **그리고** 아이들이 있습니까?

(=Is John married? And does he have kids?)

일어나라. **그리고** 아침 먹어라.

(=Wake up and eat breakfast.)

우리 같이 도서관에 가자. **그리고** 숙제도 같이 하자.

(=Let's go to the library together and do our homework together, too.)

(2) Linking different sentence types

메리가 방탄소년단을 좋아합니다. **그리고** 존도 방탄소년단을 좋아합니까? (NOT OK)

(=Mary likes BTS. Does John like BTS, too?)

메리가 방탄소년단을 좋아합니까? **그리고** 존도 방탄소년단을 좋아합니다. (NOT OK)

(=Does Mary like BTS? John likes BTS, too.)

존이 아침 일찍 일어난다. **그리고** 아침 먹어라. (NOT OK)

(=John gets up early in the morning. Eat breakfast.)

일어나라. **그리고** 존이 아침을 먹는다. (NOT OK)

(=Wake up. John eats breakfast.)

지금 어디 있어? **그리고** 같이 공부하자. (NOT OK)

(=Where are you now? Let's study together.)

같이 갑시다. **그리고** 언제 저녁을 먹습니까? (NOT OK)

(=Let's go together. When are we eating dinner?)

2. Expressing "However": 그러나

Function	Expressing "However"
Form	**그러나**
Meaning	However

"그러나" can be used to contrast two different sentences, which can be rendered as "however." Due to its formality, however, it is more likely to be used in written text or in formal speech.

존이 수영을 잘한다. **그러나** 여동생이 수영을 못한다.
(=John is good at swimming. However, his younger sister isn't.)

존이 공부를 열심히 했다. **그러나** 시험 성적이 별로 좋지 않았다.
(=John studied hard. However, his final test grade was not that good.)

존이 잘생겼다. **그러나** 남동생이 못생겼다.
(=John is handsome. However, his younger brother is ugly.)

존이 돈은 많다. **그러나** 남에게 전혀 베풀 줄을 모른다.
(=John has a lot of money. However, he doesn't spend money for others at all.)

메리가 얼굴이 예쁘다. **그러나** 너무 말랐다.
(=Mary has a pretty face. However, she is too skinny.)

내일은 전국이 대체로 맑겠습니다. **그러나** 오후 한 때 비가 조금 내리겠습니다.
(=Tomorrow it must be mostly clear nationwide. However, it must be raining occasionally in the afternoon.)

Although "그러나" is compatible with most sentence types, it cannot be used if the following sentence is a question.

존이 메리를 만났다. **그러나** 아무 말도 하지 않았다. (Statement)
(=John met Mary. However, he didn't say a word to her.)

시장하시겠습니다. **그러나** 조금만 더 기다리세요. (Imperative)
(=You must be hungry. However, please wait a little more.)

시간이 별로 없다. **그러나** 좀 더 기다려 보자. (Proposition)
(=We don't have much time. However, let's wait for him/her a little more.)

존이 키가 작습니다. **그러나** 농구를 잘 합니까? (Question: NOT OK)
(=John is short. However, is he good at basketball?)

존이 부자입니다. **그러나** 다른 사람들을 위해 돈을 씁니까? (Question: NOT OK)
(=John is rich. However, does he spend money on others?)

In the case that the following sentence is a question, "그렇지만 (But even so)" or "그런데 (But/By the way)," which are more or less equivalent to "그러나," can be used instead.

존이 키가 작습니다. **그렇지만** 농구를 잘 합니까?

(=John is short. But even so, is he good at basketball?)

존이 부자입니다. **그렇지만** 다른 사람들을 위해 돈을 씁니까?

(=John is rich. But even so, does he spend money on others?)

존이 키가 작습니다. **그런데** 농구를 잘 합니까?

(=John is short. But is he good at basketball?)

존이 부자입니다. **그런데** 다른 사람들을 위해 돈을 씁니까?

(=John is rich. But does he spend money on others?)

3. Expressing "But even so": 그렇지만, 하지만

Function	Expressing "But even so"	
Form	그렇지만	하지만
Meaning	But even so	

"그렇지만, 하지만" can be used to contrast two different sentences by conceding the situation in the preceding sentence, which can be rendered as "But even so." "그렇지만" can be freely used in both written text and conversation, whereas "하지만" is more likely to be used in conversation.

컴퓨터를 사고 싶어요. **그렇지만/하지만** 돈이 없어요.

(=I want to buy a computer. But even so, I don't have money.)

존은 부자가 아니다. **그렇지만/하지만** 항상 가난한 사람들을 도와준다.

(=John is not a rich man. But even so, he always helps poor people.)

날씨가 춥다. **그렇지만/하지만** 존은 항상 반바지만 입는다.

(=The weather is cold. But even so, John always wears short pants.)

메리는 똑똑하다. **그렇지만/하지만** 남들한테 자랑을 하지 않는다.

(=Mary is smart. But even so, she does not brag about herself to others.)

지난달 물가가 3%나 올랐다. **그렇지만/하지만** 정부는 아무 대책도 취하지 않고 있다. (=Last month the prices of commodities went up by 3%. But even so, the government has not been taking any countermeasures.)

4. Expressing "But/By the way": 그런데

Function	Expressing "But/By the way"	
Form	그런데	
Meaning	But	By the way

"그런데" carries two different functions depending on the sentence type of the following sentence. If the following sentence is a statement, its function is to contrast the situation in the following sentence with the given situation in the preceding sentence, which can be rendered as "But."

메리는 지금 도서관에서 공부합니다. **그런데** 존은 밖에서 놉니다.
(=Mary is studying in the library. But John is playing outside.)

존은 키가 작다. **그런데** 농구를 잘한다.
(=John is short. But he is good at basketball.)

존은 사람은 착하다. **그런데** 말이 너무 많다.
(=John is kind-hearted. But he is too talkative.)

메리는 열심히 공부했다. **그런데** 시험에 떨어졌다.
(=Mary studied hard. But she failed the test.)

메리는 그날 아침 일찍 집을 떠났다. **그런데** 며칠째 행방불명이다.
(=Mary left her house early in the morning on that day. But she has been missing for several days.)

On the other hand, if the following sentence is a question, its function is to change the topic of a conversation by asking the question in the following sentence, which can be rendered as "By the way."

존이 아주 잘생겼어요. **그런데** 직업이 뭐예요?

(=John looks very handsome. By the way, what does he do for a living?)

한국말을 아주 잘하시네요. **그런데** 얼마 동안 한국말을 공부했어요?

(=Wow, you speak Korean very well. By the way, how long have you studied Korean?)

가격은 괜찮은 것 같습니다. **그런데** 품질은 어떻습니까?

(=The price seems to be ok to me. By the way, how about the quality?)

피로연 음식을 준비하는데 손이 모자라요. **그런데** 메리는 지금 어디에 있어요?

(=We are short of hands to prepare food for the wedding reception party. By the way, where is Mary now?)

5. Providing the reason for a given situation: 그래서, 그렇기 때문에

Function	Providing the reason for a given situation	
Form	그래서	그렇기 때문에
Meaning	So	

"그래서, 그렇기 때문에" can be used to express that the preceding sentence is the reason for the given situation in the following sentence, which can be rendered as "So." "그래서" can be freely used in written text and conversation, whereas "그렇기 때문에" is typically used in conversation.

저는 점심을 늦게 먹었습니다. **그래서/그렇기 때문에** 배가 고프지 않습니다.

(=I had a late lunch. So I am not hungry.)

존은 열심히 공부했습니다. **그래서/그렇기 때문에** 공무원 시험에 합격했습니다.

(=John studied hard. So he passed the civil service exam.)

존이 많이 도와줬습니다. **그래서/그렇기 때문에** 일을 빨리 끝낼 수 있었습니다.

(=John helped me a lot. So I could finish the work quickly.)

오늘 날씨가 아주 좋습니다. **그래서/그렇기 때문에** 기분이 좋습니다.

(=The weather is very good today. So I am in a good mood.)

어제는 너무 피곤했습니다. **그래서/그렇기 때문에** 일찍 잤습니다.

(=I was so tired yesterday. So I went to bed early.)

이 물건은 면세품입니다. **그래서/그렇기 때문에** 세금을 내지 않아도 됩니다.

(=This is a duty-free item. So you don't have to pay tax.)

6. Providing the main reason for a given situation: 그러니까

Function	Providing the main reason for a given situation
Form	그러니까
Meaning	Because of that

"그러니까" can be used to express that the situation in the preceding sentence is the main reason for the given situation in the following sentence, which can be rendered as "Because of that."

존은 돈을 아주 많이 벌었다. **그러니까** 강남에 집을 살 수 있었다.

(=John made a huge amount of money. Because of that, he was able to buy a house in the Gangnam district.)

우리나라 출산율이 계속해서 떨어지고 있다. **그러니까** 정부에서는 이에 대한 대책을 마련해야 한다.

(=Our country's birth rate has continued to drop. Because of that, the government must prepare a countermeasure.)

학교폭력이 갈수록 심각해지고 있다. **그러니까** 많은 학생들이 학교에 가는 것조차 두려워하고 있다.

(=School violence is getting more serious as time goes by. Because of that, many students are afraid of even going to school.)

A: 벌써 돈이 다 떨어졌어요.

(=I already ran out of money.)

B: **그러니까** 내가 뭐랬니? 아껴쓰라고 했잖아.

(=Because of that, what did I say to you? I asked you to be frugal.)

"그러니까" can also be used with the sentence ending "~는 말이다" to rephrase what one just said in the preceding sentence to clarify his/her point of discussion, which can be rendered as "So what one is saying/asking/suggesting is that _"

존은 일이 잘못되면 항상 다른 사람 탓만 한다. **그러니까** 같이 일하기가 힘들다**는 말이다**.

(=John always blames others if things go wrong. So what I am saying is that it is hard to work with him.)

A: 존이 많이 다쳐서 병원에 실려 갔어요.

(=John was taken to a hospital because he got severely injured.)

B: 뭐? **그러니까** 존이 지금 병원에 있다**는 말이지**?

(=What? So what you are saying is that he is now in the hospital, right?)

이 일은 혼자 하기에는 너무 벅차다. **그러니까** 시간이 있으면 메리를 좀 도와주라**는 말이다**.

(=This is too much work for one person. So what I am asking is that you must help Mary if you have time.)

나도 내일 서울에 간다. **그러니까** 나랑 같이 거기에 가자**는 말이다**.

(=I am also going to Seoul tomorrow. So what I am suggesting is that we go there together.)

7. Expressing logical reasoning: 그러므로

Function	Expressing logical reasoning
Form	**그러므로**
Meaning	Therefore

"그러므로" can be used to express a logical relationship between two adjoining sentences in which the situation in the preceding sentence is the main reason for the situation in the following sentence. It can be rendered as "Therefore." It can also be used in the syllogism (삼단논법). However, due to its formality, it is typically used in written text or in formal speech.

인간은 누구나 평등하다. **그러므로** 어떠한 차별도 받아서는 안 된다.

(=All human beings are equal. Therefore, we should not be discriminated against in any circumstances.)

모든 동물은 죽는다. 개는 동물이다. **그러므로** 모든 개는 다 죽어야 할 운명이다.

(=All animals die. Dogs are animals. Therefore, all dogs are destined to die.)

8. Expressing the cause for a negative outcome: 그러느라(고)

Function	Expressing the cause for a negative outcome
Form	그러느라(고)
Meaning	Because of doing that

"그러느라(고)" can be used to express that one is to carry out the action in the preceding sentence, which results in the negative outcome in the following sentence, which can be rendered as "Because of doing that."

어제 밤새도록 숙제를 했습니다. **그러느라(고)** 한 숨도 못 잤습니다.

(=I did my homework all night long yesterday. Because of doing that, I could not sleep at all.)

메리는 공무원 시험 준비 때문에 아주 바쁩니다. **그러느라(고)** 다른 건 신경쓸 겨를도 없습니다.

(=Mary is busy preparing for her civil service exam. Because of doing that, she doesn't have time to think about other things.)

오늘은 가게에 손님들이 많아서 하루 종일 일만 했습니다. **그러느라(고)** 점심도 못 먹었습니다.

(=Today I had worked all day long because I had so many customers at the store. Because of doing that, I even skipped lunch.)

9. Expressing a negative outcome due to an uncontrollable situation:

그러는 바람에

Function	Expressing a negative outcome due to an uncontrollable situation
Form	그러는 바람에
Meaning	Because of that

"그러는 바람에" can be used to express that the negative outcome in the following sentence occurs due to the uncontrollable, undesirable, or unfavorable situation in the preceding sentence, which can be rendered as "Because of that."

집에 돌아오는 길에 돌에 걸려 넘어졌다. **그러는 바람에** 발목을 삐었다.
(=I tripped over a stone on my way home. Because of that, I sprained my ankle.)

나는 서둘러서 집을 나왔다. **그러는 바람에** 집에 지갑을 두고 왔다.
(=I was in a hurry to get out of my house. Because of that, I left my wallet at home.)

고등학교 때 아버님 회사가 부도가 났습니다. **그러는 바람에** 대학에 진학할 수 없었습니다.
(=My father's company went bankrupt when I was a high school student. Because of that, I could not go to college.)

10. Expressing "Just for that reason":

그 이유로, 그러한/그런 이유로, 그런 저런 이유로

Function	Expressing "Just for that reason"		
Form	그 이유로	그러한/그런 이유로	그런 저런 이유로
Meaning	Just for that reason	For that kind of reason	For such and such reasons

"그 이유로" can be used to express that the situation in the preceding sentence is the sole reason for the situation in the following sentence, which can be rendered as "Just for that reason." 그러한 이유로" and its contraction form "그런 이유로" can be used in the case that the situation in the preceding sentence is the kind of reason for the situation in the following sentence, which can be rendered as "For that kind of reason." Lastly, "그런 저런 이유로" can be used to express that the situation in the preceding sentence is one of the many reasons for the situation in the following sentence, which can be rendered as "For such and such reasons."

존은 회사 기밀 정보를 유출했다. **그 이유로/그러한 이유로/그런 저런 이유로** 해고됐다.
(=John leaked his company's confidential information. For that reason/For that kind of reason/For such and such reasons, he got fired.)

많은 사람들이 회사로부터 부당한 대우를 받았다. **그 이유로/그런 이유로/그런 저런 이유로** 회사를 상대로 집단소송을 걸었다
(=Many people received poor treatment from the company. For that reason/For that kind of reason/For such and such reasons, they filed a class action lawsuit against the company.)

그 사건과 관련해 재판이 현재 진행 중입니다. **그 이유로/그러한 이유로/그런 저런 이유로** 재판과 관련된 것에 대해서는 말씀드릴 수 없습니다.
(=The trial related to that case is currently ongoing. For that reason/For that kind of reason/For such and such reasons, I cannot tell you anything that is related to the trial.)

정부가 아직 차세대 전투기 사업 예산을 확보하지 못했다. **그 이유로/그런 이유로/그런 저런 이유로** 계획이 늦어지고 있다.
(=The government has not secured the budget for the next generation fighter jet project yet. For that reason/For that kind of reason/For such and such reasons, the project has been delayed.)

11. Expressing "Concurrent actions or states": 그러면서

Function	Expressing "Concurrent actions or states"	
Form	그러면서	
Meaning	At the same time	While doing so/By doing so

"그러면서" can be used to express that the action or state in the preceding sentence takes place more or less at the same time that another action or state in the following sentences occurs, which can be rendered as "At the same time."

> 존이 공부를 잘한다. **그러면서** 운동도 잘한다.
> (=John is good at study. At the same time, he is also good at sports.)
>
> 이 집은 거실이 아주 넓습니다. **그러면서** 전망도 좋습니다.
> (=This house has a large living room. At the same time, it also has a good view.)
>
> 메리가 똑똑합니다. **그러면서** 마음씨도 착합니다.
> (=Mary is smart. At the same time, she is also kind-hearted.)

"그러면서" requires that the subject of the preceding sentence must be the same as the subject of the following sentence which is usually deleted.

> 존이 축구를 잘한다. **그러면서** 공부를 잘한다.
> 존이 축구를 잘한다. **그러면서** 메리가 공부를 잘한다. (NOT OK)
> (=John is good at soccer. At the same time, he is good at study.)
>
> 존이 똑똑합니다. **그러면서** 마음씨가 따뜻합니다.
> 존이 똑똑합니다. **그러면서** 메리가 마음씨가 따뜻합니다. (NOT OK)
> (=John is smart. At the same time, he is kind-hearted.)

"그러면서" can also be used to express that the subject is holding two different titles at the same time if the verbs of the preceding and following sentences are the copula "~이다."

> 존이 시인이다. **그러면서** 소설가다.
> (=John is a poet, and at the same time he is a novelist.)
>
> 메리가 치과의사다. **그러면서** 대학교수다.
> (=Mary is a dentist, and at the same time she is a college professor.)

Another function of "그러면서" is to express that the ongoing action in the following sentence occurs simultaneously with another ongoing action in the preceding clause, which can be rendered as "While doing so."

존이 K-드라마를 봅니다. **그러면서** 한국말을 공부합니다.

(=John is watching a Korean drama. While doing so, he is studying Korean.)

메리가 지금 K-팝을 듣고 있습니다. **그러면서** 가사를 한국말로 적고 있습니다.

(=Mary is now listening to K-pop songs. While doing so, she is transcribing the lyrics in Korean.)

존이 무대에서 노래를 부릅니다. **그러면서** 춤을 춥니다.

(=John is singing on the stage. While doing so, he is dancing.)

존은 아무 일도 안 한다. **그러면서** 다른 사람한테는 이것 저것 시킨다.

(=John is not doing anything. While doing so, he is ordering other people to do this or that.)

It can also be used to express that the continuing action in the preceding sentence brings a certain change of state in the following sentence, which can be rendered as "By doing so."

존은 한 달 전부터 운동을 시작했다. **그러면서** 몸이 아주 좋아졌다.

(=John started his workouts a month ago. By having done so, he has gotten in better shape.)

12. Expressing "Upon the completion of an action":
그리고 (나서), 그리고(서)

Function	Expressing "Upon the completion of an action"
Form	그리고 나서, 그리고서, 그리고
Meaning	After that

"그리고 나서" and its contraction forms "그리고서, 그리고" can be used to express that the action in the following sentence takes place upon the completion of the action in the preceding sentence, which can be rendered as "After that."

존이 탄 비행기가 방금 이륙했다. **그리고 나서/그리고서/그리고** 메리가 공항에 도착했다.

(=The airplane that John is on board just took off. After that, Mary arrived at the airport.)

존은 메리와 저녁을 먹었다. **그리고 나서/그리고서/그리고** 스타벅스에 갔다.

(=John ate dinner with Mary. After that, he went Starbucks.)

메리는 숙제를 했다. **그리고 나서/그리고서/그리고** TV를 봤다.

(=Mary did her homework. After that, she watched TV.)

존은 일을 다 끝냈다. **그리고 나서/그리고서/그리고** 집에 갔다.

(=John finished his work. After that, he went back home.)

메리는 올림픽에서 금메달을 땄다. **그리고 나서/그리고서/그리고** 관중들 앞에서 흐느껴 울었다.

(=Mary won the gold medal at the Olympics. After that, she was sobbing in front of the audience.)

13. Expressing "Soon after the completion of an action": 그리고 (나)(서)는

Function	Expressing "Soon after the completion of an action"
Form	그리고 나서는, 그리고서는, 그리고는
Meaning	Soon after that

"그리고 나서는" and its contraction forms "그리고서는, 그리고는" can be used to express that the situation in the following sentence happens soon after the completion of the action in the preceding sentence, which can be rendered as "Soon after that."

존은 나한테 화풀이를 했다. **그리고 나서는/그리고서는/그리고는** 밖으로 나갔다.

(=John took his anger out on me. Soon after that, he went outside.)

메리는 소주를 마셨다. **그리고 나서는/그리고서는/그리고는** 갑자기 소리를 지르기 시작했다.

(=Mary drank soju. Soon after that, she suddenly started shouting.)

존은 메리가 다른 남자친구가 있다는 사실을 알았다. **그리고 나서는/그리고서는/그리고는** 무척 화를 냈다.

(=John found out that Mary has another boyfriend. Soon after that, he went off the deep end.)

메리는 존의 입장을 이해했다. **그리고 나서는/그리고서는/그리고는** 용서해 주기로 했다.
(=Mary understood John's situation. Soon after that, she decided to forgive him.)

14. Expressing "Before/After": 그 전에, 그 다음에/그 후에

Function	Expressing "Before/After"	
Form	그 전에	그 다음에/그 후에
Meaning	Before that	After that

"그 전에" can be used to express the sequence of two different events in which the event in the following sentence occurred before the event in the preceding sentence, which can be rendered as "Before that."

존은 작년에 한국에 왔습니다. **그 전에** 대학교에서 육 개월 동안 한국말을 배웠습니다.
(=John came to Korea last year. Before that, he studied Korean at college for six months.)

메리는 지난달에 존과 결혼했습니다. **그 전에** 다른 남자친구가 있었습니다.
(=Mary married John last month. Before that, she had another boyfriend.)

존은 메리와 음악회에 갔다. **그 전에** 가까운 식당에서 같이 저녁을 먹었다.
(=John went to a concert with Mary. Before that, they ate dinner together at a nearby restaurant.)

On the other hand, "그 다음에/그 후에" can be used to express that the event in the following sentence occurs after the event in the preceding sentence, which can be rendered as "After that." They are freely interchangeable, but differ slightly in terms of formality. "그 다음에" can be freely used in both written text and conversation, whereas "그 후에" is more likely to be used in written text and formal speech.

존이 도둑을 잡았습니다. 그 **다음에/그 후에** 경찰에 신고했습니다.
(=John caught the burglar. After that, he called the police.)

메리는 몇달 전에 집을 팔았습니다. 그 **다음에/그 후에** 아파트로 이사 갔습니다.
(=Mary sold her house several months ago. After that, she moved into an apartment.)

메리는 집안 청소를 했다. 그 **다음에/그 후에** 마트에 가서 장을 봤다.
(=Mary cleaned the house. After that, she went to the market and bought some groceries.)

15. Expressing "In the middle of carrying out an action":
그러는 중에, 그러던 중(에)

Function	Expressing "In the middle of carrying out an action"	
Form	그러는 중에	그러던 중(에)
Meaning	While doing so	While one was doing so

"그러는 중에" and its past tense form "그러던 중(에)" can be used to express that the situation in the following sentence occurs at some point while carrying out the action in the preceding sentence, which can be rendered as "While doing so, While one was doing so," respectively.

존은 아침 일찍 학교에 갑니다. **그러는 중에** 메리를 자주 봅니다.
(=John goes to school early in the morning. While doing so, he often sees Mary.)

메리는 피아노를 치고 있습니다. **그러는 중에** 동생이 자꾸 방해를 합니다.
(=Mary is playing the piano. While doing so, her younger sibling repeatedly disturbs her.)

존은 운동장에서 축구를 하고 있었습니다. **그러던 중(에)** 발목을 삐었습니다.
(=John was playing soccer at the playground. While he was doing so, he sprained his ankle.)

메리는 백화점에서 쇼핑을 하고 있었습니다. **그러던 중(에)** 고등학교 때 친구를 만났습니다.
(=Mary was shopping at a department store. While she was doing so, she met her high school friend.)

존은 도서관에서 공부하고 있었습니다. **그러던 중(에)** 갑자기 전기가 나갔습니다.
(=John was studying in the library. While he was doing so, all of a sudden the power went out.)

16. Expressing "At that time": 그럴 때(에)

Function	Expressing "At that time"
Form	그럴 때(에)
Meaning	At that time

"그럴 때(에)" can be used to express that the situation in the following sentence happens when the action or state in the preceding sentence takes place, which can be rendered as "At that time."

메리는 항상 웃습니다. **그럴 때(에)** 정말 귀엽습니다.
(=Mary always smiles. At that time, she looks so cute.)

존은 일주일에 한 번 메리와 데이트를 합니다. **그럴 때(에)** 항상 그 레스토랑에 간다.
(=John goes on a date with Mary once a week. At that time, he always goes to that restaurant.)

시간이 있으면 나는 종종 낚시를 합니다. **그럴 때(에)** 이곳을 찾습니다.
(=When I have time, I often go fishing. At that time, I come to this place.)

17. Expressing "During a given period of time":
그러는 동안(에), 그럴 동안(에)

Function	Expressing "During a given period of time"	
Form	그러는 동안(에)	그럴 동안(에)
Meaning	During that time	In the meantime

"그러는 동안(에)" can be used to express that the situation in the following sentence happens during the period of time of one's carrying out the action in the preceding sentence, which can be rendered as "During that time."

존은 메리와 오랫동안 떨어져 살았다. **그러는 동안(에)** 한 번도 연락을 안 했다.
(=John had been living apart from Mary for a long time. During that time, he had never contacted Mary.)

메리는 서울에서 대학교를 다니고 있었다. <u>**그러는 동안(에)**</u> 아버님이 돌아가셨다.

(=Mary had been attending college in Seoul. During that time, her father died.)

On the other hand, "그럴 동안(에)" can be used to express that the situation in the following sentence happens during the continuing state of the action in the preceding sentence, which can be rendered as "In the meantime."

존이 거실에서 TV를 보고 있다. <u>**그럴 동안(에)**</u> 빨리 숙제를 해야겠다.

(=John is watching TV in the living room. In the meantime, I need to quickly finish my homework.)

북한의 핵미사일 개발이 거의 완성단계에 있다. <u>**그럴 동안에**</u> 우리 정부는 뭐하고 있었는지 도무지 이해가 안 간다.

(=North Korea's development of nuclear missiles is almost at the final stage of completion. I cannot understand what our government has done in the meantime.)

18. Expressing "When/Until/Whenever that happens":

그럴 때(에)(는), 그럴 때까지, 그럴 때마다

Function	Expressing "When/Until/Whenever that happens"		
Form	그럴 때(에)(는)	그럴 때까지	그럴 때마다
Meaning	When that happens	Until that happens	Whenever that happens

"그럴 때(에)(는)" can be used to express that the situation in the following sentence applies when the situation in the preceding sentence happens, which can be rendered as "When that happens."

저는 가끔 편두통이 심합니다. <u>**그럴 때에는/그럴 때는/그럴 때에/그럴 때**</u> 이 약을 먹습니다.

(=Sometimes I have a severe migraine. When that happens, I take this medicine.)

요즘 미세먼지 주의보가 자주 발령됩니다. <u>**그럴 때에는/그럴 때는/그럴 때에/그럴 때**</u> 가급적 외출을 자제하세요.

(=A micro dust advisory warning has been issued quite often these days. When that happens, please don't go out whenever possible.)

"그럴 때까지" can be used to express that the situation in the following sentence applies until the completion of the action in the preceding sentence, which can be rendered as "until that happens."

조금 있으면 회의가 끝날 겁니다. **그럴 때까지** 밖에서 기다리세요.
(=The meeting will be over soon. Please wait outside until that happens.)
(=The meeting will be over soon. Please wait outside until then.)

이번 낚시배 사고로 모두 15명이 목숨을 잃었습니다. **그럴 때까지** 긴급구조대는 도대체 뭘 했습니까?
(=Altogether fifteen people lost their lives due to this fishing boat accident. Until that happened, what on earth had the emergency rescue team done?)

On the other hand, "그럴 때마다" can be used to express that the situation in the following sentence applies whenever the situation in the preceding sentence happens, which can be rendered as "Whenever that happens."

당분간 심한 통증이 계속 있을 겁니다. **그럴 때마다** 이 진통제를 드세요.
(=You might continue to have a sharp pain for a while. Whenever that happens, take this pain reliever.)

존은 일주일에 한 번 용돈을 받는다. **그럴 때마다** 바로 다 써버린다.
(=John receives his allowance once a week. Whenever he gets the money, he immediately spends it.)

19. Expressing "When that happens": 그럴 적에

Function	Expressing "When that happens"
Form	**그럴 적에**
Meaning	When that happens

"그럴 적에" can be used to express that the situation in the following sentence occurs when the situation in the preceding sentence happens, which can be rendered as "When that happens." It is more likely to be used in conversation, whereas the equivalent expression "그럴 때(에)(는) (When that happens)" can be freely used in both written text and conversation.

> 요즘 메리가 무척 보고 싶습니다. **그럴 적에** 저는 메리의 사진을 보면서 외로움을 달랩니다.
> (=I miss Mary a lot these days. When that happens, I ease my loneliness by looking at her pictures.)

> 존이 제가 없는 동안 인터넷만 할 거예요. **그럴 적에** 혼 좀 내 주세요.
> (=John is going to surf the internet all the time while I am away. When that happens, please scold him.)

20. Expressing "Right at that moment": 그러는 순간(에), 그러는 찰나에

Function	Expressing "Right at that moment"
Form	**그러는 순간(에), 그러는 찰나에**
Meaning	Right at that moment

"그러는 순간(에), 그러는 찰나에" can be used to express that the situation in the following sentence occured right at the moment that the situation in the preceding sentence happened, which can be rendered as "Right at that moment." "그러는 순간(에)" is more commonly used in both written text and conversation, whereas "그러는 찰나에" is more likely to be used in casual speech.

> 기차가 막 역에 도착하고 있었습니다. **그러는 순간(에)/그러는 찰나에** 그 사람이 갑자기 철로에 뛰어들었다.
> (=The train was about to arrive at the station. Right at that moment, all of a sudden the person jumped onto the railway track.)

> 잠깐 한 눈을 팔았다. **그러는 순간(에)/그러는 찰나에** 앞차를 들이받았다.
> (=I took my eyes off the road for a second. Right at that moment, I crashed into the car in front of me.)

> 다리가 아파서 벤치에 앉으려고 했습니다. **그러는 순간(에)/그러는 찰나에** 누가 내 가방을 빼앗아 달아났습니다.
> (=I was trying to sit on the bench because my legs hurt. Right at that moment, some-

body snatched my bag and ran away.)

납치범이 졸기 시작했습니다. **그러는 순간(에)/그러는 찰나에** 재빨리 도망쳐 나왔습니다.
(=The kidnapper started dozing off. Right at that moment, I quickly ran away from him.)

적이 잠깐 방심하고 있었습니다. **그러는 순간(에)/그러는 찰나에** 기습공격을 했습니다.
(=The enemy forces were off guard for a moment. Right at that moment, we made a surprise attack.)

21. Expressing "At the same time": 그러는 동시에

Function	Expressing "At the same time"
Form	그러는 동시에
Meaning	At the same time

"그러는 동시에" can be used to express that the situation in the following sentence occurs simultaneously with the situation in the preceding sentence, which can be rendered as "At the same time."

존은 대학을 졸업했다. **그러는 동시에** 삼성에 취직이 됐다.
(=John graduated from college. At the same time, he got a job at Samsung.)

수상한 사람이 그 집에 들어갔어요. **그러는 동시에** 갑자기 비명소리가 들렸어요.
(=A suspicious person broke into the house. At the same time, all of a sudden I heard screaming.)

북한은 지금까지 여섯 차례에 걸쳐 핵실험을 계속하고 있다. **그러는 동시에** ICBM 개발에도 박차를 가하고 있다.
(=North Korea has continued to conduct nuclear tests over six times. At the same time, it is also spurring on the development of ICBMs.)

On the other hand, "그러는 동시에" can also be used to express that that the situation in the following sentence applies in addition to the situation in the preceding sentence, which can also be rendered as "At the same time."

이 약은 고혈압을 치료하는데 아주 효과적이다. **그러는 동시에** 우울증도 치료해 준다.
(=This medicine has a great effect on curing high blood pressure. At the same time, it can also cure depression.)

이 제품은 품질이 아주 좋다. **그러는 동시에** 가격도 합리적이다.
(=This product is of very good quality. At the same time, its price is also reasonable.)

22. Expressing "Right after that/Soon after that":

그러자마자, 그러자

Function	Expressing "Right after that/Soon after that"	
Form	그러자마자	그러자
Meaning	Right after that	Soon after that

"그러자마자" can be used to express that the situation in the following sentence takes place immediately upon the completion of the action in the preceding sentence, which can be rendered as "Right after that."

방탄소년단이 새 앨범을 발표했습니다. **그러자마자** 세계 각국에서 인기가 폭발하고 있습니다.
(=BTS released a new album. Right after that, it has been gaining huge popularity around the world.)

학교 앞에서 교통사고가 났습니다. **그러자마자** 경찰이 사고 현장에 도착했습니다.
(=A traffic accident occurred in front of the school. Right after that, the police arrived at the accident site.)

메리의 결혼식이 끝났습니다. **그러자마자** 메리는 신혼여행을 떠났습니다.
(=Mary's wedding ceremony was over. Right after that, she left for her honeymoon trip.)

On the other hand, "그러자" can be used to express that the situation in the following sentence occurs after a certain period of time, but not immediately, after the completion of the situation in the preceding sentence, which can be rendered as "Soon after that."

존은 복권에 당첨됐습니다. **그러자** 부모님께 집을 하나 사 드렸습니다.

(=John won the lottery. Soon after that, he bought a house for his parents.)

메리한테 남자친구가 생겼습니다. **그러자** 공부를 소홀히 하기 시작했습니다.

(=Mary got a boyfriend. Soon after that, she started neglecting her study.)

존이 대학교에 입학했습니다. **그러자** 등록금을 마련하지 못해서 1년 동안 휴학계를 냈습니다.

(=John entered college. Soon after that, he took a gap year because he could not afford the tuition.)

23. Expressing "About that time": 그럴 쯤에, 그럴 무렵에, 그럴 즈음에

Function	Expressing "About that time"		
Form	그럴 쯤에	그럴 무렵에	그럴 즈음에
Meaning	About that time		

"그럴 쯤에, 그럴 무렵에, 그럴 즈음에" can be used to express that the situation in the following sentence occurs about the time when the situation in the preceding sentence happens, which can be rendered as "about that time." "그럴 쯤에" is more likely to be used in conversation, whereas "그럴 무렵에, 그럴 즈음에" are typically used in written text.

우리 회사가 올해 초 재정적으로 어려움을 겪고 있었습니다. **그럴 쯤에/그럴 무렵에/그럴 즈음에** 새 투자자들이 나타나서 위기를 극복할 수 있었습니다.

(=My company was going through financial difficulty at the beginning of this year. About that time, new investors came forward, and we were able to overcome the financial crisis.)

한국전쟁 당시 불과 두세 달 만에 거의 전국이 북한군의 손에 넘어가게 되었다. **그럴 쯤에/그럴 무렵에/그럴 즈음에** 맥아더 장군이 이끄는 유엔군이 인천상륙작전을 개시했다.

(=At the time of the Korean War, the entire nation almost fell into the hands of the North Korean military within two to three months. About that time, the UN forces led by General MacArthur launched the Inchon Landing Operation.)

24. Expressing the precondition for a given situation: 그래야(지)만

Function	Expressing the precondition for a given situation	
Form	그래야지만	그래야만
Meaning	Only by doing that	

"그래야지만" and its contraction forms "그래야만" can be used to express that the situation in the preceding sentence is the precondition for the given situation in the following sentence, which can be rendered as "Only by doing that."

먼저 숙제를 끝내야겠다. **그래야지만/그래야만** 마음이 편할 것 같다.

(=I need to finish my homework first. Only by doing that, I may feel relieved.)

돈을 아껴 써야 한다. **그래야지만/그래야만** 차도 사고 집도 살 수 있다.

(=You must spend money frugally. Only by doing that, you can buy a car and a house.)

25. Expressing the precondition for carrying out an action:

그러지 않고(서)는 ~(으)ㄹ 수 없다

Function	Expressing the precondition for carrying out an action
Form	그러지 않고(서)는 ~(으)ㄹ 수 없다
Meaning	Without doing that, _ cannot

"그러지 않고서는" and its contraction form "그러지 않고는" can be used with "~(으)ㄹ 수 없다" to express that the situation in the preceding sentence is the precondition for carrying out the action in the following sentence, which can be rendered as "Without doing that, _ cannot."

메리는 마침내 부모님의 허락을 받았다. **그러지 않고(서)는** 존과 결혼할 수 없었다.

(=Mary finally got permission from her parents. Without doing that, she could not marry John.)

존은 수면제를 먹었다. **그러지 않고(서)는** 잠을 **잘 수 없다**.

(=John took a sleeping pill. Without doing that, he cannot sleep.)

존은 수술을 받았다. **그러지 않고(서)는** 오래 **살 수가 없다**.

(=John had the surgery. Without doing that, he cannot live long.)

메리는 신분증을 보여줬다. **그러지 않고(서)는** 거기에 출입**할 수가 없었다**.

(=Mary showed her ID. Without doing that, she could not have in-and-out privileges.)

26. Expressing "Not meeting one's expectation":

이래/그래/저래 가지고(서)는 ~(으)ㄹ 수 없다

Function	Expressing "Not meeting one's expectation"
Form	이래/그래/저래 가지고(서)는 ~(으)ㄹ 수 없다
Meaning	If one keeps doing it like this/that/that way, _ cannot

"이래/그래/저래 가지고(서)는" can be used with "~(으)ㄹ 수 없다" to express that the situation in the preceding sentence does not meet the expectations of one who foresees the possible future situation in the following sentence, which can be rendered as "If one keeps doing it like this/that/that way, _ cannot."

현재까지 우리 팀 성적이 1승 2패다. **이래 가지고(서)는** 예선전도 통과**할 수 없다**.

(=Our team record is 1 win and 2 losses up until now. If we keep doing it like this, we cannot even pass the preliminary round.)

존은 일주일에 두 시간 쯤 한국말 공부를 한다. **그래 가지고(서)는** TOPIK 시험에 합격**할 수 없다**.

(=John studies Korean about two hours a week. If he keeps doing it like that, he cannot pass the TOPIK test.)

메리는 저렇게 시간만 보내고 있다. **저래 가지고(서)는** 대학에 들어**갈 수 없다**.

(=Mary is just killing time that way. If she keeps doing that, she cannot enter college.)

27. Expressing an unexpected situation in a given condition: 그래도

Function	Expressing an unexpected situation in a given condition
Form	**그래도**
Meaning	Even so

"그래도" can be used to express that the situation in the following sentence cannot be normally expected from the given condition in the preceding sentence, but it happens anyway regardless of the situation in the preceding sentence, which can be rendered as "Even so."

존은 말썽꾸러기다. <u>**그래도**</u> 공부는 잘한다.

(=John is a trouble maker. Even so, he studies very well.)

이 프로젝트는 정말 시간이 많이 걸린다. <u>**그래도**</u> 반드시 끝내겠다.

(=This project takes so much time. Even so, I will finish it without fail.)

메리는 많이 먹는다. <u>**그래도**</u> 살이 안 찐다.

(=Mary eats a lot. Even so, she doesn't gain weight.)

존은 부자가 아니다. <u>**그래도**</u> 항상 가난한 사람들을 도와준다.

(=John is not rich. Even so, he always helps the poor.)

밖에 날씨가 아주 춥다. <u>**그래도**</u> 존은 반바지만 입는다.

(=The weather is very cold outside. Even so, John only wears short pants.)

메리는 아주 똑똑하다. <u>**그래도**</u> 남들한테 자랑을 하지 않는다.

(=Mary is very smart. Even so, she does not brag about herself to others.)

28. Even after considering that:

그럴지라도, 그렇다(고) 하더라도, 그렇더라도, 그렇다(손) 치더라도

"그럴지라도, 그렇다(고) 하더라도, 그렇더라도, 그렇다(손) 치더라도" can be used to express that the situation in the following sentence applies even after considering the given situation in the preceding sentence, which can be rendered as "Even though that is the case." "그럴지라도, 그렇다(고) 하더라도, 그렇더라도" can be freely used in both written text and conversation. But "그렇다손 치더라도" and its contraction form "그렇다 치더라도" are more likely to be used in conversation. "그렇다손 치더라도" is now on the verge of becoming an archaic expression.

Function	Even after considering that		
Form	그럴지라도	그렇다(고) 하더라도 그렇더라도	그렇다손 치더라도 그렇다 치더라도
Meaning	Even though that is the case		

조금 있으면 연말보너스를 받는다. **그럴지라도/그렇다(고) 하더라도/그렇더라도/그렇다손 치더라도/그렇다 치더라도** 생활이 여전히 빠듯할 것 같다.
(=I am going to get a year-end bonus soon. Even though that is the case, it will be still hard to make ends meet.)

존이 지금 공항으로 떠난다고 한다. **그럴지라도/그렇다(고) 하더라도/그렇더라도/그렇다손 치더라도/그렇다 치더라도** 메리를 만날 수 없을 거다.
(=John is saying that he is leaving for the airport now. Even though that is the case, he cannot see Mary.)

회사가 어려운 줄 안다. **그럴지라도/그렇다(고) 하더라도/그렇더라도/그렇다손 치더라도/그렇다 치더라도** 직원들을 해고하면 안 된다.
(=I know the company is facing a financial difficulty. Even though that is the case, we should not lay off our employees.)

내가 좀 잘못했다. **그럴지라도/그렇다(고) 하더라도/그렇더라도/그렇다손 치더라도/그렇다 치더라도** 이건 너무하다.
(=I know it was my fault. Even though that is the case, this is too harsh.)

한국은 이번 월드컵에서 죽음의 조에 속해 있다. **그럴지라도/그렇다(고) 하더라도/그렇더라도/그렇다손 치더라도/그렇다 치더라도** 우리 선수들은 최선을 다해서 좋은 성적을 거둬야만 한다.
(=Korea belongs to the 'Group of Death' in the upcoming World Cup. Even though that is the case, our athletes must do their best to get a good result.)

존은 배가 너무 고파서 편의점에서 빵을 하나 훔쳤다. **그럴지라도/그렇다(고) 하더라도/ 그렇더라도/그렇다손 치더라도/그렇다 치더라도** 남의 물건을 훔치는 것은 정당화 될 수 없다.

(=John stole a piece of bread from a convenience store because he was so hungry. Even though that is the case, stealing something from others cannot be justified.)

그 선수는 불법 약물인 줄 모르고 스테로이드를 복용했다고 한다. **그럴지라도/그렇다 (고) 하더라도/그렇더라도/그렇다손 치더라도/그렇다 치더라도** 처벌을 받아야 한다.

(=That athlete said that he/she took the steroid without knowing that it is an illegal substance. Even though that is the case, he/she must be punished.)

한국에서도 간통은 더 이상 범죄가 아니다. **그럴지라도/그렇다(고) 하더라도/그렇더라도/ 그렇다손 치더라도/그렇다 치더라도** 바람을 피우는 것은 사회통념상 받아들이기 어렵다.

(=Adultery is no longer a crime even in Korea. Even though that is the case, it is difficult to accept an extra-marital affair according to our social consensus.)

29. Expressing one's strong refusal to carry out an action:
그럴지언정, 그럴망정

Function	Expressing one's strong refusal to carry out an action	
Form	**그럴지언정, 그럴망정**	
Meaning	One would rather do that than _	Despite that

"그럴지언정, 그럴망정" can be used to express that one is strongly refusing to carry out the action in the following sentence even at the cost of facing the unpleasant situation in the preceding sentence, which can be rendered as "One would rather do that than _." They are often used with the optional adverb "차라리 (rather)" in the preceding sentence. In addition, the following sentence must be in a negative form. "그럴지언정" is still commonly used in written text and conversation, but "그럴망정" is now on the verge of becoming an archaic expression.

제가 (차라리) 감옥에 가겠습니다. **그럴지언정/그럴망정** 제 양심을 속일 수 없습니다.

(=I would rather go to jail. I would rather do that than going against my conscience.)

저는 (차라리) 여기 남겠습니다. **그럴지언정/그럴망정** 그 사람 집에 들어가 살고 싶지 않습니다.

(=I would rather stay here. I would rather do that than living in his/her house.)

존은 (차라리) 평생 독신으로 살 겁니다. **그럴지언정/그럴망정** 그 여자와 결혼하지 않을 겁니다.

(=John would rather live as a confirmed bachelor. He would rather do that than getting married to her.)

On the other hand, "그럴지언정, 그럴망정" can also be used to express the speaker's strong refusal to take the listener's warning or advice in the preceding sentence even at the cost of accepting the unpleasant situation in the following sentence, which can be rendered as "Despite that."

A: 지금 팔지 않으면 상해서 버릴 수도 있습니다.

(=If you don't sell it now, it may get spoiled and wasted.)

B: **그럴지언정/그럴망정** 그 가격에는 안 팔겠습니다.

(=Despite that, I would not sell it at that price.)

A: 지금 자금을 확보하지 못하면 회사가 부도가 날지도 모릅니다.

(=If you don't secure the fund, there is a chance that our company may go bankrupt.)

B: **그럴지언정/그럴망정** 고리대금업자한테서는 사채를 빌려 쓰고 싶지 않습니다.

(=Despite that, I don't want to get a private loan from a loan shark.)

30. Expressing the unexpected outcome of a situation:
그럼에도 불구하고, 그런데도 (불구하고)

Function	Expressing the unexpected outcome of a situation	
Form	**그럼에도 불구하고**	**그런데도 (불구하고)**
Meaning	Nevertheless	

"그럼에도 불구하고, 그런데도 (불구하고)" can be used to express that the situation in the following sentence is not the normally expected outcome of the given situation in the preceding sentence, which can be rendered as "Nevertheless." "그럼에도 불구하고" is more likely to be used in written text and formal speech, whereas "그런데도 (불구하고)" can be more often used in conversation.

한국은 6.25 전쟁 당시 모든 것을 잃었다. **그럼에도 불구하고/그런데도 (불구하고)** 한강의 기적이라고 불리우는 인류역사상 유례없는 경제성장을 이루어 냈다.
(=Korea lost everything at the time of the Korean War. Nevertheless, it has accomplished the remarkable economic development called the Miracle of Han River, which has been unprecedented in the history of mankind.)

대통령 비서실장은 암말기 환자였다. **그럼에도 불구하고/그런데도 (불구하고)** 남북정상회담을 성사시키기 위해 최선을 다했다.
(=The president's chief of staff was the terminal stage cancer patient. Nevertheless, he/she did his/her best to close the deal to open the South and North Korean summit talk.)

유엔은 북한에 대해 전례 없는 경제제재 조치를 취했다. **그럼에도 불구하고/그런데도 (불구하고)** 김정은 정권은 계속 핵개발에 박차를 가하고 있다.
(=The UN approved the unprecedented economic sanction against North Korea. Nevertheless, the Kim Jong-un regime has continued to spur on the nuclear development.)

31. Expressing "Despite that fact": 그러면서(도)

Function	Expressing "Despite that fact"
Form	**그러면서(도)**
Meaning	Despite that fact

"그러면서도" can be used to express that the situation in the following sentence cannot be normally expected based on the fact about the situation in the preceding sentence, which can be rendered as "Despite that fact."

존은 학교에서 메리를 왕따 시켰다. **그러면서(도)** 자기는 아무 잘못한 것이 없다고 한다.
(=John bullied Mary at school. Despite that fact, he is saying that he didn't do anything wrong.)

메리는 그것에 대해 다 알고 있었다. **그러면서(도)** 아무 것도 모르는 체했다.
(=Mary knew everything about that. Despite that fact, she pretended that she didn't know anything.)

존은 지난달에 개인파산을 신청했다. **그러면서(도)** 아직 돈이 많은 척하고 다닌다.
(=John filed personal bankruptcy last month. Despite that fact, he still acts like a rich man.)

어머님은 요즘 몸이 편찮으시다. **그러면서(도)** 하루 종일 부엌에서 일하신다.
(=My mother has been sick these days. Despite that fact, she works all day long in the kitchen.)

32. Expressing one's purpose in achieving his/her goal:
그러기 위해(서)/위하여/위한

Function	Expressing one's purpose in achieving his/her goal		
Form	그러기 위해(서)	그러기 위하여	그러기 위한
Meaning	To do so		

"그러기 위해(서), 그러기 위하여" and their modifying form "그러기 위한" can be used to express that one is to carry out the action in the following sentence in order to achieve his/her goal in the preceding sentence, which can be rendered as "To do so." "그러기 위해(서)" can be freely used in both written text and conversation, whereas "그러기 위하여" is mainly used in written text and formal speech. "

존은 이번 시험에는 꼭 합격해야 한다. **그러기 위해(서)/그러기 위하여** 열심히 공부했다.
(=John must pass this upcoming exam without fail. To do so, he has studied hard.)

유족들은 피해자의 정확한 사인을 알고 싶어했다. **그러기 위해(서)/그러기 위하여** 국립과학연구소에 피해자의 부검을 실시할 것을 요청했다.
(=The bereaved family wanted to find out the precise cause of the victim's death. To do so, they requested that the National Forensic Center conduct the autopsy of the victim.)

메리는 조만간 한국에 유학을 가려고 한다. **그러기 위한** 절차를 지금 알아보고 있다.

(=Mary intends to study in Korea soon. She is now trying to find out the procedures to do so.)

33. Expressing one's purpose of carrying out an intended action: 그러려고

Function	Expressing one's purpose of carrying out an intended action
Form	그러려고
Meaning	To do so

"그러려고" can be used to express that the situation in the following sentence happens in order to carry out the intended action in the preceding sentence, which can be rendered as "To do so."

존은 내년에 한국에 여행을 갈 계획이다. **그러려고** 돈을 모으고 있다.

(=John is planning to visit Korea next year. To do so, he is saving some money.)

메리는 앞으로 십년 후에 집을 살 계획이다. **그러려고** 열심히 일하고 있다.

(=Mary is planning to buy a house ten years from now. To do so, she has been working hard.)

존은 메리에게 생일 선물로 명품 가방을 사주려고 한다. **그러려고** 여러 제품들을 알아보고 있다.

(=John intends to buy a famous brand bag for Mary as her birthday gift. To do so, he is searching for various products.)

34. Being matched with the speaker's originally planned action:

그렇지 않아도, 그러지 않아도

Function	Being matched with the speaker's originally planned action	
Form	그렇지 않아도	그러지 않아도
Meaning	As a matter of fact	

"그렇지 않아도" and its variant "그러지 않아도" can be used to express that the situation in the preceding sentence happens to be matched with the speaker's originally planned action in the following sentence. It can be rendered as "As a matter of fact."

> 존이 자기랑 같이 한국어 수업을 듣자고 했다. **그렇지 않아도/그러지 않아도** 나도 한국말을 배우고 싶었다.
>
> (=John asked me to take the Korean language class with him. As a matter of fact, I also wanted to learn the language.)

> 교수님이 시간이 나면 한 번 사무실에 들르라고 하셨다. **그렇지 않아도/그러지 않아도** 결혼식 주례를 부탁하기 위해서 찾아 뵐 계획이었다.
>
> (=My professor asked me to stop by his office once if I have time. As a matter of fact, I was planning to visit him and ask him to officiate my wedding.)

> A: 이제 그만 하고 집에 갑시다.
>
> (=Let's stop working and go home.)

> B: **그렇지 않아도/그러지 않아도** 집에 가려던 참이었어요.
>
> (=As a matter of fact, I was about to go home.)

35. Expressing "To carry out a given task": 그렇게 하는 데(에), 그러는 데(에)

Function	Expressing "To carry out a given task"	
Form	그렇게 하는 데(에)	그러는 데(에)
Meaning	To do so	

"그렇게 하는 데(에), 그러는 데(에)" can be used to express that the situation in the following sentence applies in order to carry out the task in the preceding sentence, which can be rendered as "To do so."

> 직장에서 가까운 데에 있는 집을 구하고 있습니다. **그렇게 하는 데(에)/그러는 데(에)** 시간이 좀 필요합니다.
>
> (=I am looking for a place to live near my workplace. To do so, I need more time.)

> A: 원자력발전소를 태양열, 풍력 등 친환경에너지로 대체하려면 많은 정부예산이 필요합니다.

(=A huge amount of the government budget is needed to replace nuclear power plants with environmentally friendly energy sources, such as solar power, wind power, etc.)

B: **그렇게 하는 데(에)/그러는 데(에)** 얼마만큼의 예산이 소요됩니까?

(=To do so, how much of the budget is expected to be spent?)

A: 이 차를 수리하려면 엔진을 교체해야 합니다.

(=If you want to repair this car, you must replace the engine.)

B: **그렇게 하는 데(에)/그러는 데(에)** 돈이 얼마나 듭니까?

(=To do so, how much does it cost?)

36. Expressing the speaker's response to a given condition: 그러면, 그럼

Function	Expressing the speaker's response to a given condition	
Form	그러면	그럼
Meaning	Then	

"그러면" and it conversational variant "그럼" can be used to express the speaker's response in the following sentence if the situation in the preceding sentence happens, which can be rendered as "Then."

A: 이 우유가 조금 상한 것 같아요.
(=This milk is kind of spoiled.)

B: **그러면/그럼** 드시지 마세요.
(=Then please don't drink it.)

A: 요즘은 별로 할 일이 없네요.
(=I don't have any particular things to do these days.)

B: **그러면/그럼** 저희 집에 한번 놀러 오세요.
(=Then please come over to my house once.)

A: 일기예보에 따르면 내일은 비가 온다고 하네요.
(=According to the weather forecast, it will rain tomorrow.)

B: **그러면/그럼** 집에서 좀 쉽시다.
(=Then let's rest at home.)

A: 저 다음달에 존과 결혼해요.

(=I am going to get married to John next month.)

B: **그러면/그럼** 신혼여행은 어디로 갈 거예요?

(=Then where do you want go for your honeymoon trip?)

37. Expressing "If that is not the case":

그렇지 않으면, 그러지 않으면, 안 그러면, 아니면

Function	Expressing "If that is not the case"			
Form	그렇지 않으면	그러지 않으면	안 그러면	아니면
Meaning	Otherwise			

"그렇지 않으면, 그러지 않으면, 안 그러면, 아니면" can be used to express that the situation in the following sentence applies in the case that the situation in the preceding sentence does not occur, which can be rendered as "Otherwise." "그렇지 않으면" can be freely used in both written text and conversation, whereas "그러지 않으면, 안 그러면, 아니면" are typically used in casual speech.

메리는 시간이 있으면 백화점에서 쇼핑을 한다. **그렇지 않으면/그러지 않으면/안 그러면 /아니면** 친구와 같이 극장에서 영화를 본다.

(=Mary goes shopping at a department store when she has time. Otherwise, she watches a movie with her friends at a movie theater.)

On the other hand, they can also be used to express the speaker's warning about the foreseeable unpleasant situation in the following sentence in the case that the condition in the preceding sentence is not met, which can also be rendered as "Otherwise."

우리 정부도 지진에 철저히 대비해야 한다. **그렇지 않으면/그러지 않으면/안 그러면/아니면** 대규모 지진이 일어났을 때 많은 인명피해와 재산피해가 날 수도 있다.

(=Our government also must thoroughly prepare for an earthquake. Otherwise, when a large-scale earthquake occurs, a large number of casualties may be incurred as well as a large amount of property damages.)

38. Assuming a possible situation: (만약) 그렇다면

Function	Assuming a possible situation
Form	만약 그렇다면, 그렇다면
Meaning	If that happens to be the case

"(만약) 그렇다면" can be used to express the speaker's response in the following sentence if the situation in the preceding sentence happens to be the case, which can be rendered as "If that happens to be the case."

A: 존이 앉은 자리에서 짜장면 다섯 그릇을 먹어 치웠다.

(=John ate five bowls of jajangmyeon at one sitting.)

B: **(만약) 그렇다면** 먹방대회에도 나갈 수 있겠는걸.

(=If that happens to be the case, he can even participate in an eating competition.)

A: 메리가 너 때문에 상처를 받았다.

(=You hurt Mary's feelings.)

B: **(만약) 그렇다면** 미안하다고 전해라.

(=If that happens to be the case, tell her that I am sorry.)

A: 존이 몹시 아파서 오늘 학교에 갈 수 없습니다.

(=John cannot go to school today because he is very sick.)

B: **(만약) 그렇다면** 그냥 집에서 쉬게 하세요.

(=If that happens to be the case, just let him rest at home.)

39. Expressing "If that is the case":
그렇다(고 하)면, 그러라(고 하)면, 그러자(고 하)면

Function	Expressing "If that is the case"		
Form	그렇다고 하면, 그렇다면	그러라고 하면, 그러라면	그러자고 하면, 그러자면
Meaning	If that is the case		

"그렇다고 하면, 그러라고 하면, 그러자고 하면" and their contraction forms "그렇다면, 그러라면, 그러자면," respectively, can be used to express the speaker's response in the following sentence to what one says/asks/suggests in the preceding sentence, which can be rendered as "If that is the case."

> 피고인은 고문에 의해 그것을 자백을 했다고 한다. **그렇다고 하면/그렇다면** 그것은 법적 증거로 사용될 수 없다.
>
> (=The defendant says that he/she confessed to the crime while being tortured. If that is the case, it cannot be used as legal evidence.)
>
> 부모님이 메리와 결혼하라고 할 지도 모른다. **그러라고 하면/그러라면** 차라리 혼자 살겠다고 할 거다.
>
> (=There might be a chance that my parents ask me to get married to Mary. If that is the case, I will tell them I would rather live alone.)
>
> 존이 너한테 그 프로젝트를 같이 하자고 할 거다. **그러자고 하면/그러자면** 바빠서 안 된다고 해라.
>
> (=John might ask you to work on the project together with him. If that is the case, tell him you cannot do it because you are busy.)

40. Regretting one's not taking action or not being in a certain state:

그랬더라면, 그랬다면

Function	Regretting one's not carrying out an action or not being in a certain state	
Form	**그랬더라면**	**그랬다면**
Meaning	If that had been the case	

"그랬더라면" can be used to express a belated regret of one's not carrying out the necessary action or not being in a certain state in the preceding sentence, which prevented the favorable situation in the following sentence from having happened. It can be rendered as "If that had been the case." The preceding and following sentences are typically positive sentences, but they both reflect the negative meanings that the opposite situations actually occurred. "그랬다면" carries a more or less a similar function, but it expresses the speaker's more definitive attitude toward the situation in the preceding sentence.

조금 더 빨리 도착했어야 했는데. **그랬더라면/그랬다면** 범인을 체포할 수 있었다.
(=I should have arrived here a little bit earlier. If that had been the case, I could have arrested the suspect.)

좀 더 열심히 공부했어야 했는데. **그랬더라면/그랬다면** 시험에 합격할 수 있었을텐데.
(=I should have studied a little bit harder. If that had been the case, I could have passed the exam.)

빨리 병원에 데려가야 했는데. **그랬더라면/그랬다면** 그 사람을 살릴 수 있었는데.
(=I should have taken him to the hospital quickly. If that had been the case, I could have saved his life.)

키가 조금 더 컸어야 했는데. **그랬더라면/그랬다면** 프로농구선수가 될 수 있었을텐데.
(=I should have been a little taller. If that had been the case, I could have been a professional basketball player.)

좀 더 조심했어야 했다. **그랬더라면/그랬다면** 사고를 피할 수 있었다.
(=I should have been a little more careful. If that had been the case, I could have avoided the accident.)

41. Expressing the likeliness of a situation: 그런 것 같으면, 그럴 것 같으면

Function	Expressing the likeliness of a situation	
Form	그런 것 같으면	그럴 것 같으면
Meaning	If that seems to be the case	

"그런 것 같으면" can be used to express the speaker's response in the following sentence in reaction to the situation in the preceding sentence which seems to be happening. It can be rendered as "If that seems to be the case." On the other hand, "그럴 것 같으면" can be used instead if the situation in the preceding sentence will be likely to happen, which can be rendered as "If that is going to be the case."

A: 이 프랜차이즈 치킨집은 장사가 잘되는 것 같다.

(=It seems that the business of this franchise chicken restaurant is going well.)

B: **그런 것 같으면** 나도 하나 오픈해야겠다.

(=If that seems to be the case, I also need to open one.)

A: 이 세탁기를 사기에는 돈이 좀 부족한 것 같다.

(=It seems that I am a little bit short of money to buy this washer.)

B: **그런 것 같으면** 내가 좀 빌려 줄게.

(=If that seems to be the case, I can lend you some money.)

A: 이 패딩코트는 존한테 좀 작을 것 같다.

(=It seems that this padding will be a little too tight for John.)

B: **그럴 것 같으면** 한 치수 큰 걸로 사라.

(=If that is going to be the case, buy the one in the next size up.)

42. Expressing a precondition for one's intended/planned action:
그러려(고 하)면, 그렇게 하려거든, 그러(고)자 (하)면

"그러려고 하면" and its contraction form "그러려면" can be used to express the speaker's or the writer's suggestion in the following sentence because it is the precondition for carrying out the intended action in the preceding sentence, which can be rendered as "If one intends to do so." They can be freely used in written text and conversation.

Function	Expressing a precondition for one's intended/planned action		
Form	그러려고 하면 그러려면	그렇게 하려거든 그러려거든	그러고자 하면 그러자면
Meaning	If one intends to do so		If one plans to do so

교육부는 학교 폭력 문제를 해결하기 위한 대책 마련에 나섰습니다. **그러려고 하면/그러려면** 정부의 보다 많은 예산과 적극적인 지원이 필요합니다.

(=The Ministry of Education came forward to prepare countermeasures to prevent school violence. If it intends to do so, it needs more budget and strong support from the government.)

A: 내일 아침 일찍 출발하려고 합니다.

(=I intend to leave early in the morning tomorrow.)

B: **그러려고 하면/그러려면** 지금 주무세요.

(=If you intend to do so, please get some sleep now.)

A: 이번에는 꼭 시험에 합격할 거야.

(=I will pass the test this time without fail.)

B: **그러려고 하면/그러려면** 열심히 공부해.

(=If you intend to do so, study hard.)

"그렇게 하려거든" and its contraction form "그러려거든" can be used for the same function. But they are more likely to be used in casual speech.

A: 메리가 같이 가자고 하네.

(=Mary says she wants to join us.)

B: **그렇게 하려거든/그러려거든** 빨리 준비하라고 해.

(=If she intends to do so, tell her to get ready as soon as possible.)

A: 존이 그 일을 마치는 데 시간을 좀 더 달라고 해.

(=John is asking for more time to finish the work.)

B: **그렇게 하려거든/그러려거든** 당장 그 일에서 손 떼라고 해.

(=If he intends to do so, tell him to wash his hands of it now.)

On the other hand, "그러고자 하면" and its contraction form "그러자면" carries a similar function, but they are more likely to be used with a planned action in the preceding sentence, which can be rendered as "If one plans to do so."

A: 올해 안에 새집으로 이사 가고 싶습니다.

(=I want to move into a new house before the end of this year.)

B: **그러고자 하면/그러자면** 지금부터 집을 알아보세요.

(=If you plan to do so, try to search for a house starting now.)

43. Expressing greater likeliness of a situation: (그러면) 그럴수록

Function	Expressing greater likeliness of a situation
Form	그러면 그럴수록, 그럴수록
Meaning	The more things are going that way, the more _

"(그러면) 그럴수록" can be used to express that the situation in the following sentence is more likely to happen if the situation in the preceding sentence repeatedly occurs, which can be rendered as "The more things are going that way, the more _." "그러면" is generally optional, and it can be used only for emphasis.

존의 부모님은 잔소리를 너무 많이 하신다. (**그러면**) **그럴수록** 존은 더 반항만 한다. (=John's parents have been nitpicking him a lot. The more things are going that way, the more disobedient he becomes.)

요즘 많은 사람들이 살기가 정말 힘들다고 한다. (**그러면**) **그럴수록** 용기를 더 내야 한다. (=Many people say that it is really difficult to make ends meet these days. The more things are going that way, the more courage you must have.)

44. Expressing "In that case": 그런 경우(에), 그럴 경우(에)

Function	Expressing "In that case"	
Form	그런 경우(에)	그럴 경우(에)
Meaning	In that case	

"그런 경우(에)" can be used to express that the situation in the following sentence applies in the case that the situation in the preceding sentence occurs, which can be rendered as "In that case." On the other hand, "그럴 경우(에)" can be used instead if the condition in the preceding sentence will be likely to happen in the future.

최근 보이스피싱 때문에 많은 사람들이 금전적 피해를 당하고 있습니다. **그런 경우(에)/ 그럴 경우(에)** 가까운 범죄신고센터에 바로 연락하시기 바랍니다.

(=Recently many people incur financial losses due to voice phishing calls. In that case, please contact a nearby crime report center immediately.)

요즘 운전자들은 운전을 하면서 불필요한 행동을 하는 경우가 많습니다. **그런 경우(에)/ 그럴 경우(에)** 사고를 낼 가능성이 아주 높습니다.

(=These days many drivers are doing unnecessary actions while driving. In that case, there is a high risk of causing an accident.)

요즘 하루 걸러 미세먼지주의보가 계속 발령되고 있는데요. **그런 경우(에)/그럴 경우(에)** 외출 시에는 반드시 마스크를 쓰고 집에 돌아오자마자 더운 물로 샤워를 하셔야 합니다.

(=These days a micro dust alert has been issued every other day. In that case, you must wear a mask when you go out and take a warm shower as soon as you come back home.)

45. Expressing "If that happens/If that is the case": 그러거든, 그러거들랑

Function	Expressing "If that happens/If that is the case"	
Form	그러거든	그러거들랑
Meaning	If that happens/If that is the case	

"그러거든" can be used in imperative and propositional sentences to express that the action in the following sentence needs to be taken in reaction to the situation in the preceding sentence, which can be rendered as "If that happens/If that is the case." On the other hand, "그러거들랑" can also be used for the same function. But it is more likely to be used in casual speech.

A: 존이 하루 종일 말썽을 부렸어요.
(=John has been monkeying around all day long.)

B: **그러거든/그러거들랑** 혼 내 주세요.
(=If that happens, please scold him.)

A: 존은 다음주에 한국에 출장을 가요.
(=John is going on a business trip to Korea next week.)

B: **그러거든/그러거들랑** 용산에 있는 전쟁기념관을 가 보라고 해라.

(=If that is the case, tell him to try to visit the War Memorial of Korea located in Yongsan.)

A: 저 다음달에 열리는 한국어웅변대회에 참가해요.

(=I am going to participate in the Korean Speech Contest which is sheduled next month.)

B: **그러거든/그러거들랑** 나와 같이 한 번 연습해 보자.

(=If that is the case, let's do some practice with me.)

46. Expressing "Whatever":
그러거나 말거나/그러든지 말든지/그러든가 말든가

Function	Expressing "Whatever"		
Form	그러거나 말거나	그러든지 말든지	그러든가 말든가
Meaning	Whatever		

"그러거나 말거나, 그러든지 말든지, 그러든가 말든가" can be used to express that the situation in the following sentence is the speaker's negative reaction to the situation in the preceding sentence, which can be rendered as "Whatever."

A: 존이 또 사고를 쳤어요.

(=John got into trouble again.)

B: **그러거나 말거나/그러든지 말든지/그러든가 말든가** 이젠 지긋지긋해요.

(Whatever. I am sick and tired of it.)

A: 존하고 메리하고 또 싸워요.

(=John and Mary are fighting again.)

B: **그러거나 말거나/그러든지 말든지/그러든가 말든가** 너는 상관하지 마.

(=Whatever. Just stay out of it.)

47. Enumerating alternative options: 또는, 혹은

Function	Enumerating alternative options	
Form	또는	혹은
Meaning	Or	

"또는, 혹은" can be used to express that the situation in the following sentence is the alternative option to the situation in the preceding sentence, which can be rendered as "or." They are typically used to enumerate the stereotypical examples of the available options that the speaker can freely choose from. "또는" can be freely used in both written text and conversation, whereas "혹은" are typically used in written text and formal speech.

> 메리는 시간이 있으면 백화점에 쇼핑을 하러 간다. **또는/혹은** 친구와 같이 음악회에 간다.
> (=Mary goes shopping at a department store when she has time, or she goes to a concert with her friends.)

> 나는 돈을 많이 벌면 고아원을 세워서 부모 없는 아이들을 돌보고 싶다. **또는/혹은** 갈 곳 없는 지역사회 노인들을 위해 봉사하고 싶다.
> (=If I make a lot of money, I want to build an orphanage to take care of the children without parents, or I want to serve the elderly people in my local community who have nowhere to go.)

48. Expressing "Accordingly": 그런 만큼

Function	Expressing "Accordingly"
Form	그런 만큼
Meaning	Accordingly

"그런 만큼" can be used to express that the action in the following sentence must be carried out in the given situation in the preceding sentence, which can be rendered as "Accordingly."

모든 국민이 남북평화통일을 염원하고 있다. **그런 만큼** 정부는 조속한 시일 내에 통일에 대한 로드맵을 제시해야 한다.

(=All the people are praying for the peaceful unification between South and North Korea. Accordingly, the government should provide a road map for unification very soon.)

저희 회사는 고객여러분들로부터 끊임 없는 성원을 받아 왔습니다. **그런 만큼** 앞으로도 더 낳은 서비스로 고객 여러분들을 모시는 데 최선을 다 하도록 하겠습니다.

(=Our company has received the unending support from our highly-valued customers. Accordingly, we will continue to do our best to serve you with better service.)

올해 정부의 최대 과제는 청년 일자리 창출이다. **그런 만큼** 정부에서는 여러 가지 대책을 세워 고용 기회를 꾸준히 늘려 나가야 한다.

(=This year's biggest challenge for our government is to create jobs for young people. Accordingly, the government must establish various kinds of plans to steadily increase employment opportunities.)

49. Expressing "To that extent": 그럴 정도로, 그럴 만큼, 그럴 만치

Function	Expressing "To that extent"		
Form	그럴 정도로	그럴 만큼	그럴 만치
Meaning	To that extent		

"그럴 정도로, 그럴 만큼, 그럴 만치" can be used to express that the situation in the following sentence holds true to the extent that the situation in the preceding sentence describes, which can be rendered as "To that extent." "그럴 정도로" can be freely used in both written text and conversation, whereas "그럴 만큼" is more likely to be used in conversation. "그럴 만치," however, is now on the verge of becoming an archaic expression.

이 일은 초보자도 쉽게 할 수 있다. **그럴 정도로/그럴 만큼/그럴 만치** 아주 단순하다.

(=Even the beginner can easily handle this job. To that extent, it's very simple.)

존은 집에 오자마자 인사불성이 되었다. **그럴 정도로/그럴 만큼/그럴 만치** 술을 아주 많이 마셨다.

(=John passed out as soon as he came back home. To that extent, he drank a lot.)

존과 나는 개인적인 이야기를 자주 한다. **그럴 정도로/그럴 만큼/그럴 만치** 우리는 서로 친하다.

(=John and I often talk about personal matters. To that extent, we are close to each other.)

아인슈타인의 상대성이론은 그 당시 물리학계를 충격에 빠뜨렸다. **그럴 정도로/그럴 만큼/그럴 만치** 획기적인 이론이었다.

(=Einstein's theory of relativity shocked the field of physics at that time. To that extent, it was a groundbreaking theory.)

50. Expressing "As long as that happens/happened":

그러는 이상, 그런 이상, 그렇게 된 이상

Function	Expressing "As long as that happens/happened"		
Form	그러는 이상	그런 이상	그렇게 된 이상
Meaning	As long as that happens	As long as that happened	As long as it has turned out to be that way

"그러는 이상" can be used to express that the situation in the following sentence applies as long as the situation in the preceding sentence actually occurs, which can be rendered as "As long as that happens." "그런 이상" can be used instead if the situation in the preceding sentence has already been completed, which can be rendered as "As long as that happened."

팀장이 그 프로젝트를 반대한다. **그러는 이상** 더 이상 밀어붙일 수 없다.
(=The team leader disapproves of the project. As long as that happens, we can no longer push it forward.)

드디어 적의 허점을 찾아냈다. **그런 이상** 적 진지에 대한 공격을 더 이상 늦출 수 없다.
(=We finally found the weak spot of the enemy forces. As long as that happened, we can no longer delay our attack on the enemy post.)

On the other hand, "그렇게 된 이상" can be used to express that the situation in the following sentence applies because an unexpected situation in the preceding sentence already happened, which can be rendered as "As long as it has turned out to be that way."

우리 군사작전 계획이 적 첩보부대에 노출됐다. **그렇게 된 이상** 이번 작전을 포기할 수밖에 없다.

(=Our military operation plan has been leaked to the enemy intelligence unit. As long as it has turned out to be that way, we have no choice but to give up this operation.)

51. Expressing the main reason for taking action: 그러(느)니 만큼

Function	Expressing the main reason for taking action
Form	그러느니 만큼, 그러니 만큼
Meaning	Mainly because of that

"그러느니 만큼" and its contraction form ""그러니 만큼" can be used to express that the action in the following sentence must be carried out because of the main reason in the preceding sentence, which can be rendered as "Mainly because of that."

이 문제는 국가의 안보가 걸려 있다. **그러느니 만큼/그러니 만큼** 단호하게 대처해야 한다.
(=Our national security depends on this issue. Mainly because of that, we must take decisive measures.)

올 봄에는 심한 가뭄이 예상된다. **그러느니 만큼/그러니 만큼** 최대한 물을 아껴써야 한다.
(=We are expecting a severe drought this spring. Mainly because of that, we must conserve water as much as possible.)

이 일은 시간을 다투는 일이다. **그러느니 만큼/그러니 만큼** 가능한 한 빨리 끝내야 한다.
(=This is time-sensitive work. Mainly because of that, we must finish that as quickly as possible.)

한 나라의 대통령은 그 나라를 대표한다. **그러느니 만큼/그러니 만큼** 품위를 지켜야 한다.
(=A president represents his/her nation. Mainly because of that, he/she must maintain decency.)

한국말 공부를 남들보다 늦게 시작했다. **그러느니 만큼/그러니 만큼** 배로 노력해야 한다.
(=I started learning Korean later than others. Mainly because of that, I must double my efforts.)

52. Expressing "As well": 그럴 뿐(만) 아니라

Function	Expressing "As well"
Form	그럴 뿐만 아니라, 그럴 뿐 아니라
Meaning	As well

"그럴 뿐만 아니라" and its contraction form "그럴 뿐 아니라" can be used to express that the situation in the following sentence holds true in addition to the situation in the preceding sentence, which can be rendered as "As well." It puts more emphasis on the situation in the following sentence.

존은 3점슛을 잘 넣는다. **그럴 뿐(만) 아니라** 리바운드도 잘한다.
(=John is good at making three-point shots. He is good at catching rebounds as well.)

존은 공부를 아주 잘한다. **그럴 뿐(만) 아니라** 봉사활동도 열심히 한다.
(=John studies very well. He works hard for his community service as well.)

메리는 얼굴이 예쁘다. **그럴 뿐(만) 하니라** 몸매도 날씬하다.
(=Mary is pretty. She is slender as well.)

지난번 총격사건은 정전협정을 위반했다. **그럴 뿐(만) 아니라** 남북 간의 긴장을 고조시키고 있다.
(=The last shooting incident violated the truce treaty. It continues to heighten the tension between South and North Korea as well.)

53. Expressing "Not going beyond a given situation":

그렇다 뿐이지, 그랬다 뿐이지

Function	Expressing "Not going beyond a given situation"
Form	그렇다 뿐이지, 그랬다 뿐이지
Meaning	Other than that

"그렇다 뿐이지" and its past tense form "그랬다 뿐이지" can be used to express that the situation in the following sentence holds true in that the situation in the preceding sentence does not go beyond what is being described, which can be rendered as "Other than that."

나는 그저 당신만 믿고 있습니다. **그렇다 뿐이지** 별다른 해결책이 없습니다.
(=I just trust you. Other than that, there is no other solution.)

이 휴대폰은 조금 오래됐습니다. **그렇다 뿐이지** 아직까지 잘 작동됩니다.
(=This cell phone is a little bit old. Other than that, it still works fine.)

메리는 얼굴이 예쁩니다. **그렇다 뿐이지** 스스로 할 줄 아는 게 아무것도 없습니다.
(=Mary has a pretty face. Other than that, there is nothing that she can do by herself.)

범퍼에 살짝 기스만 났습니다. **그렇다 뿐이지** 별 다른 문제는 없습니다.
(=It just got a light scratch on the bumper. Other than that, there is no serious problem.)

그 남자와 전화 통화만 한 번 했습니다. **그랬다 뿐이지** 한 번도 만난 적이 없습니다.
(=I just had a telephone conversation with him. Other than that, I have never met him before.)

남들보다 좀 더 열심히 일을 했습니다. **그랬다 뿐이지** 특별한 성공의 비결은 없습니다.
(=I have just worked harder than others. Other than that, there is no other special secret to my success.)

저는 그저 다친 사람을 도와 주었습니다. **그랬다 뿐이지** 이번 범죄사건과 아무 관련이 없습니다.
(=I just helped the injured person. Other than that, I have nothing to do with this criminal case.)

54. Expressing "While one is at it": 그러는 김에

Function	Expressing "While one is at it"
Form	그러는 김에
Meaning	While one is at it

"그러는 김에" can be used to express that the action in the following sentence is to be carried out as a free ride given the situation that the action in the preceding sentence is being carried out, which can be rendered as "While one is at it."

존이 다음달에 새 집으로 이사한다. **그러는 김에** 가구를 모두 새로 바꾸려고 한다.
(=John is moving into a new house next month. While he is at it, he is planning to replace all the furniture with new ones.)

메리는 대학교에서 한국말을 오랫동안 공부해 왔다. **그러는 김에** 한국으로 유학을 갈 계획이다.
(=Mary has studied Korean at her college for a long time. While she is at it, she is planning to study in Korea.)

존은 다음주에 서울에 출장을 간다. **그러는 김에** 여기 저기 구경할 계획이다.
(=John is going on a business trip to Seoul next week. While he is at it, he is planning to look around various places.)

55. Talking about something that has just been said: 그래서 말인데

Function	Talking about something that has just been said
Form	그래서 말인데
Meaning	Speaking of which

"그래서 말인데" can be used to express that the speaker is trying to initiate a conversation about a given situation in the preceding sentence focusing on the situation in the following sentence, which can be rendered as "Speaking of which."

나 내일까지 카드 빚을 갚아야 해. **그래서 말인데** 한 오십만 원만 빌려줄 수 있겠니?

(=I must pay my credit card bill by tomorrow. Speaking of which, could you lend me just five hundred thousand won.)

나 지금 알바를 찾고 있거든. **그래서 말인데** 어디 좋은 알바 자리 하나 없을까?

(=I am looking for a part-time job. Speaking of which, do you happen to know of a good part-time job?)

56. Expressing "On top of that": 그런 데다(가)

Function	Expressing "On top of that"
Form	그런 데다가, 그런 데다
Meaning	On top of that

"그런 데다가" and its contraction form "그런 데다" can be used to express that the situation in the following sentence holds true on top of the situation in the preceding sentence, which can be rendered as "On top of that."

존은 돈이 많다. **그런 데다가/그런 데다** 얼굴도 잘생겼다.

(=John is rich. On top of that, he is also handsome.)

메리는 얼굴이 예쁘다. **그런 데다가/그런 데다** 공부도 잘한다.

(=Mary is pretty. On top of that, she also studies well.)

이 프로젝트는 돈이 많이 든다. **그런 데다가/그런 데다** 완성하는데 시간도 많이 걸린다.

(=This project costs a lot of money. On top of that, it also takes a long time to complete it.)

이 중고차는 너무 오래됐다. **그런 데다가/그런 데다** 값도 터무니 없다.

(=This used car is too old. On top of that, the price tag is also ridiculous.)

57. Expressing "Besides": 게다가, 더구나, 더군다나

Function	Expressing "Besides"		
Form	게다가	더구나	더군다나
Meaning	Besides		

"게다가, 더구나, 더군다나" can be used to express that the situation in the following sentence holds true in addition to the situation in the preceding sentence, which can be rendered as "Besides."

서울은 지금 아주 덥습니다. **게다가/더구나/더군다나** 습도도 높습니다.

(=It's very hot in Seoul now. Besides, the humidity is also high.)

존은 일을 아주 열심히 합니다. **게다가/더구나/더군다나** 경험도 아주 많습니다.

(=John works really hard. Besides, he also has a lot of experience.)

메리는 한국말을 아주 잘한다. **게다가/더구나/더군다나** 한국문화에 대해서도 많이 알고 있다.

(=Mary speaks Korean very well. Besides, she knows a lot about Korean culture.)

58. Expressing "In compensation for that": 그 대신(에), 그런 대신(에)

Function	Expressing "In compensation for that"
Form	그 대신(에), 그런 대신(에)
Meaning	In compensation for that

"그 대신(에), 그런 대신(에)" can used to express that the situation in the following sentence occurs in compensation for the situation in the preceding sentence, which can be rendered as "In compensation for that."

존은 머리가 그다지 좋지 않다. **그 대신(에)/그런 대신(에)** 노력을 아주 많이 한다.

(=John is not that smart. In compensation for that, he is putting a lot of effort into his studies)

메리는 여동생의 옷을 빌려 입었다. **그 대신(에)/그런 대신(에)** 저녁을 사 줬다.

(=Mary borrowed her younger sister's clothes. In compensation for that, she treated her to dinner.)

존은 메리의 숙제를 도와 주겠다고 했다. **그 대신(에)/그런 대신(에)** 자기와 데이트를 하자고 했다.

(=John said he was going to help Mary with her homework. In compensation for that, he asked her to date him.)

당분간 그 컴퓨터를 그냥 써라. **그 대신(에)/그런 대신(에)** 다음에 아주 좋은 걸로 사 줄게.

(=Just use that computer for the time being. In compensation for that, I will buy you a good one next time.)

59. Expressing the outcome of a past action/The subsequent change on a situation: 그러더니(만)

Function	The outcome of a past action	The subsequent change on a situation
Form	그러더니만, 그러더니	
Meaning	As a result of that	But then

"그러더니만" and its contraction form "그러더니" can be used to express that the situation in the following sentence is the direct outcome of the past situation in the preceding sentence, which can be rendered as "As a result of that."

존은 아주 열심히 공부했다. **그러더니만/그러더니** 시험에 합격했다.
(=John had studied really hard. As a result of that, he passed the exam.)

메리는 너무 무리하게 사업을 확장했다. **그러더니만/그러더니** 지난달에 파산을 신청했다.
(=Mary had excessively expanded her business. As a result of that, she filed a bankruptcy claim last month.)

할머니가 오랫동안 병환으로 고생하셨다. **그러시더니만/그러시더니** 작년에 돌아가셨다.
(=My grandmother had suffered from her illness for a long time. As a result of that, she passed away last year.)

On the other hand, "그러더니(만)" can also be used to express that the subsequent change in the following sentence has been made since the speaker's last observation in the preceding sentence, which can be rendered as "But then."

존은 고등학교 때까지 열심히 공부했다. **그러더니만/그러더니** 지금은 공부를 안 한다.
(=John had studied hard until he was in high school. But then he doesn't study now.)

메리는 결혼하기 전에는 비싼 것만 썼다. **그러더니만/그러더니** 지금은 아주 검소해졌다.
(=Mary had used only expensive things before she got married. But then she became very frugal now.)

존은 어렸을 때 말썽만 부렸다. **그러더니만/그러더니** 지금은 아주 점잖아졌다.
(=John had been a trouble maker when he was a kid. But then he became very gentle now.)

이 곳은 전에는 버려진 곳이었다. **그러더니만/그러더니** 지금은 여기에 고층빌딩이 많이 들어서고 있다.
(=This place was a deserted area before. But then many high-rise buildings are being built here now.)

메리는 어렸을 땐 못생겼다. **그러더니만/그러더니** 지금은 아주 예뻐졌다.
(=Mary was ugly when she was a little girl. But then she became very pretty now.)

지난주에는 아주 더웠다. **그러더니만/그러더니** 오늘은 날씨가 제법 쌀쌀해졌다.
(=It was very hot last week. But then it became a little bit chilly today.)

조금 전까지 복도가 아주 시끄러웠다. **그러더니만/그러더니** 갑자기 조용해졌다.
(=The hallway was very loud until a moment ago. But then it suddenly became quiet.)

"그랬더니(만)," the past tense form of "그러더니(만)," can be optionally used to emphasize the completion of the action or state in the preceding sentence.

존은 아주 열심히 공부했다. **그랬더니만/그랬더니** 시험에 합격했다.
(=John had studied really hard. As a result of that, he passed the exam.)

메리는 어렸을 땐 못생겼다. **그랬더니만/그랬더니** 지금은 아주 예뻐졌다.
(=Mary was ugly when she was a little girl. But then she became very pretty now.)

60. Expressing a change in the course of an action:

그러다(가), 그러다(가) 말고

Function	Expressing a change in the course of an action	
Form	그러다가, 그러다	그러다가 말고, 그러다 말고
Meaning	While doing so	After one stopped doing that

"그러다(가)" can be used to express that the action in the preceding sentence undergoes a sudden change into the action in the following sentence, which can be rendered as "While doing so."

존은 TV를 보고 있었다. **그러다가/그러다** 잠이 들었다.

(=John was watching TV. While doing so, he fell asleep.)

메리는 갑자기 비틀거렸다. **그러다가/그러다** 땅바닥에 쓰러졌다.

(=Mary was suddenly staggering. While doing so, she fell down on the ground.)

존은 노래를 불렀다. **그러다가/그러다** 갑자기 춤을 추기 시작했다.

(=John was singing a song. While doing so, he suddenly started dancing.)

메리는 어머님께 편지를 쓰고 있었다. **그러다가/그러다** 갑자기 눈물을 흘렸다.

(=Mary was writing a letter to her mother. While doing so, she suddenly shed tears.)

존은 전 재산을 주식에 투자했다. **그러다가/그러다** 망했다.

(=John invested all of his money in stocks. While doing so, he become bankrupt.)

"그랬다가," the past tense form of "그러다(가)," can be optionally used to emphasize the completion of the situation in the preceding sentence, which can be rendered as "After having done so."

존은 TV를 보고 있었다. **그랬다가** 잠이 들었다.

(=John was watching TV. After having done so, he fell asleep.)

메리는 갑자기 비틀거렸다. **그랬다가** 땅바닥에 쓰러졌다.

(=Mary was suddenly staggering. After having done so, she fell down on the ground.)

On the other hand, "그러다(가)" can also be used with the negative expression "말고 (stop)" to emphasize that the action in the preceding sentence is completely halted before taking another action in the following sentence, which can be rendered as "After one stopped doing that"

존은 밥을 먹고 있었다. **그러다가 말고/그러다 말고** 갑자기 자기 방으로 들어갔다.
(=John was eating his meal. After he stopped eating that, he suddenly went into his room.)

메리는 숙제를 하고 있었다. **그러다가 말고/그러다 말고** 밖에 나가서 친구하고 놀았다.
(=Mary was doing her homework. After she stopped doing that, she went outside and played with her friends.)

61. Expressing the discovery of a new fact:
그러고 보니(까), 그러다(가) 보니(까)

Function	Expressing the discovery of a new fact	
Form	그러고 보니까, 그러고 보니	그러다가 보니까, 그러다가 보니 그러다 보니까, 그러다 보니
Meaning	After I did that, I found out that_/ Come to think of it	While I was doing that, I found out that _

"그러고 보니까" and its contraction form "그러고 보니" can be used to express that the speaker has discovered a new fact in the following sentence after he/she carried out the action in the preceding sentence; otherwise, it might have gone unnoticed. It can be rendered as "After I did that, I found out that _."

존하고 여러 가지 이야기를 해 봤다. **그러고 보니(까)** 아주 능력 있는 사람인 것 같았다.
(=I talked to John about various kinds of things. After I did that, I found out that he is a very capable person.)

메리의 이야기를 자세히 들어 봤다. **그러고 보니(까)** 내가 너무 했던 것 같다.
(=I carefully listened to what Mary said. After I did that, I found out that I was too harsh on her.)

이번 실험 결과를 다시 한 번 살펴봤다. **그러고 보니(까)** 여기에서 실수를 한 것 같다.

(=I carefully reviewed the result of this experiment once again. After I did that, I found out that I made a mistake here.)

"그러다(가) 보니(까)" can be basically used for the same function, which can be rendered as "While I was doing that, I found out that _."

나는 한국에 오랫동안 살았다. **그러다(가) 보니(까)** 한국사람이 다 된 것 같다.

(=I have lived in Korea for a long time. While I was doing that, I found out that I almost became a Korean.)

메리하고 서울 시내 곳곳을 구경했다. **그러다(가) 보니(까)** 너무 재미있어서 시간 가는 줄 몰랐다.

(=I looked around here and there in downtown Seoul with Mary. While I was doing that, I found out that I didn't realize how much time had passed because we had a lot of fun.)

On the other hand, "그러고 보니(까)" can also be used in the middle of a conversation to express that the speaker discovered the fact in the following sentence that he/she just remembered, which can be rendered as "Come to think of it."

A: 존이 화가 많이 났다.

    (=John got really upset.)

B: **그러고 보니(까)** 내가 너무 심했던 것 같다.

    (=Come to think of it, it seems that I was too harsh on him.)

A: 벌써 열 시야.

    (=It's already 10 o'clock.)

B: **그러고 보니(까)** 집에 가야 할 시간이다.

    (=Come to think of it, it's time to go home.)

62. Expressing the natural outcome of a continuing action: 그러다(가) 보면

"그러다가 보면" and its contraction form "그러다 보면" can be used to express that the situation in the following sentence is the natural outcome of the continuing action in the preceding sentence, which can be rendered as "If one keeps doing that."

Function	Expressing the natural outcome of a continuing action
Form	그러다가 보면, 그러다 보면
Meaning	If one keeps doing that

존이 아주 열심히 일한다. **그러다(가) 보면** 언젠가는 성공할 거다.
(=John works really hard. If he keeps doing that, someday he will become successful.)

메리가 칼을 가지고 장난치고 있다. **그러다(가) 보면** 다칠 수도 있다.
(=Mary is playing with a knife. If she keeps doing that, she may get hurt.)

63. Expressing worry about facing an unwanted situation:

그럴까 봐(서), 그럴까 (봐) 싶어(서)

Function	Expressing worry about facing an unwanted situation		
Form	그럴까 봐서 그럴까 봐	그럴까 싶어서 그럴까 싶어	그럴까 봐 싶어서 그럴까 봐 싶어
Meaning	Because one is worried about that		

"그럴까 봐(서), 그럴까 싶어(서), 그럴까 봐 싶어(서)" can be used to express that the action in the following sentence is to be carried out because one is worried about the possibility of facing the unwanted situation in the preceding sentence, which can be rendered as "Because one is worried about that."

누가 그 돈을 훔쳐갈 수도 있다. **그럴까 봐(서)/그럴까 싶어(서)/그럴까 봐 싶어(서)** 몰래 감춰 놓았다.
(=There is a possibility that somebody might steal the money. Because I was worried about that, I hid the money secretly.)

나는 집안 내력 때문에 당뇨병에 걸릴 확률이 높다. **그럴까 봐(서)/그럴까 싶어(서)/그럴까 봐 싶어(서)** 요즘 음식을 조절하고 있다.
(=I have a high risk of getting diabetes because of my family history. Because I am worried about that, I have been on a diet these days.)

잠깐 한눈파는 사이에도 범인이 도망칠 수도 있다. **그럴까 봐(서)/그럴까 싶어(서)/그럴까 봐 싶어(서)** 수갑을 채워 놓았다.

(=The suspect might run away while I am looking away even for a moment. Because I was worried about that, I already handcuffed him.)

64. Getting prepared for an uncertain situation: 그럴 지(도) 몰라(서)

Function	Getting prepared for an uncertain situation
Form	그럴 지도 몰라서, 그럴 지도 몰라 그럴 지 몰라서, 그럴 지 몰라
Meaning	Just in case

"그럴 지(도) 몰라(서)" can be used to express that the action in the following sentence is to be carried out because one wants to get prepared for the uncertain situation in the preceding sentence, which can be rendered as "Just in case." It is frequently used with the optional adverb "혹시 (probably)" in the preceding sentence.

(혹시) 사장님이 언제든지 찾을 수도 있습니다. **그럴 지(도) 몰라(서)** 대기하고 있습니다.
(=My company president will probably look for me at any minute. Just in case, I have been standing by.)

그 서류는 (혹시) 나중에 필요할 수도 있습니다. **그럴 지(도) 몰라(서)** 잘 보관해 두었습니다.
(=We will probably need the document later. Just in case, I kept it in a safe place.)

(혹시) 갑자기 이곳을 떠날 수도 있습니다. **그럴 지(도) 몰라(서)** 미리 인사를 드립니다.
(=Probably I have to leave this place suddenly. Just in case, I have to say "goodbye" beforehand.)

65. Expressing "Before/After taking action":

그러기 전에, 그러기에 앞서, 그런 다음에, 그런 후에

Function	Expressing "Before/After taking action"	
Form	그러기 전에 그러기에 앞서	그런 다음에 그런 후에
Meaning	Before doing that	After doing that

"그러기 전에" can be used to express that the situation in the following sentence happens before the situation in the preceding sentence, which can be rendered as "Before doing that." It can be freely used in both written text and conversation, whereas the equivalent expression "그러기에 앞서" is more likely to be used in written text and formal speech.

존은 메리와 영화를 봤다. **그러기 전에** 같이 저녁을 먹었다.

(=John watched a movie with Mary. Before that, they ate dinner together.)

메리는 다음 달에 한국에 가려고 한다. **그러기 전에** 여권과 비자를 신청할 계획이다.
(=Mary intends to go to Korea next month. Before doing that, she is planning to apply for her passport and visa.)

사람들은 무슨 안 좋은 일이 생기면 남을 탓하는 경향이 있다. **그러기에 앞서** 먼저 자신을 돌아봐야 한다.
(=People tend to blame others when something bad comes up. Before doing that, they must look back at themselves.)

"그런 다음에, 그런 후에" can be used to express that the situation in the following sentence happens after the situation in the preceding sentence, which can be rendered as After doing that." "그런 다음에" is more frequently used in conversation, whereas "그런 후에" is more likely to be used in written text and formal speech.

메리는 집에 와서 숙제를 했다. **그런 다음에** TV를 봤다.
(=Mary came home and then did her homework. After that, she watched TV.)

한국전쟁 당시 맥아더 장군은 적의 전력과 배치 상황을 철저히 분석했다. **그런 후에** 드디어 인천상륙작전을 명령했다.

(=At the time of the Korean War, General MacArthur had thoroughly analyzed the enemy's military power and its deployment situation. After having done that, he finally issued the order for the Inchon Landing Operation.)

66. Expressing gratitude: 그 덕(분)에, 그 덕택에

Function	Expressing gratitude	
Form	그 덕(분)에	그 덕택에
Meaning	Thanks to that	

"그 덕(분)에, 그 덕택에" can be used to express that the situation in the following sentence happened thanks to the situation in the preceding sentence, which can be rendered as "Thanks to that."

존은 학교에서 4년 내내 장학금을 받았다. **그 덕(분)에/그 덕택에** 대학교육을 마칠 수 있었다.
(=John received a scholarship from his school for all four years. Thanks to that, he could finish his college education.)

메리가 이 일을 처음부터 끝까지 도와줬다. **그 덕(분)에/그 덕택에** 일을 끝낼 수 있었다.
(=Mary helped me on this work from the beginning to the end. Thanks to that, I was able to finish the work.)

67. Expressing "In contrast": 그러는 반면(에), 그런 반면(에)

Function	Expressing "In contrast"
Form	그러는 반면에, 그러는 반면 그런 반면에, 그런 반면
Meaning	But in contrast

"그러는 반면(에)" and its contraction form "그런 반면(에)" can be used to express that the situation in the following sentence is in contrast to the situation in the preceding sentence, which can be rendered as "But in contrast."

존은 공부를 아주 잘한다. **그러는 반면(에)/그런 반면(에)** 운동은 잘 못한다.
(=John studies very well. But in contrast, he is not good at sports.)

승진하면 봉급이 올라간다. **그러는 반면(에)/그런 반면(에)** 책임감도 더 무거워 진다.
(=When we get promoted, we get a pay raise. But in contrast, we need to take more responsibility.)

메리는 카지노에서 돈을 잃었다. **그러는 반면(에)/그런 반면(에)** 존은 많이 땄다.
(=Mary lost her money at the casino. But in contrast, John won a lot of money.)

메리는 얼굴이 예쁘다. **그러는 반면(에)/그런 반면(에)** 성격이 좀 까칠하다.
(=Mary has a pretty face. But in contrast, she is hard to please.)

68. Expressing "On the one hand _, but on the other hand _":
그러는가/그런가 하면

Function	Expressing "On the one hand _, but on the other hand _"	
Form	그러는가 하면	그런가 하면
Meaning	On the one hand _, but on the other hand _	

"그러는가 하면" and its contraction form 그런가 하면" can be used to express that both of the two contrastive situations in the preceding and following sentences hold true, which can be rendered as "On the one hand _, but on the other hand _."

세상에는 좋은 사람들이 있다. **그러는가 하면/그런가 하면** 나쁜 사람들도 많다.
(=On the one hand there are some good people living in the world, but on the other hand there are also some bad people.)

메리랑 살면서 행복했던 때가 있었습니다. **그러는가 하면/그런가 하면** 괴로웠던 때도 있었어요.
(While having lived with Mary, on the one hand there were times that I was happy, but on the other hand there were also times that I got frustrated.)

인삼이 어떤 사람에게는 몸에 좋습니다. **그러는가 하면/그런가 하면** 혈압이 높은 사람에게는 해로울 수도 있다.
(=On the one hand ginseng may be good for the health of some people, but on the other hand it also may be harmful for people with high blood pressure.)

혼자 살다 보면 어떤 때는 편합니다. **그러는가 하면/그런가 하면** 아주 외로울 때도 있어요.
(=While living alone, on the one hand there are times that I feel comfortable, but on the other hand there are also times that I feel very lonely.)

69. Expressing two different paths at the same time: 그러는 한편

Function	Expressing two different paths at the same time	
Form	그러는 한편	
Meaning	On the other hand, _ also	But on the other hand

"그러는 한편" can be used to express that one is carrying out the action in the preceding sentence, and at the same time he/she is also carrying out the action in the following sentence, which can be rendered as "On the other hand, _ also."

> 존은 K-드라마를 즐겨 본다. **그러는 한편** K-팝도 아주 좋아한다.
> (=John enjoys watching Korean dramas. On the other hand, he also likes K-pop music.)

> 메리는 오프라인 매장을 운영하고 있다. **그러는 한편** 온라인 쇼핑몰 창업을 준비하고 있다.
> (=Mary is running an offline store. On the other hand, she is also preparing to open an online shopping mall.)

> 최근 북한은 여러 차례 핵실험을 강행했다. **그러는 한편** 장거리탄도미사일 개발을 서두르고 있다.
> (=Recently North Korea has boldly carried out a series of nuclear tests. On the other hand, it is also spurring on the development of long range ballistic missiles.)

On the other hand, "그러는 한편" can also be used to express that the situation in the following sentence occurs in contrast to the given situation in the preceding sentence. It can be rendered as "But on the other hand."

메리는 열심히 공부하고 있다. **그러는 한편** 존은 밖에서 놀기만 한다.

(=Mary is studying hard. But on the other hand, John is just playing outside.)

세계경제는 지난 수년 동안 침체해 왔다. **그러는 한편** 한국경제는 지금도 꾸준히 성장하고 있다.

(=The world economy has fallen into a recession for the last several years. But on the other hand, the Korean economy has continued to grow steadily.)

70. Expressing "On the other hand": 한편

Function	Expressing "On the other hand"
Form	**한편**
Meaning	On the other hand

"한편" can be strategically used by the writer to send the reader a signal that the preceding sentence is the end of the discussion on a given topic, and the following sentence is the beginning of another topic he/she wants to talk about. It can be rendered as "On the other hand." Due to its formality, however, it is mainly used in written text or in formal speech.

이와 같이 우리 정부도 유엔의 대북경제제재에 동참하기로 했다. **한편** 북한은 유엔의 이러한 조치에도 불구하고 핵미사일 개발에 더욱더 박차를 가하고 있다.

(=Like this, our government also decided to join the UN's economic sanctions against North Korea. On the other hand, despite the UN's countermeasure, North Korea has continued to spur on the development of nuclear missiles.)

71. Expressing "In contrast": 반면(에)

Function	Expressing "In contrast"
Form	**반면(에)**
Meaning	In contrast

"반면(에)" can be used to express that the situation in the following sentence is directly in contrast with the situation in the preceding sentence, which can be rendered as "In contrast."

김정은은 호화로운 생활을 영위하고 있다. **반면(에)** 북한 주민들은 굶주림에 허덕이고 있다.

(=Kim Jong-un has been enjoying his luxurious lifestyle. In contrast, North Korean citizens have been suffering from starvation.)

최근 정부의 최저임금 인상 조치는 저임금 근로자의 소득을 증가시키는 긍정적인 효과가 있다. **반면(에)** 이들을 고용하는 소규모 영세상인들의 부담을 가중시키는 부정적인 측면 도 있다.

(=The government's recent measure to hike the minimum wage has a positive effect on the increase of the low-salaried workers' income. In contrast, it also has a negative impact on the small business owners who are hiring these workers by increasing their burdens.)

72. Expressing "Like this/that, Unlike this/that":
이/그와 같이, 이/그와(는) 달리

Function	Expressing "Like this/that"		Expressing "Unlike this/that"	
Form	이와 같이	그와 같이	이와(는) 달리	그와(는) 달리
Meaning	Like this	Like that	Unlike this	Unlike that

"이와 같이, 그와 같이" can be used to express that the situation in the preceding sentence is in line with a given situation in the following sentence, which can be rendered as "Like this, Like that," respectively.

북한은 최근 고위층 관리들을 잔인하게 공개처형하고 있다. **이와 같이/그와 같이** 김정은 정권은 공포정치를 자행하고 있다.

(=North Korea has recently carried out brutal public executions of high-ranking officials. Like this/Like that, Kim Jong-un's regime has continued to exercise scare tactics.)

On the other hand, "이와(는) 달리, 그와(는) 달리" can be used to express that the situation in the following sentence is contradictory to a given situation in the preceding sentence, which can be rendered as "Unlike this, Unlike that," respectively.

> 존은 다른 사람들 앞에서는 항상 점잖은 척한다. **이와(는) 달리**/**그와(는) 달리** 집에서는 망나니처럼 행동한다.
>
> (=John always pretends to be a gentleman in front of other people. Unlike this/Unlike that, he behaves like a maverick at home.)

73. Expressing "Together with/Aside from this/that":
이/그와 더불어, 이/그와(는) 별도로

Function	Expressing "Together with"		Expressing "Aside from this/that"	
Form	이와 더불어	그와 더불어	이와(는) 별도로	그와(는) 별도로
Meaning	Together with this	Together with that	Aside from this	Aside from that

"이와 더불어, 그와 더불어" can be used to express that the action in the following sentence is to be carried out together with action in the preceding sentence, which can be rendered as "Together with this, Together with that," respectively.

> 국방부는 국방력 강화를 위해 F-35 스텔스 전투기 40대를 도입하기로 했다. **이와 더불어**/ **그와 더불어** 아파치 헬기 1개 대대도 추가로 구입하기로 최종 결정했다.
>
> (=The Defense Ministry decided to import forty F-35 stealth fighter jets in order to strengthen our defense power. Together with this/Together with that, it also made a final decision to purchase one battalion's worth of Apache helicopters.)

On the other hand, "이와(는) 별도로, 그와(는) 별도로" can be used to express that the action in the following sentence is to be carried out separately from the action in the preceding sentence, which can be rendered as "Aside from this, Aside from that," respectively.

정부는 두 명 이상의 자녀를 키우는 가정에게 일정 금액의 양육비를 보조하기로 했습니다. **이와(는) 별도로/그와(는) 별도로** 자녀 교육비도 제공할 예정입니다.

(=The government decided to provide a set amount of child support to families raising two or more children. Aside from this/Aside from that, it is also going to provide them with educational support.)

74. Expressing "Irrespective of this/that": 이/그와(는) 상관 없이

Function	Expressing "Irrespective of this/that"	
Form	이와(는) 상관 없이	그와(는) 상관 없이
Meaning	Irrespective of this	Irrespective of that

"이와(는) 상관 없이, 그와(는) 상관 없이" can be used to express that the situation in the following sentence happens regardless of situation in the preceding sentence, which can be rendered as "Irrespective of this, Irrespective of that," respectively.

다음주부터 새로운 프로젝트를 시작합니다. **이와(는) 상관 없이/그와(는) 상관 없이** 기존의 프로젝트도 계속 진행합니다.

(=We are going to start a new project next week. Irrespective of this/Irrespective of that, we will also continue to work on the existing project.)

유엔은 북한의 6차 핵실험에 대한 일련의 조치로 대북경제제제를 시행하기로 결의했다. **이와(는) 상관 없이/그와(는) 상관 없이** 북한에 대한 인도주의적 식량지원 프로그램은 지속될 것이라고 했다.

(=The UN approved economic sanctions against North Korea as one of the counter-measures against North Korea's 6th nuclear test. Irrespective of this/Irrespective of that, the UN said its humanitarian food support program for North Korea will continue.)

75. Expressing "Anyway": 여하튼, 하여튼, 아무튼, 어쨌든, 좌우(지)간

Function	Expressing "Anyway"				
Form	여하튼	하여튼	아무튼	어쨌든	좌우(지)간
Meaning	Anyway				

"여하튼, 하여튼, 아무튼, 어쨌든, 좌우(지)간" can be used to express that the situation in the following sentence happens anyway regardless of the situation in the preceding sentence, which can be rendered as "Anyway." They differ only in terms of the degree of formality; "여하튼" is the most formal, and it is typically used in written text; "하여튼" can be freely used in both written text and conversation; "아무튼, 어쨌든" are more likely to be used in casual speech; lastly, "좌우(지)간" can be used typically in conversation between male speakers.

한반도 비핵화는 아직 갈 길이 멉니다. **여하튼/하여튼** 정부 당국자는 이를 위해 계속 최선의 노력을 다 해야 할 것입니다.
(=Nuclear disarmament on the Korean Peninsula is still a far-reaching goal. Anyway, the government authorities must continue to do their best to achieve this goal.)

존이 또 학교를 땡땡이 쳤어요. **좌우(지)간** 걔는 어떻게 할 수 없어요.
(=John ditched school again. Anyway, he is impossible to control.)

A: 존은 개인적인 일로 이번 미팅에는 참석 못 한다고 합니다.
(=John says that he cannot attend this meeting because of his personal matter.)

B: **하여튼/아무튼/어쨌든** 지금 회의를 시작하도록 합시다.
(=Anyway, let's start our meeting now.)

76. Expressing "Needless to say": 하물며

Function	Expressing "Needless to say"
Form	**하물며**
Meaning	So it is needless to say _

"하물며" can be used to express that the situation in the preceding sentence applies, and therefore it is needless to say that the situation in the following sentence also applies. It can be rendered as "So it is needless to say _."

존도 그 일을 끝내지 못 했습니다. **하물며** 저야 뭐 말할 필요가 있겠습니까?

(=Even John could not finish the work. So isn't it needless to talk about me?)

(=Even John could not finish the work. So it is needless to say that I could not finish it.)

메리도 시험에 떨어졌습니다. **하물며** 저야 두말할 필요도 없죠.

(=Even Mary failed the test. So it is nagging to talk about me again.)

(=Even Mary failed the test. So it is needless to say that I also failed.)

이 문제는 어린 아이도 금방 풀 수 있습니다. **하물며** 제가 못 풀겠습니까?

(=Even a little kid can quickly solve this problem. So isn't it needless to say that I can solve it?)

(=Even a little kid can quickly solve this problem. So it is needless to say that I can solve it.)

77. Expressing "For example": 예를 들면, 예를 들어(서), 예컨대

Function	Expressing "For example"		
Form	예를 들면	예를 들어(서)	예컨대
Meaning	For example		

"예를 들면, 예를 들어(서)" can be used to express that the situation in the following sentence is a concrete example that supports the claim in the preceding sentence, which can be rendered as "For example." "예를 들면" can be freely used in both written text and conversation, whereas "예를 들어(서)" is more likely to be used in formal conversation.

포도주가 사람의 수명을 연장시킨다는 연구결과가 나왔다. **예를 들면** 일주일에 포도주를 세 잔 이상 마시는 사람은 전혀 마시지 않은 사람에 비해 약 5년 정도 더 산다는 것이다.
(=The research result came out that says drinking wine can extend our life expectancy. For example, people who drink three glasses of wine a week can live for about five more years than people who don't drink wine at all.)

요즘 자영업자들이 많은 고통을 겪고 있습니다. **예를 들어(서)** 열에 아홉은 적자를 면하기 어렵습니다.
(=These days small business owners are suffering a lot. For example, nine out of ten cannot avoid a business loss.)

On the other hand, "예컨대" can also be used for the same function, but due to its formality, it is limited to use in written text. It is now on the verge of becoming an archaic expression.

지구온난화 문제가 갈수록 심각해지고 있다. **예컨대** 태평양에 위치한 몇몇 섬나라에서는 해수면이 매년 1.2cm씩 계속 상승하고 있다.
(=The issue of global warming is getting more serious. For example, the sea level for some island countries located in the Pacific Ocean has continued to rise by 1.2cm every year.).

78. Expressing "So to speak": 말하자면, 즉, 이를테면

Function	Expressing "So to speak"		
Form	말하자면	즉	이를테면
Meaning	So to speak		

"말하자면, 즉, 이를테면" can be used to express that the following sentence is a rephrase of what was said in the preceding sentence in simple and concrete terms to facilitate the listener's understanding, which can be rendered as "So to speak." "말하자면" can be freely used in both written text and conversation. "즉" is more likely to be used in written text, whereas "이를테면" is typically used in conversation and is now on the verge of becoming an archaic expression.

요즘 "묻지마" 살인사건이 급증하고 있다. **말하자면/즉/이를테면** 아무런 이유 없이 사람을 죽이는 사건이 늘어나고 있다는 것이다.
(=The number of random homicide cases has rapidly increased these days. So to speak, the number of murder cases without any clear motives has increased.)

최근 우리나라의 가계부채가 국가경제를 위협할 정도로 증가하고 있습니다. 말하자면/**즉/이를테면** 지난해 GDP 대비 가계부채는 이미 93%에 달했다고 합니다.
(=Our country's household debt has recently increased to the point that it might threaten our national economy. So to speak, it already reached 93% of our country's GDP last year.)

79. Expressing "In other words": 다시 말하(자)면, 달리 말하(자)면

Function	Expressing "In other words"	
Form	다시 말하자면, 다시 말하면	달리 말하자면, 달리 말하면
Meaning	In other words	

"다시 말하(자)면, 달리 말하(자)면" and their corresponding contraction forms "다시 말하면, 달리 말하면" can be used to indicate that the following sentence is rephrasing what was said in the preceding sentence, which can be rendered as "In other words." They are typically used to emphasize the importance of the previous statement by ensuring that the listener can clearly understand it. "다시 말하(자)면" can be freely used in both written text and conversation, whereas "달리 말하(자)면" is more likely to be used in written text and formal speech due to its formality.

자유는 거저 주어지는 것이 아니다. **다시 말하(자)면/달리 말하(자)면** 자유를 쟁취하는 데에는 반드시 희생이 따른다는 것이다.
(=Freedom is not given to us for free. In other words, freedom always comes with the sacrifice to acquire it.)

이 강당의 수용인원은 총 200명이다. **다시 말하(자)면/달리 말하(자)면** 200명 이상은 이 건물에 동시에 있을 수 없다는 것이다.

(=The maximum occupancy of this auditorium is 200 people in total. In other words, not more than 200 people can stay in this building at the same time.)

80. Expressing "To make a long story short":
간단히 말하(자)면, 간단히 요약하면

Function	Expressing "To make a long story short"	
Form	간단히 말하자면, 간단히 말하면	간단히 요약하면
Meaning	In short	

"간단히 말하(자)면, 간단히 요약하면" can be used to express that the following sentence is a brief summary of what was said so far, which can be rendered as "In short."

간단히 말하(자)면/간단히 요약하면 지구온난화는 환경오염에 의한 것이라는 이야기다.
(=In short, what I am saying is that global warming is caused by environmental pollution.)

간단히 말하(자)면/간단히 요약하면 물이 없으면 생명체가 존재할 수 없다는 것이다.
(=In short, what I am saying is that living organisms cannot exist without water.)

81. Expressing "To speak in more detail/precisely/simply":
구체적으로/정확히/쉽게 말하(자)면

Function	Expressing "To speak in more detail/precisely/simply"		
Form	구체적으로 말하자면 구체적으로 말하면	정확히 말하자면 정확히 말하면	쉽게 말하자면 쉽게 말하면
Meaning	To speak in more detail	To speak precisely	To speak simply

"구체적으로 말하자면, 정확히 말하자면, 쉽게 말하자면" and their corresponding contraction forms "구체적으로 말하면, 정확히 말하면, 쉽게 말하면" can be used with the optional adverb "좀 더 (more)" to indicate that the following sentence is rephrasing what was said so far, which can be rendered as "To speak in more detail, To speak more precisely, To speak more simply," respectively.

> (좀 더) **구체적으로 말하(자)면** 민주주의는 입법부, 사법부, 행정부의 삼권분립에 기초를 두고 있다.
> (=To speak in more detail, democracy is based on the balance of powers among the legislative, the judiciary, and the executive branches.)
>
> (좀 더) **정확히 말하(자)면** 우리나라 국민 4명 중 1명은 불면증에 시달리는 것으로 나타났다.
> (=To speak more precisely, it appears that one out of four citizens in our country is suffering from insomnia.)
>
> (좀 더) **쉽게 말하(자)면** 지구는 1년에 한 번 태양 주위를 돈다는 것이다.
> (=To speak more simply, what I am saying is that the Earth circles around the Sun once a year.)

82. Expressing "In conclusion":

결론적으로 (말하면), 한마디로 말해서/한마디로 말하(자)면

Function	Expressing "In conclusion"	
Form	결론적으로 말하면 결론적으로	한마디로 말해서 한마디로 말하자면 한마디로 말하면
Meaning	In conclusion	To put it in a nutshell

"결론적으로 말하면" and its contraction form "결론적으로" can be used to express that the following sentence is the conclusion of a topic that has been discussed so far, which can be rendered as "In conclusion."

> **결론적으로 (말하면)** 일관되지 못한 정부의 시책으로 많은 소규모 영세업자들이 피해를 보고 있다.

(=In conclusion, a large number of small business owners have been victimized due to the inconsistent government policy.)

On the other hand, "한마디로 말해서, 한마디로 말하(자)면" can be used to express that the following sentence is the brief summary of the preceding discussion, which can be rendered as "To put it in a nutshell."

한마디로 말해서/한마디로 말하(자)면 우리는 이미 고령화시대로 접어들었다는 것이다.
(=To put it in a nutshell, what I am saying is that we have already become an aging society.)

83. Expressing "If I am looking back": 돌이켜 생각해 보면, 돌이켜 생각하면

Function	Expressing "If I am looking back"
Form	돌이켜 생각해 보면 돌이켜 생각하면 돌이켜 보면
Meaning	If I am looking back

"돌이켜 생각해 보면" and its contraction forms "돌이켜 생각하면, 돌이켜 보면" can be used to express that the situation in the following sentence applies as the speaker is looking back about what had happened previously, which can be rendered as "If I am looking back."

돌이켜 생각해 보면/돌이켜 생각하면 내가 메리한테 좀 심하게 했던 것 같다.
(=If I am looking back, it seems that I was too harsh on Mary.)

돌이켜 생각해 보면/돌이켜 생각하면 인생을 허무함을 느끼게 된다.
(=If I am looking back, I realize the vanity of life.)

84. Expressing "Without a doubt": 틀림 없이, 의심할 여지 없이

Function	Expressing "Without a doubt"	
Form	틀림 없이	의심할 여지 없이
Meaning	Without a doubt	

"틀림 없이, 의심할 여지 없이" can be used to express that the situation in the following sentence is not questionable, which can be rendered as "Without a doubt."

틀림 없이/의심할 여지 없이 북한은 또 다시 가까운 시일 내에 핵실험을 재개할 겁니다.

(=Without a doubt, North Korea will resume its nuclear testing again in the very near future.)

85. Expressing "Even after deep thinking":
아무리 생각해 봐도, 아무리 생각해도

Function	Expressing "Even after deep thinking"	
Form	아무리 생각해 봐도	아무리 생각해도
Meaning	No matter how much I have thought about it	

"아무리 생각해 봐도, 아무리 생각해도" can be used to express that the situation in the following sentence still applies even after the speaker's deep thinking about the given situation, which can be rendered as "No matter how much I have thought about it."

아무리 생각해 봐도/아무리 생각해도 저는 잘못한 게 하나도 없습니다.

(=No matter how much I have thought about it, I didn't do anything wrong.)

아무리 생각해 봐도/아무리 생각해도 이번 작전은 성공할 확률이 너무 낮습니다.

(=No matter how much I have thought about it, this operation is very unlikely to succeed.)

86. Expressing "As I already expected": 아니나 다를까

Function	Expressing "As I already expected"
Form	**아니나 다를까**
Meaning	No wonder

"아니나 다를까" can be used to express that the situation in the following sentence happens as the speaker already expected, which can be rendered as "No wonder."

아니나 다를까 존이 또 거짓말을 하네요.

(=No wonder John is lying again.)

아니나 다를까 건물 주인이 또 집세를 올렸어요.

(=No wonder the building owner raised our rent again.)

87. Expressing "In fact": 사실

Function	Expressing "In fact"
Form	**사실**
Meaning	In fact

"사실" can be used to express that the speaker is revealing the fact that the situation in the following sentence is true, which can be rendered as "In fact."

사실 존은 아무 것도 잘못한 것이 없다.

(=In fact, John didn't do anything wrong.)

사실 메리는 그 일을 할 자격이 없다.

(=In fact, Mary is not qualified for doing the work.)

88. Expressing "To get to the point": 다름이 아니라

Function	Expressing "To get to the point"
Form	**다름이 아니라**
Meaning	To get to the point

"다름이 아니라" can be used to express that the speaker wants to emphasize that the situation in the following sentence is the main reason for a given situation, which can be rendered as "To get to the point."

다름이 아니라 메리 좀 만나러 왔습니다.

(=To get to the point, I came here to meet Mary.)

다름이 아니라 돈이 좀 필요해서요.

(=To get to the point, I need some money.)

89. Expressing "To be sure": 아닌 게 아니라

Function	Expressing "To be sure"
Form	**아닌 게 아니라**
Meaning	To be sure

"아닌 게 아니라" can be used to express that the speaker wants to confirm that the situation in the following sentence is indeed true after his/her personal observation, which can be rendered as "To be sure."

아닌 게 아니라 존이 사무실에서 그때까지 일하고 있었다.

(=To be sure, John had been working in his office until that time.)

아닌 게 아니라 메리 말이 옳았다.

(=To be sure, what Mary said was right.)

90. Expressing the speaker's point of view on a given situation:

그런 점에서, 그런 면에서

Function	Expressing the speaker's point of view on a given situation	
Form	그런 점에서	그런 면에서
Meaning	From that point	

"그런 점에서, 그런 면에서" can be used to express that the following sentence is the logical conclusion from the speaker's point of view based on the situation in the preceding sentence, which can be rendered as "From that point."

그것은 의도적인 살인사건이다. **그런 점에서/그런 면에서** 범인은 사형선고를 피할 수 없을 것 같다.

(=That is a premeditated murder case. From that point, the suspect cannot avoid getting the capital punishment.)

한국은 6.25 전쟁 폐허에서 눈부신 경제 발전을 이룩했다. **그런 점에서/그런 면에서** 한강의 기적이라고 부른다.

(=Korea has achieved remarkable economic development from the ruins after the Korean War. From that point, it is called "the miracle of Han River.")

91. Expressing "Even limiting the scope of discussion":

그것만 보더라도, 그것만 봐도

Function	Expressing "Even limiting the scope of discussion"	
Form	그것만 보더라도	그것만 봐도
Meaning	Just considering that	

"그 것만 보더라도, 그 것만 봐도" can be used to express that the following sentence is the logical conclusion from the speaker's point of view by limiting the scope of discussion to the situation in the preceding sentence, which can be rendered as "Just considering that."

지난달 북한은 또 한 차례의 핵실험을 했다. **그것만 보더라도/그것만 봐도** 이미 북한은 적어도10기 정도의 핵탄두 개발 능력을 갖추고 있다고 할 수 있다.
(=North Korea carried out another nuclear test last month. Just considering that, we can say that North Korea already has the capability of developing at least ten nuclear warheads.)

92. Explaining the main reason for a given situation:

왜냐하면 때문이다, 왜 그런가 하면/그러냐 하면

Function	Explaining the reason for a given situation	
Form	왜냐하면 ~ 때문이다/거든(요)	왜 그런가 하면 왜 그러냐 하면
Meaning	The reason is that _	The reason why it is like that is because _

"왜냐 하면" can be used to directly express the main reason in the following sentence for the situation in the preceding sentence, which can be rendered as "The reason is that _." It is typically used with the sentence endings "때문이다, ~거든(요)"

늦어서 죄송합니다. **왜냐 하면** 집에 일이 좀 생겼**기 때문입니다**.
늦어서 죄송해요. **왜냐 하면** 집에 일이 좀 생겼**거든요**.
(=I am sorry for the late. The reason is that I had something to take care of at my house.)

저는 한국어를 배우고 싶습니다. **왜냐 하면** 한국 회사에 취직하고 싶**기 때문입니다**.
저는 한국어를 배우고 싶어요. **왜냐 하면** 한국 회사에 취직하고 싶**거든요**.
(=I want to learn Korean. The reason is that I want to get a job at a Korean company.)

On the other hand, "왜 그런가 하면, 왜 그러냐 하면" can be used to express the main reason in the following sentence less straightforwardly, which can be rendered as "The reason why one is doing something like that _/The reason why it is _ like that."

A: 이 TV는 왜 그렇게 비싸요?

B: **왜 그런가 하면/왜 그러냐 하면** 다른 것보다 화질이 훨씬 뛰어나기 **때문이죠**.
(=Why is this TV so expensive like that? The reason why it is like that is because the picture quality is far better than others.)

CHAPTER 4 Sentence Connectors II (문장 접속사 II)

1. Soliciting the listener's acceptance of a given situation: 그나마

Function	Soliciting the listener's acceptance of a given situation
Form	그나마
Meaning	Nevertheless

"그나마" can be used to express that the speaker is soliciting the listener's acceptance of a situation in the following sentence even though it may not be good enough to meet the listener's expectation because of the reason in the preceding sentence. It can be rendered as "Nevertheless."

액수는 좀 적습니다. **그나마** 살림에 보탬이 되었으면 합니다.
(=This is just a small amount of money. Nevertheless, I hope this can be of some help to run your household)

별로 보잘것없습니다. **그나마** 한번 봐 주시기 바랍니다.
(=This is not that good. Nevertheless, I hope you can take a look at it.)

On the other hand, "그나마" can also be used with "다행이다 (to be lucky)" and "불행 중 다행이다 (to be lucky in the middle of mishaps)" to express that one went through an unpleasant situation in the preceding sentence, but he/she was lucky to avoid the worst-case scenario, which can be rendered as "Nevertheless, one was lucky."

존이 계단에서 넘어져서 다리를 삐었어요. **그나마** 심하게 다치지 않았으니 **다행이에요**.
(=John fell down the stairs and sprained his ankle. Nevertheless, he was lucky not to get seriously injured.)

메리가 자동차 사고로 차가 완전히 찌그러졌어요. **그나마** 안 다쳤으니 **불행 중 다행이에요**.
(=Mary's car is completely wrecked because of a car accident. Nevertheless, she was lucky not to get injured in the middle of the mishap.)

2. Expressing a probable cause: 그래서 그런지

Function	Expressing a probable cause
Form	그래서 그런지
Meaning	Probably because of that

"그래서 그런지" can be used to express that the situation in the following sentence occurs probably because of the situation in the preceding sentence, which can be rendered as "Probably because of that."

존은 너무 어려요. **그래서 그런지** 이 상황을 잘 이해 못해요.
(=John is too young. Probably because of that, he cannot understand this situation well.)

어제 너무 무리한 것 같아요. **그래서 그런지** 기운이 하나도 없네요.
(=It seems that I worked way too much yesterday. Probably because of that, I don't have any energy left.)

시험이 너무 어려웠어요. **그래서 그런지** 성적이 별로 좋지 않네요.
(=The test was too difficult. Probably because of that, the test scores are not that good.)

3. Expressing the aftermath of an action:
그러고 나서야/나서도/났는데도/나면/나니(까)

"그러고 나서야" can be used to express that the situation in the following sentence occurs only after the situation in the preceding sentence happened, which can be rendered as "Only after that."

Function	Expressing the aftermath of an action			
Form	그러고 나서야	그러고 나서도 그러고 났는데도	그러고 나면	그러고 나니(까)
Meaning	Only after that	Even after that	Upon doing that	Since having done that

메리는 화가 나서 동생을 한 대 때렸다. **그러고 나서야** 직성이 풀렸다.

(=Mary punched her younger sibling because she got upset. Only after that, she could calm down.)

On the other hand, "그러고 나서도, 그러고 났는데도" can be used to express that the existing situation continues in the following sentence even after the situation in the preceding sentence, which can be rendered as "Even after that." They are more or less interchangeable, but "그러고 났는데도" is used to emphasize the completion of the situation in the preceding sentence.

존은 지난달에 취직을 했다. **그러고 나서도** 부모님께 계속 돈을 달라고 한다.

(=John got a job last month. Even after that, he continues to ask his parents for money.)

어제 잠을 충분히 잤다. **그러고 났는데도** 아직 피로가 풀리지 않는다.

(=I had a good night's sleep last night. Even after that, I still cannot recover from fatigue.)

In addition, "그러고 나면, 그러고 나니(까)" can be used to express that the situation in the following sentence happens after the completion of an action in the preceding sentence, which can be rendered as "Upon doing that, Since having done that," respectively.

이 감기약 먹고 잠 좀 푹 자라. **그러고 나면** 괜찮아 질 거다.

(=Take this cold medicine and get some deep sleep. Upon doing that, you will get better.)

이제 그 프로젝트를 끝냈다. **그러고 나니(까)** 속이 다 후련하다.

(=Now I finished the project. Since having done that, I have unburdened my mind.)

4. Carrying out an action immediately: 그러기가 무섭게

Function	Carrying out an action immediately
Form	그러기가 무섭게
Meaning	Immediately after that

"그러기가 무섭게" can be used to express that the action in the following sentence is to be carried out immediately after the situation in the preceding sentence happens, which can be rendered as "Immediately after that."

종이 울렸다. **그러기가 무섭게** 존은 화장실로 달려 갔다.

(=The bell rang. Immediately after that, John rushed to the restroom.)

북한군이 군사분계선을 넘어오는 귀순병을 향해 사격하기 시작했다. **그러기가 무섭게** 우리 군도 즉각 대응사격을 했다.

(=North Korean troops started firing at the defector who was crossing the Military Demarcation Line. Immediately after that, our military also returned fire.)

5. Expressing "During a short period of time": 그러는 사이(에)

Function	Expressing "During a short period of time"
Form	그러는 사이(에)
Meaning	Just at that moment

"그러는 사이(에)" can be used to express that the situation in the following sentence happens just for the moment that the situation in the preceding sentence occurs, which can be rendered as "Just at that moment." It is more or less interchangeable with "그러는 순간(에), 그러는 찰나(에) (Right at that moment)," which we already discussed in the previous chapter.

납치범이 잠깐 잠이 들었다. **그러는 사이(에)** 몰래 빠져 나왔다.

(=The kidnapper fell asleep for a moment. Just at that moment, I escaped from him secretly)

적이 잠깐 방심하고 있었다. **그러는 사이(에)** 기습공격을 했다.

(=The enemy forces were off guard for a moment. Just at that moment, we made a surprise attack.)

벤치에 앉아서 잠깐 눈을 감았다. **그러는 사이(에)** 누군가가 내 가방을 훔쳐 갔다.

(=I sat on the bench and closed my eyes for a moment. Just at that moment, somebody stole my bag.)

경찰관이 용의자에게서 잠깐 눈을 돌렸다. **그러는 사이(에)** 용의자가 갑자기 도망치기 시작했다.

(=The police officer looked away from the suspect for a moment. Just at that moment, the suspect suddenly started running away.)

6. Expressing "At the end of": 그러던 끝에

Function	Expressing "At the end of"
Form	그러던 끝에
Meaning	At the end of having done that

"그러던 끝에" can be used to express that the situation in the following sentence finally happened at the cost of one's effort in the preceding sentence, which can be rendered as "At the end of having done that."

오랫동안 항암치료를 받아 왔다. **그러던 끝에** 이제는 암이 완치됐다.

(=I had received chemotherapy for a long time. At the end of having done that, now I have fully recovered from cancer.)

범인이 숨은 곳을 한참 찾아다녔다. **그러던 끝에** 드디어 범인을 잡았다.

(=I had searched for the suspect's hideout for a long time. At the end of having done that, I finally captured the suspect.)

오랫동안 망설였다. **그러던 끝에** 이번 선거에 출마하기로 결심했다.

(=I had hesitated for a long time. At the end of having done that, I finally decided to run for this election.)

7. Expressing "Throughout a period of time": 그러는 내내

Function	Expressing "Throughout a period of time"
Form	그러는 내내
Meaning	Throughout that period of time

"그러는 내내" can be used to express that the situation in the following sentence continues to happen during the entire period of time while the action in the preceding sentence is being carried out, which can be rendered as "throughout that period of time."

존은 하루 종일 일을 했다. **그러는 내내** 계속 불평만 했다.

(=John had worked all day long. Throughout that period of time, he had continued to complain.)

메리는 매일 한 시간씩 운동한다. **그러는 내내** 항상 K-pop을 듣는다.

(=Mary does exercise for an hour every day. Throughout that period of time, she always listens to K-pop music.)

8. Taking a better option in a given situation: 그러느니, 그럴 바에야/바에는

Function	Taking a better option in a given situation		
Form	그러느니	그럴 바에야	그럴 바에는
Meaning	Rather than doing that		

"그러느니, 그럴 바에야, 그럴 바에는" can be used to express that the speaker prefers to carry out the action in the following sentence rather than accepting the unpleasant situation in the preceding sentence, which can be rendered as "Rather than doing that." It is often used with the optional adverb "차라리 (rather)" in the following sentence.

존한테 이 일을 맡길 수 없다. **그러느니/그럴 바에야/그럴 바에는** (차라리) 내가 하겠다.

(=I cannot let John do this work. Rather than doing that, I would do it by myself.)

여기서 한 없이 기다릴 수는 없다. **그러느니/그럴 바에야/그럴 바에는** (차라리) 내가 혼자 가 보겠다.

(=I cannot wait here endlessly. Rather than doing that, I would try to go by myself.)

여기서 이렇게 개 죽음을 당할 수 없다. **그러느니/그럴 바에야/그럴 바에는** (차라리) 전선에서 용감히 싸우다 죽겠다.

(=I don't want to die here for nothing. Rather than doing that, I would fight bravely and die on the front lines.)

이런 수모를 더 이상 당할 수 없다. **그러느니/그럴 바에야/그럴 바에는** (차라리) 다른 직장을 알아보는 것이 더 낫겠다.

(=I don't want to get humiliated like this any more. Rather than doing that, it would be better to find a job at some other place.)

9. Expressing an effort that will be in vain:

그래 봐야/보았자/봤자/보았댔자/봤댔자

Function	Expressing an effort that will be in vain		
Form	그래 봐야	그래 보았자/그래 봤자	그래 보았댔자/그래 봤댔자
Meaning	Even though one tries to do that	Even though one tried to do that	Even though one has kept trying to do that

"그래 봐야" can be used to express that one's effort in the preceding sentence will be in vain as in the following sentence, which can be rendered as "Even though one tries to do that."

존한테 한 번 이야기는 해 보겠다. **그래 봐야** 내 말을 듣지 않을 거다.

(=At least I will try to talk to John about it. Even though I try to do that, he won't listen to me.)

On the other hand, "그래 보았자, 그래 보았댔자" and their corresponding contraction forms ""그래 봤자, 그래 봤댔자" carry the same function, which can be rendered as "Even though one tried to do that, Even though one has kept trying to do that," respectively.

메리한테 좀 도와달라고 사정사정해 보았다. **그래 보았자/봤자** 전혀 꿈쩍도 안 했다.
(=I tried to beg Mary for some help. Even though I tried to do that, she didn't budge at all.)

잘해 보려고 열심히 일을 해 왔다. **그래 보았댔자/봤댔자** 변한 것은 아무 것도 없었다.
(=I have worked hard to make things go well. Even though I have kept trying to do that, nothing has been changed at all.)

10. Expressing "Just for doing something/To have no choice but to accept it": 그러는 데야/그러는데야

Function	Just for doing something	To have no choice but to accept it
Form	그러는 데야	그러는데야
Meaning	Just for doing that	Because one is saying that

"그러는 데야" can be used to express that the situation in the following sentence is just good enough for taking the action in the preceding sentence, which can be rendered as "Just for doing that."

저는 보통 컴퓨터로 인터넷만 합니다. **그러는 데야** 이 컴퓨터면 충분합니다.
(=I usually use my computer just for surfing the internet. Just for doing that, this computer is more than enough.)

저는 보통 출퇴근용으로 차가 필요합니다. **그러는 데야** 이 차가 안성맞춤이죠.
(=I usually need a car just for commuting. Just for doing that, this car is a perfect match.)

On the other hand, "그러는데야" can also be used to express that one has no choice but to accept the situation in the following sentence because of a given situation in the preceding sentence, which can be rendered as "Because one is saying that."

존이 그 일을 자기가 하겠다고 합니다. **그러는데야** 제가 뭘 어떻게 합니까?
(=John is saying that he wants to do the work. Because he is saying that, what am I supposed to do?)

집주인이 갑자기 집을 안 팔겠다고 합니다. **그러는데야** 제가 할 수 있는 게 아무 것도 없죠.

(=All of a sudden the home owner said he/she is not going to sell the house. Because he/she is saying that, there's nothing I can do about it.)

존이 자기 인생은 자기가 책임진다고 해요. **그러는데야** 그냥 놔둘 수 밖에 없죠.

(=John is saying that he is going to take full responsibility for his own life. Because he is saying that, I have no choice but to leave him alone.)

메리가 존하고는 절대로 결혼 안 한다고 해요. **그러는데야** 더 이상 강요할 수는 없죠.

(=Mary is saying that she is never going to marry John. Because she is saying that, I have no choice but to stop pushing her.)

11. Expressing the unacceptability of a given situation: 그런대서야

Function	Expressing the unacceptability of a given situation
Form	그런대서야
Meaning	Once one does so

"그런대서야" can be used to express that the situation in the following sentence applies once the unacceptable situation in the preceding sentence happens, which can be rendered as "Once one does so."

존은 돈을 위해서라면 둘도 없는 친구마저도 배신할 수 있어요. **그런대서야** 사람의 도리가 아니죠.

(=John may even betray his closest friend for money. Once he does so, it is unethical.)

제 남편은 모든 걸 쉽게 포기해요. **그런대서야** 어떻게 우리 가족을 부양할 수 있겠어요?

(=My husband easily gives up on everything. Once he does so, how can he support my family?)

이 중대한 시국에 여야가 서로 싸움만 하고 있어요. **그런대서야** 어떻게 이 경제위기를 극복할 수 있겠습니까?

(=The ruling party and the opposition party are just fighting against each other at this critical juncture. Once they are doing so, how can we overcome this economic crisis?)

12. Expressing "In that case": 그러면야, 그렇다면야

Function	Expressing "In that case"	
Form	그러면야	그렇다면야
Meaning	If that happens to be the case	

"그러면야, 그렇다면야" can be used to express that the situation in the following sentence applies if the situation in the preceding sentence happens to be the case, which can be rendered as "If that happens to be the case."

A: 제가 대신 그 일을 할 게요.
(=I will do it instead of you.)

B: **그러면야/그렇다면야** 저는 더할 나위 없이 좋죠.
(=If that happens to be the case, it couldn't be better for me.)

A: 저는 이 기계를 어떻게 사용하는 지 몰라요.
(=I don't know how to use this machine.)

B: **그러면야/그렇다면야** 제가 도와드려야죠.
(=If that happens to be the case, I will help you.)

13. Reporting the reason for a given situation:

그런 이유로, 그런다는/그랬다는 이유로

Function	Reporting the reason for a given situation		
Form	그런 이유로	그런다는 이유로	그랬다는 이유로
Meaning	Because of that reason		

"그런 이유로" can be used to express that the speaker is reporting to the listener that one is going through the situation in the following sentence because of the situation in the preceding sentence, which can be rendered as "Because of that reason."

존은 회사돈을 횡령한 혐의를 받고 있다. **그런 이유로** 지금 조사를 받고 있다.

(=John is under suspicion that he embezzled money from his company. Because of that reason, he is now under investigation.)

On the other hand, "그런다는 이유로" can also be used for the same function. It is specially used if the reason in the preceding sentence is due to one's habitual action. Its past tense form "그랬다는 이유로" is used instead if the reason in the preceding sentence is due to one's completed action.

메리는 상사에게 자주 말대꾸를 한다. **그런다는 이유로** 징계를 받았다.

(=Mary often talks back at her boss. Because of that reason, she received a reprimand.)

존은 학교에서 항상 다른 학생들을 괴롭혔다. **그랬다는 이유로** 학교에서 퇴학을 당했다.

(=John had always bullied other students at school. Because of that reason, he got kicked out of school.)

14. Expressing an unacceptable justification for a given situation: 그러기로서니

Function	Expressing an unacceptable justification for a given situation
Form	그러기로서니
Meaning	But even so

"그러기로서니" can be used to express that the situation in the following sentence cannot be justified even though the situation in the preceding sentence holds true, which can be rendered as "But even so."

A: 요즘 제가 아주 바빠요.

(=I have been so busy these days.)

B: **그러기로서니** 같이 저녁 먹을 시간도 없단 말이에요?

(=But even so, don't you have time to have dinner with me?)

It is typically used with the optional adverb "아무리 (no matter how)," and the combination can be rendered as "No matter what."

A: 죄송합니다. 너무 화가 나서 그랬어요.

(=I am sorry about that. I did it because I got so upset.)

B: 아무리 **그러기로서니** 다른 사람한테 화풀이를 하면 안 되죠.

(=No matter what, you are not supposed to take your anger out on someone else.)

15. Expressing a speaker's warning against one's unacceptable action:
그러다가는, 그랬다가는

Function	Expressing a speaker's warning against one's unacceptable action	
Form	그러다가는	그랬다가는
Meaning	If one keeps doing that	Once one does that

"그러다가는" can be used to express that the preceding sentence is the speaker's warning against one's unacceptable ongoing action that may result in the unpleasant situation in the following sentence. It can be rendered as "If one keeps doing that."

빨리 서둘러야 한다. **그러다가는** 비행기를 놓칠 수도 있다.

(=You must hurry up. If you keep doing that, you may miss the flight.)

너무 잘난 척하지 마라. **그러다가는** 큰 코 다친다.

(=Don't brag about yourself too much. If you keep doing that, you may run into a big trouble.)

On the other hand, "그랬다가는" can also be used for the same function. But it is used when the unacceptable action in the preceding sentence has not taken place yet, but may possibly be carried out in the near future. It can be rendered as "Once one does that."

이건 건드릴 생각도 하지 말아라. **그랬다가는** 할아버지한테 야단 맞는다.

(=Don't even think of touching this. Once you do that, you are going to get scolded by grandfather.)

수업시간에 졸면 안 된다. **그랬다가는** 선생님한테 혼난다.
(=Don't doze off during class. Once you do that, you are going to get scolded by teacher.)

16. Expressing a sudden change from a continuing situation: 이러/그러/저러다가도

Function	Expressing a sudden change from a continuing situation		
Form	이러다가도	그러다가도	저러다가도
Meaning	Even after one is/does like this for a while	Even after one is/does like that for a while	

"이러다가도" can be used to express that the situation in the preceding sentence continues for a while, and then it undergoes a sudden change into the situation in the following sentence, which can be rendered as "Even after one is like this for a while, Even after one does it like this for a while" depending on the context. It is typically used with the adverb "갑자기 (suddenly)" in the following sentence.

날씨가 아주 변덕스러워요. **이러다가도** 갑자기 소나기가 내려요.
(=The weather is very treacherous. Even after it is like this for a while, all of a sudden a shower pours down.)

"그러다가도/저러다가도" can be used for the same function, which can be rendered as "Even after one is like that for a while, Even after one does it like that for a while" depending on the context. They are also typically used with the adverb "갑자기 (suddenly)" in the following sentence.

존은 보통 때는 멀쩡해요. **그러다가도** 갑자기 미친 사람처럼 행동해요.
(=John is usually clear minded. Even after he is like that for a while, he suddenly acts like a crazy person.)

메리는 가만 놔두면 저렇게 일을 열심히 해요. **저러다가도** 갑자기 엉뚱한 짓을 해요.
(=Mary works hard like that if I leave her alone. Even after she does it like that for a while, she suddenly does a weird thing.)

17. Being unable to keep a situation under control: 그러다(가) 못해(서)

Function	Being unable to keep a situation under control	
Form	그러다가 못해서, 그러다가 못해, 그러다 못해서, 그러다 못해	
Meaning	Because one could no longer do that	After having kept doing that

"그러다가 못해서" and it contraction forms "그러다가 못해, 그러다 못해서, 그러다 못해 "can be used to express that the situation in the following sentence happened because one could no longer keep the situation in the preceding sentence under control, which can be rendered as "Because one could no longer do that."

존은 항암치료의 극심한 고통을 견디어 왔다. **그러다(가) 못해(서)** 의사에게 안락사를 시켜달라고 요구했다.

(=John has kept enduring extreme pain from chemotheraphy. Because he could no longer do that, he asked his doctor for euthanasia.)

지금까지 존의 잘못된 행동을 참아 왔다. **그러다(가) 못해(서)** 주먹으로 한대 때려줬다.
(=I have kept tolerating John's wrong behavior up until now. Because I could no longer do that, I hit him once with my fist.)

지금까지 상황을 가만히 지켜 보았다. **그러다(가) 못해(서)** 내가 직접 문제를 해결하기로 했다.
(=I have kept observing the situation quietly so far. Because I could no longer do that, I decided to solve the problem by myself.)

On the other hand, "그러다(가) 못해(서)" can also be used to express that the ongoing situation in the preceding sentence gets out of control and takes one step further to the extreme situation in the following sentence, which can be rendered as "After having kept doing that."

존은 나한테 거짓말을 해왔다. **그러다(가) 못해(서)** 이젠 나를 갖고 놀기까지 한다.
(=John has kept lying to me. After having kept doing that, he is now even making fun of me.)

존은 나를 함부로 대한다. **그러다(가) 못해(서)** 이젠 때리기까지 한다.
(=John walks all over me. After having kept doing that, now he even beats me.)

18. Expressing a worst-case scenario: 그러는 날에는

Function	Expressing a worst-case scenario
Form	그러는 날에는
Meaning	If that happens

"그러는 날에는" can be used to express that the situation in the following sentence is the purportedly worst-case scenario that may occur if the situation in the preceding sentence happens, which can be rendered as "If that happens."

그러다가 다시 쓰러질 수도 있습니다. **그러는 날에는** 회복하기가 불가능합니다.

(=You may collapse if you keep doing so. If that happens, it will be impossible to recover from it.)

이번 선거에서 질 수도 있다. **그러는 날에는** 우리 모두 끝장이다.

(=We may lose this upcoming election. If that happens, it is going to be the end of the world for us.)

한반도에서 핵전쟁이 일어날 수도 있다. **그러는 날에는** 남한 인구의 절반 정도가 살아남기 힘들 거다.

(=A nuclear war may break out on the Korean peninsula. If that happens, half of the South Korean population might not survive.)

19. Expressing the benefit of the doubt: 그러겠냐마는, 그러랴마는

Function	Expressing the benefit of the doubt	
Form	그러겠냐마는	그러랴마는
Meaning	I doubt it, but _	

"그러겠냐마는" can be used to express that the situation in the following sentence applies even though the speaker doubts that the situation in the preceding sentence will actually occur, which can be rendered as "I doubt it, but _." It is often used with the optional adverb "설마 (It can't be true)" at the beginning of the sentence. Its past-tense form

"그랬겠냐마는" can be used to emphasize the completion of the action in the preceding sentence.

A: 우리 중에 배신자가 있는 것 같습니다.

(=It seems that there is a traitor among us.)

B: (설마) **그러겠냐마는** 한 번 알아 볼 필요는 있지.

(=I doubt it, but it might at least be necessary to find that out.)

A: 아무리 생각해도 제가 실수한 것 같아요.

(=No matter how many times I thought about it, it seems that I made a mistake.)

B: (설마) **그랬겠냐마는** 다시 한 번 확인해 보자.

(=I doubt it, but let's double check.)

On the other hand, "그러랴마는" and its past tense form 그랬으랴마는" can also be used for the same function, but they are now on the verge of becoming an archaic expression.

A: 이러다 굶어 죽을 수도 있어요.

(=We may starve to death if things keep going like this.)

B: (설마) **그러랴마는** 요즘 먹고 살기가 진짜 힘들다.

(=I doubt it, but it is really hard to make ends meet these days.)

A: 존이 또 음주운전을 한 것 같아요.

(=It seems that John was driving his car under the influence again.)

B: (설마) **그랬으랴마는** 한 번 알아보자.

(=I doubt it, but let's find that out.)

20. Expressing "Because of the expected outcome": 그럴진대

Function	Expressing "Because of the expected outcome"
Form	그럴진대
Meaning	Because of that

"그럴진대" can be used to express that the situation in the following sentence is the speaker's response to a given situation because of the expected outcome in the preceding sentence, which can be rendered as "Because of that." It is now on the verge of becoming an archaic expression.

나라의 앞날이 위험합니다. **그럴진대** 가만히 책상 앞에 앉아 공부만 할 수 없어요.
(=Our country's future is in danger. Because of that, I cannot just study sitting in front of a desk.)

누가 그랬는지 불을 보듯 뻔합니다. **그럴진대** 왜 아직도 그 사람을 안 잡아들이는지 모르겠네요.
(=It is so clear who did it. Because of that, I don't know why they don't arrest the person yet.)

김정은이 핵버튼을 누르면 북한은 지구상에서 영원히 사라질 수도 있습니다. **그럴진대** 쉽게 핵공격을 감행하지 못합니다.
(=If Kim Jong-un presses the nuclear button, North Korea may disappear from the earth forever. Because of that, he cannot easily carry out a nuclear attack.)

21. Expressing "At the time of carrying out an intended action":
그러(려)던 차에/참에

Function	Expressing "At the time of carrying out an intended action"	
Form	그러던 차에 그러던 참에	그러려던 차에 그러려던 참에
Meaning	At that time	

"그러던 차에, 그러던 참에" can be used to express that the situation in the following sentence just occured at the time of carrying out the action in the preceding sentence, which can be rendered as "At that time." "그러던 차에" can be freely used in both written text and conversation, whereas "그러던 참에" is more likely to be used in conversation.

가게 문을 닫고 나가던 중이었다. **그러던 차에/그러던 참에** 손님들이 막 들이닥쳤다.
(=I was going out after closing the store. At that time, customers just rushed in.)

막 퇴근하던 참이었다. **그러던 차에**/**그러던 참에** 팀장님한테서 전화가 왔다.

(=I was getting off work. At that time, my team leader called me.)

숙제를 하던 중이었다. **그러던 차에**/**그러던 참에** 갑자기 전기가 나갔다.

(=I was doing my homework. At that time, suddenly the power went out.)

On the other hand, "그러려던 차에, 그러려던 참에" can be used to express that the situation in the following sentence just occured when one was about to carry out the intended action in the preceding sentence, which can also be rendered as "At that time."

가게 문을 닫고 나가려던 중이었다. **그러려던 차에**/**그러려던 참에** 손님들이 막 들이닥쳤다.

(=I was about to go out after closing the store. At that time, customers just rushed in.)

막 퇴근하려던 참이었다. **그러려던 차에**/**그러려던 참에** 팀장님한테서 전화가 왔다.

(=I was about to get off work. At that time, my team leader called me.)

숙제를 하려던 중이었다. **그러려던 차에**/**그러려던 참에** 갑자기 전기가 나갔다.

(=I was about to do my homework. At that time, suddenly the power went out.)

22. Expressing "As a result of an uncontrollable ongoing situation":
그러는 통에

Function	Expressing "As a result of an uncontrollable ongoing situation"
Form	그러는 통에
Meaning	Because of that

"그러는 통에" can be used to express that the negative outcome in the following sentence occurs due to an uncontrollable, undesirable, or unfavorable ongoing situation in the preceding sentence, which can be rendered as "Because of that."

태풍이 전국을 강타하고 있다. **그러는 통에** 모든 비행기가 결항되었다.

(=The typhoon has been smashing the entire nation. Because of that, all the flights were cancelled.)

존이 자기 방식대로 하기를 원하다. **그러는 통에** 모든 일이 지체되고 있다.
(=John wants to do it his way. Because of that, all the things are being delayed.)

갑자기 배가 뒤집혔다. **그러는 통에** 사상자가 급속도로 늘고 있다.
(=Suddenly the boat capsized. Because of that, the number of casualties has been rapidly increasing.)

23. Expressing "Even in the middle of a situation":
그러는 중에도/가운데도/와중에도, 그런 중에도/가운데도/와중에도

Function	Even in the middle of a situation		Even in the middle of the turmoil
Form	그러는 중에도 그러는 가운데도	그런 중에도 그런 가운데도	그러는 와중에도 그런 와중에도
Meaning	Even in that situation		

"그러는 중에도, 그러는 가운데도" can be used to express that the situation in the following sentence occurs even in the middle of another ongoing situation in the preceding sentence, which can be rendered as "Even in that situation."

메리는 병원에 입원해 있다. **그러는 중에도/그러는 가운데도** 한국말을 공부하고 있다.
(=Mary is hospitalized. Even in that situation, she is studying Korean.)

Their corresponding past tense forms are "그런 중에도, 그런 가운데도. They can be used to express that the situation in the following sentence occurred even in the middle of the situation in the preceding sentence that had continued in the past, which can also be rendered as "Even in that situation."

존은 어렸을 때 집이 가난했다. **그런 중에도/그런 가운데도** 열심히 공부했다.
(=John's family was poor when he was a kid. Even in that situation, he studied hard.)

On the other hand, "그러는 와중에도" and its past tense form "그런 와중에도" can be used to express that the situation in the following sentence occurs/occurred even during the turmoil in the preceding sentence, which can also be rendered as "Even in that situation."

메리의 어머님이 항암치료를 받고 계신다. **그러시는 와중에도** 메리의 앞날만 걱정하신다.
(=Mary's mother has been receiving chemotheraphy. Even in that situation, she is always worried about Mary's future.)

존은 한 달 전에 암 말기 진단을 받았다. **그런 와중에도** 자기 임무를 완수했다.
(=John was diagnosed with terminal stage cancer a month ago. Even in that situation, he accomplished his mission.)

24. Considering a critical situation: 이런 마당에, 그런 마당에

Function	Considering a critical situation	
Form	이런 마당에	그런 마당에
Meaning	Given a situation like this	Given a situation like that

"이런 마당에, 그런 마당에" can be used to express that the situation in the following sentence is the speaker's negative response to the listener in consideration of the critical situation in the preceding sentence, which can be rendered as "Given a situation like this, Given a situation like that," respectively.

지금 모두가 죽느냐 사느냐 하고 있습니다. **이런 마당에** 제가 뭘 어떻게 하란 말입니까?
(=Everyone is facing a life-or-death situation. Given a situation like this, what am I supposed to do?)

지금은 나 자신도 못 믿겠습니다. **이런 마당에** 누구를 믿으란 말입니까?
(=Now I cannot even trust myself. Given a situation like this, how can I trust others?)

회사가 파산 직전에 있습니다. **그런 마당에** 어떻게 봉급을 올려달라고 합니까?
(=Our company is on the verge of going bankrupt. Given a situation like that, how can I ask for my pay raise?)

제 입에 풀칠하기도 어렵습니다. **그런 마당에** 지금 남을 도와 줄 형편이 안 됩니다.
(=I am having a hard time making ends meet. Given a situation like that, I don't think I can help others now.)

25. Showing the speaker's frustration with an intended action:

그러려고 하니까, 그러려니까

Function	Showing the speaker's frustration with an intended action	
Form	그러려고 하니까	그러려니까
Meaning	Because I intend to do that	

"그러려고 하니까" can be used to express that the speaker is showing frustration in the following sentence because he/she intends to carry out the action in the preceding sentence, which can be rendered as "Because I intend to do that." Its contaction form "그러려니까" is more likely to be used in casual speech.

> 내가 꼭 다른 사람의 기회를 빼앗는 것 같다. **그러려고 하니까/그러려니까** 좀 마음에 걸린다.
>
> (=It is just like I am depriving someone of his/her opportunity. Because I intend to do that, it has been weighing on my mind.)

> 이번 일은 저 혼자 하려고 합니다. **그러려고 하니까/그러려니까** 생각한 것보다 시간이 많이 걸리네요.
>
> (=I am trying to do this work by myself. Because I intend to do that, it takes more time than I thought.)

26. Showing the speaker's frustration with a planned action: 그러자니(까)

Function	Showing the speaker's frustration with a planned action
Form	그러자니까, 그러자니
Meaning	Because one is planning to do that

"그러자니까" and its contraction form "그러자니" can be used to express that the speaker is showing frustration in the following sentence because he/she is planning to carry out the action in the preceding sentence, which can be rendered as "Because I am planning to do that." "그러자니" is more likely to be used in casual speech.

이번에는 존한테 승진 기회를 주고 싶다. **그러자니까/그러자니** 메리가 샘을 낼 것 같아 신경이 쓰인다.

(=This time I want to give John the promotion opportunity. Because I am planning to do that, it's getting on my nerves that Mary may become jealous of him.)

딸 아이가 공부를 아주 잘 해서 자사고에 보내려고 한다. **그러자니까/그러자니** 비싼 학비 때문에 걱정이다.

(=My daughter studies very well, and so I am thinking of sending her to a private high school. Because I am planning to do that, I am worried about the expensive tuition.)

27. Expressing "Based on one's observation of a situation":
그러는 걸 보니(까), 그런 걸 보니(까)

Function	Expressing "Based on one's observation of a situation"
Form	그러는 걸 보니까, 그러는 걸 보니 그런 걸 보니까, 그런 걸 보니
Meaning	Judging from that

"그러는 걸 보니까" and its contraction form "그러는 걸 보니" can be used to express that the situation in the following sentence is the speaker's response to a given situation based on his/her personal observation of the situation in the preceding sentence, which can be rendered as "Judging from that."

존이 아직 그 일을 하고 있다. **그러는 걸 보니까/그러는 걸 보니** 오늘 끝내기가 어려울 것 같다.

(=John is still working on it. Judging from that, it seems unlikely that he can finish it by today.)

여기 저기에서 얼음이 녹고 있다. **그러는 걸 보니까/그러는 걸 보니** 벌써 봄이 온 것 같다.

(=Ice is melting here and there. Judging from that, it seems likely that spring had already come.)

Their corresponding past tense forms are "그런 걸 보니까, 그런 걸 보니," respectively.

메리가 멤버들 간의 갈등 문제를 해결했다. **그런 걸 보니까/그런 걸 보니** 메리의 리더십이 훌륭한 것 같다.

(=Mary resolved the conflicts among the members. Judging from that, she seems to show excellent leadership.)

그 가게는 손님들로 꽉 차 있었다. **그런 걸 보니까/그런 걸 보니** 장사가 아주 잘 되는 것 같다.

(=That store was fully packed with customers. Judging from that, its business seems to be going well.)

28. Expressing the cause of a negative outcome: 그런 탓에

Function	Expressing the cause of a negative outcome
Form	그런 탓에
Meaning	Because of that

"그런 탓에" can be used to express that the negative outcome in the following sentence can be directly attributed to the situation in the preceding sentence, which can be rendered as "Because of that."

존은 편식을 많이 한다. **그런 탓에** 건강이 안 좋다.

(=John is a very picky eater. Because of that, he is not healthy.)

약속시간에 늦어서 급하게 집을 나왔다. **그런 탓에** 중요한 서류를 집에 두고 왔다.

(=I was in a hurry to get out of my house because I was late for an appointment. Because of that, I left an important document at home.)

존은 전과자다. **그런 탓에** 취직하기가 힘들다.

(=John is an ex-convict. Because of that, it will be hard for him to get a job.)

29. Expressing the probable cause of a negative outcome: 그런 탓인지

Function	Expressing the probable cause of a negative outcome
Form	그런 탓인지
Meaning	Probably because of that

"그런 탓인지" can be used to express that the situation in the following sentence is the negative outcome which is probably caused by the situation in the preceding sentence. It can be rendered as "Probably because of that."

존은 주로 혼밥, 혼술을 한다. **그런 탓인지** 항상 외로워 보인다.
(=John eats alone and drinks alone most of the time. Probably because of that, he always looks lonely.)

오늘은 날씨가 무덥다. **그런 탓인지** 식욕이 하나도 없다.
(=The weather is hot and muggy today. Probably because of that, I don't have any appetite at all.)

30. Expressing the direct cause of a negative outcome: 그런 나머지

Function	Expressing the direct cause of a negative outcome
Form	그런 나머지
Meaning	As a result of that

"그런 나머지" can be used to express that the situation in the following sentence was directly caused by the situation in the preceding sentence, which can be rendered as "As a result of that."

메리는 직장에서 스트레스를 굉장히 많이 받았다. **그런 나머지** 결국 회사를 그만뒀다.
(=Mary received a tremondous amount of stress at her workplace. As a result of that, she ended up quitting her job.)

존은 무리하게 사업을 확장했다. **그런 나머지** 빚더미에 올라 앉았다.
(=John expanded his business beyond his control. As a result of that, he became indebted up to his eyeballs.)

그 영화배우는 우울증으로 오랫동안 고생했다. **그런 나머지** 결국 자살을 했다.

(=The movie actor had suffered from depression for a long time. As a result of that, he ended up committing suicide.)

그 물건은 단가가 터무니 없이 낮다. **그런 나머지** 팔 때마다 오히려 손해를 본다.

(=The unit price of that product is ridiculously low. As a result of that, we lose money whenever we sell it.)

31. Expressing "Because of a pre-existing condition":
그러는 터라(서), 그러던 터라(서)

Function	Expressing "Because of a pre-existing condition"	
Form	그러는 터라서 그러는 터라	그러던 터라서 그러던 터라
Meaning	Because of that	

"그러는 터라서" and its contraction form 그러는 터라" can be used to express that the situation in the following clause happens because of a pre-existing condition in the preceding clause, which can be rendered as "Because of that."

저는 지금 혼자 가족을 부양하고 있습니다. **그러는 터라서/그러는 터라** 군입대를 연기해야만 합니다.

(=I have been financially supporting my family all by myself. Because of that reason, I must postpone my military enlistment.)

저는 지금 새로운 프로그램을 개발하고 있습니다. **그러는 터라서/그러는 터라** 다른 곳에 신경쓸 겨를이 없습니다.

(=I am now developing a new program. Because of that, I have no time to think about other things.)

Their corresponding past tense forms are "그러던 터라서, 그러던 터라," respectively.

이 원자력 발전소 건설에 이미 많은 정부 예산을 투입했습니다. **그러던 터라서/그러던 터라** 지금 공사를 중단하기가 쉽지 않습니다.

(=We have already spent a huge amount of the government budget to build this nuclear power plant. Because of that, it is not easy to stop the construction now.)

저는 어려서부터 온갖 역경을 극복해 왔습니다. **그러던 터라서/그러던 터라** 이 정도 어려움은 저에게는 아무 것도 아닙니다.

(=I have overcome all kinds of hardships since I was young. Because of that, this kind of ordeal is almost nothing to me.)

32. Expressing "Because of one's characteristics/the nature of a situation": 그래 가지고(서)

Function	Because of one's personal characteristics	Because of the nature of a situation
Form	그래 가지고서	그래 가지고
Meaning	Because of that	Given that situation

"그래 가지고서" and its contraction form "그래 가지고" can be used to express that the situation in the following sentence can be attributed to one's specific personal characteristics in the preceding sentence, which can be rendered as "Because of that." They are typically used in casual speech.

존은 욕심이 많다. **그래 가지고(서)** 항상 모든 걸 다 자기 혼자 가지려고 한다.
(=John is very greedy. Because of that, he always wants to take it all.)

메리는 성격이 급하다. **그래 가지고(서)** 모든 일을 빨리만 하려고 한다.
(=Mary is always in a rush. Because of that, she wants to just get everything done quickly.)

On the other hand, "그래 가지고(서)" can also be used to express the speaker's response in the following sentence because of the nature of the given situation in the preceding sentence, which can be rendered as "Given that situation." Again, it is typically used in casual speech.

존이 자기가 해야 할 일을 나한테 하라고 하잖아. **그래 가지고(서)** 내가 싫다고 했어.
(=John asked me to do the thing that he was supposed to do. Given that situation,

I said no to him.)

메리가 비트코인에 투자하면 떼돈을 번다고 하잖아. **그래 가지고(서)** 나는 관심이 없다고 했어.

(=Mary told me that I can win a jackpot if I invest in Bitcoin. Given that situation, I told her I am not interested in it.)

In addition, "그래 가지고" can also be used to express the speaker's curiosity to elicit more information from the interlocutor, which can be rendered as "And then?" It can be freely repeated until one gets all the information that he/she wants to know.

A: 메리가 어제 존하고 이혼을 했대. (=Mary divorced John yesterday.)
B: **그래 가지고** (=And then?)

A: 존이 다른 여자와 바람을 핀 것 같아.
(=It appears that John had an affair with another woman.)
B: **그래 가지고** (=And then?)

A: 어제 대판 싸움을 하고 이혼서류를 접수했대.
(=They had a big fight and filed a divorce suit.)
B: **그래 가지고** (=And then?)

A: 나도 거기까지 밖에 몰라. (=That's all I know.)

33. Expressing the reason for a given situation: 그런 까닭에

Function	Expressing the reason for a given situation
Form	그런 까닭에
Meaning	Because of that reason

"그런 까닭에" can be used to express that the situation in the preceding sentence is the main reason for the situation in the following sentence, which can be rendered as "Because of that reason."

저는 커피를 마시면 잠을 못 잡니다. **그런 까닭에** 커피를 안 마십니다.

(=I cannot sleep if I drink coffee. Because of that reason, I don't drink it.)

부모님한테서 좀 재산을 물려받았습니다. **그런 까닭에** 집을 장만할 수 있었습니다.
(=I inherited some properities from my parents. Because of that reason, I was able to buy a house.)

한국 가는 비행기표를 몇 달 전에 구입했습니다. **그런 까닭에** 아주 싸게 살 수 있었습니다.
(=I purchased the airplane ticket to Korea several months ago. Because of that reason, I was able to buy it at a very low price.)

메리는 성격이 좋습니다. **그런 까닭에** 주위에 친구가 많습니다.
(=Mary has a good personality. Because of that reason, she has many friends around her.)

서울은 물가가 아주 비쌉니다. **그런 까닭에** 생활비가 많이 듭니다.
(=The prices of commodities are very expensive in Seoul. Because of that reason, the cost of living in Seoul is very high.)

존은 돈이 하나도 없었습니다. **그런 까닭에** 치료를 제대로 받지 못했습니다.
(=John did not have money at all. Because of that reason, he could not receive proper medical treatment.)

34. Matching with one's experience: 아시다시피, 보시다시피, 들으셨다시피

Function	Matching with one's experience		
Form	아시다시피 알다시피	보시다시피 보다시피	들으셨다시피 들었다시피
Meaning	As you know	As you can see	As you may have heard

"아시다시피, 보시다시피, 들으셨다시피" and their corresponding blunt forms "알다시피, 보다시피, 들었다시피" can be used to express that the speaker assumes that the situation in the following sentence matches the listener's personal experience to support his/her claim in the preceding sentence, which can be rendered as "As you know," "As you can see," "As you may have heard," respectively.

한국이 가까운 미래에 통일이 될 것 같아요. **아시다시피** 지금 남북정상회담이 열리고 있잖아요.

한국이 가까운 미래에 통일이 될 것 같아. **알다시피** 지금 남북정상회담이 열리고 있잖아.
(=Korea will become unified in the very near future. As you know, the summit talk between South and North Korea is being held now.)

지금은 시간이 없어요. **보시다시피** 지금 일이 밀려서 눈코 뜰새 없이 바빠요.
지금은 시간이 없어. **보다시피** 지금 일이 밀려서 눈코 뜰새 없이 바빠.
(=I don't have time now. As you can see, I am extremely busy because I am behind on my work schedule.)

가뭄 때문에 걱정이에요. **들으셨다시피** 거의 모든 저수지가 바닥이 드러났대요.
가뭄 때문에 걱정이야. **들었다시피** 거의 모든 저수지가 바닥이 드러났대.
(=I am worried about the drought. As you may have heard, almost all reservoirs have dried up.)

35. Expressing an action contradictory to the original commitment:
그런다/그러겠다(고 하)더니

Function	Expressing an action contradictory to the original commitment	
Form	그런다고 하더니 그런다더니	그러겠다고 하더니 그러겠다더니
Meaning	After having said that _	

"그런다고 하더니, 그러겠다고 하더니" and their contraction forms "그런다더니, 그러겠다더니" can be used to express that the situation in the following sentence actually occurred, which contradicts one's original commitment in the preceding sentence, which can be rendered as "After having said that _."

존은 이 일을 자기가 한다고 했다. **그런다고 하더니/그런다더니** 갑자기 나한테 하라고 한다.
(=John said that he was going to do this work. After having said that, suddenly he is asking me to do it.)

메리는 나한테 존과 결혼한다고 했다. **그런다고 하더니/그런다더니** 결국 다른 남자와 결혼했다.

(=Mary said that she was planning to marry John. After having said that, she ended up having married another man.)

정부는 내년부터 법인세를 올리겠다고 했다. **그러겠다고 하더니/그러겠다더니** 결국 포기하고 말았다.

(=The government said that it will raise the corporate tax rate starting from next year. After having said that, it ended up having given it up.)

36. Expressing "Even by taking the less preferred option":
그러고(서)라도, 그래서라도

Function	Expressing "Even by taking the less preferred option"	
Form	그러고서라도, 그러고라도	그래서라도
Meaning	Even by doing so	Even by doing so (as a last resort)

"그러고서라도" and its contraction form "그러고라도" can be used to express that the action in the preceding sentence is not the preferred option, but it needs to be taken anyway to carry out the action in the following sentence, which can be rendered as "Even by doing so."

은행 융자라도 받아야겠다. **그러고서라도/그러고라도** 즉시 계약을 하는 게 좋겠다.
(=I even need to get a bank loan. Even by doing so, it would be better to sign the contract immediately.)

수면제라도 몇 알 먹어야겠다. **그러고서라도/그러고라도** 잠을 좀 자야겠다.
(=I even need to take some sleeping pills. Even by doing so, I need to get some sleep.)

On the other hand, "그래서라도" can be used to express that the action in the preceding sentence is the least preferred option, but it needs to be taken anyway as a last resort to carry out the action in the following sentence, which can be rendered as "Even by doing so (as a last resort)."

집이라도 처분해야겠다. **그래서라도** 빚을 정리하는 게 좋겠다.

(=I even need to sell my house. Even by doing so, it would be better to pay off the debt.)

정부는 부동산 보유세를 올려야 한다. **그래서라도** 과열된 부동산 투기를 막는 것이 시급하다.

(=The government must raise its property tax rate. Even by doing so, it is urgent to curb the heated real estate speculation.)

37. Expressing "At all costs":

어떻게 해서라도, 어떻게 (해서)든(지), 무슨 수를 쓰더라도,

무슨 수를 써서라도, 무슨 수를 쓰든지

Function	Expressing "At all costs"	
Form	어떻게 해서라도 어떻게 해서든(지) 어떻게든(지)	무슨 수를 쓰더라도 무슨 수를 써서라도 무슨 수를 쓴(지)
Meaning	One way or another	Whatever it costs

"어떻게 해서라도" can be used to express that the situation in the following sentence must be achieved anyway given the situation in the preceding sentence, which can be rendered as "One way or another." It can be freely used in written text and conversation, whereas "어떻게 해서든(지)" and its contraction form "어떻게든(지)" are more likely to be used in conversation.

최근 청년 실업률이 급상승하고 있습니다. **어떻게 해서라도** 정부는 청년 일자리 창출을 위한 확고한 대책을 세워야 합니다.

(=Recently the unemployment rate of young people has been rapidly increasing. One way or another, the government must come up with a decisive countermeasure to create more jobs for young people.)

가능한 한 빨리 한반도의 비핵화를 이루어야 한다. **어떻게 해서라도** 북한을 대화의 장으로 끌어들여야 한다.

(=We must accomplish nuclear disarmament on the Korean Peninsula as soon as possible. One way or another, we must bring North Korea to the table.)

A: 공사 마감일이 한 달밖에 안 남았습니다.

(=We have only one month left before the construction deadline.)

B: **어떻게 해서라도/어떻게 해서든(지)/어떻게든(지)** 마감일 전에 공사를 끝내야 합니다.

(=One way or another, we must complete the construction before the deadline.

On the other hand, "무슨 수를 쓰더라도" can be used for a similar function. But they emphasize that the situation in the following sentence must be achieved at all costs given the situation in the preceding sentence, which can be rendered as "Whatever it costs." It can be freely used in written text and conversation, whereas "무슨 수를 써서라도, 무슨 수를 쓰든(지)" are more likely to be used in conversation.

최근 청년 실업률이 급상승하고 있습니다. **무슨 수를 쓰더라도** 정부는 청년 일자리 창출을 위한 확고한 대책을 세워야 합니다.

(=Recently the unemployment rate of young people has been rapidly increasing. Whatever it costs, the government must come up with a decisive countermeasure to create more jobs for young people.)

가능한 한 빨리 한반도의 비핵화를 이루어야 한다. **무슨 수를 쓰더라도** 북한을 대화의 장으로 끌어들여야 한다.

(=We must accomplish nuclear disarmament on the Korean Peninsula as soon as possible. Whatever it costs, we must bring North Korea to the table.)

A: 공사 마감일이 한 달밖에 안 남았습니다.

(=We have only one month left before the construction deadline.)

B: **무슨 수를 쓰더라도/무슨 수를 써서라도/무슨 수를 쓰든(지)** 빨리 공사를 끝내야 합니다.

(=Whatever it costs, we must complete the construction quickly.

38. Expressing one's simple response to a given situation: 그러기에, 그러길래

Function	Expressing one's simple response to a given situation	
Form	그러기에	그러길래
Meaning	Just because of that	

"그러기에, 그러길래" can be used to express that the situation in the following sentence is one's simple response to a given situation in the preceding sentence, which can be rendered as "Just because of that." "그러기에" can be freely used in both written text and conversation, whereas "그러길래" is more likely to be used in conversation.

존이 나한테 물어봤어. **그러기에/그러길래** 그렇게 말해줬을 뿐이야.
(=John asked me about it. Just because of that, I told him so.)

그 남자가 아는 척을 했어. **그러기에/그러길래** 그냥 인사만 했을 뿐이야.
(=The man pretended to know me. Just because of that, I said hello to him.)

존이 밥 먹을 돈도 없다고 했다. **그러기에/그러길래** 메리가 돈을 좀 빌려줬다.
(=John said he did not even have money for food. Just because of that, Mary lent him some money.)

39. Expressing one's simple response to a given situation:
그런다기에/길래, 그렇다기에/길래

Function	Expressing one's simple response to a given situation	
Form	그런다기에 그런다길래	그렇다기에 그렇다길래
Meaning	Just because one says so	

"그런다기에, 그런다길래" can be used to express that the situation in the following sentence is one's simple response to a given situation in the preceding sentence, which can be rendered as "Just because one says so." The verb in the preceding sentence must be an action verb. "그런다기에" can be freely used in both written text and conversation, whereas "그런다길래" is more likely to be used in conversation. Their corresponding past tense and future tense forms are "그랬다기에/그랬다길래, 그러겠다기에/그러겠다길래," respectively.

존이 저녁을 나중에 먹는다고 한다. **그런다기에/그런다길래** 알아서 하라고 했다.
(=John says that he is going to eat dinner later. Just because he says so, I told him it's up to him.)

메리가 옆 집에 사람이 이사 왔다고 했다. **그랬다기에/그랬다길래** 인사를 하러 갔다. (=Mary said my next-door neighbor moved in. Just because she said that, I went there to say hello to them.)

메리가 아파서 오늘 집에서 쉬겠다고 한다. **그러겠다기에/그러겠다길래** 그렇게 하라고 했다.
(=Mary is saying that she will take a rest at home because she is sick. Just because she says so, I told her to do so.)

존이 내일까지 숙제를 제출하겠다고 한다. **그러겠다기에/그러겠다길래** 안 된다고 했다.
(=John is saying that he will submit his homework by tomorrow. Just because he says so, I told him it's not acceptable.)

On the other hand, "그렇다기에, 그렇다길래" can be used for the same function, but the verb in the preceding sentence must be a stative verb. "그렇다기에" can be freely used in both written text and conversation, whereas "그렇다길래" is more likely to be used in conversation.

존이 그 영화가 아주 재미있다고 한다. **그렇다기에/그렇다길래** 나도 한 번 보려고 한다.
(=John says that the movie is very interesting. Just because he says so, I also want to watch it.)

일기예보에 따르면 내일은 날씨가 아주 덥다고 한다. **그렇다기에/그렇다길래** 해운대 바닷가에 가 볼까 한다.
(=According to the weather report, it will be very hot tomorrow. Just because it says so, I am thinking about going to Haeundae Beach.)

40. Expressing "Lucky to avoid the worst-case scenario":
그러기에/길래 망정이지

Function	Expressing "Lucky to avoid the worst-case scenario"
Form	그러기에 망정이지
Meaning	One is lucky, otherwise, _

"그러기에 망정이지, 그러길래 망정이지" and their corresponding past tense forms "그랬기에 망정이지, 그랬길래 망정이지" can be used to express that one is/was lucky to avoid the worst-case scenario in the following sentence thanks to the situation in the preceding sentence, which can be rendered as "One is lucky, otherwise _. "

여기 빵이 좀 남아 있다. **그러기에 망정이지/그러길래 망정이지** 우리 모두 굶어 죽을 뻔했다.

(=We have some leftover bread here. We are lucky, otherwise we might all have starved to death.)

메리가 일을 도와줬어요. **그랬기에 망정이지/그랬길래 망정이지** 일을 제 시간에 못 끝낼 뻔했어요.

(=Mary helped me with the work. I was lucky, otherwise I could not have finished the work on time.)

컴퓨터를 찾았어요. **그랬기에 망정이지/그랬길래 망정이지** 지금까지 일한 거 다 날라갈 뻔했어요.

(=I found my computer. I was lucky, otherwise I might have lost all the work I had done.)

41. Expressing an undesirable condition for a pleasant situation:
이/그/저래서는, 이/그/저래서야

Function	Expressing an undesirable condition for a pleasant situation	
Form	이래서는, 그래서는, 저래서는	이래서야, 그래서야, 저래서야
Meaning	Given this/that	If one is like this/that If one does this/that

"이래서는, 그래서는, 저래서는" can be used to express that an undesirable situation in the preceding sentence will result in the unpleasant situation in the following sentence, which can be rendered as "Given this/that." The following sentence is typically a negative statement.

이 음식점은 음식 맛이 별로다. **이래서는** 손님이 다시는 안 올 거다.

(=The food of this restaurant is not good at all. Given this, people are never going to come again.)

그 영화배우는 연기를 너무 못한다. **그래서는** 유명해 질 수가 없다.

(=That movie star is not good at acting at all. Given that, he/she cannot not become famous.)

존은 손님한테 저렇게 불친절하다. **저래서는** 손님들을 다 놓치고 만다.

(=John is so rude to his customers like that. Given that, he will lose all the customers.)

On the other hand, "이래서야, 그래서야, 저래서야" can be used instead if the following sentence is a question, more specifically a rhetorical question, which can be rendered as "If it is like this/that." In this case, the question can be rephrased into its corresponding negative statement like the sentences above.

이 음식점은 음식 맛이 별로예요. **이래서야** 손님이 다시 오겠어요?

(=The food at this restaurant is not good at all. If it is like this, do you think people are going to come here again.)

그 영화배우는 연기를 너무 못해요. **그래서야** 어디 유명해 질 수가 있겠어요?

(=That movie star is not good at acting at all. If his/her acting is like that, do you think he/she will possibly become famous?)

존은 손님한테 저렇게 불친절해요. **저래서야** 어디 장사가 되겠어요?

(=John is so rude to his customers like that. If he does that, do you think his business will go well?)

42. Taking the necessary option for a desired result: 그래야(지)

Function	Taking the necessary option for a desired result	
Form	그래야	그래야지
Meaning	Only by doing that	Only by doing that/ That should be done/ It should be that way

"그래야지" and its contraction form "그래야" can be used to express that the action in the preceding sentence must be carried out because it is the only option to get the desired result in the following sentence. It can be rendered as "Only by doing that."

일단 일을 시작했으니까 끝을 봐야겠다. **그래야지/그래야** 나중에 후회가 없을 것 같다.
(=Because I already started working on it, I need to see it through to the end. Only by doing that, I will not regret it later.)

이번에는 존을 따끔하게 혼내 줘야겠다. **그래야지/그래야** 나쁜 버릇을 고칠 수 있을 것 같다.
(=I need to scold him harshly this time. Only by doing that, I can break his bad habits.)

직원들 봉급을 올려 줘야 한다. **그래야지/그래야** 더 열심히 일할 거다.
(=You must give your employees a pay raise. Only by doing that, they will work harder.)

On the other hand, "그래야지," but not "그래야," can also be used to express that one is thinking about carrying out an alternative action in the preceding sentence instead of accepting the situation in the following sentence, which can be rendered as "That should be done." The following sentence is typically in negative form.

무슨 수를 쓰던가 해야겠다. **그래야지** 이대로 마냥 기다릴 수는 없다.
(=We need to do something. That should be done. We cannot just wait like this endlessly.)

빨리 결정을 내리셔야 합니다. **그래야지** 이대로 포기할 수는 없습니다.
(=You must make a quick decision. That should be done. We cannot give up like this.)

However, this usage of "그래야지" is different from the one above. It should be treated as a filler, not as a sentence connector because its main function is to simply make a smooth transition between the two adjoining sentences. It is, therefore, even possible to delete it without breaking any logical relationship between the two sentences.

무슨 수를 쓰던가 해야겠다. 이대로 마냥 기다릴 수는 없다. (OK)
(=We need to do something. We cannot just wait like this endlessly.)

빨리 결정을 내리셔야 합니다. 이대로 포기할 수는 없습니다. (OK)

(=You must make a quick decision. We cannot give up like this.)

In addition, "그래야지" can also be used to express one's arrogant acceptance of a situation in the preceding sentence, which can be rendered as "It should be that way." It is typically used with the optional adverbs "그럼/아무렴/당연히 (of course)."

A: 이 문제는 제가 해결하겠습니다. (=I will take care of this matter.)

B: **그럼/아무렴/당연히 그래야지**. (=Of course, it should be that way.)

43. Expressing the speaker's negative reaction to a given situation:

그런다고/그렇다고 (해서)

Function	Expressing the speaker's negative reaction to a given situation	
Form	**그런다고 (해서)**	**그렇다고 (해서)**
Meaning	But even so/But even by doing so	

"그런다고 해서, 그렇다고 해서" and their corresponding contraction forms "그런다고, 그렇다고" can be used to express that the situation in the following sentence is the speaker's negative reaction to the situation in the preceding sentence, which can be rendered as "But even so/But even by doing so."

A: 존이 앞으로 도박을 끊겠다고 합니다.

(=John says that he will quit gambling from now on.)

B: **그런다고 해서/그런다고/그렇다고 해서/그렇다고** 그걸 믿으세요?

(=But even so, do you believe that?)

메리는 아주 똑똑합니다. **그런다고 해서/그런다고/그렇다고 해서/그렇다고** 공부를 잘하는 것은 아닙니다.

(=Mary is very smart. But even so, she does not study well.)

이 수입차는 값이 아주 비쌉니다. **그런다고 해서/그런다고/그렇다고 해서/그렇다고** 국산 차보다 성능이 좋은 건 아닙니다.

(=This import car is very expensive. But even so, its performance is not far any better than our domestic cars.)

유엔사무총장이 북한에 대해 전례 없는 경제제재 조치를 발표했습니다. **그런다고 해서/ 그런다고/그렇다고 해서/그렇다고** 과연 북한이 핵개발 계획을 포기할까요?

(=The Secretary-General of the United Nations announced unprecedented economic sanctions against North Korea. But even by doing so, do you think North Korea will give up its nuclear development plan?)

44. Expressing "Even so": 그런다고/그렇다고 해도

Function	Expressing "Even so"	
Form	그런다고 해도	그렇다고 해도
Meaning	Even so	

"그런다고 해도" can be used to express that the situation in the following sentence applies regardless of the situation in the preceding clause, which can be rendered as "Even so." The verb in the preceding sentence must be an action verb.

A: 다시는 안 그러겠습니다.
(=I will never do that again.)

B: **그런다고 해도** 이번에는 용서할 수 없다.
(=Even so, I cannot forgive you this time.)

On the other hand, "그렇다고 해도" can be used for the same function, but the verb in the preceding sentence must be a stative verb.

A: 오늘 몸이 좀 안 좋습니다.
(=Today I am not in good condition.)

B: **그렇다고 해도** 오늘은 반드시 출근해야 합니다.
(=Even so, you must come to work today.)

"그런다고 해도, 그렇다고 해도" can be freely used with the optional adverb "아무리 (No matter how)," and the combination can be rendered as "No matter what."

A: 메리가 자기만 믿으라고 하네요.
(=Mary told me to just trust her.)

B: **아무리 그런다고 해도** 절대 믿지 마세요.
(=No matter what, never trust her.)

A: 메리가 지금 아주 피곤하다고 합니다.
(=Mary says that she is very tired now.)

B: **아무리 그렇다고 해도** 자기 전에 숙제는 해야 한다.
(=No matter what, she must do her homework before she goes to bed.)

45. Expressing "Not a game changer": 그렇게 한들, 그런들, 그렇다 한들

Function	Expressing "Not a game changer"	
Form	그렇게 한들, 그런들	그렇다 한들
Meaning	Even though one does/did so	Even though that is true

"그렇게 한들" and its contraction form "그런들" can be used to express that the situation in the preceding sentence happened, but it will not make any change to the given situation in the preceding sentence, which can be rendered as "Even though one does/did so." The verb in the preceding sentence must be an action verb.

메리가 존을 명예훼손으로 고소했다. **그렇게 한들/그런들** 재판에서 이길 수 있을 것 같지 않다.
(=Mary filed a defamation lawsuit against John. Even though she did so, it is not likely that she will win the case at the court.)

범인이 은신처에 숨어버렸다. **그렇게 한들/그런들** 이제는 독 안에 든 쥐다.
(=The suspect hid himself/herself in his/her hideout. Even though he/she did so, he/she is like a rat in a trap.)

On the other hand, "그렇다 한들" can be used for the same function, but the verb in the preceding sentence must be a stative verb.

존은 아주 똑똑하다. **그렇다 한들** 이 문제는 풀 수 없다.

(=John is very smart. Even though that is true, he cannot solve this problem.)

이 스포츠카는 아주 환상적이다. **그렇다 한들** 그 가격에는 쉽게 팔리지 않을 것 같다

(=This sports car is so fantastic. Even though that is true, it seems that it will not be sold easily at that price.)

46. Discovering the fact by looking back on a given situation: 그러고 보면

Function	Discovering the fact by looking back on a given situation
Form	**그러고 보면**
Meaning	If I am looking back on that

"그러고 보면" can be used to express that the speaker discovered the situation in the following sentence by looking back on a given situation in the preceding sentence, which can be rendered as "If I am looking back on that."

한국에 온 지 벌써 10년이 지났네. **그러고 보면** 세월이 참 빠르다.

(=Wow, ten years have already passed since I came to Korea. If I am looking back on that, time flies.)

나는 아무 것도 가진 게 없는 것 같다. **그러고 보면** 인생은 참 불공평하다.

(=It seems that I have nothing. If I am looking back on that, life is truly unfair.)

47. Getting an unintended outcome from an action: 그런다는 것이 (그만)

Function	Getting an unintended outcome from an action
Form	**그런다는 것이 (그만)**
Meaning	But instead of doing that, _ ended up -ing

"그런다는 것이 (그만)" can be used to express that the situation in the following sentence accidently happened because the intended action in the preceding sentence was not appropriately carried out, which can be rendered as "But instead of doing that, _ ended up -ing."

커피에 설탕을 좀 넣으려고 했어요. **그런다는 것이 (그만)** 소금을 넣어 버렸네요.
(=I was going to put some sugar in the coffee. But instead of doing that, I accidently ended up putting salt in it.)

뉴욕 지사에 소포를 보내려고 했어요. **그런다는 것이 (그만)** 시카고 지사로 보내고 말았어요.
(=I was going to send the package to the New York branch office. But instead of doing that, I accidently ended up sending it to the Chicago branch office.)

The adverb "그만 (in the end)" can sometimes be replaced with another optional adverb "도리어 (on the contrary)" in the case that the resulting situation in the following sentence is directly opposite to one's intention in the preceding sentence.

도와 드리려고 했어요. **그런다는 것이 (도리어)** 방해만 되었네요.
(=I was trying to help you. But instead of doing that, on the contrary it only disturbed you.)

48. Expressing one reason on top of another one: 그러기도 하려니와

Function	Expressing one reason on top of another one
Form	그러기도 하려니와
Meaning	On top of that

"그러기도 하려니와" can be used to express that the situation in the following sentence is another reason for a given situation on top of the reason in the preceding sentence, which can be rendered as "On top of that."

지금은 돈이 없어요. **그러기도 하려니와** 너무 바빠서 도저히 시간을 낼 수 없어요.
(=I don't have any money now. On top of that, I cannot afford the time at all because

I am too busy.)

오늘은 너무 피곤하네요. **그러기도 하려니와** 배가 고파서 말할 기운도 없어요.
(=I am too tired today. On top of that, I don't even have any energy left to talk because I am so hungry.)

밖에 날씨가 무척 더워요. **그러기도 하려니와** 날이 어두워지고 있어서 오늘은 여기서 그만 해야겠어요.
(=The weather is sizzling hot outside. On top of that, we need to call it a day because it's getting dark.)

49. Expressing the speaker's response to one's excessive request/behavior: 그러면/그랬으면 됐지

Function	Expressing the speaker's response to one's excessive request/behavior
Form	**그러면 됐지, 그랬으면 됐지**
Meaning	That's enough of it, but _

"그러면 됐지" can be used to express that the situation in the following sentence is the speaker's negative reaction to one's excessive request/behavior that went beyond the situation in the preceding sentence, which can be rendered as "That's enough of it, but _."

저도 할 만큼 했어요. **그러면 됐지** 뭐를 더 어떻게 하란 말입니까?
(=I did it as much as I could do. That's enough of it, but what am I supposed to do if you ask me to do more?)

"그랬으면 됐지" can be used to emphasize the completion of the action in the preceding sentence.

지금까지 불평 한 번 하지 않고 기다려 왔어요. **그랬으면 됐지** 더 기다리라고요?
(=I have been waiting for that without making any complaint. That's enough of it, but are you asking me to wait more?)

50. Expressing the speaker's response to one's change of mind over a done deal: 그랬으면 그만이지

Function	Expressing the speaker's response to one's change of mind over a done deal
Form	그랬으면 그만이지
Meaning	That's a done deal, but _

"그랬으면 그만이지" can be used to express that the situation in the following sentence is the speaker's negative reaction to one's change of mind over the done deal in the preceding sentence, which can be rendered as "That's a done deal, but _."

존이 메리에게 다이어 반지를 선물로 줬다. **그랬으면 그만이지** 이제와서 다시 돌려 달라고 한다.

(=John gave a diamond ring to Mary as a present. That's a done deal, but he is now asking her to give it back to him.)

메리가 아파트를 계약했다. **그랬으면 그만이지** 그 계약을 취소하고 싶다고 한다.

(=Mary signed the contract for her apartment. That's a done deal, but she wants to cancel the contract.)

51. Expressing "Regardless of that":
그러거나 말거나/그러든지 말든지/그러든가 말든가 (간에)

Function	Expressing "Regardless of that"		
Form	그러거나 말거나 (간에)	그러든지 말든지 (간에)	그러든가 말든가 (간에)
Meaning	Regardless of that		

"그러거나 말거나 (간에), 그러든지 말든지 (간에), 그러든가 말든가 (간에)" can be used to express that the situation in the following sentence always applies regardless of whether the situation in the preceding sentence occurs or not, which can be rendered as "Regardless of that."

존이 바빠서 못 온다고 한다. **그러거나 말거나 (간에)** /**그러든지 말든지 (간에)** /**그러든가 말든가 (간에)** 우리는 우리 할 일을 하자.

(=John says he cannot come because he is busy. Regardless of that, let's do what we need to do.)

메리가 또 말썽을 부린다. **그러거나 말거나 (간에)** /**그러든지 말든지 (간에)** /**그러든가 말든가 (간에)** 신경 쓰지 말아라.

(=Mary is causing trouble again. Regardless of that, don't pay attention to it.)

52. Expressing "Because of the speaker's strong intention to carry out an action": 그럴 테니(까)

Function	Expressing "Because of the speaker's intention to carry out an action"
Form	그럴 테니(까)
Meaning	Because I will do so

"그럴 테니(까)" can be used to express that the speaker asks the the listener to carry out the action in the following sentence because he/she has the strong intention to carry out the action in the preceding sentence, which can be rendered as "Because I will do so."

저는 나중에 먹을 게요. **그럴 테니(까)** 먼저 드세요.

(=I will eat later. Because I will do so, please help yourself first.)

제가 대신 할 게요. **그럴 테니(까)** 좀 쉬세요.

(=I will do it instead of you. Because I will do so, please get some rest.)

제가 존한테 이야기 해 볼게요. **그럴 테니(까)** 걱정하지 마세요.

(=I will talk to John about it. Because I will do so, please don't worry.)

53. Expressing the speaker's positive reaction to one's request:
그렇게 하도록

Function	Expressing the speaker's positive reaction to one's request
Form	그렇게 하도록, 그러도록
Meaning	To make sure of that

"그렇게 하도록" and its contraction form "그러도록" can be used to express the speaker's positive reaction to a given situation by accepting one's request in the preceding sentence, which can be rendered as "To make sure of that."

A: 손님들을 좀 더 친절히 대하세요.

(=You must treat our customers friendlier.)

B: **그렇게 하도록/그러도록** 최선을 다 하겠습니다.

(=To make sure of that, I will do my best.)

"그렇게 하도록" can also be used in the conversational idiom "그렇게 하도록 하세요," which can be rendered as "Please do so."

A: 집에 일이 있어서 일찍 들어가 봐야겠습니다.

(=I must go home early because I have something to take care of.)

B: **그렇게 하도록** 하세요.

(=Please do so.)

54. Expressing the speaker's negative reaction to one's negligence:
그렇게 되도록

Function	Expressing the speaker's negative reaction to one's negligence
Form	그렇게 되도록, 그러도록
Meaning	Until that happened

"그렇게 되도록" and its contraction form "그러도록" can be used to express the speaker's negative reaction to a given situation by complaining about one's belated action in the preceding sentence, which can be rendered as "Until that happened."

A: 존이 열이 많이 나서 응급실에 데려 갔어요.

(=Because John has high fever, I took him to an emergency room.)

B: **그렇게 되도록**/**그러도록** 도대체 집에서 뭐 했어요?

(=Until that happened, what on earth did you do at home?)

55. Expressing the speaker's strong suggestion for a better option: 그럴 것이/게 아니라

Function	Expressing the speaker's strong suggestion for a better option	
Form	그럴 것이 아니라	그럴 게 아니라
Meaning	One is not supposed to do that, but rather _	

"그럴 것이 아니라" and its contraction form "그럴 게 아니라 can be used to express that the speaker is strongly suggesting to the listener to take a better option in the following sentence rather than taking the less preferred option in the preceding sentence, which can be rendered as "One is not supposed to do that, but rather _."

A: 조금만 더 기다려 봅시다.

(=Let's wait a little longer.)

B: **그럴 것이 아니라**/**그럴 게 아니라** 더 늦기 전에 지금 당장 단호한 조치를 취해야 합니다.

(=We are not supposed to do that, but rather we must carry out a decisive action now before it gets too late.)

A: 한 번만 더 존에게 기회를 줍시다.

(=Why don't we give John one more chance?)

B: **그럴 것이 아니라**/**그럴 게 아니라** 모든 사람한테 공평해야죠.

(=We are not supposed to do that, but rather we must be fair to everyone.)

56. Making an excuse for a given situation: 그런답시고, 그렇답시고

Function	Making an excuse for a given situation	
Form	그런답시고	그렇답시고
Meaning	By making that excuse	

"그런답시고" can be used to express that one is to carry out the action in the following sentence while making an excuse for the given situation in the preceding sentence, which can be rendered as "By making that excuse." The verb in the preceding sentence must be an action verb.

> 새로 온 부장님이 근무환경을 쇄신한다고 해요. **그런답시고** 부서직원들을 함부로 대하고 있어요.
> (=The new department chief says he is going to revamp our work environment. By making that excuse, he has been treating the employees in our department improperly.)

On the other hand, "그렇답시고" can be used for the same function, but the verb in the preceding sentence must be a stative verb.

> 우리 가게 주인은 요즘 장사가 형편없다고 해요. **그렇답시고** 알바생들을 모두 해고했어요.
> (=Our store owner says that his business is not going well. By making that excuse, he laid off all the part-time employees.)

57. Expressing "Not going beyond a given situation":
그러기만 할 뿐, 그러기만 하지

Function	Expressing "Not going beyond a given situation"	
Form	그러기만 할 뿐	그러기만 하지
Meaning	Othe than just doing that	

"그러기만 할 뿐" and its past tense form "그러기만 했을 뿐" can be used to express that one is just to carry out the action in the preceding sentence, but not go beyond that, which can be rendered as "Other than just doing that." The following sentence is typically in negative form. They can be freely used in both written text and conversation.

> 존은 내가 묻는 말에만 대답하고 있다. **그러기만 할 뿐** 자기 생각이 뭔지 이야기를 안 한다.
>
> (=John is just answering the questions that I ask him. Other than just doing that, he is not talking about what he is thinking.)
>
> 메리는 내가 말하는 것을 가만히 듣고만 있었다. **그러기만 했을 뿐** 아무런 변명도 하지 않았다.
>
> (=Mary was just quietly listening to what I said to her. Other than just doing that, she did not make any excuses.)

On the other hand, "그러기만 하지" and its past tense form 그러기만 했지" can be used for the same function, but they are more likely to be used in conversation.

> 존은 그저 웃기만 한다. **그러기만 하지** 아무 것도 도와주지 않는다.
>
> (=John is just smiling. Other than just doing that, he is not helping me at all.)
>
> 메리는 화가 나서 존을 째려 보았다. **그러기만 했지** 왜 화가 났는 지에 대해서 말을 하지 않았다.
>
> (=Mary stared at John because she got angry. Other than just doing that, she didn't say why she got angry at him.)

58. Expressing acknowledgment of a given situation:

그렇기는 하지만, 그렇기야 하지만

Function	Expressing acknowledgment of a given situation	
Form	그렇기는 하지만, 그렇긴 하지만	그렇기야 하지만
Meaning	Even though that is the case	Even though that is really the case

"그렇기는 하지만" and its contraction form "그렇긴 하지만" can be used to express that the situation in the following sentence applies even though the speaker is acknowledging the situation in the preceding sentence with some reservation, which can be rendered as "Even though that is the case."

> 저는 누가 했는지 알고 있어요. **그렇기는 하지만/그렇긴 하지만** 말씀 드릴 수가 없어요.
> (=I know who did it. Even though that is the case, I cannot tell you about it.)
>
> 이 TV는 화질이 아주 뛰어나네요. **그렇기는 하지만/그렇긴 하지만** 값이 너무 비싸서 살 수가 없네요.
> (=The picture quality of this TV is excellent. Even though that is the case, I cannot buy it because it's too expensive.)

On the other hand, "그렇기야 하지만" carries the same function, which can be rendered as "Even though that is really the case." Unlike "그렇기는 하지만," it expresses the speaker's full acknowledgment of the situation in the preceding sentence.

> A: 한국말 배워 보니까 재미있지?
> (=It's fun to learn Korean, right?)
>
> B: **그렇기야 하지만** 한국어 문법이 너무 어려워요.
> (=Even though that is really the case, Korean grammar is too difficult to learn.)

59. Disapproving of the original expectation: 그러기는/긴 커녕

Function	Disapproving of the original expectation	
Form	그러기는 커녕	그러긴 커녕
Meaning	Not at all, but _	

"그러기는 커녕" and its contraction form "그러긴 커녕" can be used to express that the originally-expected outcome in the preceding sentence did not come out at all, but instead the unexpected situation in the following sentence actually happened, which can be rendered as "Not at all, but _."

> A: 그 약 먹으니까 좀 났지?
> (=You feel better after taking the medicine, right?)
>
> B: **그러기는 커녕/그러긴 커녕** 오히려 더 심해졌어.
> (=Not at all, but rather it's getting worse.)

A: 메리와 데이트하니까 좋지?

(=You liked dating Mary, right?)

B: **그러기는 커녕/그러긴 커녕** 말 한마디조차 못 건네 봤다.

(=Not at all, but I did not even have a chance to talk to her.)

A: 도박장에서 돈 좀 땄어?

(=Did you win some money at the casino?)

B: **그러기는 커녕/그러긴 커녕** 있는 돈까지 몽땅 날려 버렸어요.

(=Not at all, but I even lost all the money that I had.)

60. Expressing the condition for an immediate outcome: 그러기만 하면

Function	Expressing the condition for an immediate outcome	
Form	그러기만 하면	
Meaning	Once one does that	Only if that is the case

"그러기만 하면" can be used to express that the situation in the following sentence immediately follows once one carries out the action in the preceding sentence, which can be rendered as "Once one does that."

이 약 한 번 드셔 보세요. **그러기만 하면** 금방 나으실 거예요.

(=Why don't you take this medicine? Once you do that, you will get better immediately.)

이 주식에 한 번 투자해 보세요. **그러기만 하면** 금방 많은 돈을 벌 수 있을 거예요.

(=Why don't you invest your money in this stock? Once you do that, you can make a lot of money soon.)

On the other hand, it can also be used to express that the situation in the following sentence will happen if the condition in the preceding sentence is met because all other necessary conditions are already met, which can be rendered as "Only if that is the case."

집이 좀 컸으면 좋겠어요. **그러기만 하면** 다 좋은데.

(=I wish the house could be a little bigger. Only if that is the case, everything would be good.)

존이 돈을 좀 많이 벌어 왔으면 좋겠어요. **그러기만 하면** 생활이 더 나아질텐데요.
(=I wish John could make and bring home more money. Only if that is the case, our living condition will get better.)

61. Expressing the only exception for a given situation:
그러면 모르(겠)지만, 그러면 몰라도

Function	Expressing the only exception for a given situation	
Form	그러면 모르(겠)지만	그러면 몰라도
Meaning	Otherwise	

"그러면 모르(겠)지만, 그러면 몰라도" can be used to express that the situation in the following sentence holds true unless the situation in the preceding sentence happens, which can be rendered as "Otherwise." "그러면 모르(겠)지만" can be freely used in both written text and conversation, whereas "그러면 몰라도" is more likely to be used in conversation.

물건 값을 올릴 수 밖에 없어요. **그러면 모르(겠)지만/그러면 몰라도** 알바생들 최저임금을 감당할 수가 없어요.
(=I have no choice but to raise the prices. Otherwise, I cannot guarantee the minimum wage for my part-time workers.)

정부에서 대체에너지 개발에 대한 계획을 세워야 합니다. **그러면 모르(겠)지만/그러면 몰라도** 그냥 원전을 폐쇄하는 것을 올바른 정책이 아니에요.
(=The government must establish a plan for alternative energy development. Otherwise, it is not the right policy to simply shut down nuclear power plants.)

62. Expressing the premise of one's reaction: 그러거늘 (하물며)

Function	Expressing the premise of one's reaction
Form	**그러거늘 (하물며)**
Meaning	Granted that

"그러거늘" can be used to express that the situation in the following sentence is the speaker's legimate reaction to a given situation judging from the common sense statement in the preceding sentence, which can be rendered as "Granted that." It is often used with the optional adverb "하물며 (it is needless to say)." However, it is now on the verge of becoming an archaic expression in favor of the more frequently used expression "그런데 (Given that)."

짚신도 짝이 있어요. **그러거늘 하물며** 제 신부감이라고 없겠어요?

(=Every Jack has his Jill. Granted that, isn't it needless to say that I can find my bride?)

짐승도 자기 새끼를 거둔다. **그러거늘 하물며** 인간으로서 자기 자식을 죽인다는 것은 도저히 용납이 안 된다.

(=Even animals take care of their own babies. Granted that, it is needless to say that it is not acceptable to kill one's own child if he/she is a human being.)

63. Talking about a different subject: 그건 그렇고

Function	Talking about a different subject
Form	**그건 그렇고**
Meaning	(That's enough of it.) Anyway

"그건 그렇고" can be used to express that the speaker wants to talk about a different subject in the following sentence rather than continuing to talk about the situation in the preceding sentence, which can be rendered as "(That's enough of it.) Anyway."

나는 취직 때문에 걱정이야. **그건 그렇고** 너 요즘 어떻게 지내니?

(=I am worried about finding a job. (That's enough of it.) Anyway, how have you been lately?)

우리 아들이 프린스턴 대학에 합격했어. **그건 그렇고** 등록금을 어떻게 마련할 지 걱정이야.

(=My son got admitted to Princeton University. (That's enough of it.) Anyway, I am worried about how to pay his tuition.)

존은 지난달에 결혼했다. **그건 그렇고** 너는 언제 결혼할 거니?

(=John got married last month. (That's enough of it.) Anyway, when are you going to get married?)

64. Drawing the listener's attention to a contrasting situation:

그런데 말이다/말이야/말이지

Function	Drawing the listener's attention to a contrasting situation		
Form	그런데 말이다	그런데 말이야	그런데 말이지
Meaning	By the way		

"그런데 말이다, 그런데 말이야, 그런데 말이지" and their honorific variant forms "그런데 말입니다, 그런데 말이에요" can be used to express that the speaker wants to draw the listener's attention to a contrasting situation in the following sentence rather than the existing situation in the preceding sentence, which can be rendered as "By the way."

존은 군대에 가기 전까지 말썽만 부렸어. **그런데 말이다/그런데 말이야/그런데 말이지** 걔가 완전히 달라졌어.

(=John was a troublemaker before he joined the military. By the way, he has been completely changed into a different person.)

메리는 결혼하기 전까지 날씬했어요. **그런데 말입니다/그런데 말이에요** 요즘 살이 많이 쪘어요.

(=Mary was slender before she got married. By the way, she gained a lot of weight these days.)

65. Making an explanation for a given situation:

그게 말이다/말이야/말이지

Function	Making an explanation for a given situation		
Form	그게 말이다	그게 말이야	그게 말이지
Meaning	The thing is,		

"그게 말이다, 그게 말이야, 그게 말이지" and their honorific variant forms "그게 말입니다, 그게 말이에요" can be used to express that the speaker is trying to make an explanation for the given situation in the preceding sentence by providing the comment in the following sentence, which can be rendered as "The thing is."

A: 이 꽃병 누가 깼니?
(=Who broke this flower vase?)

B: **그게 말이다/그게 말이야/그게 말이지** 내가 실수로 깼어.
(=The thing is, I broke it by mistake.)

A: 존이 오늘 학교에 안 왔네요.
(=John didn't come to school today.)

B: **그게 말입니다/그게 말이에요** 독감에 걸려서 못 갔어요.
(=The thing is, he couldn't go to school because he got the flu.)

REFERENCES (참고문헌)

국립국어원. (2005). 외국인을 위한 한국어문법 1: *체계편*. 커뮤니케이션북스.

_____. (2005). 외국인을 위한 한국어문법 2: *용법편*. 커뮤니케이션북스.

서정수. (1996). *국어문법*. 한양대학교출판원.

최현배. (1937). *우리말본*. 정음사.

허 웅. (1995). *20세기 우리말의 형태론*. 샘문화사.

Ahn, Jean-Myung. et al. (2010). *Korean Grammar in Use: Beginning to Early Intermediate*. Darakwon.

_____. (2011). *Korean Grammar in Use: Intermediate*. Darakwon.

_____. (2014). *Korean Grammar in Use: Advanced*. Darakwon.

Aissen Judith. L. (1992). Topic and focus in Mayan. Language 68:43-80.

Byon, Andrew. Sangpil. (2008). *Basic Korean: A Grammar and Workbook*. Routledge.

_____. (2009). *Intermediate Korean: A Grammar and Workbook*. Routledge.

Defense Language Institute. Korean Basic Course. Unit 1-14. DLIFLC.

Gundel, Jeanette. (1985). Shared Knowledge and Topicality. *Journal of Pragmatics* 9:1, 83-107.

Halliday, Michael. A. K. (1967). Notes on transitivity and theme in English (part II). Journal of Linguistics 3:199-244.

Han, Chung-hye. (1998). Asymmetry in the Interpretation of -(n)un in Korean. Japanese/Korean Linguistics. vol 7.

Im, Ho Bin. et al. (1988). *Korean Grammar for International Learners*. Yonsei University Press.

_____. (2001). *Korean Grammar for International Learners*. Yonsei University Press.

Kuno, Susumu. (1973). *The Structure of the Japanese Language*. The MIT Press.

Lambrecht, Knud. (1994). *Information structure and sentence form*. Cambridge University Press.

McCawley, James. D. (1988). The Syntactic Phenomena of English Volume 1 & 2. The University of Chicago Press.

Perlmutter, David. M. (Ed.). (1983). *Studies in Relational Grammar 1*. The University of Chicago Press.

Perlmutter, David. M. & Rosen, Carol. (Eds.). (1984). *Studies in Relational Grammar 2*. The University of Chicago Press.

Postal, Paul. M. & Joseph, Brian. D. (Eds.). (1990). *Studies in Relational Grammar 3*. The University of Chicago Press.

Reinhart, Tanya. (1981). Pragmatics and linguistics: An analysis of sentence topics. Philosophica 27:53-94.

Yeon, Jaehoon. & Brown, Lucien. (2011). *Korean: A Comprehensive Grammar*. Routledge

INDEX (색인)

ㅈ

ㅌ